Praise for *Muscular Portfolios*

"Livingston has used his computer savvy to crack Wall Street's money-making secrets and make them freely available to investors at every stage of life."

**AL ZMYSLOWSKI, Board of Directors,
American Association of Individual Investors—Silicon Valley Chapter**

"Overall the book looks great! I love the idea of empowering people to take control of their own investing."

**DANIEL SOTIROFF, ETF Specialist columnist and analyst,
Morningstar Inc.**

"There's a wealth of information in this book that can help every do-it-yourself investor."

**WES GRAY, PhD,
CEO of Alpha Architect**

"In his inimitable way, Livingston has taken a tough problem—investing—broken it into component parts, analyzed the living daylights out of them with sophisticated computer runs, then extracted strategies that are both easy to understand and demonstrably superior."

**WOODY LEONHARD,
best-selling author of *Windows All-In-One For Dummies***

"The book does a great job of delivering important information to the individual investor in a very straightforward manner."

**STEPHEN JONES,
Financial and Economic Analyst**

"As I was reading, I kept a list of questions, but by the time I reached the end, all my questions had been answered. Nice job."

**BOB NEW, Engineer,
HP Inc.**

Affiliations are listed for identification purposes only.

MUSCULAR PORTFOLIOS

THE INVESTING REVOLUTION
FOR SUPERIOR RETURNS WITH LOWER RISK

BRIAN LIVINGSTON

BenBella Books, Inc.
Dallas, TX

BenBella Books, Inc.
10440 N. Central Expressway, Suite 800
Dallas, TX 75231
www.benbellabooks.com
Send feedback to feedback@benbellabooks.com

Printed in the United States of America
10 9 8 7 6 5 4 3 2 1

Library of Congress Cataloging-in-Publication Data is available upon request.
LCCN 2018019445 (print) | LCCN 2018028595 (ebook)

ISBN 9781946885388 (paper over board: alk. paper) | ISBN 9781946885630 (electronic)

Editing by Alexa Stevenson
Copyediting by Scott Calamar
Interior design by John D. Berry
Interior typesetting by Aaron Edmiston

Final layout by Karen Mason Creative
Front cover design by Marc Whitaker/MTWdesign.net
Full cover design by Sarah Avinger
Indexing by WordCo Indexing Services

Distributed to the trade by Two Rivers Distribution, an Ingram brand
www.tworiversdistribution.com

Special discounts for bulk sales (minimum of 25 copies) are available.
Please contact Aida Herrera at aida@benbellabooks.com

Before you begin . . .

Get FREE updates to this book

Be notified of new developments via email once a month.

Sign up for the FREE newsletter at: **MuscularPortfolios.com.**

Follow the footnotes for more information

Every footnote links to a longer document with more details.

» Enter **bri.li/1000** into any browser to see an example.
» Enter **bri.li/1001** to see the first footnote in this book.
» Enter **bri.li/1200** to see the 200th footnote, and so forth.

To preview the destination, add a hyphen (-) to the end, like this: **bri.li/1000-**

The 2nd edition of this book will use links that begin with "2," and so forth.

Follow the Twitter feed: @Brian_Livin

The best ways to read this book

1 · Speed read (60 minutes)

First, read the illustrations and captions, and then go back and read the parts of the text that interest you.

2 · Deep read (an easy weekend)

Go through the book, page by page. You only need to read it in sequence if you want to understand the information.

You can get value out of this book by reading it either way.

A note to readers outside the US

To keep this book simple, it refers only to United States laws and financial products. Other countries may have different regulations and product names.

Fortunately, Muscular Portfolios can be managed outside the US. Low-cost index funds that track global asset classes are available in many countries. Because non-US funds can use the same indexes as US funds, investors everywhere should enjoy roughly the same performance.

A word from the author
(actually, a few words)

For two decades—1990 through 2010—I worked as an investigative journalist, revealing the secrets of the computer industry. I exposed products that didn't work, features advertised on the packaging that weren't actually in the software yet, spammers, fraudsters—you name it.

Since then, I've turned my gaze toward the investing business—and it's 10 times worse. What we laughingly call the financial "services" industry is a cesspool filled with sharks intent on siphoning your money away and making it their own.

The good news is that it is absolutely possible to grow your savings with **no fear** of financial sharks or stock-market crashes. In the past few years, we've seen an explosion of low-cost index funds, along with serious mathematical breakthroughs in how to combine these funds into low-risk portfolios.

Top Wall Street bankers know all about this, but seldom reveal the facts to individual investors. Most people have never heard of the scientific papers detailing the evidence behind these methods. Sure, they're posted in obscure places on the Web, but they rarely make the headlines of newspapers or even blogs.

Can individual investors understand these basic principles well enough to manage their own money successfully? And can they do this without turning investing into a second job? This book shows that the answer is **"Yes!"**

This book shows you how. In fact, you can begin today. You don't need millions of dollars to take advantage of low-cost, low-risk investing. You can start with just a little money and make it grow.

I know it's hard to save money if you barely make enough to keep body and soul together.

I wish I could hire everyone who reads this book and give you a raise. But I can't.

The best I can do is help you commit to your own success. Seek out lifelong education, strive to improve your earnings, save as much as possible, and multiply your gains by investing wisely.

One of the nicest things ever said to me was by a reader of the manuscript: "My husband and I paid off our credit cards and started saving money, because of your book and your damn charts."

That's my goal. Now you have the book in front of you. I hope you like the whole damn thing.

—Brian Livingston
July 2018

Executive summary of the book
Muscular Portfolios

» **Old investing strategies** that became conventional wisdom in the 1970s and 1980s have proven them-selves to be failures, subjecting investors to unacceptable losses.

» **These debunked theories**—known as Lazy Portfolios, because their fixed holdings never change—caused investors to lose 35% to 50% **twice in a single decade** during the crashes of 2000–2002 and 2007–2009.

» **Individuals experience a "behavioral pain point"** after their portfolios have lost more than 25% in value, compelling them to sell their holdings.

» **Without devoting 80% or more to bonds,** you can't design a Lazy Portfolio that loses less than 25% after inflation, so investors lag the market. After a crash ravages their nest eggs, investors' survival instincts make them sell, locking in the loss and ensuring they miss much of the next bull market.

» **Hundreds of peer-reviewed studies** since 1993 have shown that stocks, bonds, real estate, commodities, and other asset types all follow a Momentum Rule: asset classes that have risen for 3 to 12 months tend to continue rising for another month or more.

» **Momentum is a centuries-old market factor**—an example of evidence-based investing—so basic that any investor can use it, given this book and the free Web pages updated daily at MuscularPortfolios.com.

» **Adapting a portfolio** to market conditions is a principle that has won the Nobel Prize in Economics. Dated 20th-century theories are being replaced by a new Dynamic Portfolio Model that forms the basis of Muscular Portfolios.

» **The Index Investing Revolution**—ultralow trading costs, tiny fees, and a scientific consensus about momentum—now lets us design Muscular Portfolios that keep losses below the 25% pain point while delivering robust returns.

» **Muscular Portfolios:**

a · produce great returns when measured over complete bear-bull market cycles;

b · embrace automatic, mechanical investing;

c · avoid any trading based on opinion;

d · reject active investing and market timing;

e · require only 15 minutes per month; and

f · are fully disclosed at no charge.

» **MuscularPortfolios.com** is a disruptive website that is helping drive the price of investing advice to zero.

Contents

The tale of Goldilocks and the three bankers

Once upon a time, in a forest near her village, Goldilocks stumbled through a doorway at the end of a dark path by a long brick wall.

Inside the dimly lit room, on a big oval table, she saw three shiny bowls. The smallest of the bowls was filled with money. The second bowl, which was larger, held even more money. And the third and largest bowl held the most money of all.

Beside each bowl was a printed card. Goldilocks picked up the cards, which each described a formula for investing. The formulas were called the Mama Bear, the Papa Bear, and the Baby Bear.

Each formula was as simple as simple could be. Goldilocks realized that she could choose to follow whichever one was just right for her.

Suddenly, three Wall Street bankers burst into the room, wearing woolly coats and golden watches. "You've read our secret formulas!" they cried. "We won't be able to sell them to the peasants anymore!"

Goldilocks consoled them as best she could. She would not pay for the formulas, since they were so simple. But, she told them, with all the money she'd make, perhaps she would return one day and open an account at one of their giant Wall Street banks.

She ran to the village, faster than a corpulent CEO ever could. She gave the formulas away, and everyone lived happily ever after.

But the Wall Street bankers had to find new jobs.

Illustration: "Goldilocks" by Jed Dunkerley

1 Goldilocks investing: Not too risky, not too tame, just great gains

"No invention has been more disruptive to the asset-management industry in the last quarter century than the exchange-traded fund. Its tradability, tax efficiency, and cost ignited the low fee revolution."

CRYSTAL KIM in *Barron's* (Nov. 20, 2017)[1001]

Over the centuries— since the Amsterdam Stock Exchange became the first trading pit in 1602—a huge wealth-management industry has arisen.

When we see a poisonous snake, we instinctively leap out of its way. But faced with the Wall Street gambling den—crawling with financial vipers—our impulse is to jump right in.

A small army of salespeople and brokers use every psychological trick in the book to convince us to part with our money in the market casino.

Too many people become gamblers with their life savings, certain they can beat the house. This overconfidence blinds us.

University of California professor Terrance Odean analyzed 10,000 randomly selected accounts at a national discount brokerage firm. When people sold one stock and bought another, the stock they bought went up in the next 12 months an average of 5.7%. But the discarded stock soared 9.0%! Our opinions deceive us.[1002]

Luckily for us, the financial world is being turned upside down by an Index Investing Revolution. Only in the 21st century have individuals been able to buy a full set of ultra-low-cost exchange traded funds (ETFs). These new vehicles deliver almost 100% of the return of market indexes.

This book, *Muscular Portfolios,* has some things in common with the popular Goldilocks theme:

» **In the Goldilocks fable,** a young woman finds one bowl of porridge that's too hot, another that's too cold, and finally one that's just right.

» **A so-called Goldilocks planet**—much sought-after by astronomers—is not too close to its sun and not too far, but at just the right distance to support life. (We happen to live on one.)

» **Goldilocks investing** is a research project to find and publish Muscular Portfolios. These are investment strategies that are not too risky but not too tame, earning double-digit returns while protecting you from steep losses.

Don't play unwinnable games against the supercomputers of Wall Street (Figures 1-1 and 1-2). With the latest information, you yourself can be the best investment adviser you'll ever have.

Cats are compelled to chase red laser dots that look like prey

FIGURE 1-1

Humans are compelled to chase jagged lines that look like profit

FIGURE 1-2

It's up to individuals to make their own way in the world of Wall Street

Today, whether you're a business owner, an employee, a retiree, or a student—anyone with two coins to rub together—you are largely expected to manage your own nest egg with little help.

Thirty years ago, more than 175,000 company-sponsored pension plans spanned the US. These professionally managed accounts guaranteed employees a steady flow of income for life. But by 2007, fewer than 25,000 pension plans remained.[1003]

In 1979, about 38% of American workers participated in a pension plan. By 2011, that number was down to only 14%.[1004]

During that same period, enrollment in 401(k) plans—plans at the mercy of the market, offering no guarantees—rose from 17% to 42%.

Brooke Harrington, author of the 2016 book *Capital without Borders,* explains how individual investors became stock speculators:

"Once limited to a tiny elite among America's wealthiest families—the 1 percent of adults who owned stocks in 1900, which by 1952 had risen to just 4 percent— investing in stocks became a mass activity, involving over half the US adult population by the end of the twentieth century. . . . As economic anthropologist Keith Hart points out—'economics has become the religion of our secular scientific civilization.'"[1005] (Figure 1-3)

ACADEMICS SAY

Economics has become the religion of our secular scientific civilization

FIGURE 1-3

Transitioning from pensions to 401(k)s and IRAs allowed employers to avoid the risk of accounts running dry. Instead, the responsibility increasingly fell on the shoulders of individuals. But most people have never received even the most basic instruction on how to invest to safely reap gains without suffering devastating market crashes.

Unsurprisingly, teaching individuals how to manage their own money for free is not a high priority for the financial industry. Thousands of firms are happy to charge consumers big fees for advice of little value.

Constructing a portfolio that grows steadily while minimizing risk is a skill that even many paid investment advisers haven't mastered. Can the average investor do a better job?

The answer is a definite **"Yes!"** This book shows you simple, profitable, do-it-yourself portfolios. Best of all, you don't have to pay any fees to set them up or maintain them, keeping more of your money in your own pocket.

People aren't born understanding financial principles. In 2014, two researchers had pollsters ask consumers in various countries three simple questions about investing—softballs like:

"Imagine that the interest rate on your savings account is 1% per year and inflation is 2% per year. After one year would you be able to buy with the money in this account more than today, less than today, or the same as today?"

Seventy percent of Americans couldn't give correct answers to all three questions.[1006] That's worse than respondents in Germany, Switzerland, or France. And yet 70% of the Americans rated themselves a 4 or better on a 1-to-7 scale of their "financial knowledge."[1007]

Take the test yourself. It's in Figure 1-4.

Don't worry if you flub any of the answers. You'll know how to handle much more difficult problems than these by the end of this book.

FIGURE 1-4

Can you answer three questions about money?

1 · Suppose you had $100 in a savings account and the interest rate was 2% per year. After five years, how much do you think you would have in the account if you left the money to grow?

☐ A) More than $102
☐ B) Exactly $102
☐ C) Less than $102
☐ D) Do not know

2 · Imagine that the interest rate on your savings account is 1% per year and inflation is 2% per year. After one year, would you be able to buy with the money in this account:

☐ A) More than today
☐ B) Less than today
☐ C) The same as today
☐ D) Do not know

3 · Do you think that the following statement is true or false? "Buying a single company stock usually provides a safer return than a stock mutual fund."

☐ A) True
☐ B) False
☐ C) Do not know

Answers are in Figure 1-5.

Source: Annamaria Lusardi and Olivia Mitchell, *Journal of Economic Literature*, 2014

Bear markets can ruin your life, but you can manage them

FIGURE 1-5
Three money answers

The questions are in Figure 1-4

1 · A You'd have **more** than $102 in your savings account after five years if the interest rate was 2% per year. The actual balance would be $110.41. Your $100 would be multiplied by 1.02 five times.

2 · B After one year, you'd be able to buy **less than today**, if the interest rate on your savings account was 1% per year and inflation was 2% per year.

3 · C Any single company might go bankrupt, causing its stock price to drop to zero. It's much less likely that every one of the companies in a diversified stock mutual fund would go broke. That means the fund is **safer** than any individual company.

Crashes of 30%, 40%, 50%, or more are a permanent feature of free markets.

As an investor, your primary job is to minimize these wipeouts of your wealth.

Know your enemy! Up and down markets have been called bulls and bears since the 1700s (Figure 1-6).

Based on the S&P 500's "headline price," not adjusted for dividends or inflation, major swings are defined as follows:

» **A bull market** is a gain of 20% or more.

» **A correction** is a loss of 10% to 19.9% during bull markets, which "correct" about once a year.[1008]

» **A bear market** is a loss of 20% or more. This strikes about once every eight years (i.e., 15 times in the 126 years 1892–2017).[1009] The average decline is awful: 45%.[1010]

» **A crash** is a dive of 30% or more. Eight of the last 10 S&P bear markets qualify as crashes (one per decade).

FIGURE 1-6
Frankfurt Stock Exchange

» **A severe crash** that burns up 40% or more of investors' money hits every 18 years, on average.[1011]

Figure 1-7 shows the last five severe crashes, adjusted for inflation. Real bear-market losses are usually worse than headlined.

The S&P 500 is crash prone —it consists of a single, risky type of asset (only the US's largest companies).

Mere 10% corrections should be ignored. But bear markets and crashes are performance killers you must intelligently manage.

> **» KEY CONCEPT**
> ## drawdown
> Investors hate drawdowns: a portfolio's loss from its highest point to its lowest subsequent point, based on monthly or daily closes.

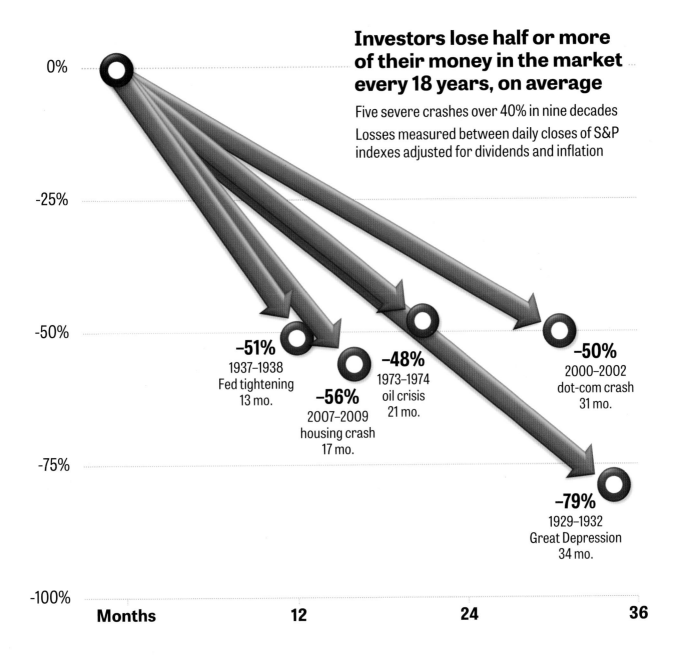

Investors lose half or more of their money in the market every 18 years, on average

Five severe crashes over 40% in nine decades

Losses measured between daily closes of S&P indexes adjusted for dividends and inflation

−51%
1937–1938
Fed tightening
13 mo.

−56%
2007–2009
housing crash
17 mo.

−48%
1973–1974
oil crisis
21 mo.

−50%
2000–2002
dot-com crash
31 mo.

−79%
1929–1932
Great Depression
34 mo.

Months   12   24   36

FIGURE 1-7 | Source: Jill Mislinski/Advisor Perspective[1012]

There's no secret that prevents you from becoming an informed investor

The foundation of all modern investing is *The Intelligent Investor* by Benjamin Graham. He produced four editions of this book between 1949 and 1973.

Graham taught a finance course at Columbia University in New York City for 28 years. Many of his students went on to become wealthy investors—the most famous of whom is Warren Buffett.

Graham died in 1976, but an updated version of his book was released in 2003. Buffett himself wrote the preface, declaring Graham's work "by far the best book on investing ever written."[1013]

Besides teaching, Graham also managed a very successful mutual fund that proved his principles Jason Zweig, a columnist for the *Wall Street Journal*, calculated that Graham's mutual fund had earned 14.7% annualized from 1936 through 1956. The market overall had gained only 12.2%. "One of the best long-term track records in Wall Street history," Zweig noted.[1014]

Graham maintained that investing success or failure was determined by the effort you put into the game. He defined two types of market players:

» **The defensive or passive investor** aims for "freedom from effort, annoyance, and the need for making frequent decisions."

» **The enterprising investor** is willing "to devote time and care to the selection of securities that are both sound and more attractive than the average."

The enterprising investor, Graham concluded, "could expect a worthwhile reward for his extra skill and effort, in the form of a better average return than that realized by the passive investor."

Think of 21st century investing as having **three** types:

» **The full-time day trader/speculator** darts in and out of securities, holding them only for days, hours, or milliseconds, looking for a fleeting "edge."

» **The armchair investor** pays little attention to the market. He or she doesn't update a portfolio until headlines announce a bear market. By that point, it's too late to adapt.

» **The informed investor** takes the time to study the science of investing (Figure 1-8). Using the latest research, informed investors make occasional adjustments to their portfolios, adapting them as market conditions change.

This book is for informed investors—and armchair investors who would like to **become** informed.

Do you have enough skill to buy a plane ticket on the Web? If so, you're perfectly qualified to handle your own portfolio, as described in this book.

Managing a portfolio takes just 15 minutes a month—and that's a ticket to watch your nest egg fly for life.

» **KEY CONCEPT**

the informed investor

Any person who studies the latest science on investing can learn enough to prevent their portfolio from crashing.

Informed investors sharpen their skills by reading the latest research on personal finance

FIGURE 1-8

The S&P 500 is not your friend— don't bet your life on it

The S&P 500 has long been used as a "benchmark" representing the performance of the broad market.

Some pundits suggest that individuals should simply buy an index fund based on the S&P 500 and do nothing else. This **buy-and-hold** strategy would supposedly grow your money steadily.

So, what if you'd sunk your entire nest egg into a buy-and-hold of the S&P 500 at the market top in March 2000?

Figure 1-9 shows the S&P 500 adjusted for inflation, showing the **real rate of return.**

In real dollars—the kind you buy groceries with—the S&P 500 **halved** your portfolio's value in just 2½ years during the 2000–2002 dot-com crash. In Wall Street jargon, you had a 50% **real drawdown**, a loss of half your purchasing power from the peak to the bottom.

Your portfolio took a full five years—from October 2002 to October 2007—to **almost** get back to even in original buying power.

The index then walloped your life savings during the 2007–2009 bear market. You were down 58.5%, measured from

the all-time peak back in March 2000. That 58.5% was your **maximum drawdown**— your greatest loss between two daily closes.

During a bull market, you hear a lot about the market's big gains. But in truth, the S&P 500 gave buy-and-hold investors **no gain whatsoever** for 13½ years, starting from the market top in 2000.

It didn't matter whether you bought the S&P in 1980 or 1990. You still wouldn't have any real gain in 2000 through 2013.

Individuals feel intense pressure to "cry uncle" during a bear market. They begin selling their financial assets at steep losses when the decline exceeds a **behavioral pain point** of about 25%. Selling converts a paper loss into a **permanent loss of capital**. (Evidence of the pain point is in Chapter 14.)

Figure 1-9 uses the low-cost Vanguard Five Hundred Index (VFINX) to track a buy-and-hold investment in the S&P 500. VFINX is a low-cost mutual fund that's indexed the S&P 500 since 1976.

It's easy for individuals to buy shares of VFINX. It's impossible to buy a theoretical index like the S&P 500. Graphing VFINX also adjusts correctly for the annual fees actual investors paid to hold the S&P 500.

» TECH TALK

total returns include dividends

Company dividends represent about 2 percentage points of the S&P 500's return each year. Figure 1-9 correctly adjusts for dividends, as calculated by Yahoo Finance.

Returns that include dividends are called **total returns.**

Beware! If graphs don't include dividends, you're seeing only the **price return,** which is less.

» KEY CONCEPT

real means inflation-adjusted

A "real" gain or loss has been adjusted to remove the effect of inflation.

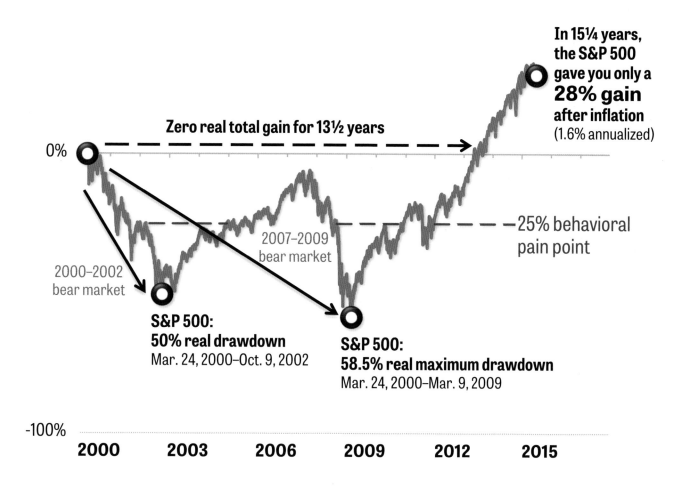

100% ···· **A buy-and-hold of the S&P 500 gave you in 13½ years a <u>zero</u> real total gain—nothing to live on!**

Real total gain, adjusted for dividends, inflation, and fees (VFINX)
Mar. 24, 2000–June 30, 2015 daily closes

In 15¼ years, the S&P 500 gave you only a **28% gain** after inflation (1.6% annualized)

Zero real total gain for 13½ years

0%

25% behavioral pain point

2007–2009 bear market

2000–2002 bear market

S&P 500: 50% real drawdown
Mar. 24, 2000–Oct. 9, 2002

S&P 500: 58.5% real maximum drawdown
Mar. 24, 2000–Mar. 9, 2009

-100%

2000   **2003**   **2006**   **2009**   **2012**   **2015**

FIGURE 1-9 | Data source: Yahoo Finance

The inflated gains you read about can leave you holding an empty bag

People who retired from their jobs in 2000—thinking that investing their nest eggs in the "hot" S&P 500 would ensure them a comfortable lifestyle—were in for a rude awakening.

If they didn't bail out during either of the two subsequent market crashes—if they held on across the entire 15¼ years—they still experienced a huge disappointment.

From Mar. 24, 2000, through June 30, 2015, the buy-and-hold return was a measly 1.6% per year, adjusted for dividends and inflation. That 1.6% is the **annualized rate of return** (abbreviated "ann'd"), a synonym for the **compound annual growth rate** (CAGR). Your $100 turned into only $128 of real purchasing power.

Gaining $28 might sound OK. But across 15¼ years, it's not. You would have gained **twice as much** by simply holding a long-term Treasury bond fund instead. That's why "buy and hold" is often called "buy and hope."[1015]

Both of the lines representing the S&P 500 in Figure 1-10 include dividends. This compares apples to apples. The only difference between the two lines is that the **real** return—shown in orange—is adjusted for inflation.

What's called the **nominal** return—shown in gray—is **not** adjusted for inflation. You usually read in newspapers and blogs the exaggerated gain of the nominal return.

Investors uncomfortable with the risks of the S&P 500 have long been told that lowering their risk means anemic gains. You've certainly heard the myth: "You must **increase** your risk to boost your gain!"

That dogma helps Wall Street sell risky securities, charging big fees for the privilege.

But, believe it or not, **reducing** your portfolio's risk is the best way to **increase** your investing gain. You don't have to choose between volatile stocks and low-yielding bonds. Today, it's easy for investors to take advantage of a well-diversified menu of global asset classes.

You don't have to be a financial genius. If you can commit just 15 minutes each month to checking in on your portfolio and giving it an occasional course correction, you can watch your savings grow safely.

The 21st-century approach to investing is called Muscular Portfolios—investing strategies that are designed to lose no more than 20% or 25%, even during the worst market crashes.

Best of all, the formula for Muscular Portfolios is fully disclosed, free of charge, in this book and at Muscular Portfolios.com. There's no need to pay anyone for pricey investing advice ever again.

>> KEY CONCEPT
annualized rate of return equals compound annual growth rate
A portfolio's CAGR or annualized return represents the growth rate of a straight line from the portfolio's start value to its end value.

>> KEY CONCEPT
nominal
Not inflation-adjusted. Think of "nominal" as "not modified for inflation at all."

The S&P 500 'headline rate' didn't give you much purchasing power after inflation

Real total gain, adjusted for dividends, inflation, and fees (VFINX)
Mar. 24, 2000–June 30, 2015 daily closes

3.9% NOMINAL annualized rate of return

1.6% REAL annualized rate of return

**S&P 500:
3.9% NOMINAL**
annualized
rate of return
(mostly inflation)

**S&P 500:
1.6% REAL**
annualized
rate of return,
after inflation

2000–2002
bear market

2007–2009
bear market

**S&P 500:
50% real drawdown**
Mar. 24, 2000–Oct. 9, 2002

**S&P 500:
58.5% real maximum drawdown**
Mar. 24, 2000–Mar. 9, 2009

100%

0%

-100%

2000   2003   2006   2009   2012   2015

FIGURE 1-10 | Data source: Yahoo Finance

The informed investor has three important principles for success

Informed investors have three goals in common:

1 · Achieve stock-like returns or better for the remainder of one's lifetime

This goal is obvious. Who wouldn't want to reap the soaring gains that the global equity markets have generated in decades past?

The problem is that stock markets are risky and prone to crashes. But these pitfalls can be eliminated by following some simple rules and committing 15 minutes per month to adjusting your portfolio as needed, as we'll see.

2 · Require portfolio changes no more than once per month—ideally, less often

In 2000, two business professors examined 78,000 accounts at a discount bro-kerage firm from 1991 through 1996. They divided the investors into five groups, sorted by how much they traded. The results are in Figure 1-11.

The one-fifth of investors who made the fewest trades had the highest annualized return: 18.5%. That beat a stock index fund, which returned 17.9% during this bullish period. Those with the highest trading volume reaped only 11.4%.[1016]

Frequent traders suffer all kinds of "trading friction." That includes commissions and other expenses, which add up before you realize it.

3 · Keep losses low, but avoid market timing

"Market timing" means **switching from 100% stocks to 100% cash based on an indicator** (such as a percentage loss). In a bull market, you may think, "The market can't go any higher." But the Federal Reserve could stimulate a rally, or any of a million other things could push the market up still more.

Evidence of how rarely market timing works comes from Mark Hulbert, editor of the *Hulbert Financial Digest* from 1980 to 2016. He subscribed to scores of investment newsletters and calculated how much you'd have made if you'd followed the advice they contained. The results weren't good:

"Just 11 of the 81 stock-market timers—those advisers who try to predict when to get into or out of the market to sidestep declines and participate in rallies—actually made money during the bear market that began after the Internet bubble burst in March 2000 and ended in October 2002.

"These market timers have lost so much since then that, on average, they are in the red over the entire period since March 2000 [through July 2014], having chalked up a 0.8% annualized loss.

"A simple buy-and-hold approach using the Wilshire 5000 over the same period, by contrast, gained an annualized 4.2%, including reinvested dividends."[1017]

» **KEY CONCEPT**

trade once a month or less
Infrequent portfolio changes are enough to achieve outperformance.

» **KEY CONCEPT**

don't try to time the market
With all the ways the Federal Reserve can stimulate a bull market, it ain't over 'til the Fed lady sings.

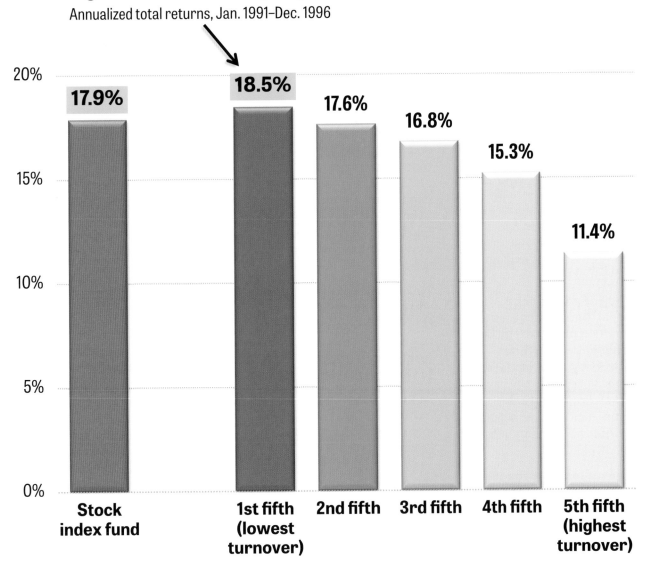

Investors who make the fewest trades have higher returns than people who trade often

Annualized total returns, Jan. 1991–Dec. 1996

- Stock index fund: 17.9%
- 1st fifth (lowest turnover): 18.5%
- 2nd fifth: 17.6%
- 3rd fifth: 16.8%
- 4th fifth: 15.3%
- 5th fifth (highest turnover): 11.4%

FIGURE 1-11 | Source: Barber & Odean (2000)[1018]

Three megatrends have sparked the Index Investing Revolution

The Index Investing Revolution

Only since 2000 have three megatrends converged:

» **The bargain-brokerage megatrend.** As recently as 1975, trading costs consumed over 2% of your money when you bought and sold a stock. Today, trades cost as little as $4. At some commission-free brokerages, trades can cost nothing. Saving your money when you trade is explained in Chapter 17.

» **The ETF megatrend.** Many mutual funds charge annual fees of 1% or more. The best exchange-traded funds boast fees as low as 0.05%. That's serious money in your pocket. Some of the ETFs in this book's model portfolios opened to the public as recently as 2014.

» **The momentum megatrend.** Academics proved in the mid-1990s that assets with recent price gains—momentum—tend to gain in the coming month or longer.

The ETF megatrend: market returns, low fees

Open-end mutual funds have been offered in the US since 1924. By contrast, the first exchange-traded fund (ETF) opened as recently as 1993. Many investors don't realize the big advantages of ETFs:

» **ETFs subject you to little or no tax** until you actually sell shares. By contrast, mutual funds are required to "distribute" (declare) dividends and capital gains once a year. In a taxable account, you must pay tax on any "distributions" by mutual funds, even though you sold no shares.

These "phantom gains" make you pay tax each year on 0.98% to 2.08% of the value of mutual funds you hold in taxable accounts, according to Lipper Associates.[1019]

At the extreme, the average mutual fund that specializes in emerging-market stocks declares a distribution each year of 6.46%, says ETF.com. But emerging-market ETFs declare only 0.01%.[1020]

Many ETFs haven't declared a distribution in years. That's a relief at tax time.[1021]

» **No entry, exit, or marketing fees.** Some mutual funds charge you a "front-end load" when you buy shares. For instance, at this writing,

Vanguard's Long-Term Corporate Bond mutual fund (VLTCX) charges a 1% "purchase fee." You're better off buying Vanguard's Long-Term Corporate Bond ETF (VCLT). It has the exact same holdings but—like every ETF—imposes no front-end load.

Mutual funds may also charge a "redemption fee" of 1% or more if you sell shares before five years. Another bite is an annual "12b-1 fee." You pay up to 1% each year, some of which is kicked back to brokers who promote such funds.[1022]

ETFs never charge any of the above fees.

» **ETFs have lower expense ratios.** The average annual fee charged by the ETFs in this book is less than 0.2%. That's only $2 per year on a $1,000 balance (Figure 1-12). The simple average of equity mutual-fund expense ratios was 1.33% in 2014, according to the 2015 Investment Company Fact Book.[1023]

» **ETFs are cheap to buy and sell.** When you buy a stock or an ETF, you pay the "ask" price. When you sell, you get the "bid" price. The difference (the "bid-ask spread") is the profit margin collected by a professional market maker. Small

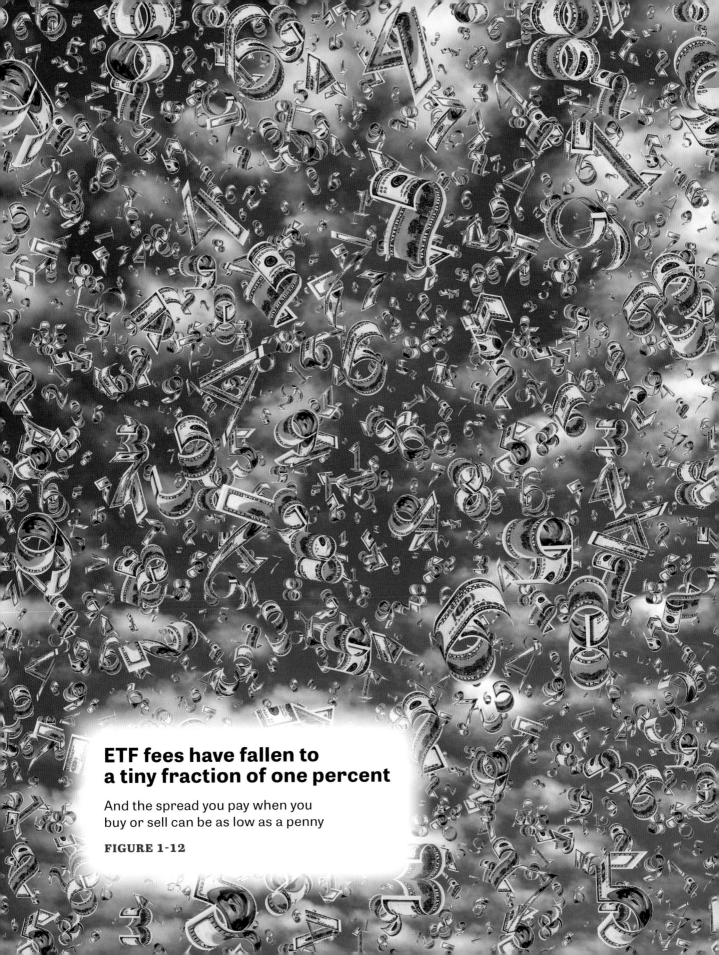

**ETF fees have fallen to
a tiny fraction of one percent**

And the spread you pay when you
buy or sell can be as low as a penny

FIGURE 1-12

stocks can easily have spreads of 1% or more. The most popular ETFs have tiny spreads: under 0.1%. (See Chapter 17 for details.)

» Buy any time during the day. You can check the price of any ETF whenever the market is open. You can look at 3 PM Eastern and buy an ETF that has good momentum before the market closes at 4.

You can't see a mutual fund's price until hours after the close. This delays your decision by one full day.

Most corporate 401(k) savings plans still include only mutual funds, not ETFs.[1024] But that's changing.

Investors kept $18.2 trillion in US-based mutual funds but only $2.0 trillion in ETFs in 2014.[1025] However, people moved $680 billion out of mutual funds and into ETFs in the 8.3 years ending April 2015.[1026]

Our prospects have forever been changed by momentum

The third megatrend—proof of momentum—is the most crucial to understand.

As long ago as 1837, author James Grant revealed in his book *The Great Metropolis* the "golden rules" by which British economist David Ricardo amassed a huge fortune in the stock market:

"Cut short your losses, Let your profits run on."[1027]

This sounds obvious—but in practice, most investors do the opposite. They hold losing investments too long and dispose of winning securities too quickly. Behavioral finance experts call this the "disposition effect." It's a wealth-destroying and all-too-human trait.[1028]

How can investors overcome this tendency? How can we tell how long an investment should be held?

The answer is science. Evidence-based rules can help us purchase asset classes that have the best odds of rising in the months to come. They can also tell us when to let go of assets whose odds are no longer so good (Figure 1-13).

In 1993, two UCLA researchers statistically confirmed the existence of an objective standard. It's called the momentum factor. An asset class whose price has risen over the past 3 to 12 months **tends to continue to rise** for the following month or more.

The researchers, Narasimhan Jegadeesh and Sheridan Titman, found "significant profits" in the NYSE and AMEX markets predicted by this factor. They looked as far back as 1927—an unbroken 62 years of evidence.[1029]

These findings have survived the test of time. In a 2014 metastudy of momentum, certified investment management analyst David Garff stated:

"This theory has been one of the most strongly tested in all of modern finance, with more than 300 academic and practical papers, including 150 in the past five years."[1030]

» KEY CONCEPT

the momentum factor
Asset classes that have risen in price for the past 3 to 12 months tend to continue to rise for another month or more.

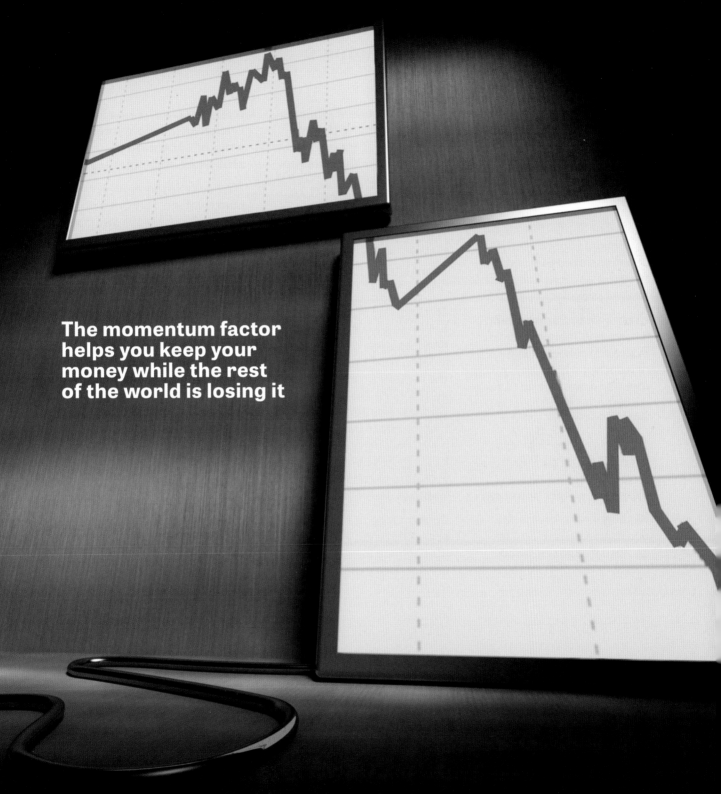

The momentum factor helps you keep your money while the rest of the world is losing it

FIGURE 1-13

The momentum factor is one of the strongest influences in economics

The evidence of momentum in free markets faced a powerful headwind from the so-called Efficient Market Hypothesis (EMH). This theory was published in 1970 by Eugene Fama, a finance professor at the University of Chicago (Figure 1-14). His paper asserted that "security prices at any time 'fully reflect' all available information."[1031]

In other words, everything known about an investment is already reflected in its price. Supposedly, that price must be rational, and human trading decisions must be rational as well.

This theory was disproved in a 1981 paper by Robert Shiller, an economics professor at Yale University.

Writing in the *American Economic Review*, Shiller showed that stock-price volatility was "five to thirteen times too high" to support the conclusion that humans were making purely logical calculations:

"The failure of the efficient markets model is thus so dramatic that it would seem impossible to attribute the failure to such things as data errors, price index problems, or changes in tax laws."[1032]

In 2011, the *Review* named Shiller's paper one of the top 20 articles in its 100-year history.[1033]

The final nail in the coffin of EMH was a wave of behavioral-finance research. Beginning in 1985, Werner De Bondt of the University of Wisconsin and Richard Thaler of Cornell University published evidence that investors overreact to news, making security prices lurch. Prices can take three to five years to return to a "rational" level.[1034]

Confirmation by hundreds of such studies caused a U-turn in economic thinking. If people are not purely rational, there might be factors that are **not** already reflected in a security's price. To their credit, Fama and his coauthor Kenneth French of Dartmouth began publishing a series of papers on momentum.

In a 2007 study, Fama and French called momentum **a major exception to efficiency,** writing:

"The premier anomaly is momentum. . . . Stocks with low returns over the last year tend to have low returns for the next few months and stocks with high past returns tend to have high future returns."[1035]

Fama and French found that momentum predicted gains over the next month or so more strongly than any other factor they identified. Along with coauthors like Mark Carhart, they showed that securities with momentum tend to rise.

In 2011, after studying decades of historical market data from North America, Europe, and Asia, they declared that "there is return momentum everywhere."[1036]

> **» KEY CONCEPT**
> ## evidence-based investing
> Nobel laureates like Shiller and Fama show that only a few market factors—momentum chief among them—have predictive ability.

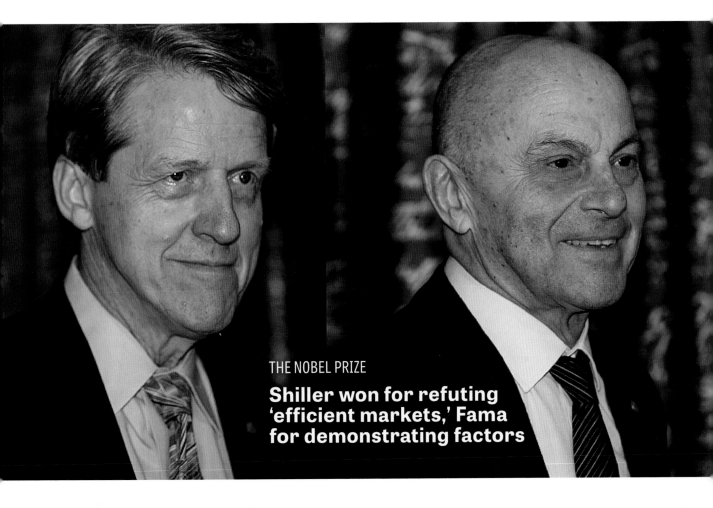

THE NOBEL PRIZE

Shiller won for refuting 'efficient markets,' Fama for demonstrating factors

FIGURE 1-14 | Stockholm, Sweden, 2013

Every country of the 23 they examined exhibited momentum (with the exception of Japan, for whatever reason).

In 2013, both Fama and Shiller received the Nobel Prize in Economics. The selection committee's official report never even mentioned the discarded Efficient Market Hypothesis, since it's a bit of an embarrassment among economists these days.[1037]

Instead, the prize was awarded to Shiller for **disproving** the hypothesis and Fama for subsequently **moving beyond it.**

Nobel winners reveal how we behave irrationally about money

A key to the Index Investing Revolution is a breakthrough in understanding our own minds.

Economists used to think human beings were walking calculators. They called us *Homo economicus.* We supposedly made every decision about money using nothing but pure logic. That view is sometimes called **neoclassical economics.**

This dogma has largely been replaced by **behavioral economics.** Study after study shows that we all deal with financial data in wildly illogical ways.

If someone said, "Everyone chooses a mate using only rational decision-making," you'd laugh. Well, it turns out that money activates many of the same emotions as sex. There's nothing logical about the way we approach financial decisions.

In 2002, the Nobel Prize in Economics was awarded to psychologist Daniel Kahneman (Figure 1-15) and economist Vernon Smith for their revelations about behavioral finance. Kahneman wrote much of his early work with Amos Tversky (Figure 1-16), who died in 1996.[1038]

Praise for behavioral finance continues to mount. The 2017 Nobel went to pioneer Richard Thaler, who, in 2008 with Cass Sunstein, cowrote the influential book *Nudge.*[1039]

Kahneman and Tversky's studies explain why our decision-making about investing fails us. We're not the cool, rational creatures we think we are.

In his bestselling 2011 book, *Thinking, Fast and Slow,* Kahneman explains that we all use at least two kinds of thinking:

Quick! Add two plus two. You can do this automatically. Kahneman calls that "System 1 thinking." It provides rapid, nearly unconscious answers to simple situations.[1040]

Now—when you're about to make a left turn against oncoming traffic—try to multiply 17 by 23 in your head. Wait, don't actually do it! The conscious thought process required to multiply those two numbers would impair your ability to drive.[1041]

This second math problem is an example of "System 2 thinking." (Hat-tip to Laurence Siegel of Advisor Perspectives for these examples of System 1 and 2.)

System 2 thinking involves more advanced multistep thought. This means more opportunity for the kind of cognitive errors that humans can't help but make. Alas, we aren't computers—but we do all have some common glitches:

» **A loss hurts us worse than a gain thrills us.** We feel the pain of loss more than twice as much as we enjoy the prospect of an equal gain. (This is called "prospect theory.")

» **We notice what confirms our views and not what challenges them.** We tend to filter out new information unless it reinforces our own beliefs ("confirmation bias").[1042]

Behavioral biases like these affect investment decisions. They make people seriously underperform the market. Evidence of this is in Chapter 14.

How can you overcome these biases? One way is to follow scientific methods of asset selection that don't rely on your own opinions. Helping you do so is the goal of this book.

Kahneman and his coauthor Tversky uncovered our behavioral biases

FIGURE 1-15
Digital Life Design conference, Munich, 2009

Amos Tversky, 1937–1996

FIGURE 1-16

Muscular Portfolios require low maintenance but offer great returns

Muscular Portfolios offer less risk of crashing but perform long term like the broad market or better.

The two Muscular Portfolios in this book select from menus of 9 to 13 ETFs. Each month, followers of the portfolios tune up their holdings using a specific Momentum Rule.

No one can predict exactly which asset class will be number one next month or any month. But that degree of precision isn't necessary.

Figure 1-17 is a 43-year historical model. It was developed using a computer program called the Quant simulator. The software is given out to subscribers of The Idea Farm newsletter, edited by Mebane Faber, coauthor of *The Ivy Portfolio.*

Quant calculates the return on all major asset classes. The program is sometimes referred to as a "backtester," but it's more accurately called a simulator. That's because Quant doesn't use prices of individual stocks. Instead, it models the asset classes that are tracked by today's low-cost index ETFs.

Figure 1-17 shows diamond markers where the S&P 500 subjected investors to four crashes—declines of 30% or more—in 43 years.

Notice the other diamond markers. The Mama Bear Portfolio lost only 18% and the Papa Bear Portfolio no more than 25%, measured between month-ends. That's far better than the S&P 500 and Lazy Portfolios, which have delivered intolerable losses of 30% to 51% over the same period.

Muscular Portfolios are **clones** of strategies developed by financial experts. A clone is a translation of a proven methodology into a free model that any individual can easily use. The Mama Bear Portfolio clones a strategy published by Steve LeCompte of CXO Advisory; The Papa Bear Portfolio mirrors a peer-reviewed whitepaper by Mebane Faber. Both are described in Chapters 5 and 6.

Obviously, the gains shown in a simulation cannot be guaranteed. For this reason, your best approach is to estimate **how badly a strategy may hurt you in years to come.** A portfolio that's made investors suffer losses of 30%, 40%, or 50% in the past will subject them to the same intolerable losses in the future.

Investors can't stomach strategies that cause that much pain. Survivable losses help you stay the course. Avoid the human tendency to lock in your losses by selling during a bear market.

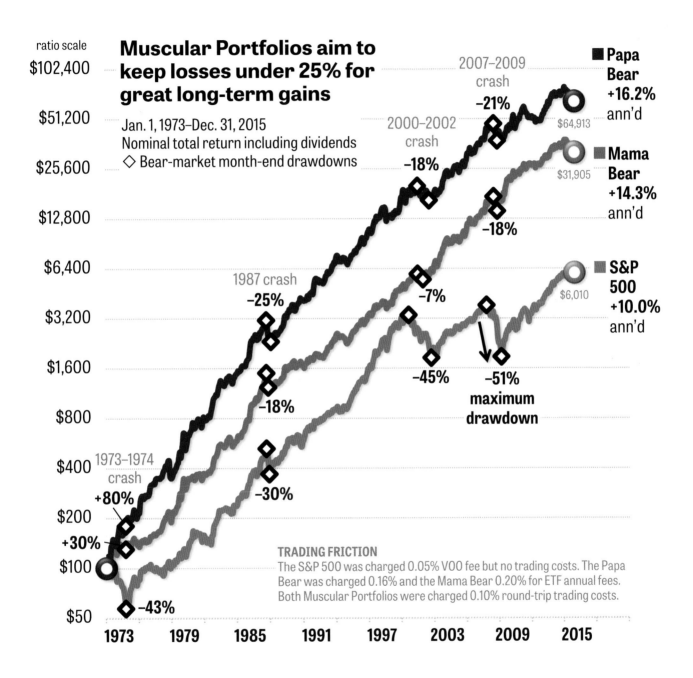

Muscular Portfolios aim to keep losses under 25% for great long-term gains

Jan. 1, 1973–Dec. 31, 2015
Nominal total return including dividends
◇ Bear-market month-end drawdowns

ratio scale

$102,400
$51,200
$25,600
$12,800
$6,400
$3,200
$1,600
$800
$400
$200
$100
$50

1973 1979 1985 1991 1997 2003 2009 2015

2007–2009 crash
−21%

2000–2002 crash
−18%

1987 crash
−25%

−18%

−7%

−45%

−51%
maximum drawdown

1973–1974 crash
+80%
+30%
−43%

−18%

−30%

$64,913
$31,905
$6,010

■ Papa Bear +16.2% ann'd
■ Mama Bear +14.3% ann'd
■ S&P 500 +10.0% ann'd

TRADING FRICTION
The S&P 500 was charged 0.05% VOO fee but no trading costs. The Papa Bear was charged 0.16% and the Mama Bear 0.20% for ETF annual fees. Both Muscular Portfolios were charged 0.10% round-trip trading costs.

FIGURE 1-17 | Source: Quant simulator

The Baby Bear matches the S&P 500 but subjects you to less risk

The Baby Bear is a starter portfolio for accounts under $10,000. Commissions of even $100 would eat 1% of that amount, so the Baby Bear holds down costs by requiring only an annual rebalance.

The Baby Bear clones a recommendation made for more than two decades by Jack Bogle, founder of the Vanguard Group. It's described in Chapter 7.

The Baby Bear is ultrasimple: 50% stocks and 50% bonds. (A 60/40 split is also common, but according to Bogle, this delivers returns similar to 50/50.)[1043]

Figure 1-18 shows a 43-year Quant model.

The S&P 500's annualized return was **10.0%.** Bonds returned **8.9%.** Notice that the Baby Bear did not return the **average** of the two, which would have been **9.45%.** Instead, it returned a higher **9.8%.** That's because bonds often go up when stocks go down, lessening crashes. The Baby Bear's simple two-ETF strategy gave it a return within a mere 0.2 point of the S&P 500.

> **» TECH TALK**
>
> ## no one guarantees simulated results
>
> **» Models are not track records.** Simulations compute historical data using current trading costs. ETFs didn't even exist back in 1973. Focus on a portfolio's maximum loss, which is certain to recur.
>
> **» Today's trading costs are under 0.10%.** Commissions and bid-ask spreads for major ETFs are both below 0.05% round-trip (Chapter 20). In simulations, Muscular Portfolios are therefore charged 0.10% round-trip per transaction.

Pundits often joke about the "Holy Grail of Investing"—a strategy with market-like returns but only bond-like volatility. What does that mean?

» "Market-like returns" are results within 1 percentage point of the S&P 500 over complete bear-bull market cycles.

» "Bond-like volatility" means losses less than Treasury funds. One Vanguard government bond fund, EDV, fell 40% when interest rates rose (Dec. 26, 2008–June 10, 2009).[1044] Your portfolio has bond-like volatility if it never falls more than 40%.

The easy-peasy Baby Bear fits both definitions. Enjoying market-like returns with smaller losses than the S&P 500 is not a fantasy. It's simple math.

So should everyone follow the Baby Bear? No. Bogle himself says stocks are pricey and bond yields are low. Bogle estimates that a 50/50 portfolio will eke out a return of only 3.5% or 4.5% in the 10 years ending 2025 (see Chapter 13). Inflation will probably eat away a lot of that.[1045, 1046]

If you can spend 15 minutes a month, you'll do better with a Muscular Portfolio.

> **» KEY CONCEPT**
> ## market-like returns, bond-like volatility
> Even a simple 50/50 portfolio delivers S&P 500–sized returns with smaller losses.

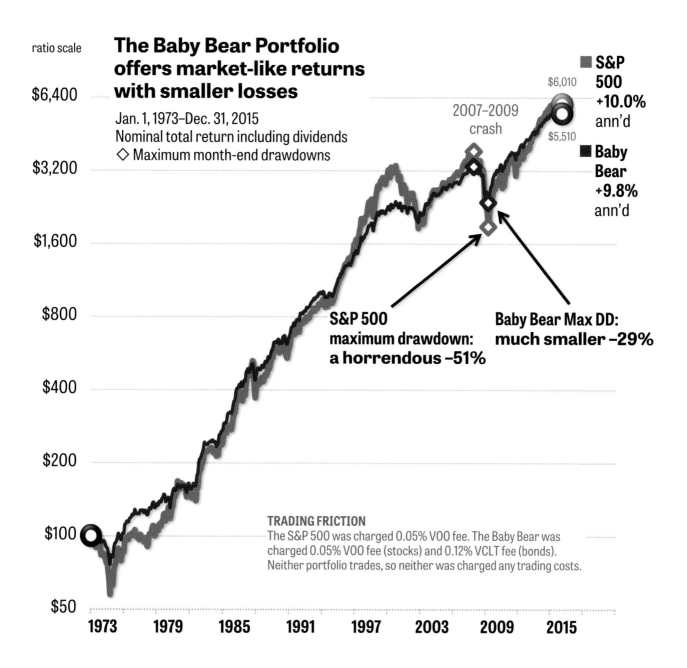

ratio scale

The Baby Bear Portfolio offers market-like returns with smaller losses

Jan. 1, 1973–Dec. 31, 2015
Nominal total return including dividends
◇ Maximum month-end drawdowns

$6,400

$3,200

2007–2009
crash

$6,010

■ S&P
500
+10.0%
ann'd

$5,510

■ Baby
Bear
+9.8%
ann'd

$1,600

$800

**S&P 500
maximum drawdown:
a horrendous –51%**

**Baby Bear Max DD:
much smaller –29%**

$400

$200

$100

TRADING FRICTION
The S&P 500 was charged 0.05% VOO fee. The Baby Bear was
charged 0.05% VOO fee (stocks) and 0.12% VCLT fee (bonds).
Neither portfolio trades, so neither was charged any trading costs.

$50

1973   1979   1985   1991   1997   2003   2009   2015

FIGURE 1-18 | Source: Quant simulator

Portfolios benefit from diversification, but Lazy Portfolios use assets passively

"Index" mutual funds emerged in the 1980s and 1990s. These funds provided an alternative to the picking of individual stocks. Investors could hold an assortment of securities representing a particular type of asset, such as corporate bonds or European stocks.

How many different asset classes are there? Well, you can divide the world into an unlimited number. But 9 to 13 asset classes are generally enough for any portfolio to select from. Figure 1-19 shows nine major asset classes, which can be carved into many minor categories.

The emergence of index funds sparked an idea in the minds of some financial professionals. "Why don't we simply hold a lot of different asset classes in our portfolios? The diversification will keep us safe when the S&P 500 crashes!"[1047]

The idea was to allocate your money to a diverse set of index funds in static proportions at all times. This system was called a Lazy Portfolio (after a 2004 book on the subject, as we'll see in Chapter 3).

The main attraction of Lazy Portfolios was that you never had to alter the weight allocated to any index fund. Simply "rebalance" each fund back to its original percentage of the portfolio's value once a year, perhaps in December or January. In Wall Street jargon, a Lazy Portfolio is called a "strategic" or "static" asset allocation (SAA).

There was one exception to the strict allocation policy. A follower might be told to increase the percentage of fixed-income assets—like bonds or money-market funds—each year as he or she grew closer to retirement age. This gradually lowers a portfolio's volatility—but usually also reduces its gains.

Each of the most common Lazy Portfolios was designed during one of the longest bullish streaks in American history: the 18-year party that raged from 1982 to 2000 (interrupted only by the two-month crash of 1987).

Unfortunately, both the 2000–2002 dot-com bear market and the 2007–2009 financial crisis revealed the fatal flaw of Lazy Portfolios. While they may protect you from the risk of holding only one asset type, a broad market crash still packs a devastating punch to your savings.

Mere diversification didn't keep Lazy Portfolios from crashing 35% to 50%. Many shell-shocked investors liquidated their holdings near the bottom, locking in huge losses.

» **KEY CONCEPT**

asset classes
ETFs now track every kind of security around the world, offering diversification that can protect you from any one asset crashing.

How many asset classes are there?

Let's start with these nine categories:

Equities

» US stocks

» Developed-market stocks

» Emerging-market stocks

Hard assets
(also called "alternatives")

» Real-estate investment trusts (REITs)

» Commodities (energy, agriculture, metals)

» Gold

Fixed-income

» Government bonds

» Investment-grade corporate bonds

» Cash (money-market funds)

FIGURE 1-19

Lazy Portfolios subject you to unacceptable losses and lag the market

Muscular Portfolios gradually rotate into the strongest asset classes, making one change every one or two months. Lazy Portfolios, by contrast, always hold the same five or more assets, never adapting—even when some ETFs clearly offer better performance than others.

Lazy Portfolios subject you to two major performance headaches:

» **They tend to lag the S&P 500 rather than providing you with market-like returns; and**

» **They suffer bear-market losses far worse than the 25% pain point that compels investors to throw in the towel, harming their long-term performance.**

Figure 1-20 shows a Quant simulation of a typical Lazy Portfolio. It's called the Aggressive ETF Bucket Portfolio because it holds a static asset allocation of 10 ETFs in three "mental buckets" of money:

» 65.33% in stocks and junk bonds

» 26.67% in Treasury and high-quality bonds

» 8% in cash (money-market funds)

The Bucket Portfolio is regularly posted on the website of Morningstar, Inc., an investment management firm. It's often presented by Christine Benz, the firm's director of personal finance.[1048] Its specific holdings are listed in Appendix C and in a white-paper by the author of this book.[1049]

How would this Lazy Portfolio have done over the past four bear-bull market cycles, simulated under the same conditions as the Mama Bear and the Papa Bear?

Figure 1-20 graphs the results. The Bucket Portfolio would have underperformed the S&P 500 by almost one full percentage point: 9.1% annualized vs. the S&P 500's 10.0%.

That difference would have given your tax-deferred account an ending balance—over a 43-year working career—28% smaller than a buy-and-hold of an S&P 500 index fund like Vanguard's VOO. (You'd have $433,300 vs. $601,000, for example.)

Even worse, the Bucket Portfolio would have subjected followers to intolerable losses almost as dire as the S&P 500's. The portfolio would have been down 34% during the financial crisis—far beyond the 25% behavioral pain point.

You'd have been better off with the super-simple Baby Bear Portfolio. It lost no more than 29% but gave you an ending balance 27% higher than Morningstar's. (You'd have $551,000 vs. $433,300.)

No one can predict the future, of course. But one thing is certain: Strategies that don't work in theory aren't likely to work when you put serious money into them. A portfolio that performs poorly in simulations will disappoint you in real life.

This is not to pick on the Bucket Portfolio. The nine most popular Lazy Portfolios are all graphed in Chapter 3.

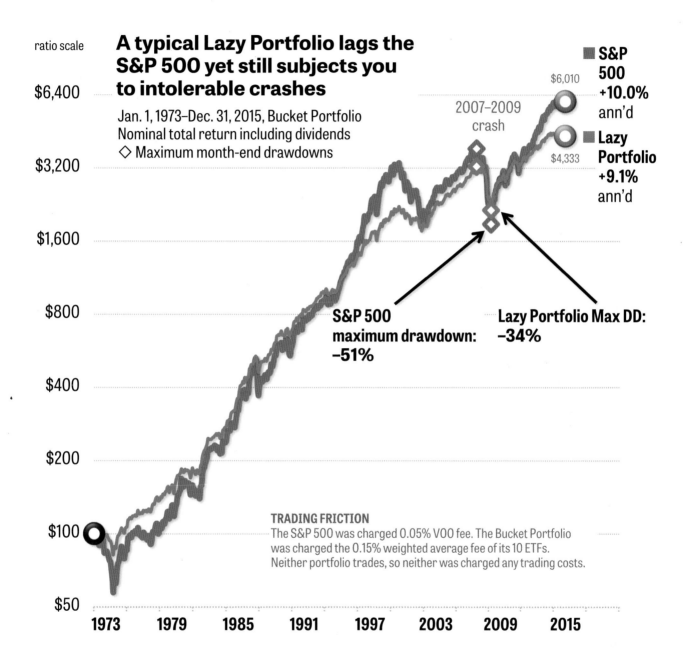

A typical Lazy Portfolio lags the S&P 500 yet still subjects you to intolerable crashes

Jan. 1, 1973–Dec. 31, 2015, Bucket Portfolio
Nominal total return including dividends
◇ Maximum month-end drawdowns

ratio scale

2007–2009 crash

$6,010

$4,333

■ S&P 500 +10.0% ann'd

■ Lazy Portfolio +9.1% ann'd

S&P 500 maximum drawdown: –51%

Lazy Portfolio Max DD: –34%

TRADING FRICTION
The S&P 500 was charged 0.05% VOO fee. The Bucket Portfolio was charged the 0.15% weighted average fee of its 10 ETFs. Neither portfolio trades, so neither was charged any trading costs.

$6,400 · $3,200 · $1,600 · $800 · $400 · $200 · $100 · $50

1973 · 1979 · 1985 · 1991 · 1997 · 2003 · 2009 · 2015

FIGURE 1-20 | Source: Quant simulator

Because it contradicts human nature, momentum is unlikely to burn out

After all the evidence is in, the model portfolios in this book face the question: "If these things work so well, won't everyone start using them? And won't that make them stop working?"

If too many big-money players pile into the Next Big Thing—whether it's dot-coms in 2000 or subprime mortgages in 2007—a strategy can become overgrazed and ineffective.

This concern is understandable. But several features of Muscular Portfolios make this fear unwarranted:

1 · Using momentum violates basic human traits

A powerful self-protective instinct is baked into our DNA. This instinct pushes us to buy stocks when the market is exciting and sell stocks when the market is scary. This is the essence of buying high and selling low.

The mountain of money that people lose this way is called the **Behavior Gap**. Acting on their opinions hurt average investors by about 2 percentage points of return each year, 1991–2003, according to Jason Hsu, vice chairman of Research Affiliates. (Evidence is in Chapter 14.)

Hsu studied the money flow into and out of US equity mutual funds. The funds returned 8.81%, but only 6.87% was realized by investors due to millions of them buying high and selling low. Ouch![1050]

Armchair investors are constantly looking for some trick that would make it easy to "buy low, sell high." But any such formula would soon attract billion-dollar traders and their supercomputers. Then the trick would vanish.

Muscular Portfolios are "buy high, sell higher" strategies. They don't tilt toward an asset class until it's risen for the past 3 to 12 months. At that point, armchair investors see the gain in price and say, "That's too hot." Informed investors say, "That's just right," and buy the trend.

Most individuals are instinct-bound to buy in good times and sell in bad times. The momentum factor acts to reverse this compulsion. Whenever Muscular Portfolio users trade, there will be millions of armchair investors doing the opposite.

2 · Giant hedge funds can't promote simple strategies

High-risk trading speculators can't promote an ultrasimple strategy to manage money. They know that complex strategies impress wealthy prospects.

To raise money, hedge funds must attract high-net-worth individuals with millions to invest. It isn't sexy to say, "We'll use your money to buy three index funds and change one of them every month or two." That wouldn't impress affluent clients who are told rapid trading means profits (Figure 1-21).

All that trading doesn't actually do hedge funds' clients any good. The big joke in the wealth-management game is hedge funds' terrible track record.

In 2007, Warren Buffett made a challenge of $1 million—to be donated to charity—that over the next 10 years an S&P 500 index fund would outperform any five hedge funds a challenger selected.[1051]

The bet was accepted by Ted Seides. He was, at the time, president of Protégé Partners, a New York asset-management firm that specializes in evaluating money managers. The hedge funds' gains were measured after subtracting their fees, which varied from 1.0% to

Why hedge funds won't overuse Muscular Portfolios

FIGURE 1-21 | Illustration by Randy Wood. Text by Brian Livingston

1.5% of assets and 5% to 20% of profits.[1052]

Buffett won easily. The hedge funds rose only 22% in 10 years. The S&P 500 index fund had climbed more than 85%—almost quadruple the gain! The index returned 7.1% annualized, while the "best of class" hedge funds returned only 2.2%.[1053]

Some hedge funds do well. Most do not.

For the 10+ years ending Feb. 16, 2016, the HFRX Equity Hedge Index—a universe of long/short hedge funds—**lost** 6.4% (a loss rate of −0.6% annualized). In the same period, the S&P 500 **gained** 97.6% (+6.3% annualized).[1054]

The hedge-fund industry must keep making up stories that they can beat the market on the way up **and** down.

That's a "yeti portfolio," named for the mythical beast said to hide in the Himalayan Mountains. And, like the yeti, it doesn't exist. Any formula that actually beat the market **all the time** would be detected by traders' supercomputers and quickly become overused. If it worked once, it would soon become extinct (Figure 1-22).

3 · Large institutions often have a written policy against asset rotation

"The individual investor has a distinct advantage over the institution in terms of flexibility," says James Cloonan, the chairman of the American Association of Individual Investors (AAII) from 1979 to 2017. That's putting it mildly![1055]

Institutional pension funds, for instance, have a barrier against adopting Muscular Portfolios. It's called the Policy Committee. No giant pension fund—beset by employers, employees, and conflicting stakeholders on all sides—will ever allow sizable shifts from one asset to another. Institutions are all about stability, even if it hurts performance.

A good example is CalPERS, the California Public Employees' Retirement System. It's America's largest pension fund, managing about **$300 billion**.[1056]

CalPERS's board-mandated investment policy is 58 pages long. Among many other things, the policy requires that the pension fund's allocation to equities remains between 36% and 51% at all times. The allocation to real-estate securities must always be exactly 10% of assets—no more, no less.[1057]

Let's just say most pension funds won't be adopting asset-rotation formulas any time this century.

But an individual can easily do so, selling one ETF and buying some other one with a few clicks of a mouse.

4 · Even a million dollars doesn't move the global markets

Obviously, no investment strategy would continue to work if everyone in the world decided to invest in exactly the same way. But that isn't a serious objection. Everyone in the world can't even agree which side of the road to drive on.

Let's say you're a trust-fund baby. You follow the Papa Bear with a cool $3 million. One day, the Momentum Rule

» **KEY CONCEPT**
individuals have flexibility that institutions do not
Individuals can easily change their asset allocation whereas giant institutions can't.

A yeti portfolio supposedly beats the S&P 500 going up <u>and</u> down—but such a thing would soon become extinct

IN BEAR MARKETS

	you crash	you beat the S&P 500
IN BULL MARKETS — you lag the S&P 500	**Lazy Portfolios** poor in the long-term	**Muscular Portfolios** good in the long-term
IN BULL MARKETS — you beat the S&P 500	**High-Risk Portfolios** levered and crash-prone	**Yeti Portfolios** dream on — not likely to exist

FIGURE 1-22 | Illustration by Pieter Tandjung

calls for you to sell $1 million of an equity ETF and buy $1 million of a bond ETF instead.

Oooh, a million dollars! That sounds like a lot. Well, it isn't. Not in the global market casino.

The Muscular Portfolios in this book use some of the world's most liquid ETFs with hugely traded underlying assets.

Imagine you're at the Summer Games. You're standing next to an Olympic-size swimming pool. Filled two meters deep, the pool holds 2.6 million quarts (2.5 million liters). Talk about liquidity.

The value of all the world's equities is **$67 trillion.**[1058] Your $1 million sale is an invisible fraction of that. It's like three tablespoons of water compared to the pool (Figure 1-23).

Now imagine you convince 1,000 of your closest billionaire friends to each sell the same thing. They would unload ETF shares worth $1 billion. That would be like

a total of 36 quart jars of water.

What if your friends poured 36 quarts into the pool's 2.6 million quarts? No one would even notice a change in water level.

Buying and selling ETFs isn't like splashing water into a pool. Exchange-traded funds, um, trade on an exchange. Liquidity—the ability to buy and sell at any time without significantly moving a security's price—is another way ETFs outshine mutual funds.

When you buy or sell ETF shares, your buyer could be anyone. Selling shares of an ETF to a random buyer usually doesn't require the sale of any underlying assets.[1059]

Selling shares of a mutual fund is different. You can only sell shares back to the mutual fund's sponsor. It must dip into its cash reserves to pay out your money. If the reserves are not sufficient, a mutual fund must raise cash by liquidating some company's stock, pushing down its price.

When you buy or sell a **bond** ETF, you're even less likely to make a splash. All of the issued bonds in the world total **$88 trillion**—nearly one-third more than global equities.[1060]

That doesn't mean no one could **ever** move the market. If CalPERS went insane and dumped **$100 billion** of a Treasury ETF, yes, the price that day would go bonkers. Then it would recover. An ETF's price reverts to its underlying asset value.

Even CalPERS's crazy sale would represent less than half a day's trading. The average daily volume of Treasury debt securities was **$203 billion** in January 2016.[1061] And that doesn't include corporate bonds or sovereign bonds in every other country of the world.

So don't worry that your $1,000 or $1,000,000 or whatever will sink an ETF. Market glitches can and do arise—but your trade won't be the cause.

Everybody into the pool!

> **LIVINGSTON'S LAW OF INFORMED INVESTING**
> *The S&P is not for me,*
> *Too much crashing and volatility.*

One million dollars of an ETF compared to the global equity market is like three tablespoons of water to an Olympic-size pool

FIGURE 1-23

2 How do you know whether your portfolio is lazy or muscular?

"Don't speculate unless you can make it a full-time job."

BERNARD M. BARUCH (1870–1965), American millionaire trader, in *Wall Street People* (2001)[1062]

How would you recognize an investing strategy that was perfect for your needs if you saw it?

With the new 21st-century knowledge we now have available to us, there are several criteria that this chapter lays out:

» **Use one weird trick** Warren Buffett has taken advantage of for years to pile up his massive gains.

» **Recognize that the formula** is not specific to any complex stock-picking method, and it doesn't require you to be any kind of a financial genius.

» **Learn how little value** there is in the track records of 1, 3, 5, and 10 years that Wall Street brokers like to show you.

» **Recognize the damage** that jumping from one strategy to another based on short-term results can cause.

» **Understand that larger and larger losses** require longer and longer periods just to get your portfolio back to where it started.

» **See how very simple strategies** win out over complex systems, when you give them a chance to work (Figure 2-1).

Don't accept a strategy unless it works for you

FIGURE 2-1

The trick of a great return is revealed by Warren Buffett's performance

Warren Buffett is one of the most successful investors of our time. But a simple trick behind his great performance is not widely discussed.

Figure 2-2 graphs the 15¼ years from March 24, 2000, through June 30, 2015. This period began with the dotcom bear market, followed by a bull market. Then came the financial crisis, with its especially surly bear market, followed by a second bull market.

The orange line in the graph is the S&P 500 (represented by Vanguard's index mutual fund, VFINX). The blue line is Buffett's portfolio, Berkshire Hathaway. (The symbol for Berkshire's main share class is variously spelled BRK.A, BRK/A, and BRK-A.)

The graph is adjusted for dividends and inflation (i.e., it shows real total return). VFINX automatically deducts its annual fee, which is currently an ultra-low 0.05%. Using tradable securities like this gives the graph a commonsense link to reality.

Buffett has a record most investors would kill for. Over this period, his portfolio turned $100,000 into $269,000 in real dollars. The S&P 500 grew to only $128,000. (If inflation were added, the ending values would be $374,000 and $178,000.)

Buffett's real annualized rate of return was a phenomenal 6.7%. The S&P 500's real return, remember, was only 1.6%. (With inflation, the returns were 9.0% for Buffett and 3.9% for the S&P 500.)

Choose your response to the question posed in Figure 2-2. The answer is in Figure 2-3.

» **TECH TALK**

let's all make honest graphs

Sales brochures and academic studies often omit crucial graph features. In this book, unless otherwise noted, graphs reflect all of the following essentials:

» **Adjust for splits and dividends** (use total return)

» **Subtract realistic current transaction costs**

» **Subtract the current ETF or mutual fund annual fees** (actual investors buy funds, not indexes)

» **Use a ratio scale (aka semilog) on the left axis** if any values double and then double again

» **Show before-tax and after-tax performance**

After-tax performances for the Muscular Portfolios in this book are provided in Chapter 19.

» **KEY CONCEPT**

gain and rate of return are two different things

Let's say your account balance grew from $100 to $144 in 24 months.

• You had a two-year GAIN of 44%.

• Your annualized RETURN was 20%, because: $100 x 1.20 x 1.20 = $144.

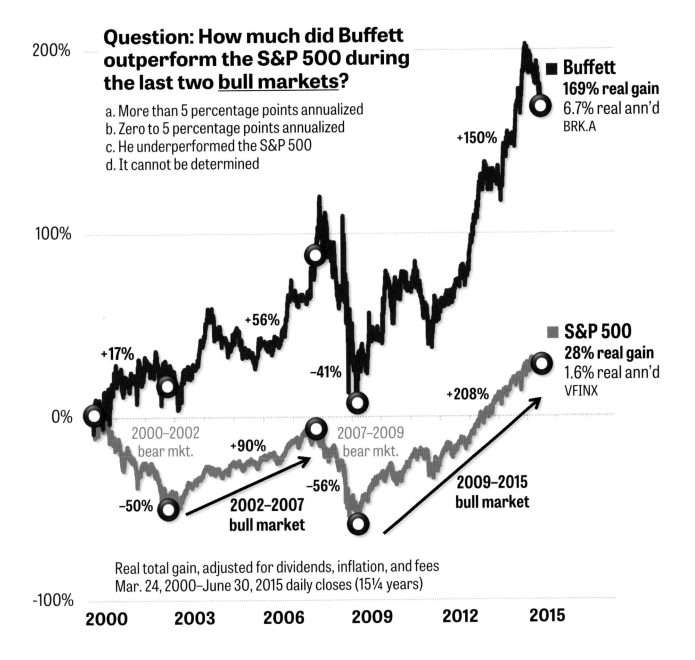

Question: How much did Buffett outperform the S&P 500 during the last two <u>bull markets</u>?

a. More than 5 percentage points annualized
b. Zero to 5 percentage points annualized
c. He underperformed the S&P 500
d. It cannot be determined

+150%

■ **Buffett**
169% real gain
6.7% real ann'd
BRK.A

+56%

+17%

−41%

■ **S&P 500**
28% real gain
1.6% real ann'd
VFINX

2000–2002
bear mkt.

+90%

2007–2009
bear mkt.

+208%

−50%

2002–2007
bull market

−56%

2009–2015
bull market

Real total gain, adjusted for dividends, inflation, and fees
Mar. 24, 2000–June 30, 2015 daily closes (15¼ years)

200%

100%

0%

−100%

2000   2003   2006   2009   2012   2015

FIGURE 2-2 | Data source: Yahoo Finance

Beating the S&P 500 during bull markets is not necessary to succeed long-term

The correct answer is "c." Warren Buffett's portfolio noticeably **underperformed** the S&P 500 during both of the bull markets we saw in Figure 2-2.

In the 2002–2007 bull market, Figure 2-3 shows that the S&P 500 gained 90% in real dollars. Buffett's portfolio gained only 56%.

In the 2009–2015 bull market (through June 30, 2015), the S&P 500 gained 208%. Buffett's gained only 150%.

His trick is what could be called **the Buffett Buffer.** All of his enormous 15¼-year outperformance came from keeping his losses low during the market's inevitable crashes and slumps.

Notice in Figure 2-3 that Buffett's portfolio gained only about **two-thirds** as much as the S&P 500 in each of the two bull markets.

With all of his skill, Buffett's enviable gains since 2000 **never** came from "beating the market" when the S&P 500 was in a bull run-up.

Did Buffett **deliberately** try to underperform in bull markets? Not a chance. His diverse portfolio simply hit a lot of singles, which added up to a very winning game.

But did Buffett get discouraged during bull markets and say, "I quit!" just because his portfolio underperformed the S&P 500 then? Absolutely not. Instead, he was patient.

Figure 2-3 is formatted as a **market-cycle graph.** Such graphs make it easy to see how a portfolio handles both bear and bull markets.

A market-cycle graph begins with a bear market. How well did each portfolio handle a down cycle?

Each account is then reset to a 0% baseline. (For example, each portfolio's dollar value might restart at $100.)

Starting over at the baseline shows us how each strategy performed in the **next** market cycle.

» KEY CONCEPT

the Buffett Buffer

Keeping your losses small during bear mar-kets means you can lag the S&P 500 during bull markets but beat it over the entire bear-bull market cycle.

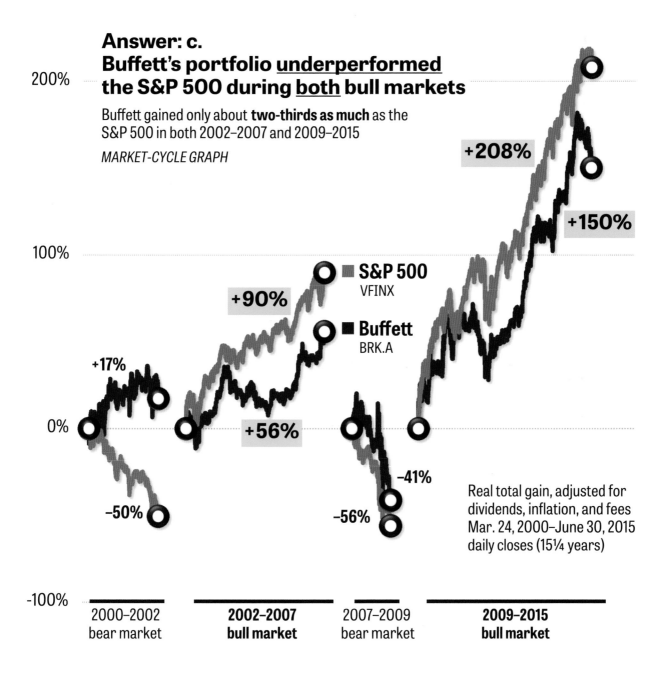

Answer: c.
Buffett's portfolio <u>underperformed</u> the S&P 500 during <u>both</u> bull markets

Buffett gained only about **two-thirds as much** as the S&P 500 in both 2002–2007 and 2009–2015

MARKET-CYCLE GRAPH

200%

+208%

+150%

100%

■ **S&P 500**
VFINX

+90%

■ **Buffett**
BRK.A

+17%

0%

+56%

–41%

–56%

–50%

Real total gain, adjusted for dividends, inflation, and fees
Mar. 24, 2000–June 30, 2015
daily closes (15¼ years)

-100%

| 2000–2002 bear market | **2002–2007 bull market** | 2007–2009 bear market | **2009–2015 bull market** |

FIGURE 2-3 | Data source: Yahoo Finance

Analysis shows that Buffett's success was expertise, not luck (but it's waning)

We've seen that the portfolio of companies Buffett chose—which kept his losses smaller than the S&P 500's—far outperformed the index.

But how do we know Buffett wasn't just lucky?

After all, in any group of 100 investors, one of them will by definition perform in the top 1%. It's possible that could entirely be chance.

In the 2001 book *Fooled by Randomness*, investment manager Nassim Nicholas Taleb makes the point a different way: (1) Take 10,000 managers. (2) Determine with a coin toss at the end of each year which managers made money or lost money. (3) Do this for five years. The result?

"We have now, simply in a fair game, 313 managers who made money for five years in a row. Out of pure luck."[1063]

More than 3% of investment managers can achieve five positive years in a row, purely at random!

Fortunately for Buffett shareholders—and the shareholders of other investors like him, as we'll see shortly—the stunning outperformance of the Berkshire Hathaway portfolio is **not** random.

Two researchers studied Berkshire's performance from 1976 through 2006. Gerald Martin and John Puthenpurackal—business professors at American University and the University of Nevada—found that "the magnitude by which the portfolio beats the market makes a luck explanation extremely unlikely." In addition:

"Collectively, our findings suggest that Berkshire Hathaway's exceptional investment record is due to investment skill and not due to luck or as compensation for high risk."[1064]

So why don't we all just buy Berkshire Hathaway stock? Why bother to learn the science of investing?

"For decades, Mr. Buffett has been warning that size is the enemy of excellence for any investor and that Berkshire's future performance was bound to decline," *Wall Street Journal* columnist Jason Zweig wrote in 2018 (Figure 2-4).[1065]

Buffett's strategy worked well for more than 50 years. Unfortunately, the trend is at its end. Figure 2-5 shows that Berkshire's trendline now barely matches the S&P 500 and no longer beats it.

In addition, as we saw in Figure 2-3, Berkshire subjected investors to a loss of 41%, adjusted for inflation, in 2007–2009. That would be intolerable for most investors.

This takes nothing away from Buffett's achievements. He's truly earned—in addition to his billions—the title of "genius."

But don't assume you can copy his stock-picking skill. We all need a simple but powerful investing method that will keep working for years to come.

> **» KEY CONCEPT**
> ## train yourself to have Buffett's patience
> Warren Buffett doesn't beat the S&P 500 during bull markets—nor should you.

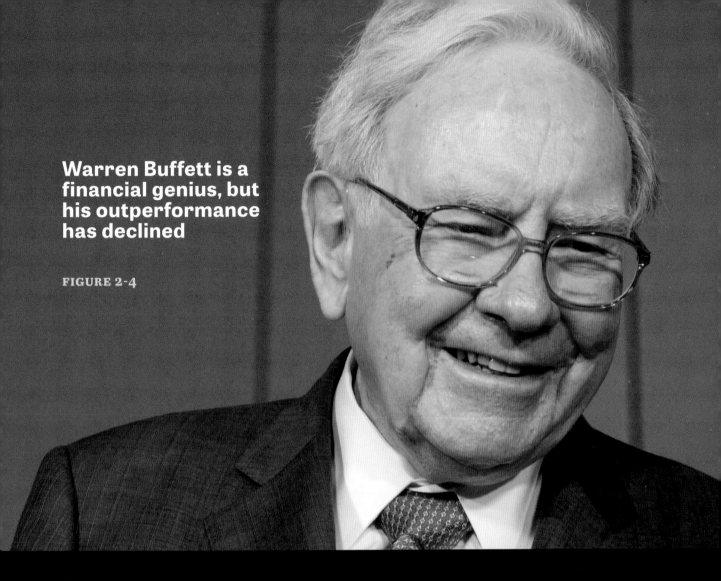

Warren Buffett is a financial genius, but his outperformance has declined

FIGURE 2-4

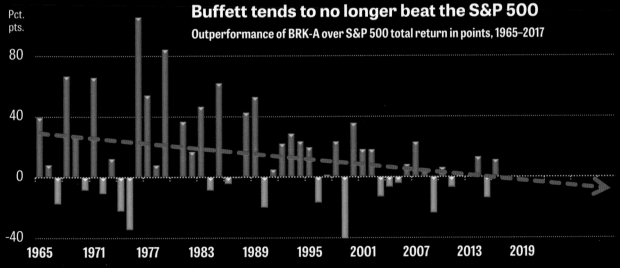

Buffett tends to no longer beat the S&P 500

Outperformance of BRK-A over S&P 500 total return in points, 1965–2017

Pct. pts.

80

40

0

-40

1965   1971   1977   1983   1989   1995   2001   2007   2013   2019

FIGURE 2-5 | Adapted from CXOAdvisory[1066]

Using Buffett-like principles doesn't require his skill, just a bit of discipline

The Buffett Buffer is simple—keep your losses small—but our human nature means it's not easy. We're our own worst enemies.

How can we mere mortals use the Buffett Buffer? Say you're scanning a mutual fund prospectus, which makes the following promise:

» **"The fund guarantees exactly two-thirds the total return of the S&P 500 . . ."**

You might say, "Yuck! Who wants only two-thirds of the index's gain?"

But wait! Reading more closely, you see that this fund is actually making you a better offer:

» **"The fund guarantees exactly two-thirds the total return of the S&P 500 in months when the index was up, AND only one-half the loss in months when the index was down."**

Figure 2-6 shows how much you'd have made from this fund's policy over 15¼ years.

This imaginary fund nearly **doubled** the S&P 500's gain, including dividends. Your money gained 146%. The S&P 500 gained only 82%.

Your fund tacked 2 percentage points on top of the S&P 500's rate of return. Your annualized rate of return was 6.1%, not just 4.0%.

Human nature compels us to focus on the short term: this year or even just this month. Investors with long-term discipline—evaluating portfolio performance only over complete bear-bull cycles—are far and few between. But you can be one of them.

» **It's tough to beat the S&P 500 during bull markets.** The index is not just the 500 largest US companies. The components are deliberately selected by Standard & Poor's Index Committee, a roomful of smart people who favor companies with strong recent profitability and growth.

This "momentum tilt" in the S&P 500 often makes it the strongest asset class and hard to outrace.[1067]

» **It's easy to lose just half of the S&P 500's declines during bear markets.** This is because the high-flying index is crash-prone. But there's no need for you to "time the market" to avoid these losses while maintaining gains. Instead, follow the basic rules outlined later in this chapter.

(Starting with Figure 2-6, returns in this book are not adjusted for inflation, unless otherwise stated. This enables you to easily compare the graphs to the "headline returns" you see in almost every publication. Subtract about 2.3 percentage points from the annualized returns in Figure 2-6 to find the inflation-adjusted annualized returns.)

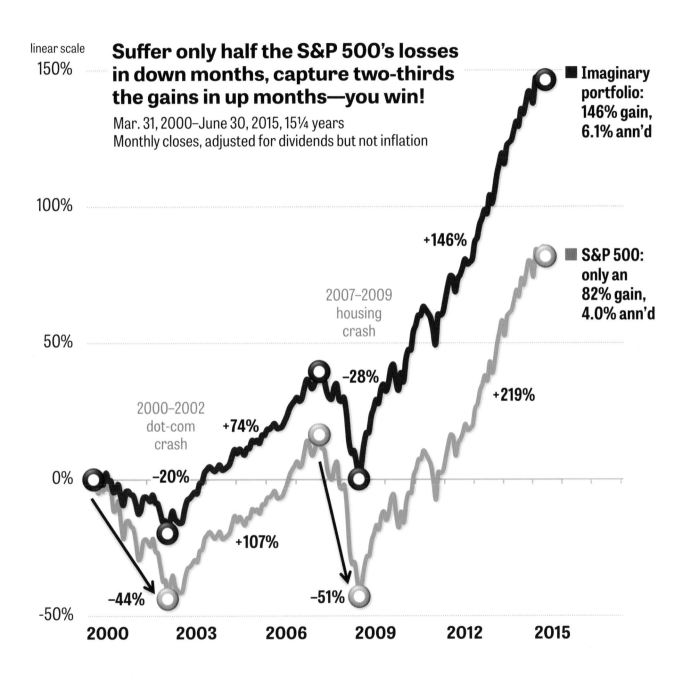

Suffer only half the S&P 500's losses in down months, capture two-thirds the gains in up months—you win!

Mar. 31, 2000–June 30, 2015, 15¼ years
Monthly closes, adjusted for dividends but not inflation

linear scale

150%

100%

50%

0%

-50%

2000 2003 2006 2009 2012 2015

2000–2002 dot-com crash

2007–2009 housing crash

+74%

−20%

−44%

+107%

−51%

−28%

+146%

+219%

■ Imaginary portfolio: 146% gain, 6.1% ann'd

■ S&P 500: only an 82% gain, 4.0% ann'd

FIGURE 2-6 | Data source: Yahoo Finance, author's calculations

Good results for fewer than 15 years do not predict future good results

So far, we've seen that we should:

» **Keep portfolio changes to no more than once per month** (ideally, less often); and

» **Refrain from market timing. Instead, remain 100% invested at all times in a diversified set of assets** (using basic rules that we'll see soon).

What about the financial newsletters that were monitored by the *Hulbert Financial Digest*? Couldn't we simply subscribe to the strategy that gained the most **last** year and follow its advice the **next** year?

A strategy in which each calendar year you followed whichever guru made the most in the previous year actually resulted in an annualized **32.2% loss.** During the 23-year period studied by Hulbert, the Wilshire 5000 index—containing virtually every US stock—returned 13.1% annualized. Strategies that soar in one year tend to dive in the following year. This is called **reversion to average.**

Not only is a single year a lousy predictor of the next 12 months' worth of performance. Hulbert found that strategies ranking in the top one-quarter for as long as 10 years had **no persistence at all.** Hulbert revealed his findings at the 2013 conference of the American Association of Individual Investors (AAII).[1068]

He examined the strategies that ranked in the top one-quarter for 1, 5, or 10 years. He found they had no more than a 25% chance—in other words, a random chance—of being in the top one-quarter for the next 1, 5, or 10 years (Figure 2-7). And yet track records of 3, 5, and 10 years are what wealth managers brag about! Here are the facts:

» **A top strategy over 1 year** had less than a random chance of repeating this performance in the next year;

» **A top strategy over 5 years** had less than a random chance of repeating for the next 5 years;

» **A top strategy over 10 years** had less than a random chance of repeating for the next 10 years.

Hulbert had to go all the way out to 15-year track records to find anything predictive at all (Figure 2-8):

» **A strategy that ranked in the top quarter over a 15-year period** had a 50/50 chance—twice as good as random chance—of being a top strategy over the following 15 years.[1069]

In a 2013 article about investing strategies, Hulbert wrote: "I used to think that five years were long enough to separate out those with genuine ability, but I have since concluded that it has to be far longer than that. I now recommend focusing on performance over at least 15 years."[1070]

Strategies that ranked in the top quarter for 1, 5, or 10 years were very likely to underperform

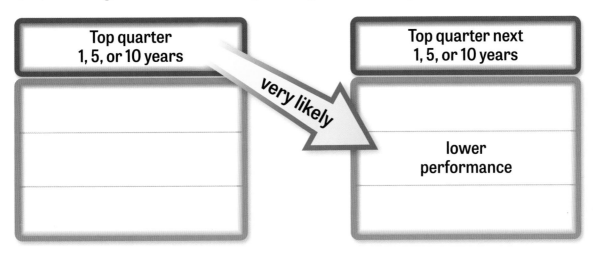

FIGURE 2-7 | Illustration by Pieter Tandjung

But if strategies were in the top quarter for as long as 15 years, they were more likely than chance to repeat

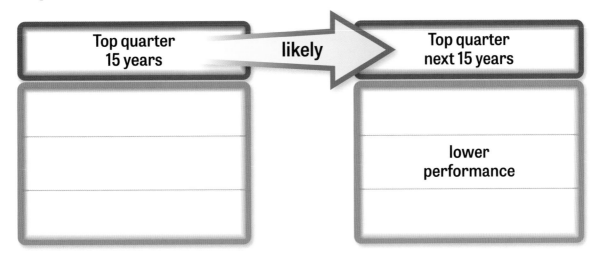

FIGURE 2-8 | Illustration by Pieter Tandjung

Past bad performance does tend to predict future bad performance

One remarkable fact in Hulbert's 23-year study (Figures 2-9 and 2-10) was that bad performance was strongly predictive of more bad performance:

» Strategies that ranked in the bottom one-quarter of performance were much more likely to repeat the bad performance—even if the track record was as short as one year!

This finding—that past bad performance has a significant tendency to predict future bad performance—has been replicated in numerous academic studies with far larger samples than Hulbert's.

For example, an influential 1997 paper by Mark Carhart of the University of Southern California examined the performance of more than 1,800 US equity mutual funds over 32 years (1962–1993).[1071]

Carhart divided the funds into the top tenth, the bottom tenth, and every tenth in between.

He found that a fund's good performance in the past one, three, and five years wasn't very predictive of future good performance.

Only the funds in the very top tenth in one year had any greater likelihood of appearing in the top tenth in the following year, and even that association was weak.

Only 17% of the funds in the top tenth repeated their accomplishment the following year. That's not very predictive, considering that 10% would have made it into that top tenth by random chance.

However, funds in the **bottom** tenth in one year had a 46% chance of repeating their bottom-tenth performance. Some disappeared entirely. (Funds disappear mostly because they're shut down or merged out of existence due to bad performance. To avoid biasing the database toward survivors, Carhart corrected for funds that vanished.)

So, portfolios with **past** bad performance—defined as the bottom one-tenth—were 4.6 times more likely than chance to have **future** bad performance. Now **that's** significant!

For another example, analysts at the National Bureau of Economic Research released a paper in 2007 on mutual-fund performance persistence or the lack of it.

They called funds that had similar performance for two years in a row "seasoned." Each one-tenth of the funds is a "decile." The researchers wrote:

"For seasoned funds in the bottom decile, poor performance over one three-year period at the fund level persists over the subsequent three-year period. No equivalent evidence of persistence exists in the top decile."[1072]

Bad performance turns out to be a powerful decision-making tool. It's impossible to predict which asset classes will have the **best** performance in the next few years. But you can eliminate a lot of pain in your portfolio by avoiding asset classes and investing strategies that have had **poor** performance.

Strategies in the basement for as little as 1, 5, or 10 years were much more likely than chance to stay in the basement

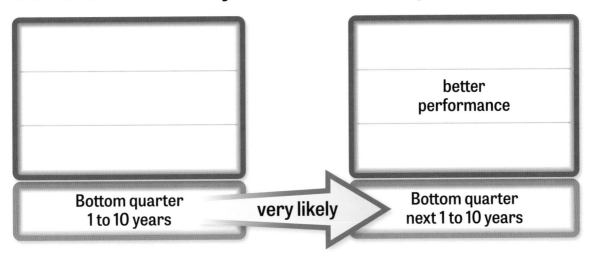

	better performance

| Bottom quarter 1 to 10 years | very likely | Bottom quarter next 1 to 10 years |

FIGURE 2-9 | Illustration by Pieter Tandjung

Mark Hulbert has studied investment advisers for more than three decades

FIGURE 2-10

We're only human—tempted by the quick fix of short-termism

Wall Street encourages "short-termism." The biggest myth Wall Street sells is that individual investors should scrutinize market moves, minute by minute.

An even more harmful belief is that an investing strategy can be rated and evaluated on the basis of a short history.

FT Remark, a research service, interviewed senior executives at 400 large investment firms and pension funds that hire outside money managers. The question was: "How long is underperformance tolerated before seeking a replacement?"[1073]

The answers showed a shocking devotion to short-termism at the expense of the institutions' own financial interests:

» **An astounding 40%** of institutions said **a single year** was all that could elapse before a lagging outside manager was up for replacement by a different one;

» **49%** said the "outperform or else" limit was **two years**; and

» **The other 11%** said underperformance was tolerated only **three years** before termination.

Professors at Emory University and Arizona State analyzed 3,400 such institutions. Over an eight-year period, the firms dismissed hundreds of outside portfolio managers and hired others. In the next three years, the fired managers **outperformed** the hired managers by almost a full percentage point![1074] (See Figure 2-11.)

As humans, we're bad at understanding randomness. To illustrate this, three researchers posed a simple problem to 700 financial professionals:

» You're given two coins. One coin is fair, the other comes up heads 60% of the time, but you don't know which coin is which.

» What is your "quick guess" of how many rounds of flips it would take for you to state, with 95% confidence, which coin is loaded?

Surprisingly, 30% of the financial professionals said only 10 rounds. The median guess was 40 rounds.

The correct answer is 143 rounds. That's how much evidence is needed just to choose with confidence between two coins! And your choice would still be wrong in 5% of the cases.[1075]

Judge portfolios by periods no shorter than complete bear-bull (or bull-bear) market cycles. The more cycles you can examine, the better.

Avoid portfolios with intolerable losses in the past (30% or worse). They're likely to subject you to more of the same in the future.

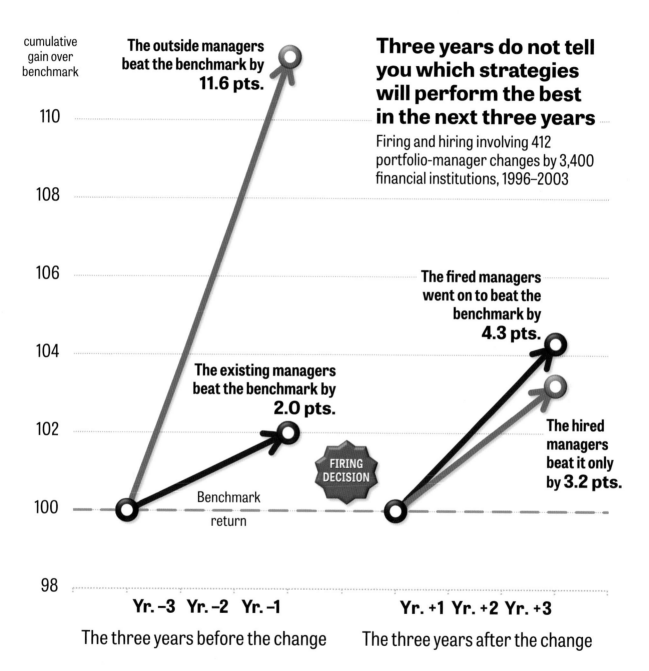

cumulative
gain over
benchmark

**The outside managers
beat the benchmark by
11.6 pts.**

**Three years do not tell
you which strategies
will perform the best
in the next three years**

Firing and hiring involving 412
portfolio-manager changes by 3,400
financial institutions, 1996–2003

110

108

106

**The fired managers
went on to beat the
benchmark by
4.3 pts.**

104

**The existing managers
beat the benchmark by
2.0 pts.**

102

**FIRING
DECISION**

**The hired
managers
beat it only
by 3.2 pts.**

100

Benchmark
return

98

Yr. –3   Yr. –2   Yr. –1

Yr. +1 Yr. +2 Yr. +3

The three years before the change

The three years after the change

FIGURE 2-11 | Source: Goyal and Wahal (2008)

Choose an investing strategy with no history of every losing more than 25%

As we've seen, outstanding investors like Warren Buffett don't have to beat the S&P 500 during bull markets. They outperform by keeping their losses small during bear markets.

This takes advantage of a principle called "recovery time." Figure 2-12 illustrates it:

» **Two portfolios start** with $100.

» **A market index crashes 50%** in a bear market, such as the 2007–2009 global financial crisis.

» **Your portfolio** loses only 25%.

» **Both portfolios grow back** at a real rate (adjusted for inflation) of 6.55% annualized. That's approximately the real total return of the Baby Bear in simulations and the actual S&P 500 from 1973 through 2015, as we saw previously.

» **It takes only 4½ years** for your portfolio to get back to your original $100.

» **It takes 11 years for the index** to get back to even.

Obviously, 11 years is a recovery time that's more than twice as long as 4½ years.

If the index fell exactly twice as much as your portfolio, why didn't the index take **exactly** twice as long to recover?

» **If your portfolio loses 25%,** a gain of only 33.3% will bring you back to even. Example: $75 to $100 is a 33.3% gain.

» **When the index loses 50%,** it requires a gain of 100% to get back to even— $50 to $100 is a 100% gain. That takes much longer.

As they say on Wall Street, "Recovery time grows geometrically." Larger and larger losses take longer and longer to recover from.

The Buffett Buffer, as we saw previously, means it's better to diversify and keep your losses small during bear markets. That's a lot easier than trying to outdo the S&P 500 when it happens to be the strongest asset class during bull markets.

As we'll see, the Baby Bear Portfolio holds only two asset classes: US stocks and US bonds.

The Mama Bear and Papa Bear have a larger menu of asset classes to choose from. And Muscular Portfolios use asset rotation to keep you out of assets that are sinking.

Avoiding the huge losses that the S&P 500 subjects investors to every 10 years or so keeps your investment strategy on track.

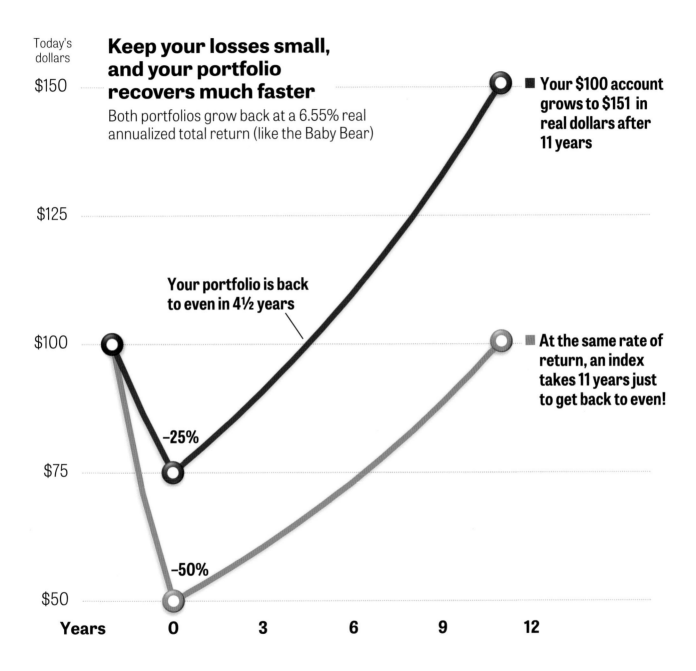

Keep your losses small, and your portfolio recovers much faster

Both portfolios grow back at a 6.55% real annualized total return (like the Baby Bear)

Today's dollars

$150

$125

$100

$75

$50

Your portfolio is back to even in 4½ years

−25%

−50%

Years   0   3   6   9   12

■ Your $100 account grows to $151 in real dollars after 11 years

■ At the same rate of return, an index takes 11 years just to get back to even!

FIGURE 2-12 | Source: Author's calculations

Don't let anyone say you can't have market-like returns and smaller losses

The S&P 500 is just a number. Never doubt that you can do as well as or better. The trick is to use simple, basic strategies and keep your costs to a bare minimum.

It's true that professional fund managers are talented. Researchers at the University of California and Carnegie Mellon found that 80% of managers show skill in security selection.[1076]

And yet the sponsors of actively managed funds must apologize, year after year, for lagging behind well-known market indexes. After fees, 93% of large-cap managers and 94% of small-cap managers underperformed their benchmarks in the 15 years ending June 30, 2017.[1077]

The complicated strategies these funds use rack up trading costs. And their high fees eat up the remaining gains. You can do better.

For an illustration, consider the Dow Jones Industrial Average (DJIA). This is a simple, actively managed index of 30 stocks. The index changes about 3% (one stock) each year.

David Blitzer, who chairs the S&P Index Committee that composes many indexes, including the Dow, says: "It is more actively managed than any other index I can think of—ours or anyone else's."[1078]

Looking way back to 1985, the DJIA has far outperformed the S&P 500. Including dividends, the Dow returned 9.1% annualized in the 32 years ending Feb. 28, 2017. The S&P 500 returned only 8.4%. In other words, the Dow turned $100 into $1,621. The S&P 500 grew to just $1,305.[1079]

Of course, neither index subtracts annual fees. And no mutual fund tracked the Dow before 1991.[1080] How about comparing two **actual** funds that charge **actual** fees to **actual** investors?

After fees, the Vanguard Balanced Index Fund (VBINX) easily beat the Vanguard 500 Index Fund—VFINX, which tracks the S&P 500—in the last two market cycles (Figure 2-13). VBINX is very similar to the Baby Bear Portfolio, which holds 50%

US stocks and 50% US bonds and is explained in the previous chapter. VBINX owns a 60/40 proportion. Vanguard's Jack Bogle has said 60/40 has "similar returns" to 50/50.[1081]

Notice that the balanced index fund rose only about two-thirds as much as the S&P 500 during bull markets. VBINX outperforms overall **solely** by keeping its losses low during bear markets.

Why don't we all buy VBINX? Well, it's tough to stay with it. The fund periodically loses intolerable amounts—33% just in 2007–2009.

Can a strategy as basic as three ETFs perform well? In investing, simple works. Muscular Portfolios enjoy index-like strength without crashes.

Tip: Benchmark your portfolio against VBINX, which is a smoother ride than the S&P 500. But invest using a Muscular Portfolio, which is superior to either index.

LIVINGSTON'S LAW OF FISCAL FITNESS

Some portfolios take you for a ride
While other portfolios stand by your side.

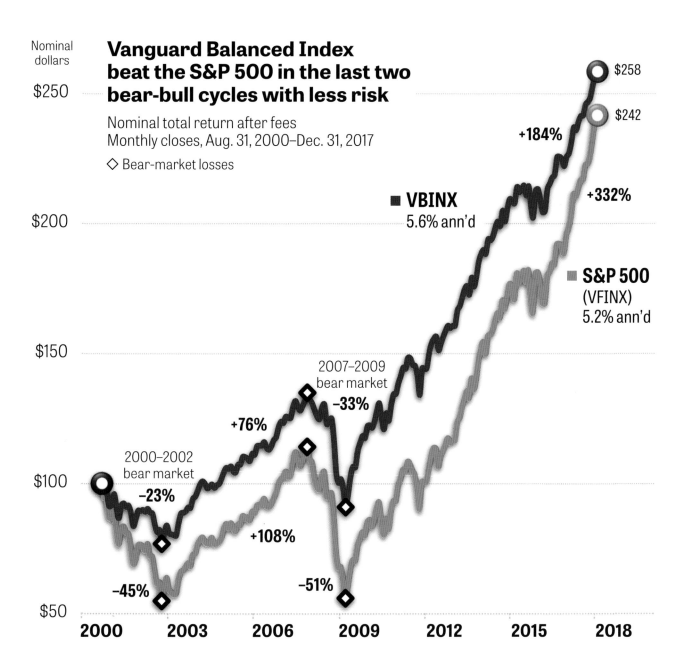

Vanguard Balanced Index beat the S&P 500 in the last two bear-bull cycles with less risk

Nominal total return after fees
Monthly closes, Aug. 31, 2000–Dec. 31, 2017

◇ Bear-market losses

Nominal dollars

$250

$200

$150

$100

$50

VBINX
5.6% ann'd

S&P 500
(VFINX)
5.2% ann'd

+184%

+332%

$258

$242

2007–2009 bear market
−33%

2000–2002 bear market
−23%

+76%

+108%

−45%

−51%

2000 2003 2006 2009 2012 2015 2018

FIGURE 2-13 | Data source: Yahoo Finance

3 When Lazy Portfolios fail you and Muscular Portfolios support you

"Diversification alone is no longer sufficient to temper risk. In the past year, we saw virtually every asset class hammered. You need something more to manage risk well."

MOHAMED EL-ERIAN, former CEO of PIMCO, in *Kiplinger's Personal Finance*, (March 2009)[1082]

The rise of low-cost mutual funds that tracked asset classes around the world spawned the investing craze known as Lazy Portfolios (Figure 3-1).

Lazy Portfolios were designed by a variety of academics and financial pundits. Each author avoided a simple stock/bond split. Instead, Lazy Portfolios typically hold five or more asset classes, attempting to benefit from the diversification.

Each Lazy Portfolio's creator determined a percentage for each asset class. This was enforced by "rebalancing" the account once per year. You'd sell some shares of any asset classes that had gone up and buy more of any that had gone down.

The 2004 book *The Lazy Person's Guide to Investing* by Paul B. Farrell described several of these models. He pursued this theme in a MarketWatch.com column that ran until 2016.[1083]

One strategy that claimed the Lazy Portfolio moniker was actually called the Couch Potato. Proposed in 1991 by Scott Burns, a columnist for the *Dallas Morning News*, the idea was that you did **almost nothing** to set up your account and **absolutely nothing** month by month. Only rebalancing the portfolio at the end of the year was required. You could sit on the couch and watch TV the rest of the time.[1084]

The Couch Potato included only two mutual funds, held in a 50/50 proportion. The two asset classes were US stocks and US bonds. Burns came out later with a three-fund variation that added non-US stocks (called the Margaritaville Portfolio).

Having only two or three assets makes strategies like the Couch Potato and Margaritaville "starter portfolios," like the Baby Bear. A true Lazy Portfolio includes five or more asset classes to take advantage of global diversification.

Jack Bogle's definition of a 50/50 portfolio—which Chapter 1 describes as the Baby Bear—is clearer and has a community forum supporting it at Bogleheads.org. So we bid farewell to the Couch Potato here.

This chapter is not about starter portfolios but the disappointing runs of the more diversified and publicized Lazy Portfolios.

Lazy Portfolios never change their positions

Perhaps they get up and rebalance once a year

FIGURE 3-1

Lazy Portfolios don't provide market-like returns but still crash

Figure 3-2 is based on MarketWatch.com's real-time tracking of eight popular portfolios.[1085] The website's records show that **every one** of the Lazy Portfolios it tracks—including the ones from Farrell's book—badly trailed the S&P 500.

With only three funds, MarketWatch's tracking includes three starter portfolios that hold fewer than five asset classes. They are the Second Grader's Starter Portfolio, the No-Brainer, and Margaritaville. The "second grader" (Allan Roth's son, Kevin), lagged the S&P 500 less over 15 years than any of MarketWatch's other listed portfolios.

The other five strategies—the true Lazy Portfolios—badly underperformed the S&P 500 over every time period. The 15-year returns of these five portfolios were 7.37% to 8.80%. By comparison, the S&P 500's 9.93% return was far superior.

The only significant stats cover 15 years (Figure 3-2's yellow column). But for a taste of what investors endured, peek at the shorter periods. The best a Lazy Portfolio could do over 10 years was a lag of 2½ points (Coffeehouse). The worst over 5 years was a lag of 9½ points (Ultimate).

Chapter 1 showed that "market-like returns" are within 1 percentage point of the S&P 500's long-term return. Lazy Portfolios don't deliver market-like returns.

Lazy Portfolios' weak showings might be accepted if these plans gave investors a much smoother ride than the S&P 500.

But Figure 3-3 shows that these theories subjected investors to nominal losses of 35% to 48%—almost as bad as the crash-prone index.

» TECH TALK

short-term vs. long-term

MarketWatch posts annualized returns for eight Lazy Portfolios every business day. However, the statistics that are posted go back only 10 years and don't report drawdowns. MarketWatch did not respond to requests for historical data on the Lazy Portfolios it's tracked.

The 15-year returns shown in Figure 3-2 were obtained with an assist from Archive.org, a nonprofit organization that records Web pages for posterity. Archive.org preserved the Lazy Portfolios' 10-year returns in December 2012. Stitching those numbers together with more recent MarketWatch statistics from December 2017 produced complete 15-year returns.

This chapter confirms the MarketWatch numbers by matching them against two other data providers—My Plan IQ and the Idea Farm's Quant simulator—in Figure 3-3.

» KEY CONCEPT

Lazy Portfolios perform poorly

A Lazy Portfolio tends to lag the S&P 500 while still subjecting investors to intolerable crashes during bear markets.

Every Lazy Portfolio lagged the S&P 500 by a wide margin over 3, 5, 10, and 15 years

Total returns for portfolios tracked by MarketWatch

Portfolio/AUTHOR Periods ending Dec. 31, 2017	Funds	3 yrs. ann'd	5 yrs. ann'd	10 yrs. ann'd	15 yrs. ann'd
S&P 500	**n/a**	**10.85%**	**16.17%**	**8.42%**	**9.93%**
Second Grader's Starter Portfolio[1086] ALLAN ROTH	3	8.89	11.84	6.05	**9.20**
Family Taxable[1087] TED ARONSON	11	7.51	8.81	5.71	**8.80**
Unconventional Success[1088] DAVID SWENSEN	6	6.37	8.50	5.94	**8.68**
No-Brainer[1089] WILLIAM BERNSTEIN	4	7.19	10.07	5.79	**8.52**
Coffeehouse[1090] BILL SCHULTHEIS	7	6.05	8.55	5.97	**7.87**
Margaritaville[1091] SCOTT BURNS	3	6.85	7.72	4.60	**7.80**
Smart Money (Coward's Portfolio)[1092] WILLIAM BERNSTEIN	9	6.21	8.35	5.29	**7.53**
Ultimate Buy-and-Hold[1093] PAUL MERRIMAN	11	5.48	6.64	4.31	**7.37**

FIGURE 3-2 | Sources: MarketWatch.com and Archive.org

Mere diversification is no help when world markets are crashing

It's important to know how much a strategy lost in the past, but MarketWatch doesn't publish that. Fortunately, we don't have to guess. A research firm named My Plan IQ rates thousands of 401(k) plans and other financial programs. The tracking includes five of MarketWatch's Lazy Portfolios. (My Plan IQ does not track MarketWatch's three starter portfolios.)

As a double check, Quant can estimate the performance of almost any portfolio—lazy or muscular—over the past four decades.

The three services will never agree exactly. For one thing, they each use different databases and methodologies.

But Figure 3-3 shows that MarketWatch, My Plan IQ, and Quant give remarkably similar return estimates over the past 15 years. The average difference is less than 1.0 percentage point.

My Plan IQ and Quant also report very similar losses by the Lazy Portfolios during the 2007–2009 bear. For example, Family Taxable crashed –39.6% in Quant's estimation and–43.5% in My Plan IQ's monthly tracking. The average difference between the two services is only 3.1 points.

Figure 3-4 graphs the Lazy Portfolios. Adjusted for inflation, the losses are even worse. Ouch! Stop the pain!

The crashes of the S&P 500 and Lazy Portfolios have earned them the title of **downer portfolios**. Investors deserve better.

Portfolio	15-year returns, 2003–2017 AVERAGE DIFFERENCE: 0.91 PCT. PTS.			Estimated drawdowns, 2007–2009 AVERAGE DIFFERENCE (MO.): 3.11 PCT. PTS.		
	Market-Watch	**My Plan IQ**	**Quant**	**My Plan IQ (daily)**	**My Plan IQ (monthly)**	**Quant (monthly)**
Family Taxable	**8.80%**	10.36%	9.16%	–48.21%	–43.48%	–39.57%
Unconventional	**8.68**	9.63	9.21	–43.49	–39.10	–40.73
Coffeehouse	**7.87**	8.28	8.66	–35.45	–31.35	–33.12
Coward's	**7.53**	7.04	9.16	–36.66	–32.10	–37.31
Ultimate	**7.37**	6.94	8.33	–37.66	–33.54	–36.56

FIGURE 3-3 | Nominal return or gain/loss. Sources: MarketWatch, Archive.org, My Plan IQ, and Quant simulator

» KEY CONCEPT

downer portfolios

Portfolios that crash 30% or more every few years—like the S&P 500 and Lazy Portfolios—compel people to liquidate, locking in huge losses.

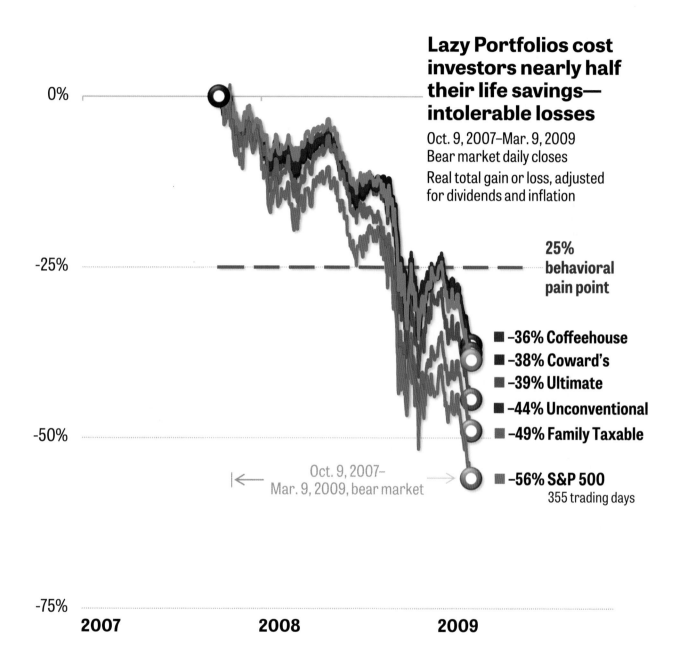

Lazy Portfolios cost investors nearly half their life savings— intolerable losses

Oct. 9, 2007–Mar. 9, 2009
Bear market daily closes

Real total gain or loss, adjusted for dividends and inflation

25% behavioral pain point

0%

-25%

-50%

-75%

■ -36% Coffeehouse
■ -38% Coward's
■ -39% Ultimate
■ -44% Unconventional
■ -49% Family Taxable

■ -56% S&P 500
355 trading days

Oct. 9, 2007–
Mar. 9, 2009, bear market

2007   2008   2009

FIGURE 3-4 | Data source: My Plan IQ

Why do Lazy Portfolios crash?
When markets are up, everything's fine.

"The people who can truly stomach the volatility of a 100% stock portfolio are either dead or catatonic," said Claude Erb, a former fund manager at the TCW Group, in an interview with the *Wall Street Journal*.[1094]

Nevertheless over 40% of Americans' IRAs are invested in a manner that's far too risky. These accounts allocate at least 80% of their portfolios to a single asset class—US stocks.[1095]

And about two-thirds of **those** IRA owners are truly gambling with their life savings, betting a full 100% on US stocks alone.

An alternative to this you-bet-your-life concentration on US stocks was provided by the development in the 1990s of index mutual funds. For the first time, American investors could easily buy not just US stocks, but stocks and bonds in other developed countries (primarily Europe and Asia) and emerging markets.

These global asset classes may provide some diversification during US equity bull markets (Figure 3-5). But when US equities crash, non-US markets tend to crash as well (Figure 3-6).

Unfortunately, mere diversification of your holdings is not enough to provide safety from heart-crushing losses.

The crashes experienced by each Lazy Portfolio reveal the Achilles' heel of all static asset allocation strategies.

To grow, your wealth needs exposure to equities. But static portfolios cannot adapt to market conditions as they change.

As a result, Lazy Portfolios burn up investors' life savings during bear markets almost as badly as the S&P 500 does.

» TECH TALK

actual fund gains and losses

The graphs in Figures 3-5, 3-6, and 3-7 show the performances of actual index mutual funds. These funds were open to the public and available for individuals to purchase during the time periods shown.

These securities automatically deduct their annual fees from their prices. This makes the graphs more true to life than graphs of purely theoretical indexes.

Figures 3-5 and 3-6 show the total gain or loss of the following Vanguard low-cost index mutual funds:

» VFINX   S&P 500
» NAESX   US small-cap stocks
» VGSIX   real-estate investment trusts
» VTMGX   developed-market stocks
» VEIEX   emerging-market stocks

Figure 3-7 adds the following funds from Vanguard, Invesco, and iShares, respectively (at this writing, Vanguard offers no hard-asset funds):

» VUSTX   30-year Treasury bonds
» DBC   commodities
» IAU   gold

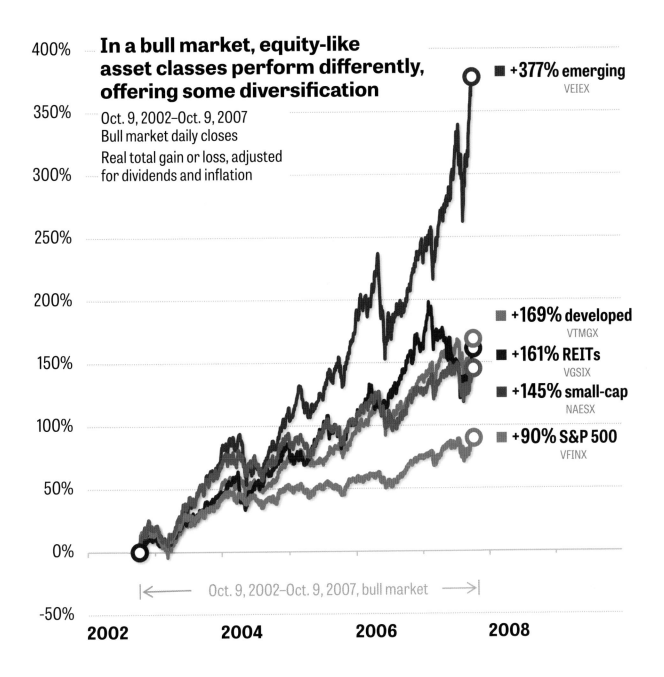

In a bull market, equity-like asset classes perform differently, offering some diversification

Oct. 9, 2002–Oct. 9, 2007
Bull market daily closes

Real total gain or loss, adjusted for dividends and inflation

■ **+377%** emerging
VEIEX

■ **+169%** developed
VTMGX

■ **+161%** REITs
VGSIX

■ **+145%** small-cap
NAESX

■ **+90%** S&P 500
VFINX

|← Oct. 9, 2002–Oct. 9, 2007, bull market →|

FIGURE 3-5 | Data source: Yahoo Finance

A static asset allocation is a disaster when equities go south

The equity markets in every corner of the world—from developed countries to emerging markets—collapsed 56% to 62% in the 2007–2009 bear, adjusted for dividends and inflation (Figure 3-6).

Real-estate investment trusts (REITs) crashed even more. A REIT trades like a stock and is considered equity-like, but REITs were supposed to protect investors with diversification. Despite this, REIT indexes fell by a horrifying 70%.

The results were massive losses for investors who thought diversification would protect their life savings from serious harm.

In Chapter 1, we learned that there's a "25% behavioral pain point." Past a 25% loss, individual investors start to liquidate their holdings, locking in their losses.

Of course, 25% is just a rule of thumb. The actual number varies from person to person and from day to day.

It's extremely difficult to tell how many people throw in the towel at any given loss percentage. That's because brokerage firms usually won't release sample data, even to qualified researchers.

The explanation given is generally "privacy," despite the fact that this data can be easily anonymized. It's hard not to suspect that brokerage firms simply don't want to reveal just how badly their customers do playing the market game.

Ben Carlson is the author of *A Wealth of Common Sense* (2015) and the director of institutional asset management at Ritholtz Wealth Management. He's witnessed the behavior of thousands of serious investors. In an interview, he described the progression he sees as clients watch the value of their hard-earned savings go down, down, down:

"In a 10% correction, people for the most part are OK.

"At 20%, people get a little edgy.

"When you get to the 30%, 40% loss range, people say, 'Get me out. I tap out. That's it.'

"That's my back-of-the-envelope personal experience of the pain point."

We don't need to know the exact loss level that will make an individual investor throw in the towel. We know for sure, thanks to behavioral finance research, that a majority of individuals find it unacceptable for their life savings ever to collapse more than 25%.

With a Lazy Portfolio, losses of more than 25% every few years are inevitable.

By contrast, a Muscular Portfolio—by its very design—keeps investors in asset classes that are in uptrends and unlikely to crash.

To keep losses under 25%, a portfolio of diverse asset classes needs the cushion that the Momentum Rule provides, as we'll see shortly.

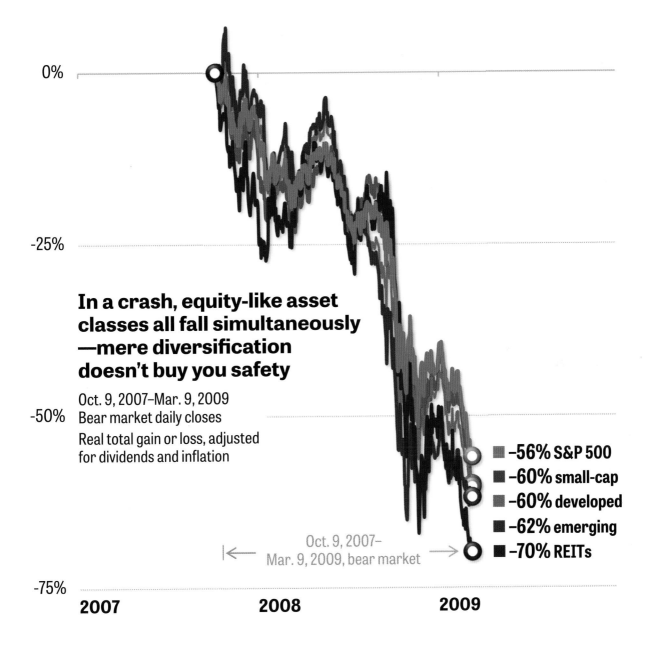

In a crash, equity-like asset classes all fall simultaneously —mere diversification doesn't buy you safety

Oct. 9, 2007–Mar. 9, 2009
Bear market daily closes

Real total gain or loss, adjusted for dividends and inflation

0%

-25%

-50%

-75%

2007   2008   2009

Oct. 9, 2007–
Mar. 9, 2009, bear market

−56% S&P 500
−60% small-cap
−60% developed
−62% emerging
−70% REITs

FIGURE 3-6 | Data source: Yahoo Finance

Bonds and commodities went up, but most Lazy Portfolios can't use them

When the equity market is going to hell in a handbasket, bonds and commodities often give shelter.

Assets that are not stocks and not bonds—for example, REITs, commodities and precious metals—are referred to as "alternatives."

Most Lazy Portfolios have no allocation to commodities and metals. A few allow a small percentage that can never be expanded.

By contrast, Muscular Portfolios include these alternatives in the menu of securities that can be bought. Even better, each portfolio's Momentum Rule automatically increases your allocation to bonds, commodities, and metals when equity markets around the world lose momentum and start to crash.

Bonds and alternatives are assets that may go up when equity markets worldwide are diving, as shown in Figure 3-7:

» **Bonds.** During the 2007–2009 equity crash, many bonds gained value. Figure 3-7 shows that long-term Treasurys gained 18%. Investors who shifted some money from stocks to bonds avoided a lot of pain.

» **Commodities.** During the first half of the crash, demand for commodities rose. This made commodity ETFs such as DBC the strongest performers. Adjusted for inflation, DBC rose an incredible 66% in only nine months. Commodities provided an excellent alternative to the global equity crash— but only for the first half of the 2007–2009 bear market.

After July 2008, the prices of commodities fell as it became clear that the US banking crisis was turning into a global recession. Between February 2008 and February 2010, about 8.7 million jobs vanished in the US alone, and other countries fared far worse.[1096] Buying pressure for commodities disappeared, and prices dove.

This is another illustration of the problem with static asset allocation: You can't entrust your money to **any** one asset class and then ignore it.

» **Gold.** Like all commodities, gold's "intrinsic value" is hard to guess. Oil, cotton, gold— none of these pay dividends or reap earnings. Their prices are set by the tough global battle of supply and demand.

Specific commodities often perform differently than the category as a whole. Gold can still diversify a portfolio. It's an asset with its own fads and fashions.

Gold rose 22% in 2007– 2009, when the S&P 500 was crashing. But a few years earlier, February 1980 through April 2001, gold in dollar terms fell more than 86%, adjusted for inflation. Whoops!

Humans like gold because it's shiny, a trait we share with crows. Treat gold strictly as an asset class with ups and downs, not a magical substance.

» KEY CONCEPT

something is always going up
If equities are crashing, bonds, commodities, and precious metals may be rising.

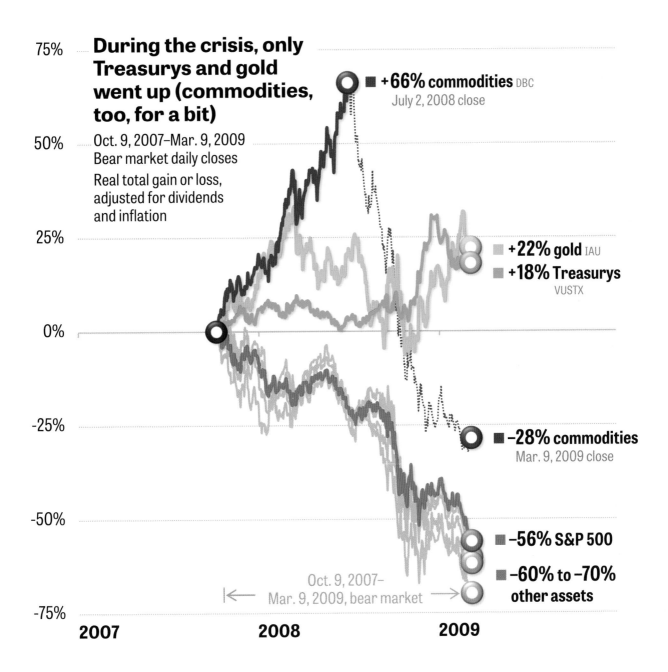

75%

During the crisis, only Treasurys and gold went up (commodities, too, for a bit)

Oct. 9, 2007–Mar. 9, 2009
Bear market daily closes

Real total gain or loss,
adjusted for dividends
and inflation

50%

25%

0%

-25%

-50%

-75%

■ **+66% commodities** DBC
July 2, 2008 close

■ **+22% gold** IAU

■ **+18% Treasurys**
VUSTX

■ **−28% commodities**
Mar. 9, 2009 close

■ **−56% S&P 500**

■ **−60% to −70%**
other assets

Oct. 9, 2007–
Mar. 9, 2009, bear market

2007   2008   2009

FIGURE 3-7 | Data source: Yahoo Finance

Captains tack their sailboats— informed investors tilt their portfolios

The informed investor is like the captain of a sailboat. On the ocean, sometimes the trade winds blow opposite the direction the captain wants to go. Sometimes the winds of the market blow the wrong way, too.

How does a sailboat manage to glide **toward** the breeze instead of being pushed away by it? How does an informed investor stay afloat when a portfolio is buffeted by cruel market storms?

Sailing toward the wind requires a trick called **tacking.** The captain angles the boat's sails to catch the wind from whatever direction it's coming, pushing the boat forward along the line of the hull.

Out on the water, a sailboat almost never glides 100% toward the wind or 100% away from it. Instead, the captain tacks a certain amount one way or the other to get to the destination (Figure 3-8).

Informed investors can learn from the captain and avoid any attempt at "market timing"—switching between 100% stocks and 100% cash. Jumping from one extreme to another is not a successful way to captain a sailboat **or** manage a portfolio.

Gradually tilting a portfolio toward asset classes that have stronger momentum is called **asset rotation.** The informed investor makes changes slowly—not every day or every week, but only once every month or two. That's plenty often for any long-term investor to take advantage of the shifting winds of the market.

It's not widely known that a sailboat with a skilled captain can actually sail across water faster than the wind. No, this doesn't require casting any magical spells or violating any laws of physics.

Remarkably, a new world record was set in 2012 by a sailboat traveling 65 knots. That was as much as 2½ times the actual wind speed.[1097]

In investing, it's possible for a skilled captain like Warren Buffett to grow his portfolio faster than the S&P 500. No, this doesn't require casting any magical spells or violating any laws of finance.

You don't have to be a genius like Buffett to enjoy great performance, any more than a captain needs to be Superman to sail faster than the wind. Muscular Portfolios are easy to use and fully disclosed, with no secret formulas. Scientific findings about the market over the past three decades give you all the tools you need.

> **»KEY CONCEPT**
> ## asset rotation
> Remain 100% invested in at least three asset classes at all times, and gradually tilt your portfolio toward the ETFs with the best momentum.

**Sailors tack with the wind.
Informed investors tilt with the trend.**

FIGURE 3-8

The small losses of Muscular Portfolios are much more tolerable in bad times

One of the things a Lazy Portfolio doesn't have is a Momentum Rule. Muscular Portfolios use such a rule to find the three ETFs that have the strongest momentum over the past 3 to 12 months. Informed investors tilt once a month into those ETFs.

Figure 3-9 shows just the 2007–2009 financial crisis. Measured from one month-end to another, the worst losses the Mama Bear Portfolio and the Papa Bear Portfolio suffered were only 18% and 22%. Drawdowns that small are survivable.

Even better, the two Muscular Portfolios rotated in late 2008 out of asset classes that were falling and into ones that were rising. By March 1, 2009, the Papa Bear was down only 12% and the Mama Bear was actually up 1%.

Investors in Muscular Portfolios were ecstatic, compared with the losses of one-third to one-half suffered by the S&P 500 and Lazy Portfolios.

Imagine you'd sunk $100,000 into the S&P 500 or a Lazy Portfolio in October 2007. By March 2009, you were left with only $44,000 to $64,000 in real dollars. In disgust, you probably would've thrown in the towel before the new bull market began.

With the Papa Bear or the Mama Bear, you'd still have had $88,000 to $101,000 in March 2009. You had a giant head start.

No intolerable losses compelled you to liquidate. You were 100% invested in rising ETFs when the next bull market began. That's what makes Muscular Portfolios outperform overall.

》TECH TALK

subtracting current costs and fees

Annual fees

In the simulations in this chapter, an annual fee of 0.05% was subtracted from the S&P 500. This represents the current cost of an index ETF such as Vanguard's VOO. ("V" is the Roman numeral for 5, get it?)

Lazy Portfolios and their momentum versions were charged an annual fee of 0.11%, which is the current average of their ETFs. Exception: The 7Twelve Portfolio holds emerging-market and commodity ETFs that charge slightly higher fees, increasing that portfolio's average annual fee to 0.15%.

Trading costs

The momentum versions of portfolios in this chapter were charged 0.10% for current round-trip costs (selling one ETF and buying another).

No trading costs were subtracted from the S&P 500 or Lazy Portfolios, even though Lazy Portfolios do incur rebalancing costs.

The costs of previous decades are not relevant. ETFs didn't even exist in 1973. The purpose of a simulation is to estimate today's costs going forward, not backward.

》KEY CONCEPT

this book's purpose

Friends don't let friends lose half of their life savings in the stock market.

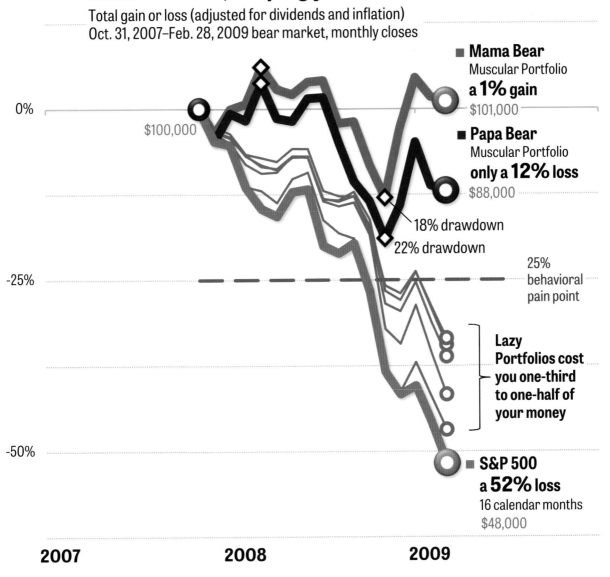

Muscular Portfolios use gradual asset rotation, keeping your losses low

Total gain or loss (adjusted for dividends and inflation)
Oct. 31, 2007–Feb. 28, 2009 bear market, monthly closes

■ **Mama Bear**
Muscular Portfolio
a 1% gain
$101,000

■ **Papa Bear**
Muscular Portfolio
only a 12% loss
$88,000

18% drawdown

22% drawdown

25% behavioral pain point

Lazy Portfolios cost you one-third to one-half of your money

■ **S&P 500**
a 52% loss
16 calendar months
$48,000

$100,000

0%

-25%

-50%

2007   2008   2009

FIGURE 3-9 | Data sources: My Plan IQ (Lazy Portfolios), CXO Advisory (Mama Bear),[1098] Quant simulator (Papa Bear)[1099]

The Momentum Rule improves Lazy Portfolios, but unpredictably

A Momentum Rule provides a great benefit to a Muscular Portfolio that's properly designed. Momentum can sometimes improve a Lazy Portfolio, but usually not as much as it improves a Muscular Portfolio.

Paul Merriman's Ultimate Buy-and-Hold Portfolio is an example. It specifies 11 asset classes, including equities, REITs, and Treasury bonds.[1100] No commodities are included. (For Ultimate's specific holdings, see Appendix C.)

The momentum version of Ultimate tilted more toward bonds in 2008

Date	Equities	Bonds
Jan. 1, 2007	100%	
Dec. 1, 2007	67%	33%
Jan. 1, 2008	33%	67%
Feb. 1, 2008	100%	
Mar. 1, 2008	33%	67%
Apr. 1, 2008	100%	
May 1, 2008	33%	67%
Aug. 1, 2008	100%	
Oct. 1, 2008	33%	67%
Dec. 1, 2008	100%	
June 1, 2009	100%	

FIGURE 3-10
Source: Quant simulator

The Ultimate Portfolio typically devotes 60% to equity-like assets—stocks and REITs—and 40% to fixed income.[1101] (Merriman has published many variations.)

Adding a Momentum Rule would have caused Ultimate's momentum version to make 10 changes in 2007 through 2009. Each change would have shifted a portion of the portfolio from equity-like assets to bonds or vice versa. (On average, that was one change every three or four months.)

The table in Figure 3-10 shows how the Momentum Rule gradually tilted the portfolio 33%, then 67%, and finally 100% toward bonds during the three years of the financial crisis. The improved portfolio had been 100% in bonds for weeks when the Lehman Brothers bankruptcy on Sept. 15, 2008, caused the market to collapse. The portfolio got 100% back into equity-like assets by June 2009—only three months after the bear market ended.

Figure 3-11 graphs the 2007–2009 bear market. The official Ultimate lost 37% in the crash. That's far past the pain point that compels investors to liquidate. The momentum version did much better. It had a survivable drawdown of only 19%.

That's an improvement, but it's not as pleasant a finish as the Muscular Portfolios delivered. Cushioning your life savings during crashes is why Muscular Portfolios outperform. We saw this over periods of more than four decades in Chapter 1.

» TECH TALK
the simulations' Momentum Rule
Unless stated otherwise, the Quant simulations in this book use the same Momentum Rule as the Papa Bear:

1 · At every month's end, you average each asset class's total return over the past 3, 6, and 12 months.

2 · The following month, you hold the three assets with the strongest momentum, equally weighted.

3 · No minimum fixed-income allocation is required.

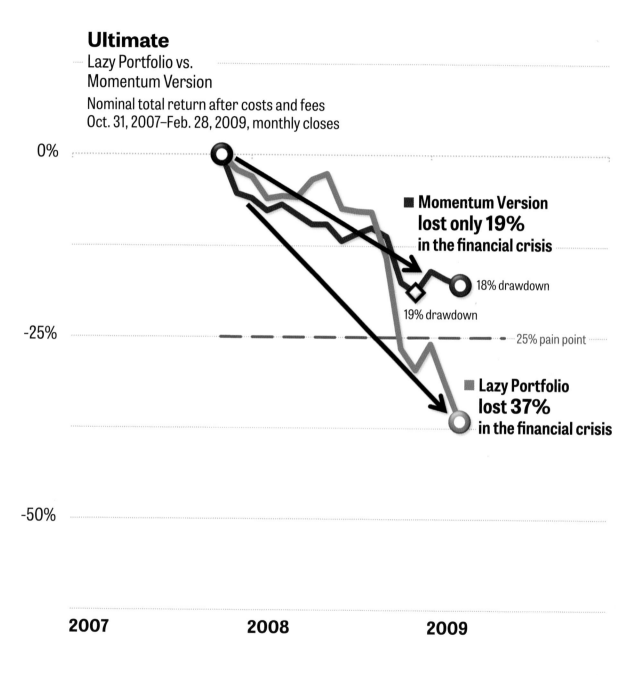

Ultimate
Lazy Portfolio vs.
Momentum Version

Nominal total return after costs and fees
Oct. 31, 2007–Feb. 28, 2009, monthly closes

0%

■ Momentum Version
lost only 19%
in the financial crisis

18% drawdown

19% drawdown

-25%

25% pain point

■ Lazy Portfolio
lost 37%
in the financial crisis

-50%

2007   2008   2009

FIGURE 3-11 | Source: Quant simulator

A 43-year simulation gives us four bear markets and four bull markets

Simulations using the 43-year period from 1973 through 2015 include four bear markets and four bull markets. This long-term perspective provides an acid test for Lazy Portfolios.

Ariel Levy, a *New Yorker* staff writer, once commented on a way to improve the taste of any dish in the *Moosewood Cookbook*, a vegetarian bible. "Pick almost any recipe . . . Now add bacon," she wrote.[1102]

Momentum—a little "bacon" —boosts the gain of every popular Lazy Portfolio. In most cases, momentum also reduces a portfolio's maximum drawdown.

The Quant simulator provides total returns from Jan. 1, 1973, to Dec. 31, 2015, for US and non-US equities and bonds, commodities, gold, and much else.

Figures 3-12 to 3-14 compare the S&P 500's 43-year return against nine of the best-known Lazy Portfolios. Each portfolio is also shown with a momentum version.

Figure 3-12 shows two portfolios:

» **The S&P 500** had a total return of 10.0% annualized. By happenstance, that's an easy-to-remember round number. (The precise total return was 10.038%.)

» **7Twelve** is an example of a Lazy Portfolio that enjoys higher returns and smaller losses when a Momentum Rule is added. It holds 12 ETFs representing seven major asset classes. The official portfolio underperformed the S&P with a return of only 9.25%. The momentum version boosted the return by a **remarkable six points** to 15.4%. Momentum also cut 7Twelve's worst loss from 41% to a survivable 20% in 1987. The improved drawdown in 2009 was even less: only 15%.

Watch for linear and ratio scales

In this chapter and elsewhere, graphs use a linear scale or a ratio scale, as appropriate. It's good to know the differences (see Figure 3-12):

» **Linear scales** are common. Values on the vertical axis rise by addition: $100, $200, $300, $400, and so forth.

» **Ratio scales** should be used whenever any portfolio rises 400% or more. A ratio scale (also called a **semilog scale**) shows a constant rate of return as a straight line, rather than an exaggerated curve pointing toward the sky. Values rise geomtrically: $100, $200, $400, $800.

Say you inherit $100,000 at age 25 and invest it until you retire at 68. Figure 3-12 shows that adding only 1.79 percentage points to your annualized performance would give you **double the money** after your 43-year working and saving career (about $12 million vs. only $6 million). Those 1.79 points do add up!

Turning this around, say a broker's fees shaved 1.79 points off your return. You'd end up with **half as much money** (a mere $6 million vs. $12 million).

Every Lazy Portfolio's rate of return improved 4 to 6 percentage points in a momentum version

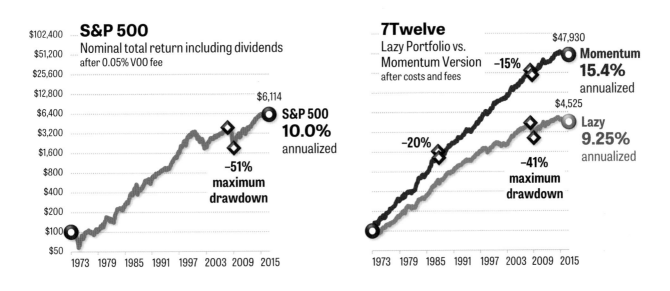

S&P 500
Nominal total return including dividends
after 0.05% VOO fee

$6,114
S&P 500
10.0%
annualized

−51%
maximum
drawdown

7Twelve
Lazy Portfolio vs.
Momentum Version
after costs and fees

$47,930
−15%
Momentum
15.4%
annualized

$4,525
Lazy
9.25%
annualized

−20%
−41%
maximum
drawdown

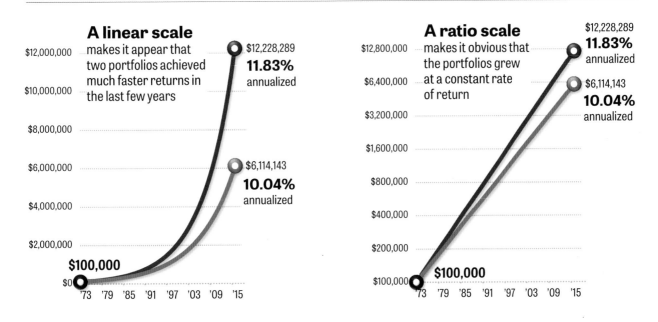

A linear scale
makes it appear that
two portfolios achieved
much faster returns in
the last few years

$12,228,289
11.83%
annualized

$6,114,143
10.04%
annualized

$100,000

A ratio scale
makes it obvious that
the portfolios grew
at a constant rate
of return

$12,228,289
11.83%
annualized

$6,114,143
10.04%
annualized

$100,000

FIGURE 3-12 | Source: Quant simulator (S&P 500, 7Twelve); author's calculations (scales)

You can't simply tack a Momentum Rule onto a Lazy Portfolio

Figure 3-13 reinforces the previous figure. Modified by the Momentum Rule, **every Lazy Portfolio enjoyed about 4 to 6 points more annualized return** in the long term.

Across a 43-year investment horizon—perhaps as long as your working career—4 to 6 percentage points would be gigantic. Adding a Momentum Rule would give you **5 to 10 times the ending dollar value** of the official Lazy Portfolios.

But you can't just bolt momentum onto a Lazy Portfolio and expect it to excel. Momentum works best with the proper mix of asset classes, as in the Mama Bear and Papa Bear Portfolios.

» The Coward's Portfolio is one of three Lazy Portfolios whose maximum drawdowns did not get better but actually worsened (−49% rather than −37%) or got no better. The portfolio (also called Smart Money, after a magazine that profiled it) holds US stocks, with an extra allocation to "value" companies. It also holds equity funds from countries around the world, US REIT funds, and short-term US fixed-income funds. Like the other eight Lazy Portfolios in this chapter, it enjoyed about four points more annualized return when improved with the Momentum Rule. But its asset classes didn't provide enough choices in the menu to keep you from crashing, even with momentum.

» The Ideal Index Portfolio's return improved from 10.5% to 14.9%. However, Ideal's maximum drawdown was **not** improved by momentum. Its worst loss was 43% in 2007–2009 in both variations.

» The Coffeehouse Portfolio raised its return to 15.1% in the momentum version rather than 10.5%. But the maximum drawdown with momentum actually worsened to 40% from 33%.

» The Nano Portfolio uses only five asset classes. Even with that relatively small menu, momentum improved the portfolio's return to 14.0% rather than 9.5%. The momentum version also lessened the maximum drawdown to 26% rather than 38%. However, a 26% loss is still unacceptable—worse than the 20% to 25% level that causes investors to throw in the towel.

There's no way to predict how much the momentum version of a Lazy Portfolio will return in the future. However, it's remarkable to see that every Lazy Portfolio's return was higher **with** a Momentum Rule than without. One simple change—holding each month the three asset classes with the **best momentum,** rather than holding every asset class—makes a huge difference.

Three of nine Lazy Portfolios suffered crashes that were <u>worse</u> or showed no improvement using momentum

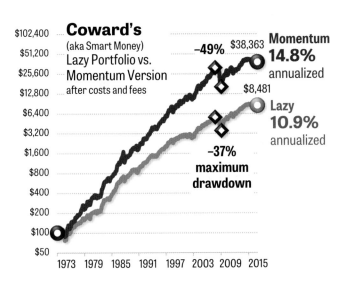

Coward's
(aka Smart Money)
Lazy Portfolio vs.
Momentum Version
after costs and fees

−49% $38,363 **Momentum 14.8%** annualized

$8,481 **Lazy 10.9%** annualized

−37% maximum drawdown

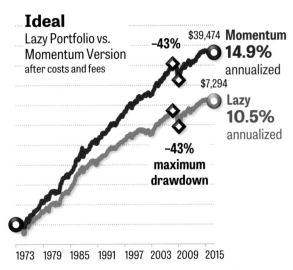

Ideal
Lazy Portfolio vs.
Momentum Version
after costs and fees

−43% $39,474 **Momentum 14.9%** annualized

$7,294 **Lazy 10.5%** annualized

−43% maximum drawdown

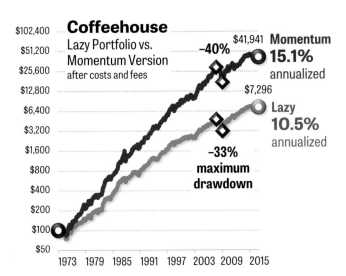

Coffeehouse
Lazy Portfolio vs.
Momentum Version
after costs and fees

−40% $41,941 **Momentum 15.1%** annualized

$7,296 **Lazy 10.5%** annualized

−33% maximum drawdown

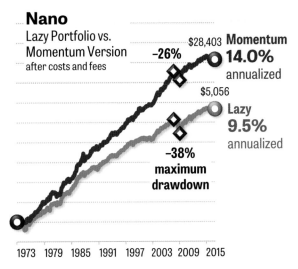

Nano
Lazy Portfolio vs.
Momentum Version
after costs and fees

−26% $28,403 **Momentum 14.0%** annualized

$5,056 **Lazy 9.5%** annualized

−38% maximum drawdown

FIGURE 3-13 | Source: Quant simulator

Momentum provides many advantages, but investors require more

Figure 3-14 shows four Lazy Portfolios that improved both their gains and their losses by adding a Momentum Rule:

» The Family Taxable Portfolio reduced its 40% crash in 2007–2009 to 18% using momentum. But momentum didn't keep the Lazy Portfolio within a tolerable dive in 1987, when it lost 29%. That's more than most people could stand.

» The Gone Fishin' Portfolio behaved similarly. Its 39% drawdown in 2007–2009 was reduced to 27%. But like the Family strategy, the momentum version of Gone Fishin' suffered its worst drawdown in 1987: a loss of 29%. Both loss levels are huge haircuts that most individual investors wouldn't tolerate.

» The Unconventional Success Portfolio saw its maximum loss reduced to a survivable level: to 24% from 41%. But the momentum version improved the portfolio's return only to 14.3%

from 9.7%. That's the third-lowest momentum-improved return among the nine portfolios shown in Figures 3-12 to 3-14.

» The Ultimate Buy-and-Hold Portfolio boasts the greatest point spurt of all the portfolios improved with momentum. A massive 6.6 point boost lifted Ultimate's annualized return to 16.6% rather than 10.0%.

That difference was entirely due to the momentum version holding losses to a minimum, a three-year close-up of which we saw earlier in this chapter. Ultimate's maximum drawdown, when using momentum, fell to the smallest of any of the nine momentum versions. The worst month-end drawdown using momentum was a mere 19%—a far cry from the painful 37% crash of the official Ultimate Buy-and-Hold Portfolio.

Ultimate reveals the true potential of adding the

Momentum Rule to a portfolio. Over a 43-year working/saving lifetime, a 6.6 point boost would have turned a $10,000 investment into $7,588,600 instead of only $610,200. Your ending value would have been **12 times higher** with a Momentum Rule. (Of course, you could have enjoyed spending some of the larger gains along the way!)

Getting such strong returns with one simple change is great. But adding a Momentum Rule to a Lazy Portfolio doesn't qualify it to be called a Muscular Portfolio. Investors also expect other important criteria to be met.

Those conditions include a financial strategy having ease of use and some kind of online support. These services should be required before investors entrust any strategy with serious money. These criteria are called Strategy Sanity (see Figure 3-15).

Momentum improved four Lazy Portfolios with better returns <u>and</u> smaller drawdowns

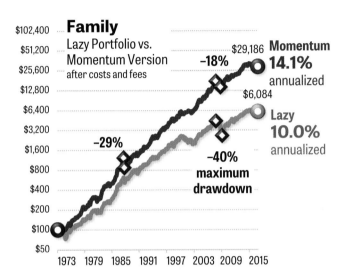

Family
Lazy Portfolio vs. Momentum Version after costs and fees

Momentum **14.1%** annualized — $29,186, −18%

Lazy **10.0%** annualized — $6,084

−29%

−40% maximum drawdown

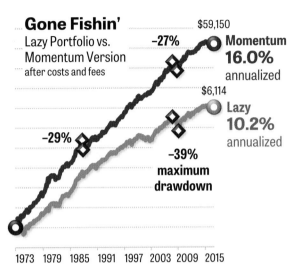

Gone Fishin'
Lazy Portfolio vs. Momentum Version after costs and fees

Momentum **16.0%** annualized — $59,150, −27%

Lazy **10.2%** annualized — $6,114

−29%

−39% maximum drawdown

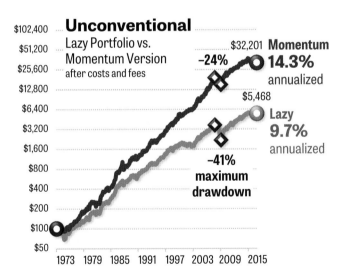

Unconventional
Lazy Portfolio vs. Momentum Version after costs and fees

Momentum **14.3%** annualized — $32,201, −24%

Lazy **9.7%** annualized — $5,468

−41% maximum drawdown

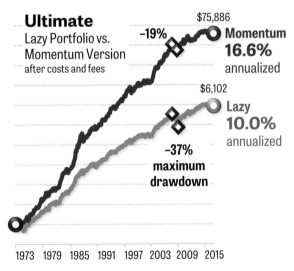

Ultimate
Lazy Portfolio vs. Momentum Version after costs and fees

Momentum **16.6%** annualized — $75,886, −19%

Lazy **10.0%** annualized — $6,102

−37% maximum drawdown

FIGURE 3-14 | Source: Quant simulator

Informed investors look for Strategy Sanity before betting their life savings

Muscular Portfolios offer great returns. But an investment strategy should never be selected on the basis of returns alone.

Figure 3-15 shows other criteria that all formulas for individual investors should meet: Strategy Sanity. In the 21st century, there's no excuse for investment strategies that are expensive, complicated, or secretive.

Some of the most important criteria are:

» **Free updated picks.** MuscularPortfolios.com is a free website that refreshes its ETF rankings every 10 minutes during market hours. It discloses which ETFs to buy and sell, using a Momentum Rule to select the strongest funds.

» **Years of use by a broad community.** Equivalents to the Mama Bear and Papa Bear have been followed in real time for years by readers of Steve LeCompte and Mebane Faber, whose portfolios are cloned in this book. Starter portfolios like the Baby Bear have been tracked for two decades by Jack Bogle with open, free-wheeling discussions at Bogleheads.org.

» **Unlikely to become over-grazed.** Muscular Portfolios require the self-control to act only once a month on a predictable schedule and to follow a mechanical formula.

According to the 43-year simulations shown in Chapter 1:

» **The Papa Bear** achieved an annualized rate of return of 16.2% with no month-end losses greater than 25% during bear markets. That's competitive with even the most-improved Lazy Portfolio and far above the official ones.

» **The Mama Bear** attained a smaller but still-excellent return of 14.3%. In exchange, month-end losses were no more than 18%—making it perfect for people with low risk tolerance.

» **The Baby Bear**—which is a starter plan, not a Muscular Portfolio—realized almost exactly the same 10% return as the S&P 500 over 43 years. Yet its much smaller drawdown of 29% puts the S&P 500's 51% loss to shame.

What if a Muscular Portfolio's return is not as high in the coming 43 years? What if a Muscular Portfolio's future return delivers only **half** as much outperformance vs. the S&P 500? What if it produces only the **same** performance as the S&P 500?

So what? Even in those cases, you would have achieved **market-like returns** with **tolerable, bond-like volatility.** Skip the horrendous losses that other strategies subject you to.

The future is unpredictable, and nothing is ever guaranteed. What we **can** say for sure is that Muscular Portfolios are a saner investment strategy than any Lazy Portfolio—even one that's been retrofitted with momentum.

Strategy Sanity: A dozen traits we demand

Any investing plan for individuals should meet at least the following minimum standards:

Feature	Why it's important
1 · Market-like returns	It's possible with highly liquid index ETFs to capture 99% of an asset class's gains.
2 · No month-end losses over 25%	Advances in portfolio design keep drawdowns tolerable.
3 · Absolutely no math	Most people will never crunch spreadsheets or compute their own statistics.
4 · Less than 15 minutes per month	Busy adults don't want to be glued to computer screens every day.
5 · No more than monthly changes	Excessive trading hurts performance and makes saving a chore.
6 · Fully disclosed	The book *Muscular Portfolios* and its website reveal every detail.
7 · Free picks updated continuously	The website refreshes its listings every 10 minutes during market hours.
8 · No registration required	Submitting an email address or purchasing tutorials is not mandatory.
9 · Years of use by actual people	Users have access to a longtime newsletter or online forum.
10 · Unlikely to become overgrazed	Muscular Portfolios take discipline that many investors don't have.
11 · Same formula at all times	Identical rules in bear and bull phases, which cannot be predicted.
12 · No shorting/borrowing	Going short and taking on debt heighten your risk of loss.

FIGURE 3-15

Lazy Portfolio authors didn't use momentum, lacking a full set of ETFs

Don't try to invent your own Lazy Portfolio and then "improve" it with your own definition of momentum. Doing so would violate several of the principles of Strategy Sanity laid out in Figure 3-15.

The designers of the portfolios that are cloned in this book are true financial experts. They produce investing strategies suitable for people from all walks of life. Don't gamble your life savings on the "hot asset class of the day."

But you may wonder: If the addition of one simple rule, academically documented in 1993, improves Lazy Portfolios so much, why didn't the original authors of these 1990s-era strategies use momentum themselves?

Asset rotation required three megatrends (as described in Chapter 1) that didn't converge until the 21st century:

» Near-zero commissions. FolioInvesting.com, for example, didn't open until 2000. At this writing, Folio charges only $4 for its patented "window trades" (or $0 with a paid membership). Until prices fell this low, asset-rotation strategies were eaten alive by commissions.

» Ultralow ETF fees and bid-ask spreads. Many ETFs today charge 0.1% or less annually.

» Evidence of momentum. It took the findings of hundreds of academic studies to convince the experts. But now momentum is considered a fundamental factor of free markets around the world.

Figure 3-16 reveals how difficult it would have been to design an asset-rotation portfolio in the 20th century:

» A few index mutual funds existed in 1990, but the development of mass-market, low-cost indexing was in its infancy.

» ETFs are ideal, mutual funds are not. Mutual funds are required to make capital gains distributions every year. In a taxable account, this forces you to pay tax on unrealized gains. Mutual funds also don't reveal their pricing until the end of each market day.

» Mutual funds for commodities, gold, and some other global asset classes had high active-management fees. The first commodity ETF that brought these fees down, DBC, opened in 2006. But it had the disadvantage of producing IRS Schedule K-1 income. That can make your gains taxable, even in a tax-deferred account. DBC's sister fund PDBC, which produces standard Form 1099 income, didn't open until 2014.

LIVINGSTON'S LAW OF LAZINESS

A Lazy Portfolio hit by a runaway train
Subjects your savings to a world of pain.

» KEY CONCEPT

just say nope to buy-and-hope

A buy-and-hold strategy that never adapts to market conditions exposes you to huge losses, which no investor should tolerate.

All 13 global index ETFs were not available until 2014

Partial listing of index mutual funds and exchange-traded funds

A few index mutual funds existed before 2000:

ERA	YEAR	
	1960	◀ first small-cap index mutual fund **NAESX**
	1976	◀ first S&P 500 index mutual fund **VFINX**
	1986	◀ 30-year Treasury bonds **VUSTX**
GHW Bush	1989	
		◀ large-cap value/large-cap growth stocks **VIVAX VIGRX**
Clinton	1993	
		◀ emerging-market stocks **VEIEX**
		◀ real estate investment trusts (REITs) **VGSIX**
	1997	
		◀ small-cap value/small-cap growth stocks **VISVX VISGX**
		◀ developed-market stocks **VTMGX**
GW Bush	2001	

ETFs for Muscular Portfolios arose 2004–2014:

ERA	YEAR	
		◀ large-cap value/growth stocks **VTV VUG** | REITs **VNQ**
	2005	◀ emerging-market stocks **VWO** | gold **IAU**
		◀ first schedule K-1 commodity ETF **DBC**
		◀ developed-market stocks **VEA** | 30-year Treasurys **EDV**
Obama	2009	◀ 10–25 year Treasurys **VGLT**
		◀ Russell 1000 **VONE** | small/value/growth **VIOO VIOV VIOG**
	2013	◀ non-US government & corporate bonds **BNDX**
		◀ first Form 1099 commodity ETF **PDBC**

FIGURE 3-16 | Illustration by Pieter Tandjung

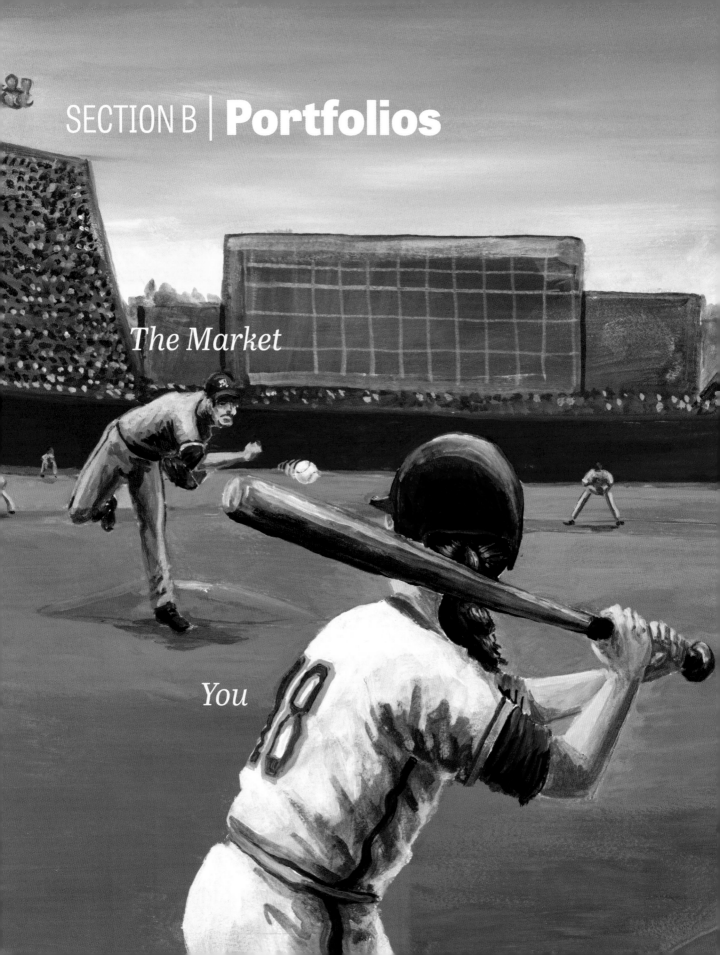

SECTION B | **Portfolios**

The Market

You

To win, just hit the ball

Imagine you're batting for the home team. In a moment, the opposing pitcher will hurl a fastball inches from your face at 100 miles per hour.

After you see the ball leave the pitcher's hand, you have one-fourth of a second to decide whether you should swing high, swing low, or not swing at all. You have three ways to cope:

» **Swinging wildly.** If the fear of being hit seizes you, you'll tighten up and flail blindly, your bat not even touching the ball.

» **Analysis paralysis.** If your mind tries to calculate the exact flight path of the throw, you'll freeze like a dummy and strike out.

» **Responding automatically.** Your only hope is to swing mechanically—the way you've trained for years to do and have practiced hundreds of times.

Emotions and overanalyzing will lose you the game for sure. That's baseball.

In investing, the market is the pitcher. You're the batter—you must deal with whatever the market throws at you.

As an investor, both swinging wildly and analysis paralysis are losing strategies. To win the game, your portfolio must **automatically** adapt to whatever the market does. You don't need to hit home runs, but you do need to hit the ball.

Over the years, financial sharks have taken billions of dollars from investors by playing to their wants and fears, which never seem to evolve.

From this section forward, you'll learn how to undo the all-too-human tendencies that make investors underperform.

Once you know the trick, it's easy to watch your nest egg grow—without agony, regret, or fear of crashes.

Illustration: "The Ball Game" by Jed Dunkerley

4 Find the investment portfolio that's just right for you

"One accurate measurement is worth a thousand expert opinions."

REAR ADMIRAL GRACE HOPPER (1906–1992), designer of UNIVAC I, the first commercial computer[1103]

The upcoming chapters describe four model investing strategies. They range from the very simplest starter portfolio—the Baby Bear, which you only rebalance once a year—to two different Muscular Portfolios, which require a 15-minute checkup once a month:

» **The Mama Bear** uses the simplest menu of asset classes of any Muscular Portfolio.

» **The Papa Bear** is a Muscular Portfolio with a slightly larger asset-class menu, but with the potential for greater gains.

» **The Baby Bear** is the easiest possible two-asset portfolio—it grows like the S&P 500 over time but with smaller drawdowns.

» **The End Game Portfolio** is a simple wealth-preservation strategy. It has a large allocation to bond ETFs (for income) and a small allocation to a Muscular Portfolio (for growth).

Four questions help you find a strategy that fits your needs

Which portfolio should you choose?

Figure 4-1 uses four simple questions to determine which portfolio you should follow.

Of course, complications such as wills, trusts, college-savings plans, family-owned businesses, or large holdings of real estate require more planning than any mere portfolio strategy can provide. And if you have a very complex financial situation, you should seek a fee-only adviser to look at your case, as described in Chapter 16.

But limiting our task to that of making your savings grow, the four questions in Figure 4-1 should be enough to give you an answer.

Once a month, visit the Web address for whichever portfolio you choose to follow:

» **MuscularPortfolios.com/mama-bear**

» **MuscularPortfolios.com/papa-bear**

» **MuscularPortfolios.com/baby-bear**

There is no Web page for the End Game Portfolio, which is simply a combination of bond ETFs and a Muscular Portfolio (Chapter 23).

The Muscular Portfolios decision tree
Four simple questions determine the correct plan

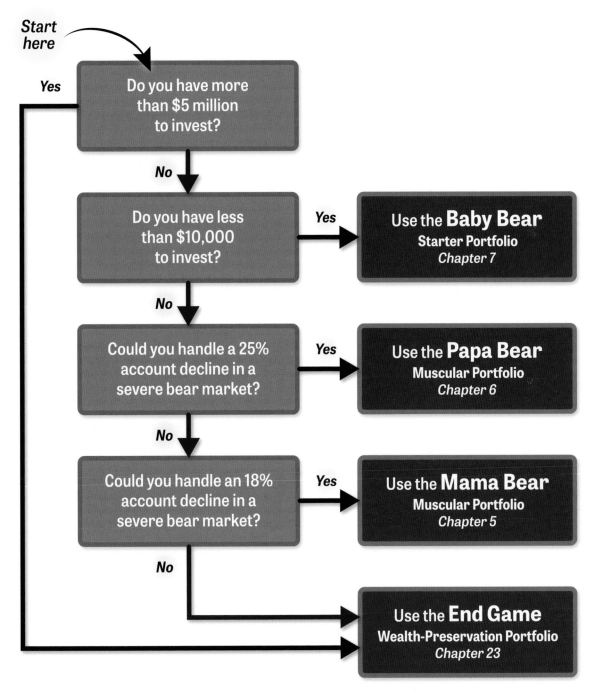

FIGURE 4-1 | If your household is in the top tax bracket—taxable income over $600,000 (couples) or $500,000 (singles)—read the advice in Chapter 19 before choosing a strategy. Illustration by Pieter Tandjung

Use the free rankings at MuscularPortfolios.com to find ETFs

The portfolios in this book are different from most other investment strategies you'll ever see. No one is charging you any fees. The portfolios are do-it-yourself solutions, but most of the work has already been done for you—at no charge.

The ETFs that rate the best for each portfolio are on MuscularPortfolios.com, along with instructions for your portfolio's holding percentages. All for free.

You don't even have to provide an email address to use the Muscular Portfolios website. (But be sure to sign up to get the free monthly newsletter that updates this book.)

To make your monthly tune-ups, simply visit the Web address. Figure 4-2 shows the Mama Bear Portfolio as an example.

You'll find plenty of detail in the upcoming chapters, but here are a few basics to keep in mind:

The ratings at the site update every 10 minutes while the markets are open, usually 9:30 AM to 4 PM Eastern Time on weekdays. Market providers delay the data approximately 20 minutes.

Because the top-ranked ETFs can remain unchanged for weeks, the exact minute you check is not important.

Visit the website any time before 3 PM Eastern Time and make your trades prior to 4 PM.

Never place a market order while the market is closed. When the market opens, market makers are sometimes able to charge you a high profit margin (called a "bid-ask spread"). See Chapter 17 for easy ways to keep these trading costs low.

What if your job doesn't allow you to make a trade while the market is open? Get an account with an online brokerage that allows you to place "window trades." One example, FolioInvesting.com, is described in Chapter 17. You can order a trade at night that Folio safely executes in the 11 AM "window" the next trading day.

Every year or two, a "flash crash" occurs for a half hour or so. A flash crash is a market glitch that makes security prices unusually high or low.

Normally, spreads for popular ETFs stay well under 0.5%. But during a flash crash, things go crazy. If you see a spread greater than 1% in the rankings at MuscularPortfolios.com, don't buy or sell at that time. Check an hour later, and trade when the spreads are below 1%.

LIVINGSTON'S LAW OF DECISION-MAKING

One plan's too hot and one plan's too cold
Pick one that's just right before you're too old.

MUSCULAR PORTFOLIOS.

The Mama Bear Portfolio

Asset class	5-mo. return	ETF symbol	Price	Bid-ask spread	Buy
Emerging-market stocks	**+7.00**	VWO	46.98	0.02%	34%
Commodities	**+6.92**	PDBC	17.77	0.06%	33%
Gold	**+4.52**	IAU	12.73	0.08%	33%
US large-cap stocks	+4.12	VONE	121.20	0.03%	—
US small-cap stocks	+3.61	VIOO	140.12	0.05%	—
Developed-market large-cap stocks	+2.60	VEA	44.25	0.02%	—
US Treasury bills, 1 to 12 mo.	+0.45	SHV	110.37	0.01%	—
US Treasury bonds, 20+ yr.	+0.38	VGLT	75.02	0.09%	—

FIGURE 4-2 | Get the picks in any browser or smartphone—no app required

5 The Mama Bear is about as simple as a Muscular Portfolio can be

"The race is not always to the swift, nor the battle to the strong, but that's the way to bet."

DAMON RUNYON, American author (1884–1946)[1104]

The Mama Bear Portfolio is the first of two Muscular Portfolios in this book. The other is the Papa Bear Portfolio, which we'll see in the next chapter.

» **The Mama Bear Portfolio is for people who:**

1 · **Will commit 15 minutes a month to tune up their account;**

2 · **Want a menu of only nine different ETFs to keep things simple; and**

3 · **Want to keep their maximum drawdowns to only 18% during wild market crashes.**

A Muscular Portfolio requires you to check a free website once a month and give your portfolio a quick tune-up based on the information there. This monthly tune-up takes, at most, 15 minutes. If no switch from one ETF to another is required, the checkup takes only one minute. That's a tiny amount of effort with an impressive return.

As we saw in Chapter 1, the Mama Bear would have returned 14.3% annualized in the 43-year period from 1973–2015, according to the Quant simulator. The Papa Bear, with its broader 13-asset menu, returned a noticeably better 16.2%. The S&P 500 including dividends returned approximately 10.0%. (See Figure 5-1.)

People who are very risk averse may prefer the Mama Bear to the Papa Bear because it offers smaller losses during crashes. The Mama Bear's maximum drawdown was 18% (tied in 1987 and 2008). The Papa Bear's was 25% (in 1987).

The Mama Bear is especially easy to manage. On average, it requires you to change your portfolio only 9 out of 12 months a year, like the Papa Bear. (For stats, see Chapter 19.)

In the other three months of the year, the Mama Bear requires no change to the top three ETFs. You would have checked the website to find there was nothing you needed to do!

The improved performance you get from the 15 minutes you spend might well be a better return on your time than that offered by any job.

» **KEY CONCEPT**

the Mama Bear Portfolio
Nine asset classes give you enough diversification to hold the three strongest ETFs—the ones that are likely to rise and not crash.

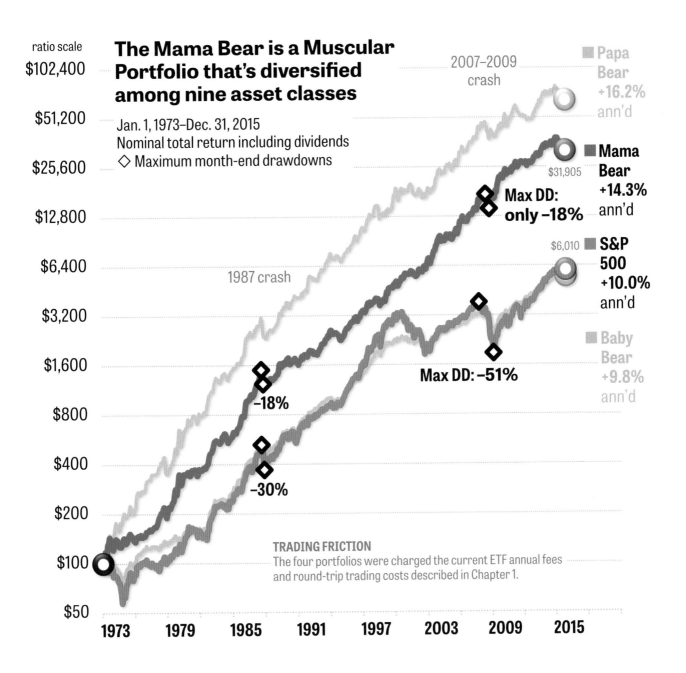

FIGURE 5-1 | Source: Quant simulator

Each month, the Mama Bear holds the three ETFs with the best momentum

The Baby Bear Portfolio, as we'll see in Chapter 7, is a starter portfolio with a menu of only two asset classes. The portfolio is split 50/50 between US stocks and US bonds. You hold at all times the two ETFs that track those assets.

Muscular Portfolios like the Mama Bear and the Papa Bear are different. A Muscular Portfolio has a full **menu** of asset classes. The Mama Bear selects from 9 ETFs and the Papa Bear selects from 13.

A Muscular Portfolio uses asset rotation without market timing. Instead, each month you hold the three ETFs that have the strongest momentum. This is determined by the Momentum Rule, as we saw in Chapter 1.

There's an important difference between a Muscular Portfolio and that portfolio's menu:

» **The Mama Bear menu** is the total set of nine asset classes to choose from.

» **The Mama Bear Portfolio** is the three ETFs each month that have the best momentum.

Figure 5-2 shows the nine ETFs that make up the Mama Bear menu. On your chosen day of the month, you simply check the following Web page:

MuscularPortfolios.com/ mama-bear

If there's been a change since last month's checkup, you sell any of your ETFs that have fallen out of the top three and buy those ETFs that have taken their place, following the rules shown in Figure 5-2. You're done!

For the annual fee of each ETF in Figure 5-2—and alternative funds you can use if these exact ETFs are not available in your 401(k) plan—see Appendix A.

The Mama Bear menu

Asset class	Security name	Symbol
US large-cap stocks	Vanguard Russell 1000 ETF	VONE
US small-cap stocks	Vanguard Small-Cap 600 ETF	VIOO
Developed-market large-cap stocks	Vanguard Europe Pacific ETF	VEA
Emerging-market stocks	Vanguard Emerging Markets ETF	VWO
Real-estate investment trusts (REITs)	Vanguard REIT ETF	VNQ
Commodities	PowerShares DB Commodity ETF	PDBC
Gold	COMEX Gold Trust ETF	IAU
US Treasury bonds, long-term	Vanguard Long-Term Govt. Bond ETF	VGLT
Cash (US T-bills, 1 to 12 months)	iShares Short-Term Treasury ETF	SHV

COLOR KEY

equities	hard assets	fixed-income

FIGURE 5-2

Strategy rules for the Mama Bear Portfolio

1 · Select a specific day to tune up your portfolio.

2 · On that day each month, check: **MuscularPortfolios.com/mama-bear.**

3 · The nine ETFs that make up the Mama Bear menu will be ranked according to momentum (five-month return). Note the top three.

4 · If you already own all three ETFs—because you purchased them in a previous month—do nothing.

5 · Sell any ETF not in the top three. Immediately buy instead any top-three ETF that you don't already hold.

6 · Exact percentages are not important. Rebalance only if any ETF is over 20% off target. (See Chapter 18.)

Analyzing the performance of thousands of studies led to the nine asset classes

The Mama Bear Portfolio is a clone of a strategy by Steve LeCompte, the founder and editor of CXOAdvisory.com. This financial analysis site calls its asset-rotation plan SACEMS (the Simple Asset Class ETF Momentum Strategy).

LeCompte previously worked in program management at IBM and as project officer on the staff of Adm. H.G. Rickover. He holds a master's degree in physics from the University of Michigan.

Today, LeCompte is most famous for conducting a study called Guru Grades. He tracked 6,582 public statements by 68 stock market experts from 1999 through 2012. He found that only 47% of their predictions came to pass. That's less than a 50/50 chance![1105]

If the gurus had simply said, "The market will be up next month," they would have been right 60% of the time. That's because the S&P 500 rises in about 60% of all months. And yet only 7 of the 68 experts (10.3%) achieved an accuracy better than 60%. That's likely just chance.

Guru Grades is just a small part of what CXO Advisory does. The site's main service is analyzing various experts' whitepapers about investing. As often as not, CXO Advisory reveals that the theories are bunk.

LeCompte must laugh his head off posting these findings. In one case, he studied Jim Cramer's popular cable TV show, *Mad Money*. After a six-month analysis, LeCompte reported that the stocks rated "sell" in the show's Lightning Round segment had gained **more than twice as much** as the stocks rated "buy"!

LeCompte concluded with a remarkable finding:

"His 'sell' recommendations in aggregate may outperform the market."[1106]

As LeCompte observes, popular investing TV shows are based "primarily on entertainment value rather than economic value."

In a statement, Cramer responded: "My popularity rides not on showmanship but on rigor on my part and success on the part of the viewers and readers who use my work."[1107]

Since 2004, LeCompte has posted more than 2,000 analyses of academic studies.

LeCompte has sacrificed hours of his time on the cross of academic literature to give us eternal freedom from the devilish details of theories that just don't work.

Steve LeCompte

Expert analyst of asset rotation

FIGURE 5-3

Don't think holding just one ETF is better than holding the top three ETFs

At this point, you might be thinking, "If holding the three ETFs with the best momentum each month is good, wouldn't holding only the top **one** be even better?"

It ain't necessarily so.

To answer this very question, CXO Advisory has, since July 31, 2006, tracked in real time the results of holding the top one, top two, or top three ETFs.

Figure 5-4 shows that the top-three ETF portfolio had a higher annualized return than the top-one portfolio—after almost 11 years of tracking.

The top-three portfolio returned 11.8% annualized while the top-one portfolio returned only 9.1%.

The reason is diversification. No one can predict **exactly** which stock, bond, or ETF will be the very best performer in the month to come. But holding three ETFs that have good odds—the ETFs with the strongest momentum— means you're likely to own at least **one** asset class that outperforms.

Best of all, the top-three portfolio protects you from intolerable losses. The maximum drawdown when holding three ETFs was only 13%. The top-one portfolio, in contrast, experienced a blood-curdling 30% loss during the same period.

In Figure 5-4, the top-one portfolio (the reddish line) sometimes zooms ahead but always falls back to or below the Top 3 Portfolio (the green line).

The moral of the story? Never put all your eggs in one ETF's basket.

LeCompte has generously provided a free list of his portfolio's menu of nine ETFs.[1108] He's also publicly disclosed his version of the Momentum Rule: simply rank each ETF by its five-month total return.[1109]

While these and some other analyses are free, paying subscribers to CXO Advisory receive the whole enchilada, including premium articles and month-end rankings for the nine ETFs. The site also covers strategies other than the momentum model. At this writing, a paid subscription—which is strongly recommended—costs $179 per year or $17.99 per month.

If you subscribe to CXO to follow its top-three ETF portfolio, be aware that CXO has chosen different specific ETFs than the Mama Bear menu. The Mama Bear uses newer ETFs with lower annual fees. The asset classes tracked, however, are the same.

At the time of writing, the eight index ETFs CXO uses, plus cash, are:

SPY, IWM, EFA, EEM, VNQ, DBC, GLD, and TLT.

The differences between the funds are small enough that the performances of the CXO Advisory ETFs and the Mama Bear ETFs should be nearly identical.

» KEY CONCEPT
three ETFs are better than one
The top-three ETF portfolio gives you a smoother ride while gaining as much or more than holding just one ETF.

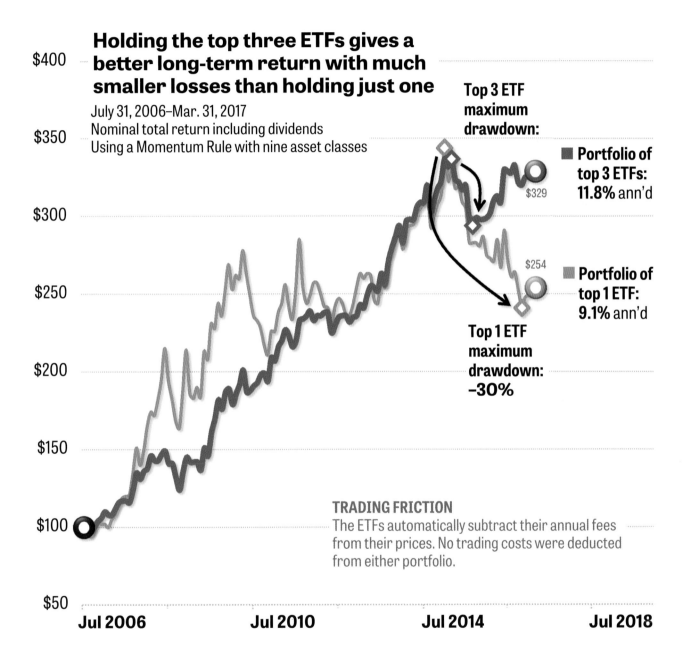

Holding the top three ETFs gives a better long-term return with much smaller losses than holding just one

July 31, 2006–Mar. 31, 2017
Nominal total return including dividends
Using a Momentum Rule with nine asset classes

Top 3 ETF maximum drawdown:

Top 1 ETF maximum drawdown: –30%

■ Portfolio of top 3 ETFs: 11.8% ann'd

$329

■ Portfolio of top 1 ETF: 9.1% ann'd

$254

TRADING FRICTION
The ETFs automatically subtract their annual fees from their prices. No trading costs were deducted from either portfolio.

$400
$350
$300
$250
$200
$150
$100
$50

Jul 2006   Jul 2010   Jul 2014   Jul 2018

FIGURE 5-4 | Source: CXO Advisory[1110]

Don't think you'll do better by adding a few more asset classes you like

There are now hundreds of ETFs tracking various asset classes. The list seems to grow every day.

Could you profitably add some other asset class to the nine used by the Mama Bear?

In a series of exhaustive tests, CXO Advisory found no significant benefit from inserting other asset classes into the menu.

LeCompte added 24 different ETFs, one at a time, into the original menu of nine. He computed the returns for each portfolio as far back as most of these ETFs existed (February 2006).

Most of the additions hurt rather than helped performance. Any improvement in annualized returns amounted to only a few tenths of a percentage point—very possibly the result of random chance. The additions also mostly worsened the portfolio's maximum drawdown.

LeCompte concluded that "there is little to be gained by small expansion of the base set of assets."[1111]

Similarly unprofitable results occurred when **subtracting** one of the nine ETFs from the menu. It often made no difference, but the worst case—leaving out the large-cap Russell 1000 index—cut the annualized return of the top-three ETF portfolio by 2 percentage points.[1112]

As we'll see in the next chapter, the Papa Bear menu adds **four** ETFs. These expand the menu to include such asset classes as US value and growth stocks, US corporate bonds, and non-US bonds. But the additions by themselves are not the primary reason the Papa Bear offers higher returns than the Mama Bear. The Papa Bear also uses a slightly different Momentum Rule. Adding a few ETFs to the Mama Bear doesn't give you the Papa Bear. (More on that portfolio in the next chapter.)

Don't assume mutual funds perform as well as ETFs

Mutual funds have been available in some form for decades, while the first ETF didn't open to the public until 1973. More importantly, the full set of index ETFs used in this book was not complete until 2014.

It's tempting to assume that mutual funds would give you the same performance as ETFs. But it doesn't work that way.

Mutual funds only **approximate** the way ETFs track assets like commodities, gold, and small-cap stocks. This is because most mutual funds, by design, generally use more costly "active management," charging higher fees that reduce your returns. (Exceptions include the Investor and Admiral mutual funds from the Vanguard Group. They and their associated ETFs are merely different share classes of the same fund and have almost identical returns.)

CXO Advisory studied asset rotation with supposedly comparable mutual funds. But using those funds, "a wide variation in performance" was found. Also, CXO's five-month Momentum Rule produced inconsistent results.[1113]

The closing price of a mutual fund can't be known until after trading has ended for the day. If you tried to buy a mutual fund based on a Momentum Rule, every purchase would always be one day behind the data.

By contrast, ETF prices are constantly updated. You can check the prices of ETFs at 3 PM Eastern and trade before the market closes at 4 PM that same day. In short, mutual funds are not a perfect substitute for the ETFs in this book.

The last trading day of the month isn't the only option for your tune-up

This book calculates performance using closing prices on the last trading day of each month. That makes the numbers compatible with numerous academic studies that compute returns the same way.

However, that doesn't mean you're required to choose the last trading day of the month to tune up a Muscular Portfolio.

CXO Advisory looked at the results of tuning up its three-ETF portfolio on every market day of the month going back almost 12 years:

» The portfolio had a one point higher annualized return if the monthly changes were made in the period from eight trading days **before** month's end to two trading days **after** month's end.

» Drawdowns were 5 to 10 percentage points smaller if changes were made in the period from seven trading days **before** to two trading days **after** month's end.[1114]

However, these small differences may have been due to random chance. As long as you tune up the Mama Bear within a few days of month's end, you should be fine.

Say you decide to tune up your portfolio on the last Friday of each month, but on that day you forgot, or you went out for an early happy hour, or whatever. The fix is simple. Just check MuscularPortfolios.com on the **next** market day. Go back to your regular checkup day the following month.

The important thing is that you shouldn't use "stale" performance numbers. You should use the most current data when you make your changes. For instance, don't check the rankings one day and execute your trades the next.

CXO found that each day of delay slightly hurts performance and worsens drawdowns.[1115]

LIVINGSTON'S LAW OF MAMA-NESS
From thousands of ETFs, you check on nine
And watch your money grow like a vine.

---

6 The Papa Bear adds a distinction between value and growth

"You need to have a disciplined check on your emotions and a methodology for doing things. Most people lack that discipline."

BARRY RITHOLTZ, famed wealth manager, in USNews.com (2016)[1116]

The Papa Bear Portfolio is the second of two Muscular Portfolios in this book. We saw the Mama Bear in the previous chapter. The Baby Bear, a starter portfolio, is in the next chapter. The End Game, a wealth-preservation portfolio, is in Chapter 23.

» **The Papa Bear Portfolio is for people who:**

1 · **Will commit 15 minutes a month to tuning up their account;**

2 · **Want the higher returns that the Papa Bear offers over the Mama Bear; and**

3 · **Will stay the course even during market crashes, when the Papa Bear may be down 25%.**

It's not as hard as it may sound to tolerate a drawdown of 25%. When that's happening to the Papa Bear, it's likely that the S&P 500 will be down 30%, 40%, 50%, or more. It's a lot easier to accept temporary weakness in your portfolio when it's outperforming the market by 10 or 20 percentage points.

Like the Mama Bear, the Papa Bear requires you to give your portfolio a tune-up once a month. On average, the Papa Bear requires you to make a change in 9 out of 12 months each year. (For stats, see Chapter 19.)

If there's a change to be made, the tune-up may take as little as 15 minutes. If, on the other hand, none of the ETFs you're holding have changed in rank, you're done as soon as you've checked the website. But it's essential that you look every month—don't let your portfolio drift unchecked.

Figure 6-1 shows a 43-year simulation of the Papa Bear. This simple, three-ETF portfolio offers long-term performance that's as good as that of some of the best professional wealth managers in the business. (See Figure 6-3 later in this chapter.)

The Papa Bear extracts as much of the "signal" as possible from the "noise" that is the market.

» KEY CONCEPT
the Papa Bear Portfolio
Using the Momentum Rule on a set of 13 ETFs gives superior returns.

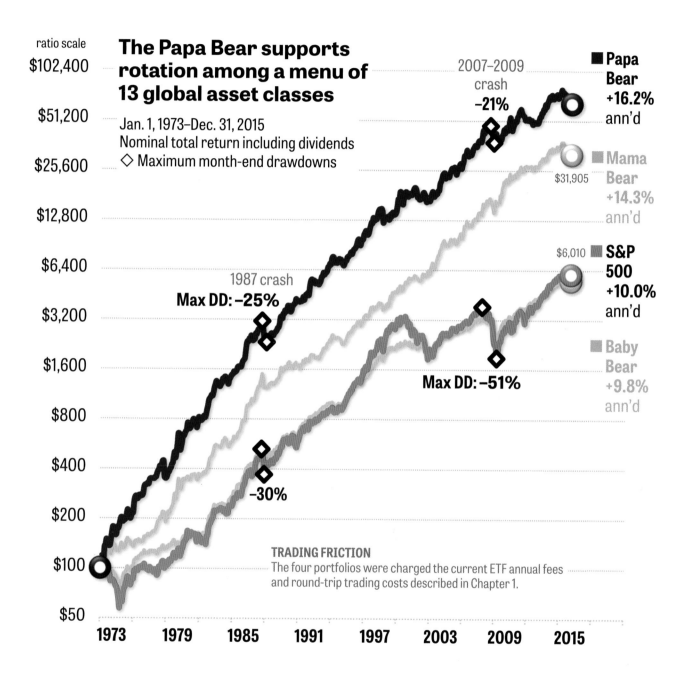

The Papa Bear supports rotation among a menu of 13 global asset classes

Jan. 1, 1973–Dec. 31, 2015
Nominal total return including dividends
◇ Maximum month-end drawdowns

ratio scale

$102,400
$51,200
$25,600
$12,800
$6,400
$3,200
$1,600
$800
$400
$200
$100
$50

1973 1979 1985 1991 1997 2003 2009 2015

2007–2009 crash **–21%**

1987 crash
Max DD: –25%

–30%

Max DD: –51%

■ **Papa Bear +16.2%** ann'd

■ **Mama Bear +14.3%** ann'd
$31,905

■ **S&P 500 +10.0%** ann'd
$6,010

■ **Baby Bear +9.8%** ann'd

TRADING FRICTION
The four portfolios were charged the current ETF annual fees
and round-trip trading costs described in Chapter 1.

FIGURE 6-1 | Source: Quant simulator

You hold the 3 out of 13 ETFs with the best odds using the Papa Bear

As we saw in the previous chapter, the Mama Bear Portfolio has a menu of nine asset classes. The Papa Bear expands this menu to include 13.

Unlike the Mama Bear, the Papa Bear makes a distinction between "value" and "growth" stocks, treating them as separate asset classes. We'll see the reasons for that later in this chapter.

The Papa Bear is similar to the Mama Bear in that each portfolio holds only three ETFs at a time. The ETFs you hold each month are the strongest three, as determined by the Momentum Rule.

For both strategies, there's an important difference between an investment strategy's **menu** and a specific **portfolio:**

» **The Papa Bear menu** is the total set of 13 asset classes that the strategy selects from.

» **The Papa Bear Portfolio** consists of the three ETFs each month that have the best momentum.

Figure 6-2 shows the 13 ETFs that make up the Papa Bear menu.

On your chosen day of the month, simply check the following Web page:

MuscularPortfolios.com/ papa-bear

If there's any change in the top three compared with last month, simply sell any ETF that has fallen out and buy any ETF that is in. You're done!

The Papa Bear uses a different Momentum Rule than the Mama Bear. Instead of ranking each ETF by its five-month total return, the Papa Bear averages each ETF's return over the past 3, 6, and 12 months.

The Papa Bear's slightly "slower" rule keeps you in rising assets longer. This helps explain the Papa Bear's higher performance. But the rule also takes more time to get out of assets whose uptrends are weakening. That's why the Papa Bear's drawdowns are slightly larger than the Mama Bear's. Picking one over the other is a matter of personal preference.

For the annual fees of each ETF in Figure 6-2—and alternative funds you can use if these exact ETFs are not available in your 401(k) plan— see Appendix A.

The Papa Bear menu

Asset class	Security name	Symbol
US large-cap value stocks	Vanguard Value ETF	VTV
US large-cap growth stocks	Vanguard Growth ETF	VUG
US small-cap value stocks	Vanguard Small-Cap 600 Value ETF	VIOV
US small-cap growth stocks	Vanguard Small-Cap 600 Growth ETF	VIOG
Developed-market stocks	Vanguard FTSE Developed Markets ETF	VEA
Emerging-market stocks	Vanguard MSCI Emerging Markets ETF	VWO
US real-estate investment trusts	Vanguard REIT ETF	VNQ
Commodities	PowerShares DB Commodity ETF	PDBC
Gold	iShares Gold Trust ETF	IAU
US Treasury bonds, 30-year	Vanguard Extended Duration Treas. ETF	EDV
US Treasury notes, 10-year	Vanguard Intermediate-Term Govt. ETF	VGIT
US investment-grade corporate bonds	Vanguard Long-Term Corp. Bond ETF	VCLT
Non-US govt. & corporate bonds	Vanguard Total International Bond ETF	BNDX

COLOR KEY

equities	hard assets	fixed-income

FIGURE 6-2

Strategy rules for the Papa Bear Portfolio

1 · Select a day to tune up your portfolio.

2 · On that day each month, check: **MuscularPortfolios.com/papa-bear.**

3 · The 13 ETFs that make up the Papa Bear asset menu will be ranked according to the strategy's Momentum Rule (the average of returns over the past 3, 6, and 12 months). Note the top three.

4 · If you already own all three ETFs—because you purchased them in a previous month—do nothing.

5 · Sell any ETF not in the top three. Immediately buy instead any top-three ETF that you don't already hold.

6 · Exact percentages are not important. Rebalance only if any ETF is over 20% off target (see Chapter 18).

The man who expanded the investing universe to 13 asset classes

The Papa Bear Portfolio is a clone of a strategy by Mebane Faber. (He's known to all as Meb.)

Our saga begins in 2006, when a young and then little-known wealth manager named Faber posted a white-paper to the Social Sciences Research Network.[1117] SSRN is a big pond filled with big fish. More than 250,000 authors have submitted papers and studies to the site. Getting Web surfers' attention is hard in the best of times.

The *Journal of Wealth Management*, a prestigious financial publication, print-ed Faber's whitepaper in its spring 2007 issue. People noticed.

Then, in 2009, Faber's fame took off as coauthor of a book called *The Ivy Portfolio.* Covering the same ground as his SSRN whitepaper, the book explored how several multibillion-dollar Ivy League university endowment funds were earning their double-digit returns.

Harvard's and Yale's endow-ments achieved annualized returns of 15.2% and 16.6%, respectively, in the 24 years ending June 30, 2008. The S&P 500 had an annual-ized total return of only 12% during the same period.

Even better, the two endow-ments' worst fiscal years (ending June 30) involved losses of no more than 2.7%. The S&P 500 lost 18% just in the fiscal year ending June 2002.

Faber's book asked, in effect, "If the Ivy League can do it, why can't individual inves-tors?" His answer was that individual investors can and should.

The Ivy Portfolio specified just five asset classes—US stocks, non-US stocks, commodities, US REITs, and 10-year Treasury notes. By tilting toward the assets with the best momentum, Faber wrote, individuals could match some of the best endowments' performances.

Though the book bore a 2009 copyright, the research was the same as that used in his 2006 working paper. Faber had publicly staked out his position well before the beginning of the 2008 global financial crisis, the worst crash since the Great Depression.

The so-called Ivy 5 powered through the crisis with flying colors. One respected analyst and blogger named Doug Short tracked Faber's five-ETF strategy in real time from the beginning of 2007 through the end of 2012. Short showed that the Ivy 5 lost only about 7% during the crash. In the same period, the S&P 500 vaporized more than 50% of investors' money.[1118]

Even more attractive were the long-term gains. The Ivy 5 gained more than 30%. The S&P 500 gained only 13%. (See Figure 6-4.)

Faber updated his study in 2013, expanding the strategy to 13 asset classes. However, the 2013 academic paper provided no list of ETFs to use. This book's Papa Bear Portfolio reveals for the first time a matching set of 13 low-cost ETFs.[1119]

Faber's 2013 whitepaper went on to become the number-one most-downloaded document in SSRN history, out of hundreds of thousands of papers.[1120]

Faber is truly a rock star among researchers.

Mebane Faber

Designer of ETF strategies

FIGURE 6-3

Faber's Ivy 5 has expanded into the more diversified Papa Bear with 13 ETFs

Almost no one foresaw the horrendous crash of 2007–2009. The bursting of the global real-estate bubble sank equity markets worldwide.

But over the same period, the asset-rotation plan known as the Ivy 5 passed its first major stress test.

Each month, Faber's strategy automatically tilted away from any of the five asset classes that had poor momentum. The Ivy 5's loss of only 7% isn't even bad enough to be called a market correction!

You may remember the horror people felt—perhaps that **you** felt—when the S&P 500 lost more than half its value. For a time, it appeared that several major Wall Street banks would collapse for lack of capital, truly destroying the economy.

Those who followed Faber's asset-rotation plan must have felt lucky indeed to see their portfolios down only 7% while the market was half gone and possibly diving further.

In 2013, Faber released a whitepaper that expanded the original five asset classes to a complete set of 13. The Papa Bear Portfolio in this book is a clone of Faber's 13-asset strategy.

In 43-year estimates by the Quant simulator, both the 9-ETF Mama Bear and the 13-ETF Papa Bear strongly outperform the original Ivy 5.

After subtracting the trading costs and fees shown in Figures 6-4 and 1-16, the annualized gains of the Mama Bear and Papa Bear were 14.3% and 16.2%, respectively.

The Ivy 5, on the other hand, would have returned 9.7%—about the same as the S&P 500's 10.0% and the Baby Bear's 9.8%.

The improved returns that come from expanding from five asset classes to 9 or 13 is well worth the slight effort of watching those additional ETFs.

» TECH TALK

the Ivy Portfolio

The Ivy Portfolio mirrored university endowment holdings by allocating 20% to each of five ETFs: US stocks (VTI), developed-market stocks (VEU), commodities (DBC), US REITs (VNQ), and US bonds (BND).

The Ivy 5 strategy used a hedging rule: If any ETF's price at month-end was below the average of the last 10 monthly closes, Treasury notes were held the next month instead of that ETF.

Neither the Mama Bear nor the Papa Bear needs such a hedging component. These two Muscular Portfolios have larger, better-diversified menus of 9 and 13 asset classes, respectively. Simply holding the three ETFs with the strongest momentum each month gives you plenty of risk reduction without hedging.

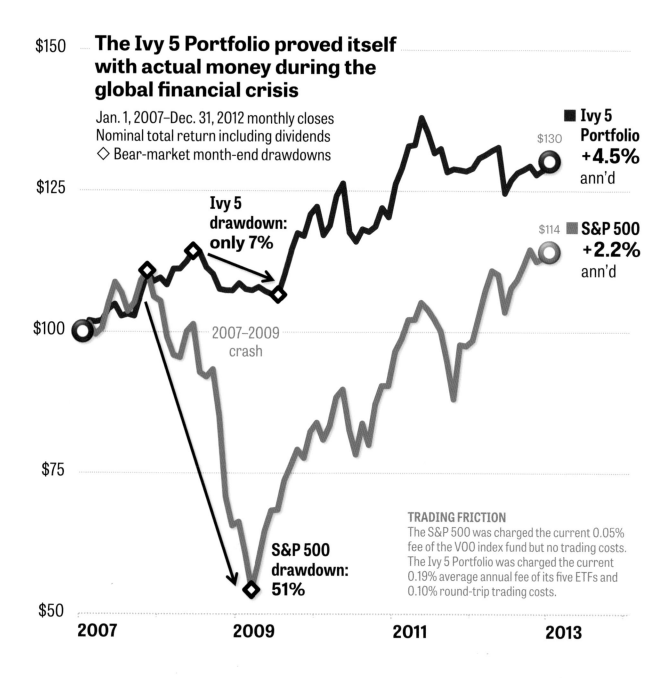

The Ivy 5 Portfolio proved itself with actual money during the global financial crisis

Jan. 1, 2007–Dec. 31, 2012 monthly closes
Nominal total return including dividends
◇ Bear-market month-end drawdowns

$150

$125

$100

$75

$50

2007   2009   2011   2013

Ivy 5
drawdown:
only 7%

2007–2009
crash

S&P 500
drawdown:
51%

$130 ■ Ivy 5
       Portfolio
       +4.5%
       ann'd

$114 ■ S&P 500
       +2.2%
       ann'd

TRADING FRICTION
The S&P 500 was charged the current 0.05%
fee of the VOO index fund but no trading costs.
The Ivy 5 Portfolio was charged the current
0.19% average annual fee of its five ETFs and
0.10% round-trip trading costs.

FIGURE 6-4 | Source: Quant simulator and Doug Short[1121]

What makes the Papa Bear's asset classes better than the Mama Bear's?

The Mama Bear menu contains nine asset classes. Portfolios with access to fewer asset classes don't seem to have the diversification necessary to take advantage of the Momentum Rule.

What benefits do the Papa Bear's extra asset classes give us?

» **Value and growth stocks.** The Mama Bear menu includes ETFs that track US large-cap stocks (VONE) and US small-cap stocks (VIOO). This allows the Mama Bear to tilt each month toward large caps or small caps, whichever asset class happens to be in an uptrend at the moment.

By contrast, the Papa Bear menu further divides large-cap and small-cap US stocks into a total of four asset classes: "large-cap value," "large-cap growth," "small-cap value," and "small-cap growth."

Value stocks have a ratio of share price to accounting book value that's in the lower half of all stocks. In other words, a company might have assets of $10 billion on its books, but buyers are pricing its shares as though it was worth only $9 billion.

Growth stocks are in the higher half of price-to-book. These companies have share prices that are far above the assets on their books. Growth stocks sometimes rise faster than value stocks, and vice versa, for decades at a time. (See the Bonus Chapter for details.)

The Papa Bear's four ETFs, therefore, give you exposure to four market factors: large cap, small cap, value, and growth.

The Momentum Rule automatically tilts the Papa Bear toward **value** stocks when they happen to be going up and toward **growth** stocks when they are in fashion instead.

You never need to have an opinion about whether value stocks or growth stocks are "better." Let the market tell you!

» **More fixed-income choices.** The Mama Bear supports **two** fixed-income

asset classes: 10- to 25-year Treasury bonds and cash (via a money-market ETF). The Papa Bear menu includes **four** fixed-income asset classes, which track:

» 30-year Treasury bonds

» 10-year Treasury notes

» US corporate investment-grade debt securities

» non-US government and corporate bonds

The non-US bond ETF in the Papa Bear Portfolio is "dollar-hedged" by its sponsor, the Vanguard Group. This means the portfolio's return on non-US bonds is not affected by changes in the dollar's value, thanks to Vanguard's hedging activity in currency markets.

Unlike the Mama Bear, the Papa Bear menu does not include cash, such as a money-market ETF. This is because Faber's 2103 white-paper proved using historical data that 10-year Treasury

» **KEY CONCEPT**
the Papa Bear treats value and growth as separate asset classes
Value stocks and growth stocks outperform each other in different years, and you can reap the benefits.

bonds perform better than a money-market fund in most cases. This is true during equity crashes as well as periods of rising interest rates.[1122]

For example, 1973–1982 was a 10-year period when interest rates rose sharply. Inflation during the decade was a rather high 9.1% annualized. Treasury bills (which offer rates close to money-market funds) returned 12.1%. However, 10-year Treasury bonds did better, shrugging off the rise in interest rates and delivering a superior 13.7%.

If equity funds and alternatives are all falling, the Papa Bear automatically rotates into whichever three fixed-income funds have the best momentum.

The Papa Bear is very similar to the Mama Bear in every other way

Many of the same principles that apply to the Mama Bear also apply to the Papa Bear. Read the previous chapter for more detailed explanations of the following points:

» **Don't add additional asset classes you may happen to like.** CXO Advisory shows that few if any single ETF additions improved the performance of the Mama Bear. The four extra ETFs in the Papa Bear have been designed by experts to work well together. Leave the choice of asset classes to the pros.

» **Don't substitute random mutual funds for ETFs.** You may have a "bad" 401(k) that doesn't give you access to the ETFs in the Papa Bear. If so, see Appendix A for a list of mutual funds that perform almost exactly like the respective ETFs. Don't think you can swap an ETF for a random mutual fund just because it has a similar-sounding name.

» **Trading on the last day of the month is not required.** As we saw in the previous chapter, CXO Advisory tested every possible day of the month to tune up the Mama Bear Portfolio. The simulated accounts had higher returns and smaller drawdowns if the monthly changes were made seven trading days **before** to two trading days **after** month end.[1123]

The Papa Bear is likely to provide very similar results. But what's most important is that you use a consistent day of the month and give your portfolio a checkup without fail.

» **If you miss a day, tune up anyway.** Maybe you got busy and forgot to check MuscularPortfolios.com on the day of the month you chose. Simply check on the **next** market day and buy whatever ETFs are the strongest then. Go back to your regular day the following month.

LIVINGSTON'S LAW OF PAPA-NESS
Expanding your menu all the way to 13
Can reap some rewards far over the mean.

---

7 The Baby Bear is a starter portfolio as easy as an annual tune-up

"It can scarcely be denied that the supreme goal of all theory is to make the irreducible basic elements as simple and as few as possible without having to surrender the adequate representation of a single datum of experience."

ALBERT EINSTEIN'S actual words in a June 10, 1933, lecture[1124]

"Make your theory as simple as possible, but no simpler."

WHAT PEOPLE SAY EINSTEIN SAID

If what you're seeking is simplicity, simplicity, simplicity, the Baby Bear is it. This portfolio holds only two asset classes—all US stocks and all US bonds—in equal proportions.

» **The Baby Bear Portfolio is for people who:**

1 · **Have less than $10,000 to invest** *or*

2 · **Can't commit 15 minutes per month to tune up a brokerage account.**

The Baby Bear is a starter portfolio that keeps trading costs low for people with less than $10,000 to invest. And unlike Muscular Portfolios, which are checked monthly, the Baby Bear requires a checkup only once a year.

If either of the two ETFs is more than 5% off its target weight at year-end, you rebalance. That means selling shares of one fund and buying shares of the other fund to bring things back to 50/50, as described later in this chapter.

Once-a-year rebalancing means the portfolio requires a maximum of two trades annually—none, in some years. If you keep your commissions as low as $5 each, two trades would cost $10. That shaves only 0.1% from a $10,000 account—a modest haircut.

Figure 7-1 shows a simulation of the Baby Bear's performance compared with an S&P 500 index fund over the 43-year period from 1973

to 2015. The Baby Bear's balance would have been higher than the cash value of the S&P 500 in 65% of the months.

The Baby Bear's return is not the mere average of whatever the stock and bond returns were. Stocks and bonds cushion each other's declines, resulting in better returns in the long run. (This was explained in the discussion of Figure 1-18.)

In academic terms, the two assets have a "low correlation." The Baby Bear simply recovers faster than the S&P 500 after market crashes.

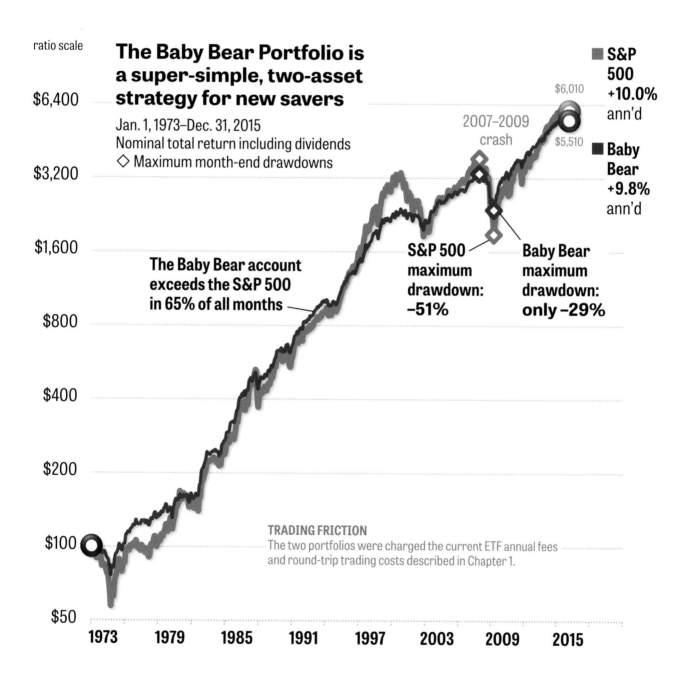

ratio scale

The Baby Bear Portfolio is a super-simple, two-asset strategy for new savers

Jan. 1, 1973–Dec. 31, 2015
Nominal total return including dividends
◇ Maximum month-end drawdowns

$6,400

$3,200

$1,600

$800

$400

$200

$100

$50

The Baby Bear account exceeds the S&P 500 in 65% of all months

■ S&P 500 +10.0% ann'd

■ Baby Bear +9.8% ann'd

$6,010

2007–2009 crash

$5,510

S&P 500 maximum drawdown: −51%

Baby Bear maximum drawdown: only −29%

TRADING FRICTION
The two portfolios were charged the current ETF annual fees and round-trip trading costs described in Chapter 1.

1973   1979   1985   1991   1997   2003   2009   2015

FIGURE 7-1 | Source: Quant simulator

The Baby Bear Portfolio is ultrasimple—but it does benefit from rebalancing

As portfolios go, the Baby Bear is stone simple.

Figure 7-2 shows the Baby Bear menu: two exchange-traded funds held in a 50/50 balance.

The Vanguard Total Stock Market Index (VTI) holds essentially all US stocks. The Vanguard Total Bond Market Index (BND) does the same for US bonds.

All you need to do to set up the Baby Bear is buy equal dollar amounts of each fund.

The only time your portfolio needs a checkup is at the end of the year. If you wish to make additions or withdrawals at other times, however, that's fine. Simply make your transaction using whichever of the two funds is the farthest from its 50% target weight.

This "cash-flow rebalancing" is the easiest way to keep the two funds balanced without making unnecessary transactions that would incur taxes in a taxable account.

At checkup time, simply compare the dollar value of each fund. If one ETF is more than 5% above its ideal 50% weight, sell some of the larger fund and use the cash to buy more of the smaller fund. Let's take a closer look at this example:

» Your portfolio's value is $2,000.

» A 50/50 split means each ETF would ideally be worth $1,000.

» Let's say the bond position has risen to $1,060.

» The stock position has fallen to $940.

» If so, your two positions are 6% off their ideal $1,000 weights.

» To rebalance, sell $60 of the bond ETF.

» Buy $60 of the stock ETF. *Voilà!* Your ETFs are now each worth $1,000.

Ask your tax preparer whether you should make these trades before Dec. 31 or after Jan. 1. Why?

» **If you sell an ETF at a loss on or before Dec. 31,** you can deduct the loss from any of your capital gains that year. You can also subtract up to $3,000 of the loss from your ordinary income that year and in subsequent years until the loss is used up.

» **If you sell at a profit after Jan. 1,** you can delay paying tax on that gain until as late as Apr. 15 of the following year. That can delay your tax payment by 12 months.

There's more explanation of how to save money on taxes in Chapters 19 and 21.

The historical results you would have achieved with a 50/50 split are explained in an analysis by Michael McKeown, a certified

The Baby Bear menu

Asset class	Security name	Symbol
All US stocks	Vanguard Total Stock Market ETF	VTI
All US bonds (govt. & corporate)	Vanguard Total Bond Market ETF	BND

COLOR KEY

equities	fixed-income

FIGURE 7-2

Strategy rules for the Baby Bear Portfolio

1 · Start out by buying equal dollar amounts of each fund.

2 · Maintaining exact percentages of 50% in each ETF every month is not important.

3 · At year-end, rebalance only if either fund is more than 5% off equal weight.

4 · In a tax-deferred account, sell and buy a few shares near year-end if rebalancing is needed.

5 · In a taxable account, ask your tax preparer whether rebalancing is worth incurring a tax bill on any gain.

financial planner for Aurum Wealth Management Group.

In the 20 years ending December 2013, McKeown states: "The returns of the 50/50 portfolio capture 95% of the upside of the S&P 500 with only about half of the volatility."

Market-like returns with smaller losses are certainly nice. However, for many human beings with actual feelings, the Baby Bear's 29% month-end loss in the 2007–2009 financial crisis (Figure 7-1) would be too painful to endure.

If you don't want that much stress, the pros and cons of following a Muscular Portfolio rather than the Baby Bear are explained later in this chapter.

How the two-asset model—50% stocks, 50% bonds—became popular

The Baby Bear Portfolio is inspired by Jack Bogle, who founded the Vanguard Group in 1974 and was its CEO until 1996. Back in 1976, he launched arguably the world's earliest fund that tracked the S&P 500: the First Index Investment Trust (now called the Vanguard 500 Index Fund).[1125]

The Baby Bear is a clone based on Bogle's 2011 white-paper, "The Lessons of History," which celebrates the simple strategy of holding 50% US stocks and 50% US bonds at all times.[1126]

Bogle presented this paper at a talk he gave to the fund managers of America's largest college endowments. Reading the transcript, you can almost hear Bogle glee-fully twisting the knife as he reminds the audience that he'd first proposed this plan to them 15 years earlier in a 1996 paper titled "My Alma Mater's Money," which spec-ified "a 50/50 portfolio using US stock and bond index funds—a balanced portfolio with extraordinary diversifi-cation and remarkably low costs."

In one of the greatest "I told you so" rants of all time, Bogle crows that the return of the 50/50 portfolio was "well above" that achieved by most endowment fund man-agers—many of whom were sitting right in front of him—after adjusting for risk.

The 50/50 portfolio suffered a bear-market loss of only 10% in the fiscal year ending June 2009. But the average endow-ment fund fell 19%—almost **twice the loss.** Avoiding that wild dive helped the 50/50 portfolio have a superior risk-adjusted performance. The managers could have enjoyed the same smooth ride if they'd taken Bogle's advice 15 years earlier.

In terms of raw perfor-mance, the average endow-ment manager achieved a 7.3% annualized return in the 15 years ending June 30, 2011. The 50/50 portfolio gained 7.1%—virtually the same.

Even better, it beat outright the performance of endow-ments with assets under half a billion. Their return was only 7.0%. These fund managers gained **nothing** from all their fancy trading.

Bogle's 1996 paper allocated 50% to Vanguard's Total Stock Market Index (VTSMX) and 50% to the Total Bond Market Index (VBMFX)—both of which are mutual funds. ETFs hadn't been invented yet.

Today, Vanguard offers matching ETFs: VTI tracks all US stocks, and BND tracks all US bonds. The Baby Bear Portfolio uses these two funds. In a taxable account, ETFs generate fewer tax bills than mutual funds.[1127]

In addition, ultralow ETF fees make a big difference in your wallet. VTI and BND cost only 0.04% and 0.06%, respec-tively.

Importantly for new inves-tors who want a starter portfolio, these cheap ETFs require **no minimums.** To get the same low annual fee as VTI using Vanguard's match-ing mutual fund, you'd

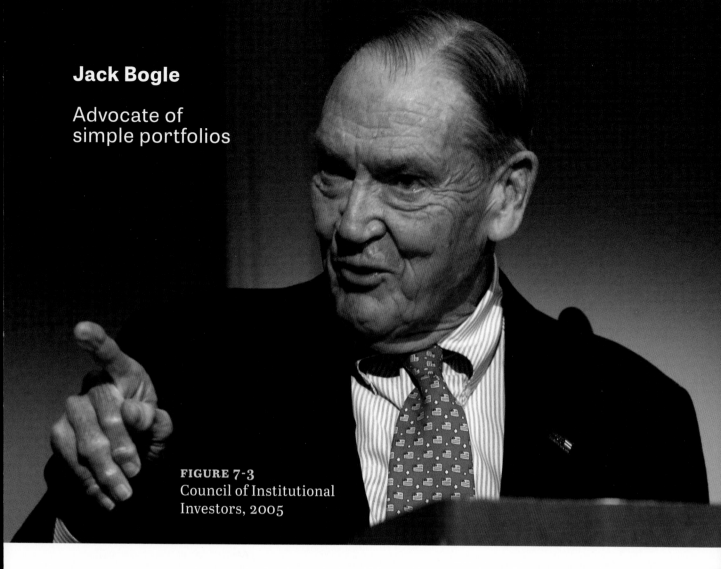

Jack Bogle

Advocate of
simple portfolios

FIGURE 7-3
Council of Institutional
Investors, 2005

be required to buy at least $10,000 worth.[1128]

The importance of keeping your costs low as an investor is driven home by the fact that Bogle's personal net worth is estimated at "only" $80 million.[1129]

That sounds like a lot, but the founders and owners of Fidelity Investments—Ned Johnson III and family—are collectively worth **$28.5 billion.**[1130]

Where did that extra $28 billion come from? Out of the higher fees Fidelity's customers paid compared to Vanguard's.

There are good reasons <u>not</u> to select the Baby Bear Portfolio

The best argument against choosing the Baby Bear is that it's not likely to produce returns as strong as a Muscular Portfolio. At this writing, bond yields are near historical lows, while stocks are selling for very rich prices. That predicts poor long-term gains for US stocks, as detailed in Chapter 13.

In the 10-year period ending 2025, Bogle himself estimates that a 50/50 portfolio will eke out only 3.5% or 4.5% of annualized return. And the **real** return will be lower—reduced by the rate of inflation.[1131,1132]

To "fix" the two-asset model, people have suggested more complex strategies—namely Lazy Portfolios, which typically hold five or more asset classes.

However, as we saw in Chapter 3, these strategies generally perform no better than the Baby Bear Portfolio, while subjecting investors to higher losses—crashes of 35%, 45%, or worse.

Most individual investors are best off committing to the mere 15 minutes a month that a Muscular Portfolio requires, and choosing the Mama Bear or the Papa Bear over the Baby Bear.

But the following section describes a few situations that might make the Baby Bear just right for you.

The Baby Bear Portfolio should be reserved for special cases

Despite the meager future returns projected for a 50/50 portfolio, the following are good reasons to choose the Baby Bear:

» Less than $10,000 to invest. With today's bargain online brokerages, you can easily keep transaction costs below 0.1% of a $100,000 account balance (see Chapter 17). But that's harder if your balance is under $10,000.

The Mama Bear and Papa Bear Portfolios—as described in the previous two chapters—require, on average, 9 or 10 portfolio changes per year.

Even if you pay only $5 per trade, selling 10 ETFs and buying 10 others in a year would cost you $100. That would represent a 1% bite of a $10,000 account. It might not be acceptable to you to give up 1% of your nest egg to trading costs.

» Serious tax aversion. If you're dead set against ever paying short-term capital gains taxes, the Baby Bear provides an answer. You always hold each ETF for 12 months plus one day (or longer). Any gains will qualify for preferential tax treatment as **long-term** capital gains.

» **New babies cry out for the Baby Bear.** If you've suddenly been blessed with twins, you should probably be spending every spare moment catching a few winks, not allocating assets.

The combined demands of your job, your commute, and your wail-watching may make you too exhausted to move. Looking up fund prices—even just once every 30 days—might be unthinkable.

» **Extreme world travel.** If you plan to, say, circle the globe in a tiny sailboat or trek across Asia on foot, your Internet access may be spotty for months at a time.

That's a good argument for checking the market only once a year. If you're lucky, you'll have more money at the end of your trip than when you began.

» **Mental decline.** The ability to make sophisticated financial decisions peaks at age 53 and decays thereafter. According to AARP, about 1 in 6 people in the US over the age of 65 are affected by Alzheimer's disease.

If your mental state is tentative, even a monthly checkup of a Muscular Portfolio might be too demanding. In that case, a legal trustee that an attorney helps you appoint could learn how to hold your funds the Baby Bear way, providing at least some growth and income for your needs.

» **You're a Nobel laureate.** One of the strangest reasons to select a 50/50 portfolio is that it's used by a winner of the Nobel Prize in Economics: Harry Markowitz.

As we'll see with more detail in the Bonus Chapter, *Wall Street Journal* columnist Jason Zweig interviewed Markowitz for a 2007 book, *Your Money or Your Brain*. Zweig asked the Nobel winner, now a consultant to wealth-management firms, how he allocated his personal money. Markowitz, then 80 years of age, replied:

"I should have computed the historical co-variances of the asset classes and drawn an efficient frontier. Instead, I visualized my grief if the stock market went way up and I wasn't in it—or if it went way down and I was completely in it. My intention was to minimize my future regret. So I split my contributions 50/50 between bonds and equities."[1133]

To keep his emotions in check, this esteemed Ph.D. chose a Baby Bear Portfolio!

The bottom line: The Baby Bear is a great alternative to Muscular Portfolios for those who need one. But if you're **not** in one of the specific situations named above, the Mama Bear and Papa Bear offer better returns and smaller drawdowns.

LIVINGSTON'S LAW OF SIMPLICITY
The Baby Bear plan is more than sublime
For those with a shortage of money or time.

How armchair investors time the market

Illustration: "I Knew It" by Jed Dunkerely
Text by Brian Livingston

8 · Compounding is the most powerful force in your investing universe

"I early inquired the rate of interest on invested money, and worried my child's brain into an understanding of the virtues and excellencies of that remarkable invention of man, compound interest."

JACK LONDON in "What Life Means to Me," 1906[1134] (*usually attributed to Albert Einstein*)[1135]

Was it Jack London or Albert Einstein who extolled the wonders of compound interest? It doesn't matter. What's indisputable is that compounding is indeed a remarkable force, and one you definitely want working **for** you instead of **against** you.

To be sure, there are people who don't need the power of compounding. Those are people who amassed enough to live on all at once—perhaps by receiving a large inheritance—and people who saved massive percentages of their take-home pay to build a nest egg in just a few years.

The latter type are part of a movement called Financial Independence Retire Early (FIRE) or Eary Retirement Extreme (ERE). This trend has its own network of websites, blogs, and a book by Jacob Lund Fisker titled—you guessed it—*Early Retirement Extreme*.[1136]

Followers of Fisker's movement strive to achieve economic independence—financial freedom—in as little as five years. The basic principles are:

1 · **Cut your expenses** to the bone.

2 · **Save 40% to 80%** of your take-home pay.

3 · **Quit any jobs you hate** and take only jobs you like (Figure 8-1) as soon as you've saved 300 times your monthly expenses.

For example, you'd need savings of $300,000 to withdraw $1,000 per month under this policy. (See Chapter 22.)

Fisker himself accomplished this between the ages of 25 and 30. But he wasn't able to pay for heat in the winter, among other expenses he chose to cut.[1137]

For the rest of us—who aren't quite so frugal—compounding over a period of years is the best way to build a nest egg.

Unfortunately, a lot of people haven't gotten the memo about how much they'll need to save or how long it'll take.

"Nearly half of all working-age families have zero retirement account savings," according to a 2016 report by the Economic Policy Institute.[1138] "The median for families with savings was $60,000." That $60,000 would give you only $200 a month to live on, using ERE's formula.

Compounding isn't a government program, so you don't have to worry about anyone repealing it. Let's put it to work.

Financial freedom means the opportunity to do whatever you want with the rest of your life

FIGURE 8-1

If you have the time, compounding has the way

It's simple to make compounding work for you:

1 · Put as much of your money as you can into an account that grows over time.

2 · Don't remove your gains prematurely; leave any gains in the account to increase even more.

3 · Use IRAs and other tax-deferred accounts to minimize the reduction of your assets by taxes.

4 · Eventually, your account will produce more money all by itself than you can earn from your job.

At that point, you can keep your job if it appeals to you, respectfully resign, or tell off your boss as you storm out the door. You can accept only work assignments you like, volunteer your time to your favorite nonprofit groups, or spend your days in the garden with a book. You're financially free.

Financial freedom is the opposite of debt slavery. Compound interest is working **against** you if you have credit card balances that are charging you annual rates of 15%, 25%, or more. They're eating up your capital and delaying the day you're free to do whatever you wish, whenever you wish.

All of the strategies in *Muscular Portfolios* make use of the power of compounding to grow your wealth. It can be a bit hard, though, for our feeble brains to grasp just how powerful this force truly is.

In the rest of this chapter, we'll see how compounding works for people as varied as teenagers (Figure 8-2), college grads in their first real job at 30 (Figure 8-3), and working people who are just now starting to save in their 50s (Figure 8-4). The following stories reveal all.

» KEY CONCEPT

financial freedom

The more you save, the sooner your portfolio will make enough each year that you can quit your job and do whatever you like.

How compounding turns a teen's seven summer paychecks into a cool one million real dollars

Imagine that a student's grand-parents explain the power of compounding. Let's say the teen then earns—and saves in a tax-free Roth account—$5,000 each summer for as few as seven years. By the age of 70, that kid will wind up with more than $1 million—in today's dollars! This seemingly impossible feat is explained in Figure 8-3.

FIGURE 8-2

A teen's $35K compounds to more than $200K deposited over a career

Here's how the teen would do it:

1 · First of all, the kid must make some earned income. The US Fair Labor Standards Act allows 14-year-olds to work.[1139] Kids younger than 14 may also legally earn money in a family business or babysitting. Check the law in your state.[1140]

2 · For minors, an adult must set up a "custodial Roth account." The student assumes control at age 18.[1141] All returns compound in a Roth. Withdrawals are untaxed, if IRS rules are met.[1142] (See Chapter 19.)

3 · A dependent—someone whose financial support is mostly from parents—may be able to earn as much as $12,000 tax free (the standard deduction in 2018). Check Publication 929 by the IRS[1143] and a guide to summer jobs by Laura Saunders.[1144]

4 · Under 2018 IRS rules, the limit on each year's Roth contribution is $5,500 or **taxable compensation,** whichever is less.[1145] (The limit is reduced or eliminated if an unmarried person's modified adjusted gross income is over $120,000, but few teens will have this problem.)[1146]

5 · How can a teen earn $5,000 a year? One way is a summer job with take-home pay of $9 an hour, 40 hours per week for 14 weeks. Another is a year-round job paying $9 an hour for 11 hours per week.

6 · A generous relative might decide to help. For example, out of each year's $5,000 of wages, the teen socks away $2,500. The relative could match it with another $2,500. (The donor should require that each match is put into the Roth, not spent.)

7 · What's a realistic rate at which the teen's account might compound? Even the simplest starter portfolio— the Baby Bear—earned 9.8% annualized in 43-year simulations. Subtracting 3.25% due to inflation, the teen's portfolio might well generate a real (inflation-adjusted) return of 6.55% annualized.

8 · The teen's balance at age 70 would be **$1.018 million in today's dollars.** (That's $1.018 million in **real** dollars. Assuming 3.25% inflation, that balance would be over $5 million in **nominal** dollars.)

Now let's compare this to an adult who begins contributing $5,000 to a Roth at age 30, and continues doing so until age 70. (Note: An employed adult might be better off with an IRA or 401[k], but let's compare Roths to Roths here.)

The teen's seven contributions would total $35,000 in real dollars. The adult saver's forty deposits would total $200,000. (Each saver must increase the $5,000 contribution each year by the rate of inflation.)

At age 70, the adult's ending real balance would be only **$948,000**—less than the teen saver's real **$1.018 million.**

Figure 8-3 shows that the teen's balance is always larger than that of an individual who begins making contributions at age 30.

When you look at numbers like that, compounding's power reaches up and slaps you in the face.

>> **KEY CONCEPT**

compounding

If you start saving today, you'll build a much larger nest egg than if you start in 10 years.

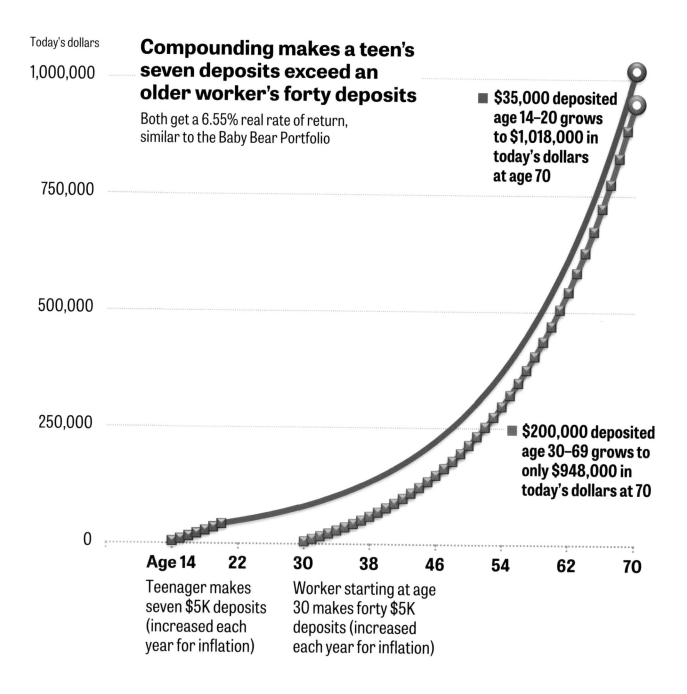

Compounding makes a teen's seven deposits exceed an older worker's forty deposits

Both get a 6.55% real rate of return, similar to the Baby Bear Portfolio

Today's dollars

1,000,000

750,000

500,000

250,000

0

■ $35,000 deposited age 14–20 grows to $1,018,000 in today's dollars at age 70

■ $200,000 deposited age 30–69 grows to only $948,000 in today's dollars at 70

Age 14   22   30   38   46   54   62   70

Teenager makes seven $5K deposits (increased each year for inflation)

Worker starting at age 30 makes forty $5K deposits (increased each year for inflation)

FIGURE 8-3 | Source: Author's calculations

Even if you didn't start at 14, you can save your way to $1 million in today's money

By working a few weeks each summer (with or without a generous parent or grandparent), a teen has enough time to build a nice nest egg while his or her tax rate is very low—and before college expenses and debt payments wipe out any surplus income.

To a teen, age 70 seems as long from now as the sun burning out. Realistically, few kids would leave the money untouched for five decades. It's more likely the funds would come out to pay for college. (Economist Brian Caplan finds that a bachelor's degree in business produces a 6% return on investment for the best students.)[1147]

Note: Teen income below $6,400 and any Roth **balances** don't reduce student aid, but Roth **withdrawals** do.[1148] Consult a counselor on Roths vs. 539-type college savings programs (Chapter 19).

A Roth account contains two "types" of money:

1 · Contributions (amounts you deposited)

Any contributions into a Roth can be withdrawn by the owner **at any time with no tax or penalty.**

2 · Gains (increases due to the market)

Any gains can be freely withdrawn (starting in the fifth tax year after you first opened any Roth) for "qualifying reasons."[1149] Those reasons include college expenses, up to $10,000 down on a first home, etc. Withdrawals of Roth gains (not contributions) before age 59½ for other reasons are penalized.

But what if it turns out that the teen **doesn't need the money for tuition?** For example, the teen might receive:

» **A full scholarship;**

» **Tuition allowance through a job;**

» **Tuition forgiveness through a public service program.**

He or she might even go straight into business—or, horrors, decide to become a **writer**—meaning no tuition expenses.

In cases like the above, the balance of the Roth could actually grow for 50 years, just as shown in Figure 8-3.

The preceding example is adapted from "Fund a Teenager's Million-Dollar Retirement" by David John Marotta using different assumptions.[1150] The power of compounding works in all such scenarios.

What if you didn't happen to be a financial wizard at age 14? Can you still use compounding to achieve a $1 million nest egg if you're in your 30s, 40s, or 50s? The answer is "yes"—if you really save.

Figure 8-4 shows the percentage of $50,000 take-home pay that you'd have to save at a 6.55% real return to end up with $1 million in today's dollars. The required percentages approximately double every 10 years you delay, so get started.

> **LIVINGSTON'S LAW OF GROWTH**
> *Your money grows just like a tree*
> *Until one day you're financially free.*

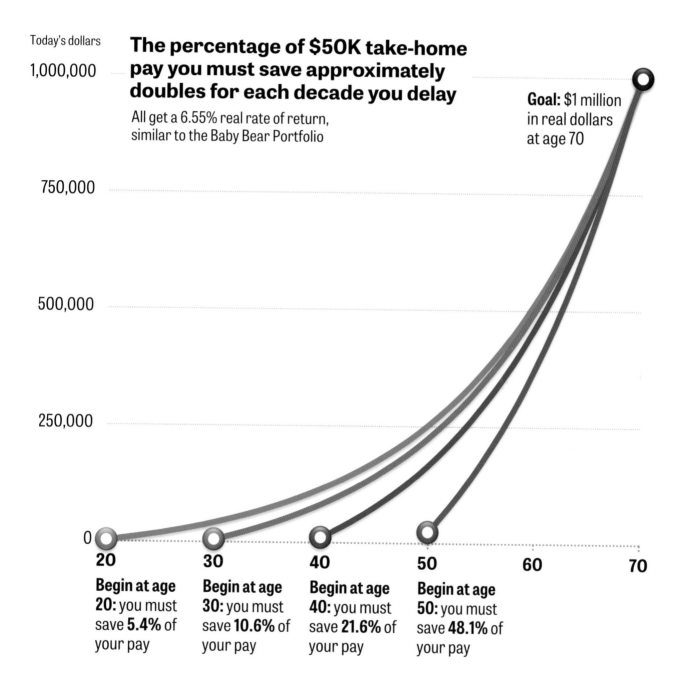

Today's dollars

The percentage of $50K take-home pay you must save approximately doubles for each decade you delay

All get a 6.55% real rate of return, similar to the Baby Bear Portfolio

1,000,000

Goal: $1 million in real dollars at age 70

750,000

500,000

250,000

0

20 · 30 · 40 · 50 · 60 · 70

Begin at age 20: you must save **5.4%** of your pay

Begin at age 30: you must save **10.6%** of your pay

Begin at age 40: you must save **21.6%** of your pay

Begin at age 50: you must save **48.1%** of your pay

FIGURE 8-4 | Source: Author's calculations

9 Diversification is the only free lunch you'll ever get

"True diversification is . . . giving up on home runs to avoid striking out."[1151]

BEN CARLSON, portfolio manager at Ritholtz Wealth Management

Diversification is the blending of different asset types into a single portfolio. This is just as important as the principle of compounding, which we read about in the previous chapter.

Holding assets other than stocks—such as bonds, real-estate investment trusts, and commodities—helps protect you from intolerable losses.

As we saw in Chapter 3, diversification alone isn't a magic bullet. The abysmal drawdown of Lazy Portfolios shows that simply holding a few different asset classes won't protect you during a crash. That's especially true if those asset classes are all equity-like.

But diversification is indeed a powerful force. Coupled with momentum, it's the key to the success of Muscular Portfolios.

Traders often say, "Diversification is the only free lunch in investing" (Figure 9-1). That's because it costs little or nothing for you to hold multiple assets rather than just one. But diversification immediately gives you the benefits of smaller losses and a smoother ride.

Diversification can not only reduce your drawdowns but improve your gains. We saw in Chapter 5 that a portfolio holding the three strongest asset classes can actually outperform an account that holds only the single strongest asset class.

How could that possibly work? Wouldn't holding just the one strongest asset class always be best?

Experts have demonstrated the magic of diversification for decades. One of the first was Harry Markowitz, author of the influential book *Portfolio Selection* (1959).[1152] He demonstrated that two different asset classes—stocks and bonds—could be combined into a single portfolio that was less volatile than either asset class by itself. That was a surprising point of view back then. (We'll see more about Markowitz in the Bonus Chapter.)

Unfortunately, the human mind isn't a walking calculator. We didn't evolve to compute the diversification benefits of even two asset classes, much less three or more.

In this chapter, we'll see a simple example, a more complex one, and finally a real-world model of how to make diversification work for you.

> **» KEY CONCEPT**
> ## diversification works in mysterious ways
> Combining different asset classes improves your portfolio, but it isn't intuitive.

Holding three different asset classes is better than entrusting your life savings to only one

FIGURE 9-1

Two funds: The simplest example of the magic of diversification

Let's start out with an artificial example—an imaginary stock exchange. Can you determine the right answer to the question illustrated in Figure 9-2?

» **This exchange** supports only two investments: a money-market fund and a single stock.

» **Money Fund A** guarantees a payout of 0.1% per month. With the benefit of compounding, that works out to be 1.2066% per year. After 96 months (eight years), your $100 would be worth $110.07.

» **Security B** is a boring stock. Its price wobbles from $100 to $85 to $70 and back every four months without really going anywhere. Your $100 would wind up being worth no more than $100—an annualized return of 0%.

Perhaps Security B is a heavily regulated utility. This imaginary, long-established company is likely to generate the same snoozer profits forever. True, its price does fluctuate as the market does. But its stock will never be worth more than $70 to $100.

Traders would say Security B is "stuck in a trading range" or "going sideways."

Money Fund A and Security B have a **low correlation**. That means Money Fund A doesn't tend to go up just because Security B goes up. Money Fund A goes up every month like clockwork, no matter what Security B is doing. As a matter of fact, A and B have **zero** correlation. Security B doesn't influence the money fund's return at all.

Knowing all of the above, what would you choose as the best investment portfolio?

In other words:

Which asset allocation will produce the highest rate of return?

» **a** · 100% in Money Fund A

» **b** · 100% in Security B

» **c** · 50% in A and 50% in B, rebalanced monthly

» **d** · It cannot be determined.

In this artificial example, rebalance trades incur today's low 0.1% round-trip transaction costs.

Make a note of your answer, and then turn to Figure 9-3.

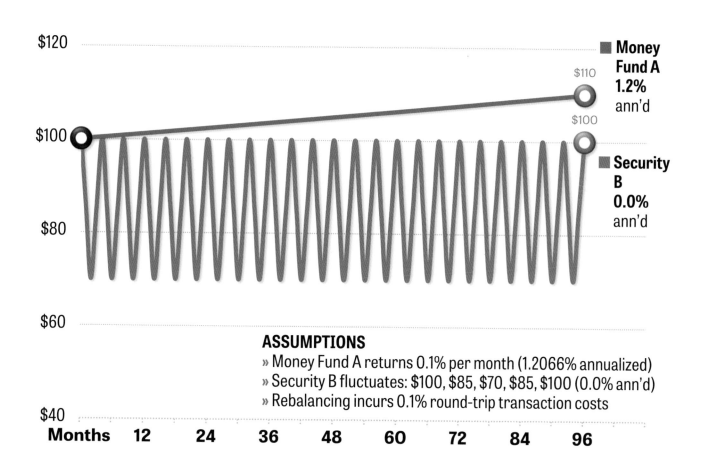

$160 — **Question: Which asset allocation will produce the highest rate of return?**

a. 100% in Money Fund A
b. 100% in Security B
c. 50% in A and 50% in B, rebalanced monthly
d. It cannot be determined

$140

$120

Money Fund A 1.2% ann'd

$110

$100

$100

Security B 0.0% ann'd

$80

$60

ASSUMPTIONS
» Money Fund A returns 0.1% per month (1.2066% annualized)
» Security B fluctuates: $100, $85, $70, $85, $100 (0.0% ann'd)
» Rebalancing incurs 0.1% round-trip transaction costs

$40

Months   12   24   36   48   60   72   84   96

FIGURE 9-2 | Adapted from Shannon's Demon

Diversification means even a going-sideways security can help a portfolio

Remarkably, the money fund's surefire 1.2% return isn't the best choice. See for yourself in Figure 9-3.

Diversifying 50/50 with a stock that's stuck in a trading range produces a better gain than a buy-and-hold of either asset by itself. This is called Shannon's Demon (see Tech Talk).

The diversified portfolio rewards a kind of discipline many individuals don't have:

» Shifting from winners to losers takes guts. Rebalancing a 50/50 portfolio guarantees you're selling a little of the asset that went up the most and buying more of the asset that didn't. That's not easy for most people!

» The diversification benefit requires patience. Notice that, in 17 out of the first 24 months, your 50/50 portfolio would have had a **lower** balance than if you'd simply held a low-yielding money fund! (In other words, the blue line was below the green line 17 times out of the first 24.)

It's only after 51 months—more than four years—that your diversified portfolio pulls ahead of the money fund for good and never falls behind.

Staying the course takes patience, even though the diversified portfolio's long-term return is more than **quadruple** the money fund—5.4% annualized vs. only 1.2%.

A Wall Street wag might say, "Any investing strategy you start following with serious money will disappoint you for the first two years."

That may not be **literally** true—but keep the saying in mind when you begin any new investing formula. The benefit of diversification takes time.

Don't confuse this example with the Mama Bear Portfolio and the Papa Bear Portfolio. Muscular Portfolios do not require rebalancing monthly—or at any arbitrary interval. Later in this chapter, we'll read about a real-world rebalancing policy.

» TECH TALK

Shannon's Demon

Claude Elwood Shannon (1916–2001) is credited with inventing the field of information theory. He was a mathematics professor at MIT for 22 years.[1153]

Shannon's Demon is a thought experiment in which a trader profits from random movements of securities. One is a volatile stock that has a low correlation with another. Diversifying between the two securities produces more profit than a buy-and-hold of either security. In the real world, the trading costs of monthly rebalancing would reduce the gains.

The term "demon," in this case, doesn't signify an evil spirit but any powerful force that works automatically.

Shannon also managed money, earning a phenomenal 28% annualized return from about 1959 through 1986, better than Warren Buffett, according to *Fortune's Formula* (2010) by William Poundstone.[1154]

» KEY CONCEPT

investor's remorse

Assume that any investing strategy you start following with serious money will disappoint you for the first two years or so.

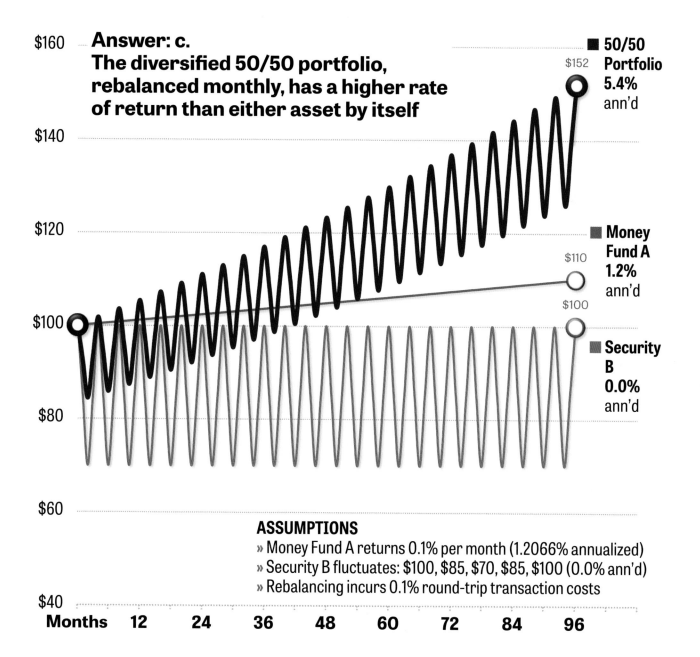

Answer: c.
The diversified 50/50 portfolio, rebalanced monthly, has a higher rate of return than either asset by itself

50/50 Portfolio 5.4% ann'd — $152

Money Fund A 1.2% ann'd — $110

Security B 0.0% ann'd — $100

ASSUMPTIONS
» Money Fund A returns 0.1% per month (1.2066% annualized)
» Security B fluctuates: $100, $85, $70, $85, $100 (0.0% ann'd)
» Rebalancing incurs 0.1% round-trip transaction costs

FIGURE 9-3 | Adapted from Shannon's Demon

Will diversification work with two securities that both have negative returns?

The example in Figure 9-3 is admittedly artificial. No securities exist that vary from $100 to $85 to $70 and back like clockwork.

So how about a scenario that's truly random? What if our made-up market offered just two stocks to invest in? Each company rises and falls based on a coin toss. Even worse, both companies are destined to decline in value in the long term.

Perhaps one firm is stuck with an inventory of obsolete BlackBerry phones, and the other is selling old Windows phones. Bummer, dude.

In Figure 9-4, these two companies go up and down each month at random under the following rules:

» **If Coin C comes up tails,** Security C's price goes down 30%. If heads, Security C rises 40%.

» **If Coin D comes up tails,** Security D's price goes down 20%. If heads, Security D rises 15%.

"Just a dang minute," you might be saying. "Security C is a good bet. It goes down only 30% and then goes back up 40%. It's a winner!"

Beware of promises you hear about gains and losses. These things aren't easy to estimate in your head. About 11 out of every 10 people hate math.

What you need to know is that 40% up doesn't beat 30% down.

Let's say Security C goes down 30%. Its price falls from $100 to $70. If the stock then rises 40%, its price would be only $98, not $100.

The stock would need to rise almost 43% to move from $70 to $100. Cursed as it is with random 30% drops and only 40% recoveries, Security C has a negative **expected return**. It's a long-term loser.

In Figure 9-4, notice that Security C has a lucky streak for the first 24 months. That's followed by an unlucky streak for the second 24 months. By contrast, Security D starts out unlucky and then has a run of luck. That's the randomness of a coin toss.

In this example, after 48 months, Security C is down to $61.58. You've lost more than one-third of your money. Security D is down to $57.72. You've lost more than 42%. Here's the question:

Which asset allocation will produce the highest rate of return?

» **a** · 100% in Security C

» **b** · 100% in Security D

» **c** · 50% in C and 50% in D, rebalanced monthly

» **d** · It cannot be determined

Make a note of your answer, and then turn to Figure 9-5.

» **KEY CONCEPT**

expected return

After thousands of random events, any asset has a typical growth rate it tends to revert to.

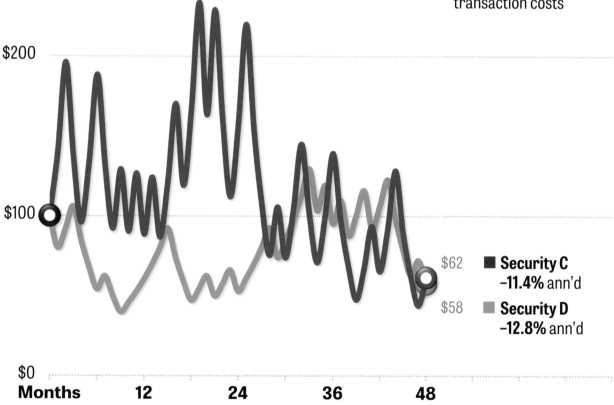

Question: Which allocation will produce the highest return?

a. 100% in Security C
b. 100% in Security D
c. 50% in C and 50% in D, rebalanced monthly
d. It cannot be determined

ASSUMPTIONS

» On a toss of Coin C, Security C returns +40% or –30% each month

» On a toss of Coin D, Security D returns +15% or –20% each month

» Rebalancing incurs 0.1% round-trip transaction costs

$300

$200

$100

$0

Months   12   24   36   48

$62   ■ **Security C** **–11.4%** ann'd

$58   ■ **Security D** **–12.8%** ann'd

FIGURE 9-4 | Adapted from "The Joy of Volatility" (2008), Dempster, Evstigneev, and Schenk-Hoppé

When you diversify a portfolio, you can turn a sow's ear into a silk purse

Figure 9-5 shows the answer. Even though Security C and Security D go up and down completely at random —they're controlled by coin tosses each month—the 50/50 portfolio rose in the long term.

» **Security C** lost 11.4% annualized.

» **Security D** lost 12.8% annualized.

» **The 50/50 portfolio** actually rose 15.4% annualized. But it never held any asset other than two securities with negative expected returns!

What makes this possible? Once again, the investor removed a bit of money each month from whichever asset had gone up the most and added that money to the other asset. (That isn't necessary with Muscular Portfolios, as we'll discuss again later.)

As in the Money Fund A/ Security B example, notice that getting a positive return required patience.

» **The 50/50 portfolio** was actually in negative territory after 12 months, while Security C was up during most of that 12 months.

» **Even after 24 months,** Security C was ahead of the 50/50 portfolio most of the time.

» **It wasn't until *two years*** into the process that the 50/50 portfolio pulled decisively ahead. Informed investors give a strategy time to work.

Will a 50/50 portfolio, periodically rebalanced, **always** return more than either one of two assets?

Absolutely not!

Flipping two coins 48 times produces more than 79 trillion quadrillion possible outcomes. (That's 79 followed by 27 zeros.) In some of these random cases, a 50/50 portfolio would win. In many other cases, Security C or D would win. One security could even come up heads 48 times in a row. That's randomness for you!

Don't invest by flipping coins. Don't risk your nest egg on wildly volatile securities. We can do a lot better than random chance. Our next example uses assets you can actually buy.

» **TECH TALK**
the joy of volatility

The benefit of diversification shows up **on average,** not in every case. In a stock exchange where actual securities are on sale, anything can and will happen.

Figures 9-4 and 9-5 are adapted from "The Joy of Volatility," published in the February 2008 issue of *Quantitative Finance* by three professors at Britain's Cambridge, Leeds, and Manchester universities. See their academic paper for the mathematical formulas these figures are based on.[1155]

» **KEY CONCEPT**
reversion to average

An investing strategy that's had a hot streak is likely to experience a cold streak.

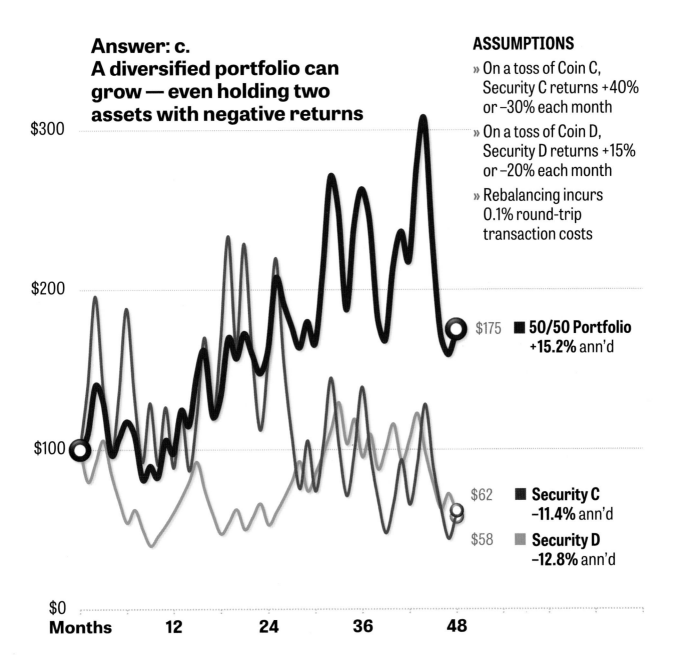

Answer: c.
A diversified portfolio can grow — even holding two assets with negative returns

ASSUMPTIONS

» On a toss of Coin C, Security C returns +40% or –30% each month

» On a toss of Coin D, Security D returns +15% or –20% each month

» Rebalancing incurs 0.1% round-trip transaction costs

$300

$200

$100

$0

Months 12 24 36 48

$175 ■ **50/50 Portfolio** **+15.2%** ann'd

$62 ■ **Security C** **–11.4%** ann'd

$58 ■ **Security D** **–12.8%** ann'd

FIGURE 9-5 | Adapted from "The Joy of Volatility" (2008), Dempster, Evstigneev, and Schenk-Hoppé

A real-world case of two asset classes and the best way to allocate them

Our final example in this chapter begins with Figure 9-6. The graph brings us face-to-face with the two largest asset classes in the US: large-cap stocks (represented by the S&P 500) and investment-grade bonds (represented by the returns you would have received from an index of high-quality debt).

There are no imaginary securities in this example. You can easily get almost the return of the S&P 500—along with that index's bone-crushing crashes—by simply purchasing an exchange-traded fund like Vanguard's VOO.

Similarly, you can achieve the same returns as a bond index with Vanguard's VCLT. That ETF holds investment-quality corporate bonds.

In the 20th century, before ETFs became widely available, you would have had to purchase Vanguard mutual funds to track these asset classes. The returns would have been about the same as ETFs, although annual fees were somewhat higher in the old days.

Bonds have had a bullish period since the 1980s, but they still underperformed the S&P 500. Figure 9-6 shows that the S&P 500 (after subtracting today's annual fees) returned 10.0% annualized. Bonds were more than 1 percentage point less rewarding, returning only 8.9%.

Notice in Figure 9-6 that a buy-and-hold portfolio of bonds would have left you behind the S&P 500 for an excruciating 14-year period: 1995 through 2008. Your bond portfolio would have lagged an S&P 500 portfolio in about 50% of all the months on the graph. Hard to take!

Here's the question:

Which asset allocation will produce the highest rate of return?

» **a** · 100% in the S&P 500

» **b** · 100% in investment-grade bonds

» **c** · A 50/50 portfolio, rebalanced monthly

» **d** · It cannot be determined

Make a note of your answer, and then turn to Figure 9-7.

» **TECH TALK**

securities you can actually buy

Figure 9-6 graphs two asset classes that have been tracked for decades by low-cost index funds.

To match the performance of the S&P 500, Vanguard has offered since 1976 a mutual fund that now bears the symbol VFINX. Today, we'd choose the ETF version, VOO, which charges an annual fee of 0.05%.

Vanguard has also offered since 1973 a low-cost investment-grade bond fund, VWESX. The matching ETF is VCLT, which has a reasonable annual fee of 0.12%.

In both cases, today's ETFs offer small investors lower fees, better tax treatment, and greater trading convenience than the older mutual funds.

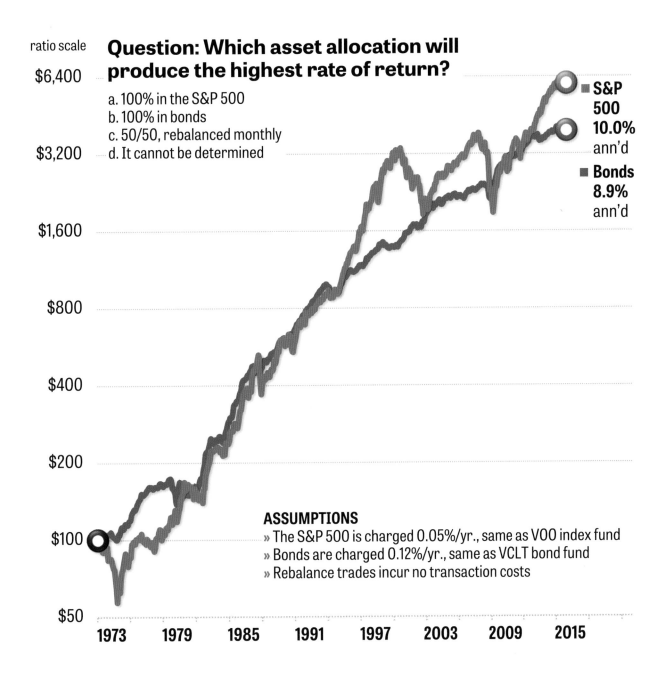

ratio scale

$6,400

Question: Which asset allocation will produce the highest rate of return?

a. 100% in the S&P 500
b. 100% in bonds
c. 50/50, rebalanced monthly
d. It cannot be determined

$3,200

$1,600

$800

$400

$200

■ S&P 500 10.0% ann'd

■ Bonds 8.9% ann'd

ASSUMPTIONS
» The S&P 500 is charged 0.05%/yr., same as VOO index fund
» Bonds are charged 0.12%/yr., same as VCLT bond fund
» Rebalance trades incur no transaction costs

$100

$50

1973 1979 1985 1991 1997 2003 2009 2015

FIGURE 9-6 | Source: Quant simulator

A simple two-asset plan beats the S&P 500 most but not all of the time

Figure 9-7 shows that diversification with only two assets doesn't exactly guarantee anything. In the last five years of the 43-year period, the S&P 500 portfolio pulled slightly ahead of an all-bond portfolio. But look at what happened along the way.

In 65% of the months, the 50/50 portfolio—which this book calls the Baby Bear—actually had a higher balance than the S&P 500 portfolio.

And your diversified portfolio would have helped you sleep better at night. The S&P 500 subjected buy-and-hold investors to an intolerable crash of 51% in the 2007–2009 bear market. (The loss was even worse if you consider inflation.)

By contrast, the 50/50 portfolio never lost more than 29%. That's still worrisome, and you can do much better with a Muscular Portfolio, as we'll see again later in this chapter. But while many investors can survive a 29% loss, losing **half** of one's life savings makes most investors throw in the towel, locking in their catastrophe.

Most importantly, the more stable 50/50 portfolio and the crash-prone stock index achieved almost the same compound annual growth rate. The Baby Bear returned 9.8% annualized. That's a rounding error compared with the S&P 500's 10.0%.

Why didn't the 50/50 portfolio merely achieve the mathematical **average** of the 8.9% return of bonds and the 10.0% return of stocks? That simple average would have been 9.45%.

What gave the 50/50 portfolio the extra oomph to reach 9.8%?

The Baby Bear returned so much more than the simple average solely because

the 50/50 portfolio kept its losses small.

This was true not only in the 2007–2009 financial crisis: In **every** bear market, the diversified portfolio subjected investors to much smaller drawdowns than the S&P 500. Smaller losses require smaller gains to recover from.

Even better, the 50/50 portfolio held on to most of the S&P 500's gains in the soaring 14-year period of 1995–2008. Notice in Figure 9-7 that the Baby Bear (the purple line) hewed closely to the S&P 500 (the orange line) in the roaring 1990s and 2000s.

» TECH TALK

more examples of diversification

Shannon's Demon and "The Joy of Volatility" were wittily analyzed in a paper by Adam Butler, the chief investment officer of Resolve Asset Management.

His article "Volatility Harvesting and the Importance of Rebalancing" adds a real-world example using Tokyo's Nikkei stock index (like New York's S&P 500).

In a slow, grinding collapse, Japanese stocks fell 48% in the years 1995–2011. But if you'd rebalanced those same stocks with low-yielding Japanese government bonds 50/50 each quarter, you'd have had a portfolio that actually **gained** 41% over the 17-year period.[1156]

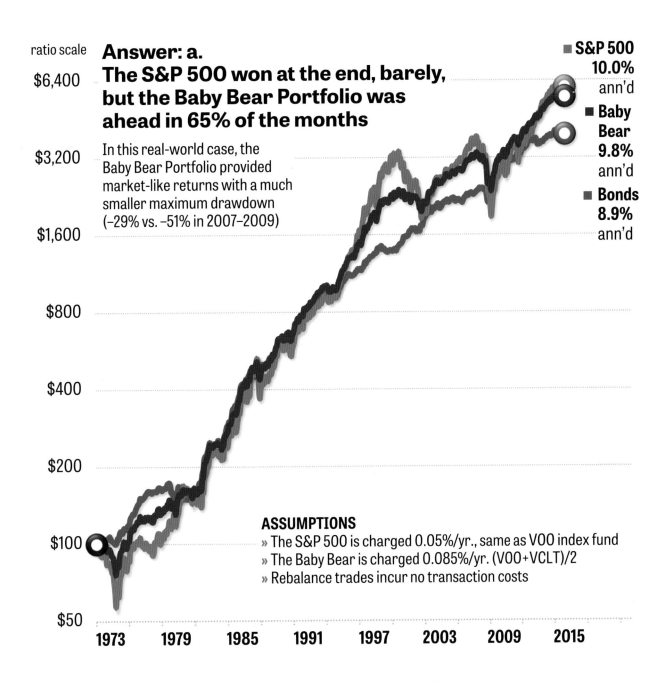

ratio scale

Answer: a.
The S&P 500 won at the end, barely,
but the Baby Bear Portfolio was
ahead in 65% of the months

$6,400

In this real-world case, the
Baby Bear Portfolio provided
market-like returns with a much
smaller maximum drawdown
(–29% vs. –51% in 2007–2009)

$3,200

$1,600

$800

$400

$200

ASSUMPTIONS
» The S&P 500 is charged 0.05%/yr., same as VOO index fund
» The Baby Bear is charged 0.085%/yr. (VOO+VCLT)/2
» Rebalance trades incur no transaction costs

$100

$50

1973   1979   1985   1991   1997   2003   2009   2015

■ **S&P 500**
10.0%
ann'd

■ **Baby**
Bear
9.8%
ann'd

■ **Bonds**
8.9%
ann'd

FIGURE 9-7 | Source: Quant simulator

Muscular Portfolios are well diversified and don't need monthly rebalancing

As we saw in Chapter 1, the Baby Bear is a starter portfolio, not a Muscular Portfolio. A simple 50/50 investing strategy like the Baby Bear is designed to keep transaction costs as low as possible for people with less than $10,000 to invest.

If you have more than $10,000, you can reap the full rewards of diversification. The benefit is greatest when your portfolio picks and chooses from among a wide range of assets.

Your returns are limited if you restrict yourself to US stocks and bonds. Instead, Muscular Portfolios expand your choices to include other low-cost index funds, some of which became available only in the 21st century.

The Mama Bear adds asset classes like US small-cap stocks, non-US stocks, real-estate investment trusts (REITs), commodities, and gold. The Papa Bear additionally supports separate investments in growth stocks and value stocks. These asset classes often behave differently, as explained in Chapter 6.

What advantage do these additional asset classes give your portfolio? The benefit is that some ETFs actually go up when the S&P 500 is crashing down. In particular, commodities, precious metals, and bonds have a low correlation with stocks. This is graphically illustrated later in this chapter in Figure 9-9.

Figure 9-8 shows the improved returns that are possible by holding the best of nine asset classes—the menu of the Mama Bear Portfolio— or 13 asset classes, as in the Papa Bear Portfolio.

Selecting the best from a global menu of very different asset classes eliminates the need to rebalance a portfolio every month. Specifically, you need to rebalance a Muscular Portfolio only when one ETF is more than 20% off its target weight. This is explained fully in Chapter 18. Keep your transaction expenses down by making rebalance trades only when necessary.

The small course corrections made by Muscular Portfolios serve a similar (though far more effective) function as the monthly rebalances that drive the artificial examples earlier in this chapter.

Over the years, the Mama Bear and Papa Bear gradually tilt toward the asset classes that have the best odds. These odds are determined by our old friend, the Momentum Rule, which is the subject of the next chapter.

Don't go wild with diversification. If Bill Gates had "diversified" into the S&P 500 instead of holding all the stock he received when Microsoft first went public, he'd have only 1/40th as much wealth today.[1157]

But the right amount of diversification is important to anyone's portfolio growth. Even Gates is gradually reducing his concentration in Microsoft stock.[1158]

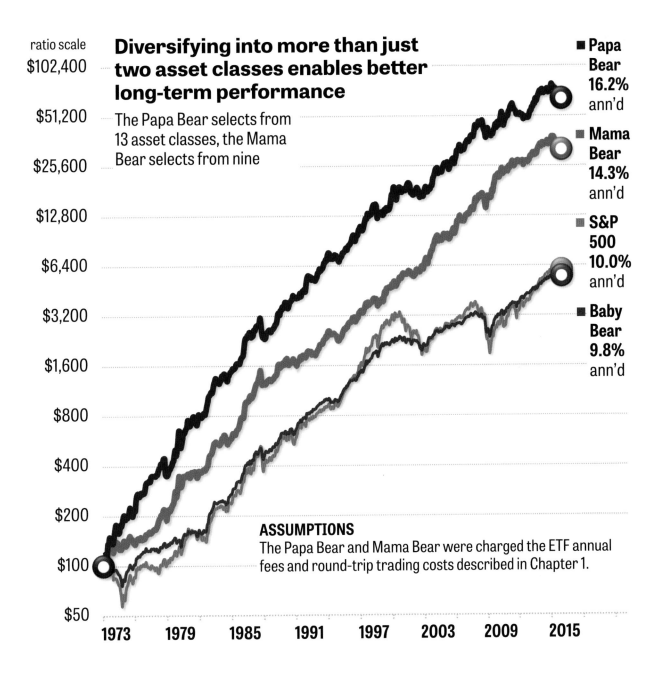

Diversifying into more than just two asset classes enables better long-term performance

The Papa Bear selects from 13 asset classes, the Mama Bear selects from nine

ratio scale

$102,400
$51,200
$25,600
$12,800
$6,400
$3,200
$1,600
$800
$400
$200
$100
$50

1973 1979 1985 1991 1997 2003 2009 2015

■ Papa Bear 16.2% ann'd

■ Mama Bear 14.3% ann'd

■ S&P 500 10.0% ann'd

■ Baby Bear 9.8% ann'd

ASSUMPTIONS
The Papa Bear and Mama Bear were charged the ETF annual fees and round-trip trading costs described in Chapter 1.

FIGURE 9-8 | Source: Quant simulator

It pays to hold some low-correlation assets during stock market collapses

"**Correlation**" **is a** fancy word, but the concept is simple. On days when Asset Class X went up, what did Asset Class Y do, and what percentage of the time did it do it?

If Y usually rises with X, then X and Y have a positive correlation. (This is what we usually mean when we say two asset classes are correlated.) If Y usually falls, then X and Y have a negative correlation. And if the behavior of X doesn't seem to predict anything about the behavior of Y, they aren't correlated at all.

Commodities, gold, and bonds can diversify your holdings, because they often move differently than the S&P 500. Muscular Portfolios include commodities and gold in their menus, but most Lazy Portfolios do not (see Appendix C). In Figure 9-9:

» **The S&P 500,** obviously, is always up when the S&P 500 is up. This large-cap index has a perfect 100% correlation with itself.

» **Small caps and developed/ emerging markets** do little to diversify large caps. These three asset classes are 85% to 93% correlated with the S&P 500. As we saw in Chapter 3, these assets crashed

60% to 62% in 2007–2009, while the S&P 500 was down 56% (adjusted for dividends and inflation).

» **Real-estate investment trusts** are 76% correlated with the S&P 500. That provides a bit of a cushion— after all, real-estate income may rise even when stocks are down. But REITs are called "equity-like" for a reason. For instance, Vanguard's REIT index fund (VGSIX) had a disastrous –70% real total return in the 2007–2009 bear.

» **Commodity index ETFs** provide strong diversification benefits. With a correla-

tion of just 44%, commodity prices are only **weakly** tied to US large-cap prices.

» **Gold and other precious metals** move almost entirely independently of the S&P 500. Gold's mere 4% ranking is essentially a correlation of zero. Precious metals may rise or fall regardless of whether stocks are soaring or crashing.

» **Corporate bonds and Treasurys** actually have a **negative** correlation to the S&P 500: minus 32% and minus 40%, respectively. In other words, bonds often rise in price when stocks fall.

» TECH TALK

correlations aren't written in stone

Be aware that correlations change all the time. Figure 9-9 uses actual index funds (after subtracting their historical fees) to show asset-class correlations over a 13-year period. However different years would generate different readings.

The illustration shows the correlation of major index funds versus the S&P 500 from November 18, 2004, through September 8, 2017. However, the commodities correlation begins on February 6, 2006—the earliest a commodity index ETF was available.

LIVINGSTON'S LAW OF DIVERSIFICATION

Holding more than two asset classes
Is a vital way your wealth amasses.

Two assets that help you diversify— commodities and precious metals— are held by few Lazy Portfolios

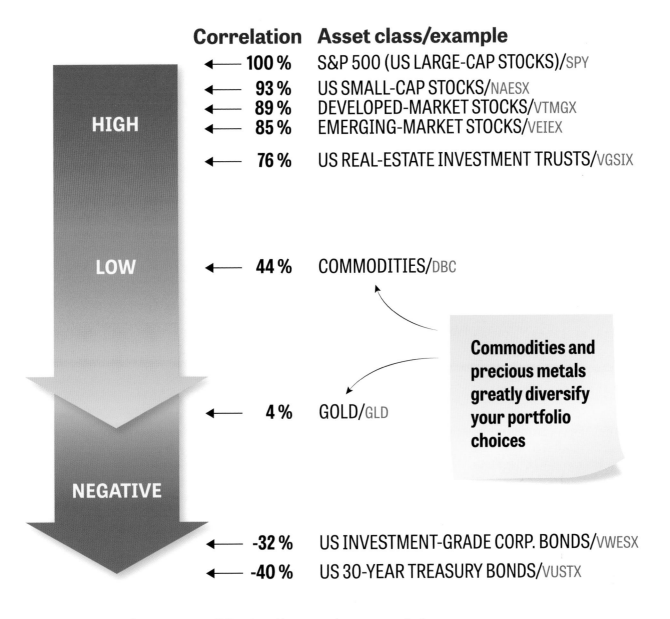

Correlation	Asset class/example
← 100 %	S&P 500 (US LARGE-CAP STOCKS)/SPY
← 93 %	US SMALL-CAP STOCKS/NAESX
← 89 %	DEVELOPED-MARKET STOCKS/VTMGX
← 85 %	EMERGING-MARKET STOCKS/VEIEX
← 76 %	US REAL-ESTATE INVESTMENT TRUSTS/VGSIX
← 44 %	COMMODITIES/DBC
← 4 %	GOLD/GLD
← -32 %	US INVESTMENT-GRADE CORP. BONDS/VWESX
← -40 %	US 30-YEAR TREASURY BONDS/VUSTX

HIGH

LOW

NEGATIVE

Commodities and precious metals greatly diversify your portfolio choices

FIGURE 9-9 | Source: PortfolioVisualizer.com/asset-correlations

10 Momentum is a trend that will forever be your best friend

"Not only is momentum the 'premier market anomaly' as per Fama & French . . . it may be the only really practical anomaly."

GARY ANTONACCI, principal, Portfolio Management Consultants[1159]

Momentum is the tendency for asset classes that have gone up in price during the past 3 to 12 months to continue to go up for the next month or more. Compounding, diversification, and momentum are the three core principles of Muscular Portfolios.

Momentum is supported by the latest research, yet is easy enough for anyone to understand (Figure 10-1). In their academic paper "Dissecting Anomalies" (2007), finance professors Eugene Fama and Kenneth French explain it like this:

"The premier anomaly is momentum . . . stocks with low returns over the last year tend to have low returns for the next few months, and stocks with high past returns tend to have high future returns."[1160]

Any reasonably diversified portfolio that you're willing to check up on once a month can benefit from momentum. Financial adviser Gary Antonacci says momentum "may be the only really practical anomaly" that is easy for individuals to exploit.[1161]

That's because price histories of the major asset classes are easy to find on the Web. The momentum calculations are even made for you—completely free of charge—at MuscularPortfolios.com.

Momentum has been a recognized factor in free markets for hundreds of years. Christopher Geczy of the University of Pennsylvania and Mikhail Samonov of Forefront Analytics assembled returns going back to 1800—when only 10 stocks traded in the US market.

The findings were stunning. Over the entire 212-year period, strong-momentum securities consistently outperformed low-momentum ones by approximately 5 percentage points annualized. The numbers don't include transaction costs—which are lost to history—but the evidence is so overwhelming that the principle shines forth.

As if this weren't enough, the authors also confirmed momentum in indexes, commodities, and other asset classes, including British stocks going back to the 1800s.[1162]

The research proving momentum may be new, but momentum itself isn't. And despite the fact that everyone knows about it, it keeps working . . . because human nature ensures it does.

An ETF in motion tends to remain in motion

—with apologies to Sir Isaac Newton

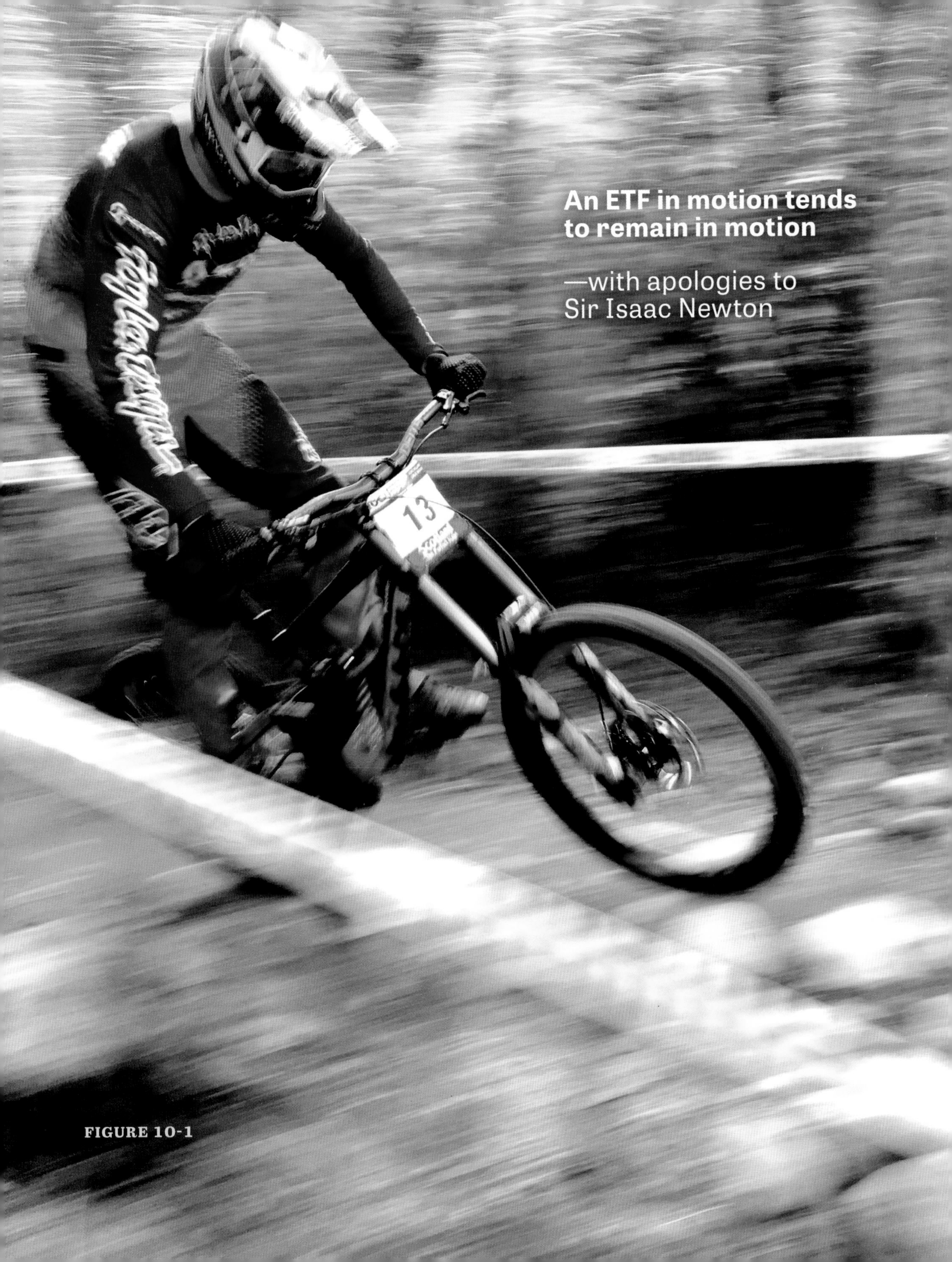

FIGURE 10-1

Momentum isn't perfect, but it gives you the best odds to grow your money

There are many market prediction systems, and most stop working once they became widely known. But traders have always recognized that security prices exhibit trends. Securities that have performed well continue to rise for a time, while poorly performing ones tend to be bad bets.

Why does momentum work century after century, even though investors have always been aware of it?

The answer is that traders are human and suffer from **behavioral biases.** People read about an asset that's soared in price over the past 12 months, and they finally buy in.

"Investors herd and they gravitate toward what is already in motion, and that reinforces the price movement," explains Mike Moody of Dorsey Wright Money Management.[1163]

Relying on a Momentum Rule is not the same as buying what is "hot." It means that instead of following your instinct or opinion, you let **science** tilt your portfolio toward asset classes that are in the midst of a trend and away from those that have ended one.

How does the Momentum Rule manage to predict anything? Figure 10-2 illustrates the findings of three researchers—Adam Butler, Michael Philbrick, and Rodrigo Gordillo—who examined the performance of 10 asset classes over more than 20 years.

Asset classes that performed in the top five over the past six months (roughly the same Momentum Rule used by the Mama Bear) were significantly more likely than chance to also be in the top five the following month.

In their 2016 book *Adaptive Asset Allocation*, the researchers reveal the results:

"Examining our 10-asset universe, the probability that a top half six-month performer . . . will deliver returns in the top half over the subsequent month is 54 percent using a sample period from January 1995 to the present. Those odds might seem minor, but the spread is statistically significant and provides a meaningful investment edge over time."[1164]

Assets in the top half in the past few months tend to be in the top half next month

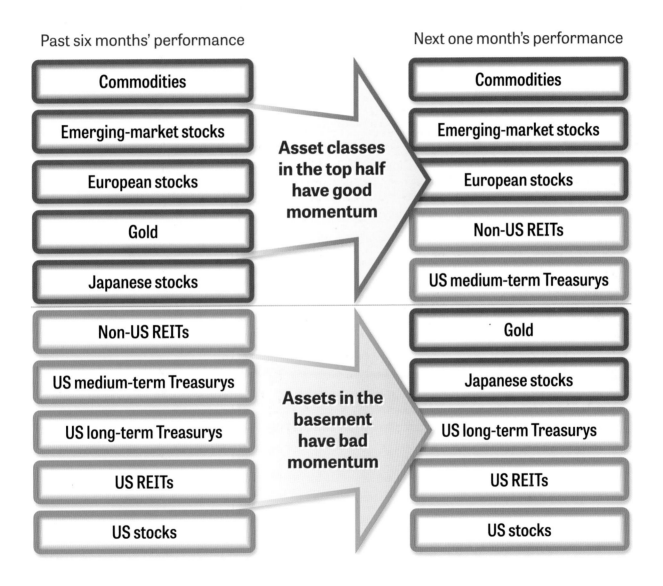

FIGURE 10-2 | Assets are listed in alphabetical order within categories. No actual returns are shown. Adapted from Adaptive Asset Allocation, Butler, Philbrick, and Gordillo (2016).[1165]

Other market factors lose their punch, but momentum keeps on keepin' on

A strategy that predicts winners 54% of the time may not seem like a big deal.

But imagine you knew that a certain roulette wheel paid off on red 54% of the time (Figure 10-3).

You could bankrupt any casino that would let you keep playing! (See Tech Talk.)

As we've seen, the Momentum Rule has worked for hundreds of years. It's not likely to become overused, because it exploits human nature.

In theory, various "market factors" predict that some securities will go up more than others. However, a study by Arnott, Beck, and Kalesnik shows that these factors lost about three-fourths of their effect after disclosure in an academic paper. The factors with more than 20 years' data since publication are shown in Figure 10-4:

» **Small caps** outpaced the market return by 7 points for 14 years. Then the effect mostly disappeared. Small caps outperfomed by just

0.8 of a point for the next 35 years. (Small caps are stocks with a market capitalization of only $200 million to $2 billion.)

» **Value stocks** boosted returns 9+ points for 30 years. But the value factor lost three-fourths of its benefit after publication. (Value stocks are those with the best ratio of book assets to market price—b/p—or the best score on a blend of measures.)

» **Low-beta stocks** dropped from 7.4 to 2.1 points of out-performance. (Low betas are those with the least fluctuation compared with the market.) [1166]

» **The momentum portfolio** outperformed the market by 5.4 points before publication. In the next 23 years, remark-ably, momentum kept over **two-thirds** of its effect, best-ing the market by 3.7 points.

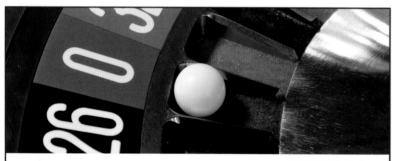

FIGURE 10-3

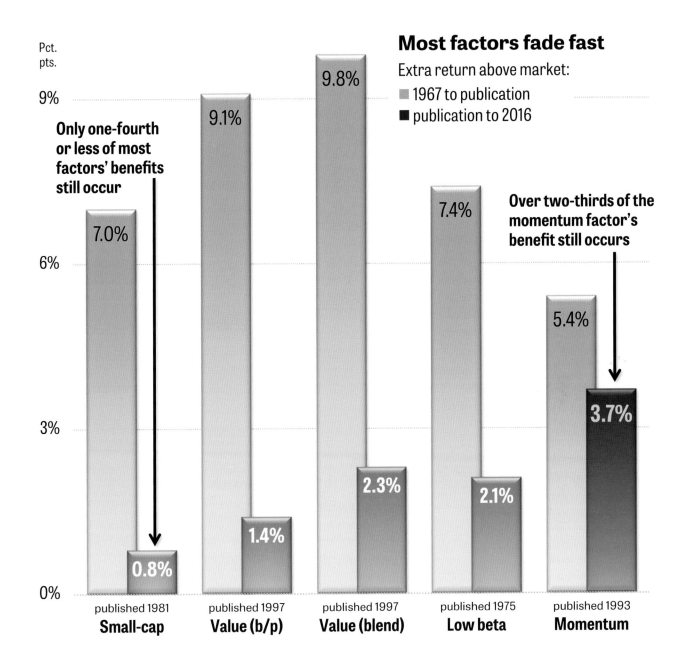

Most factors fade fast

Extra return above market:
- ■ 1967 to publication
- ■ publication to 2016

Pct. pts.

Only one-fourth or less of most factors' benefits still occur

Over two-thirds of the momentum factor's benefit still occurs

Factor	1967 to publication	publication to 2016
Small-cap (published 1981)	7.0%	0.8%
Value (b/p) (published 1997)	9.1%	1.4%
Value (blend) (published 1997)	9.8%	2.3%
Low beta (published 1975)	7.4%	2.1%
Momentum (published 1993)	5.4%	3.7%

FIGURE 10-4 | Source: Arnott, Beck, Kalesnik/Research Affiliates (2016)[1167]

Behavioral science explains why the momentum factor persists

Why did most factors in Figure 10-4 lose almost all of their predictive power? Some possible reasons:

» **A "hot streak"** occurred for each factor during the years researchers studied it; or

» **Traders overused the factor** after it was publicly disclosed, leading to inevitable underperformance in the future.

Does using a Muscular Portfolio mean you can't take advantage of hot and cold streaks for market factors like small-cap and value? Not at all:

» **The Mama Bear Portfolio** tilts **toward** small caps when they're outperforming and **away** from small caps when they're underperforming.

» **The Papa Bear Portfolio** tilts **toward** value stocks when they're hot and **away** when they're not.

Muscular Portfolios tilt by relying on a specific scientific formula, not on human instinct.

Analysts at AQR Capital Management and New York University show in Figure 10-5 how humans underreact and overreact to unexpected events.

Imagine Lehman Brothers going bankrupt or OPEC raising oil prices. Suddenly, the prices of financial institutions or energy pipelines jump one way or the other. But after an initial jolt, investors continue to adjust their expectations slowly.

Muscular Portfolios exploit this fact. Using asset rotation, you automatically purchase whatever asset has the strongest momentum. When that is no longer top rated, you buy some other asset that is.

In June 2015, Fama and French re-examined momentum and several other market factors. The momentum effect for a given asset "tends to persist for only about nine months," they wrote.[1168]

Fortunately, that's plenty of time to realize your gains.

» TECH TALK

don't assume momentum works on individual stocks

Momentum works best with asset classes, not individual stocks. Portfolio manager Gary Antonacci writes: "The stocks generating the largest momentum returns are the smallest, less liquid ones having higher trading costs . . . transaction costs negate much of the momentum profits of individual stocks."[1169]

LIVINGSTON'S LAW OF MOMENTUM

The trend is your friend
Until the trend is at its end.

Momentum works because it's human nature to underreact and overreact to new info

A stylized 'lifecycle' of a trend

- ▬ Market price
- ≡ Intrinsic value

overreaction

underreaction

trend ends

❸ **Momentum strategy sells here**

❷ **Momentum strategy buys here**

❶ **Unexpected event!**

$58

$54

$50

$46

Months   12   24   36

FIGURE 10-5 | Adapted from Brian Hurst, Yao Hua Ooi, and Lasse Heje Pedersen[1170]

Looks like something good to eat!

Investors

SECTION D | **Adaptation**

"Well-known financial frauds—starting with the South Sea Company and Mississippi Company scandals of 1720—caused amateur investors to desert the stock market for a generation or more afterwards. But the pattern has not held in the twenty-first century United States, despite evidence of rampant fraud, from the Enron accounting scandal to the role of formerly trusted institutions like Goldman Sachs and Fannie Mae in precipitating the subprime mortgage crisis. None of these events has significantly decreased Americans' participation in the stock market."

BROOKE HARRINGTON, Copenhagen Business School (2012)[1171]

Illustration: "In Deep Water" by Jed Dunkerley

11 Don't let rogue Wall Street banks tap your nest egg

"I sincerely believe, with you, that banking establishments are more dangerous than standing armies."

THOMAS JEFFERSON, letter to former US senator John Taylor (1816)[1172]

Something is seriously wrong with the moral compasses of top bank executives these days.

There are many honest bankers, but the financial crisis of 2008 revealed that the CEOs of giant Wall Street banks had orchestrated a massive fraud.

After the US real-estate bubble of the 2000s popped, it became all too obvious that banks had been gambling with their own depositors' funds, mismanaging accounts, skirting regulations, and generally making huge bets on the housing boom. When it all came undone, the bankers—desperate for money—nearly drove the world's economy into a second Great Depression.[1173]

Over five million homeowners were foreclosed on, many fraudulently, *Newsweek* reported.[1174]

According to an AP investigation in 2011, "the nation's largest banks and mortgage lenders, including JPMorgan Chase, Wells Fargo, Bank of America and an arm of Goldman Sachs" falsified signatures to foreclose on as many homes as possible (Figure 11-1).

"So far, no individuals, lenders or paperwork processors have been charged with a crime over the robo-signed signatures found on documents last year," the AP wrote. "But much of the suspect paperwork that has been filed since then is for . . . people who are in good standing" on their mortgages.[1175]

The 2011 report of the Angelides Commission, a bipartisan panel appointed by Congress, fingered the leaders of Wall Street's largest banks as the root of the financial crisis:

"We conclude dramatic failures of corporate governance and risk management at many systemically important financial institutions were a key cause of this crisis. . . . We conclude there was a systemic breakdown in accountability and ethics."[1176]

William Dudley, president of the Federal Reserve Bank of New York, said CEOs showed "deep-seated cultural and ethical failures" and lacked "respect for law, regulation and the public trust."[1177]

To raise cash, Wall Street banks foreclosed on more than five million homeowners, many of whom weren't even behind on their payments

FIGURE 11-1

The wages of sin

Wall Street's rogue banks paid over **$150 billion** in settlements for their actions (partial list).

Bank	Charges	Settlement	Plaintiffs
Bank of America *with subsidiaries Merrill Lynch and Countrywide Financial*	• Defective mortgage loans	$54,900,000,000	Various claimants
	• Financial fraud	16,650,000,000	Justice Dept.
	• Abusive foreclosure practices	11,800,000,000	Justice Dept.
	• Securities law violations	5,830,000,000	FHFA
	• Rigging US dollar exchange rates	450,000,000	US/UK/Switz.
	• Defrauding investors	170,000,000	SEC
	• Faulty disclosures, inaccurate books (Merrill, defendent)	131,800,000	SEC
	• Deliberately misleading investors (Countrywide, defendent)	22,500,000	SEC
Citigroup	• Misleading investors (DoJ, plaintiff)	$7,000,000,000	Justice Dept.
	• Rigging US dollar exchange rates	2,250,000,000	US/UK/Switz.
	• Abusive foreclosure practices	2,200,000,000	Justice Dept.
	• Securities law violations	250,000,000	FHFA
	• Misleading investors (SEC, plaintiff)	360,000,000	SEC
Credit Suisse	• Conspiracy to hide offshore assets	$2,811,000,000	Justice Dept.
	• Securities law violations	885,000,000	FHFA
	• Misleading investors	120,000,000	SEC
Deutsche Bank	• Manipulating Libor interest rates	$2,500,000,000	Justice Dept./EU
	• Securities law violations	1,925,000,000	FHFA
	• Misstating financial reports	55,000,000	SEC
	• Assisting in concealing income in Switzerland	31,000,000	Justice Dept.
Goldman Sachs	• Misconduct in mortgage securities	$5,060,000,000	Justice Dept.
	• Securities law violations	1,200,000,000	FHFA
	• Defrauding investors	550,000,000	SEC
	• Misrepresentations to Illinois pension funds	272,000,000	NECA-IBEW Fund

Bank	Charges	Settlement	Plaintiffs
JPMorgan Chase	• Misleading investors (DoJ, plaintiff)	$13,000,000,000	Justice Dept.
	• Abusive foreclosure practices	5,290,000,000	Justice Dept.
	• Securities law violations	4,000,000,000	FHFA
	• Rigging US dollar exchange rates	1,900,000,000	US/UK/Switz.
	• Misleading investors (SEC, plaintiff)	450,500,000	SEC
	• Manipulating Libor interest rates	108,000,000	Justice Dept./EU
Morgan Stanley	• Misleading investors about mortgage loans	$3,172,500,000	DoJ/NY/Illinois
	• Securities law violations	1,250,000,000	FHFA
	• Misleading investors	275,000,000	SEC
	• Losses to credit unions from residential mortgage-backed securities (RMBS)	225,000,000	NCUA
UBS	• Manipulating Libor interest rates	$1,500,000,000	Justice Dept./EU
	• Rigging US dollar exchange rates	1,300,000,000	US/UK/Switz.
	• Securities law violations	885,000,000	FHFA
	• Retaining millions payable to investors	50,000,000	SEC
Wells Fargo	• Abusive foreclosure practices	$5,350,000,000	Justice Dept.
	• Improper mortgage lending practices	1,200,000,000	Justice Dept.
	• Securities law violations	335,230,000	FHFA
	• Failure to file 100,000 legally required notices	81,600,000	Justice Dept.
	• Selling investments without disclosing risks	6,500,000	SEC

FIGURE 11-2

Sources:

Bloomberg News (BofA claimants),[1178] (abusive foreclosure practices),[1179] (rigging dollar exchange);[1180]

Federal Housing Finance Agency (FHFA);[1181]

HousingWire.com (Goldman Sachs vs. pension funds);[1182]

Justice Dept. (Bank of America),[1183] (Citigroup),[1184] (Credit Suisse),[1185] (Deutsche Bank),[1186] (Goldman Sachs),[1187] (JPMorgan Chase),[1188] (Morgan Stanley),[1189] (UBS),[1190] (Wells Fargo);[1191,1192]

New York Times (manipulating Libor interest rates);[1193]

Securities and Exchange Commission (SEC)[1194]

Wall Street banks that are repeat offenders may have your life savings

The nine biggest offenders shown in Figure 11-2 make up a Rogues' Gallery of lawlessness. In many cases, bank CEOs were never required to admit or deny guilt.

Instead, these nine banks eventually paid more than **$150 billion** in settlements. That's a lot, but not nearly enough to make people whole.

This listing is not meant to suggest that the settlement payments were sufficient punishments. Nor were the nine giant banks the only bad actors.

Let your eyes skim once again the violations in Figure 11-2. This only hints at the scale of ethical failures exhibited by "too big to jail" Wall Street CEOs. Are these the actions you really want from the people who are handling your nest egg?

» **Defrauding investors**

» **Securities law violations**

» **Abusive foreclosure practices**

» **Rigging currency exchange rates**

» **Deliberately misleading investors**

» **Manipulating interest rates**

No one should want any bank capable of such things anywhere near their life savings.

And yet millions of Americans have been persuaded to entrust **trillions** of their dollars to these same Wall Street giants.

Figure 11-3 shows that the nine banks in the laundry list of larceny are also some of America's largest wealth-management firms. These banks primarily serve households with a net worth over $8.3 million. Such families own almost one-third of America's total liquid invest-ment holdings, according to Federal Reserve figures.[1195]

When ranked by AUM (assets under management), the first five listed banks—Bank of America, Morgan Stanley, JPMorgan Chase, UBS, and Wells Fargo—are America's five largest wealth managers for high-net-worth individuals, according to *Barron's Penta*.[1196]

The four other banks—Goldman Sachs, Citigroup, Credit Suisse, and Deutsche—rank 8th or lower.

These nine Rogues' Gallery banks together control more than two-thirds of the **$7.1 trillion** of high-net-worth accounts in the hands of the country's top 40 wealth-management firms.

That's some impressively concentrated power. Perhaps this explains why these nine banks' CEOs felt comfortable running roughshod over ethics in pursuit of financial gain.

» **KEY CONCEPT**
the Rogues' Gallery
Nine giant Wall Street banks behaved unethically on a massive scale, leading to the 2008 global financial crisis and the Great Recession.

Rogues' Gallery banks control two-thirds of the wealth held by America's top 40 management firms

Sum of high-net-worth accounts over $5 million

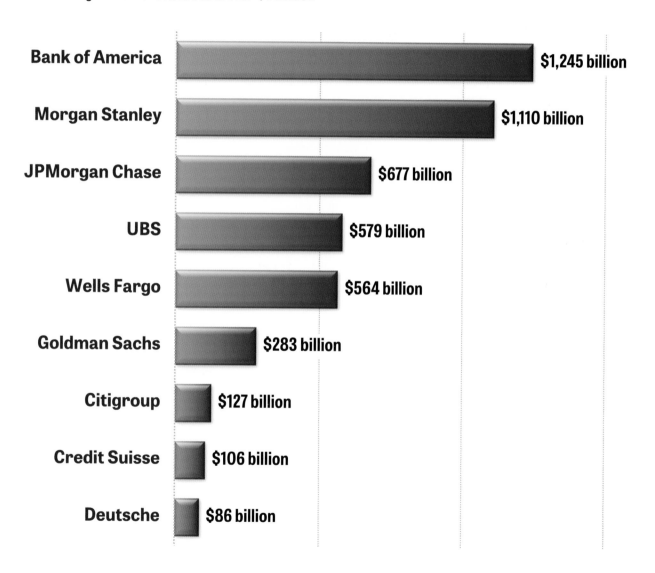

Bank of America — $1,245 billion

Morgan Stanley — $1,110 billion

JPMorgan Chase — $677 billion

UBS — $579 billion

Wells Fargo — $564 billion

Goldman Sachs — $283 billion

Citigroup — $127 billion

Credit Suisse — $106 billion

Deutsche — $86 billion

FIGURE 11-3
Source: *Barron's Penta.*[1197] All data 2017,[1198] except Credit Suisse/Deutsche, 2015[1199]

Forget outright fraud—the reliable old 'long con' is plenty profitable

Being ripped off by a pickpocket is an example of a "short con." The thief bumps into you and makes off with your wallet within mere seconds.

Pickpockets are pikers. Much larger amounts can be taken from you via the "long cons" played by Wall Street banks, making money off you by taking fees that seem small but add up to a big payday for your broker.

Figure 11-4 shows how a **full-service** firm can absorb more of your savings than you keep. This example is adapted from William Bernstein's 2010 book, *The Four Pillars of Investing, 2nd Ed.*[1200]

Let's say you receive an inheritance of $100,000. You seek out wealth managers. They explain that you can avoid paying individual commissions if you pay a yearly fee of 1% of your assets under management (AUM). This gets you a "full-service wrap account." The firm seems respectable, so you agree.

Your adviser puts your money into a typical 50% stock/50% bond mix. You could have done as much yourself, just by buying the two ETFs in the ultrasimple Baby Bear Portfolio. Assuming 3.25% inflation, that would have achieved a 6.55% annualized real return in 1973–2015, as shown in Chapter 1.

Instead, here comes the long con. The adviser doesn't use your money to buy shares of low-cost funds. To maximize its take, the firm puts your money in **house** funds—which it owns.

On top of the 1% wrap fee, these proprietary funds charge management fees of, say, 2% per year. Once your fees are booked, the firm enjoys the same 6.55% return you do—but it doesn't charge itself 3% in wrap and management fees.

The total fee percentage could be **worse** than 3%. As Bernstein notes, "it is not unusual to see accounts from which as much as 5% annually is extracted."[1201]

Extra expenses may include a one-time "front-end load fee" or "back-end redemption fee." Some mutual funds charge 3.0% to 8.5% for one fee or the other. Much of that money, of course, is kicked back to the adviser. (Figure 11-4 assumes a total bite of 3% annually, with no extra one-time fees.)

The firm's account started with $0 the day you walked in with $100,000. At Year 23, the firm's account holds $217,000 in today's dollars. But your account grew to only $214,000. At Year 30, the firm's account has **50% more money than you** ($401,800 vs. $269,000). How's **that** for full service!

Bernstein writes: "You are in fact locked in a financial life-and-death struggle with the investment industry; losing that battle puts you at increased risk of running short of assets far sooner than you'd like."[1202]

Don't assume that a fee of "only" 1% per year is trivial. **It isn't!** Paying 1% per year, plus other commissions and expenses, is a big deal. Over time, it picks your pocket.

The Department of Labor issued a "fiduciary rule" in 2016 to discourage excessive fees in retirement accounts. But—among other loopholes—firms that sell **only** their own house funds are exempt from the rule![1203]

It's far better to manage your money yourself and pay very low annual fees—or none at all.

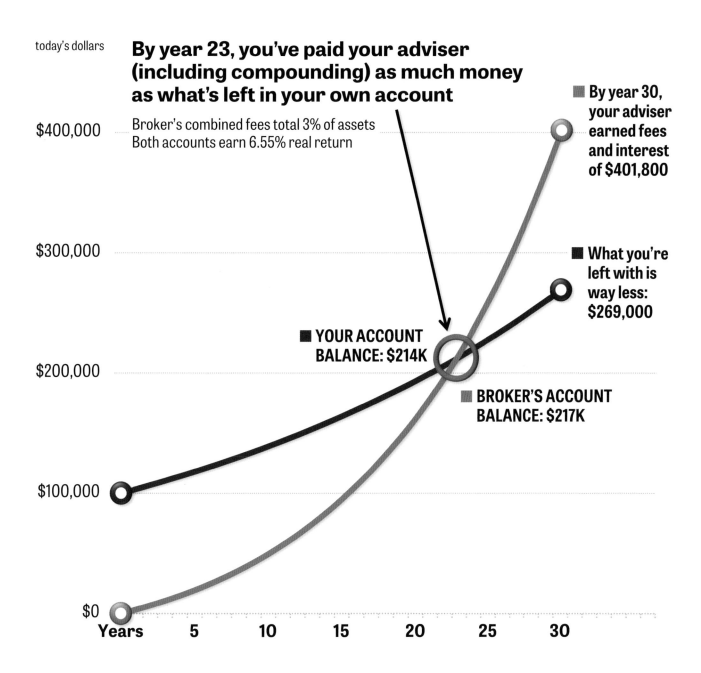

today's dollars

By year 23, you've paid your adviser (including compounding) as much money as what's left in your own account

Broker's combined fees total 3% of assets
Both accounts earn 6.55% real return

■ By year 30, your adviser earned fees and interest of $401,800

■ What you're left with is way less: $269,000

$400,000

$300,000

■ YOUR ACCOUNT BALANCE: $214K

$200,000

■ BROKER'S ACCOUNT BALANCE: $217K

$100,000

$0

Years   5   10   15   20   25   30

FIGURE 11-4 | Source: Author's calculations

The poster child for bad behavior is Goldman Sachs

Goldman Sachs is notorious for many reasons, among them its 2009 exposé by *Rolling Stone* national correspondent Matt Taibbi:

"The world's most powerful investment bank is a great vampire squid wrapped around the face of humanity, relentlessly jamming its blood funnel into anything that smells like money."[1204]

That kind of sensational language is terribly unfair to squids.

What did Goldman do that was so horrible?

» By 2006, Goldman underwrote more than $76 billion of mortgage-backed securities. One-third of that was made up of mortgages to subprime borrowers, many of whom clearly couldn't afford the payments. Goldman then shorted the securities, making profits when housing prices collapsed. One hedge-fund manager called this "the **heart** of securities fraud."[1205]

» The European debt crisis was set in motion by Goldman Sachs in 2001, when it constructed so-called currency swaps for Greece.

According to *Der Spiegel*, the securities used "fictional exchange rates."[1206] This enabled Greece to mislead European regulators as to its actual debt level. Since these "swaps" were highly likely to ultimately default, Goldman shorted them, too, as reported by Business Insider.[1207]

» Driving an entire US county to near-bankruptcy is a skill Goldman shares with other rogue banks. JPMorgan, Goldman, and others floated bonds for a Jefferson County, Alabama, sewage-treatment plant that swelled from estimates of $250 million to a price of $3 billion. Goldman profited until, at one point, JPMorgan paid it $3 million to stand aside.[1208] The former director of the Municipal Securities Rulemaking Board called this "an open-and-shut case of anti-competitive behavior."[1209] More than 20 local officials were convicted in federal court of inflating the plant's cost by taking millions in bribes.[1210] For making those payoffs, JPMorgan was forced by the SEC in 2009 to disgorge $722 million.[1211]

But you don't have to be a crooked European government or a corrupted county board to be taken advantage of by Goldman Sachs. All that's required is for you to give the firm any of your money at all:

» High fees on Goldman's proprietary mutual funds contributed to terrible performance for its clients from 2005 through 2014. Figure 11-5 shows that only 12% of Goldman's house funds beat their benchmarks, according to Morningstar.[1212] By contrast, 46% of similar funds from Vanguard outperformed, which is very good. It means you have about a 50/50 chance that Vanguard funds will deliver the returns you expect or better.

» Goldman steered customers' money into its own funds. The bank "typically put a majority of clients' cash and fixed-income investments into Goldman funds," according to the *New York Times*. Other banks were only slightly less aggressive. Until 2013, JPMorgan Chase steered about 42% of clients' money into its own funds, and Deutsche Bank about 34%.[1213]

Only 12% of Goldman Sachs's house funds outperformed their benchmarks during the past 10-year period

Vanguard funds achieved a respectable chance—nearly 50/50—of beating their benchmarks

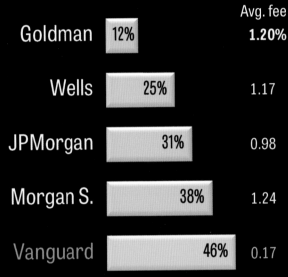

		Avg. fee
Goldman	12%	**1.20%**
Wells	25%	1.17
JPMorgan	31%	0.98
Morgan S.	38%	1.24
Vanguard	46%	0.17

FIGURE 11-5
Goldman Sachs Tower, Jersey City, NJ.
Statistics by Morningstar[1214]

Of course bankers wear nice clothes—you're picking up the tab

Considering that giant
Wall Street banks generally don't deliver better performance than a low-cost index ETF—and frequently deliver worse—why do people still entrust their life savings to these firms?

Goldman is even the butt of an old Wall Street joke:

Q. What's a good way to make $5 million in the stock market?

A. Start with $10 million at Goldman Sachs.

Alas, some people never learn. Goldman reported that it attracted $73 billion of new investor money in 2014. That boosted its wealth-management revenue 11% compared with 2013.[1215]

One explanation for people's trust in banks is the way their salespeople look.

Why do wealth managers dress like undertakers? If they're so successful, why can't financial advisers come to work in nice, comfortable polo shirts and khaki pants, like their rich clients?

Brokers wear Armani suits and silk dresses because people unconsciously obey suggestions made by anyone clothed like an authority figure.

Robert Cialdini illustrates this in *Influence: The Psychology of Persuasion*.[1216] Researchers hired a 31-year-old actor to repeatedly jaywalk across a street—against a DON'T WALK light—and found that bystanders' reactions varied depending on an interesting variable. As Cialdini explains:

"In half of the cases, he [the actor] was dressed in a freshly pressed business suit and tie; on the other occasions, he wore a work shirt and trousers. The researchers watched from a distance and counted the number of pedestrians waiting at the corner who followed the man across the street. Like the children of Hamlin who crowded after the Pied Piper, three and a half times as many people swept into traffic behind the suited jaywalker. In this case, though, the magic came not from his pipe but his pinstripes."

Three and a half times!
That's how much more likely you are to follow someone in an expensive suit. The fact that we're not conscious of this makes it all the more dangerous (Figure 11-6).

So, what should you do if your money is in the hands of a giant Wall Street bank?

Get your money out now. The most important step you can take to protect your wealth is to **disinvest**. Transfer your nest egg to a bargain brokerage (as described in Chapter 17). Use this book's model portfolios. You can manage your own money far better than any rogue bank ever will.

> **»KEY CONCEPT**
> ## disinvest now
> If your money is in the hands of any giant bank like Goldman Sachs, get it out today.

You're 3½ times more likely to follow someone in a business suit than a person in working clothes

FIGURE 11-6

The banking industry has powerful incentives to be unethical

From personal experience, we know that most retail bankers are very nice individuals. They're kind to children and pets. They're friendly to their neighbors. They greet you warmly when you visit to deposit your paycheck.

High finance, however, attracts plenty of people whose top priority is simply to become enormously wealthy as fast as possible. And at the top level of rogue Wall Street banks, the pressure for bankers to produce profits at any cost is enormous.

Perhaps unsurprisingly then, when asked to rank the personal integrity of those in various professions, the public rates wealth managers at the bottom—lower than even car salesmen and insurance dealers.[1217]

The industry as a whole fares just as badly. Jon Picoult, founder of Watermark Consulting, wrote in *Barron's* in 2015, "For the past five years, diversified financial companies [Wall Street banks] have ranked dead last in the Reputation Institute's annual consumer survey of industry reputations—scoring even lower than the widely despised cable companies."[1218]

In a study published by the journal *Nature*, 208 banking employees were asked to play a coin-flipping game. Each banker could win up to $200 if the coin tosses came out in their favor. The bankers recorded the results of the tosses themselves.

The researchers didn't watch. They couldn't tell who had recorded their results honestly. But because coins come up heads 50% of the time, they could rely on the averages over many tosses to give them the information.

Before the game, bankers in one group were asked to state their occupation. In that cohort, the researchers computed that 26% had cheated in recording their results. In the other group—players who **hadn't been reminded** that they were bankers—virtually no cheating was detected.

The researchers repeated this experiment with employees in other lines of work. Asking about their occupation beforehand made **no difference** in whether a significant number of people cheated.

As Alain Cohn, one of the researchers, told the *New York Times*, "bankers behave dishonestly only when they feel that it is expected of them."[1219] The study's summary notes, "bank employees who participated in the study work in a business culture that tends to tolerate or promote dishonest behavior."[1220]

If you've fallen prey to a smooth-talking financial adviser, don't feel alone. Even Kevin Noblet, a wealth-management editor at the *Wall Street Journal*, wasn't immune:

"So we signed on. And the trouble started right away. . . . Management fees for several of the funds my adviser used were high. Some exceeded 2% a year. How much in net gains would be left for me after a fund manager got his 2% and my adviser, his 1%?"[1221]

Noblet left his adviser after only nine months. He got off easy. Some clients never catch on.

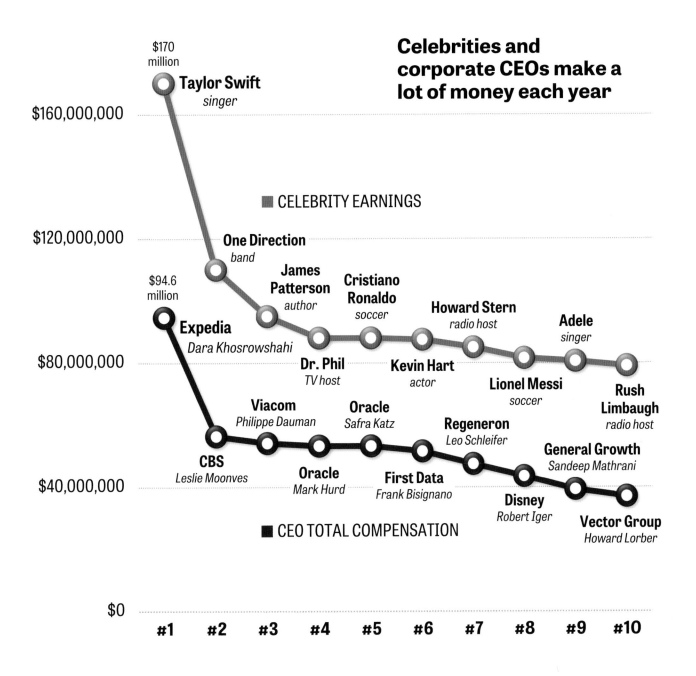

Celebrities and corporate CEOs make a lot of money each year

$170 million — Taylor Swift *singer*

$160,000,000

■ CELEBRITY EARNINGS

One Direction *band*

$120,000,000

James Patterson *author*

Cristiano Ronaldo *soccer*

Howard Stern *radio host*

Adele *singer*

$94.6 million

Expedia *Dara Khosrowshahi*

Dr. Phil *TV host*

Kevin Hart *actor*

Lionel Messi *soccer*

Rush Limbaugh *radio host*

$80,000,000

Viacom *Philippe Dauman*

Oracle *Safra Katz*

Regeneron *Leo Schleifer*

General Growth *Sandeep Mathrani*

CBS *Leslie Moonves*

Oracle *Mark Hurd*

First Data *Frank Bisignano*

Disney *Robert Iger*

Vector Group *Howard Lorber*

$40,000,000

■ CEO TOTAL COMPENSATION

$0

#1   #2   #3   #4   #5   #6   #7   #8   #9   #10

FIGURE 11-7
Sources: Equilar (CEO compensation, 2015),[1222] Forbes (celebrities, July 13, 2016)[1223]

Hedge-fund managers have the biggest incentives of all

The financial lure of wealth management is enormous. Figures 11-7 and 11-8 show what the biggest celebrities and corporate CEOs take home, compared with the financial services elite: the managers of giant hedge funds.

The best-paid corporate chief executive in a 2015 survey by Equilar was Expedia's CEO, Dara Khosrowshahi, who made a cool $94.6 million in total compensation.

Singing for your supper pays off even better. That same year, Taylor Swift made $170 million, according to *Forbes*.

But those numbers are only **one-tenth** what the top hedge-fund managers make.

Tied for first place with an almost inconceivable **$1.7 billion** annual income were Ken Griffin of Citadel LLC and James Simons of Renaissance Technologies.

Even the 10th-highest hedge-fund manager raked in more than the poor, impoverished pop star Taylor Swift, with her $170 million.

Hedge-fund managers also pay a lower rate of tax than mere celebrities and CEOs. Some manager income counts as "carried interest," for which the highest tax bracket is only 20% rather than the 37% for regular income.[1224]

Now, pretend you're a college student working toward a degree in business. Look at all those dollars! You can imagine young people—at least those whose fantasies include becoming billionaires—being attracted to a career working for a giant Wall Street bank. Especially if, as is so often the case these days, those students graduate with crushing student-loan debt.

Hedge-fund managers generate their huge payday by spreading the myth that they generate superior returns. They then charge gullible affluent people a 2% annual fee on assets under management **plus** 20% of any gains. Some funds charge less, others charge more, but "2-and-20" is pretty common.

Unfortunately, most investors don't realize how much 2-and-20 really costs them. As financial columnist Brett Arends points out:

"If the average investment portfolio earns 6% a year, your hedge fund manager has to earn 9.5% before fees before you even break even. In other words, the manager has to beat the market by about 60% per year. Good luck with that."[1225]

If you also subtract trading costs and taxes, hedge-fund accounts are even worse. Mark Kritzman, CFA, calculates that a hedge fund with a 19% **gross** annualized return would leave you with less **net** gain than an index fund with a 10% gross return.[1226]

Here's the joke—hedgies don't deliver 10%. Actual hedge-fund investors earned a dollar-weighted return of only 6% from 1980 through 2008. That was "barely above the 5.6 percent risk-free rate" of Treasury bills, according to the *Journal of Financial Economics*.[1227]

Luckily, the hedge-fund myth is dying. New tools and low-cost ETFs make it easier than ever to manage your own money, and informed investors are reclaiming control of their savings.

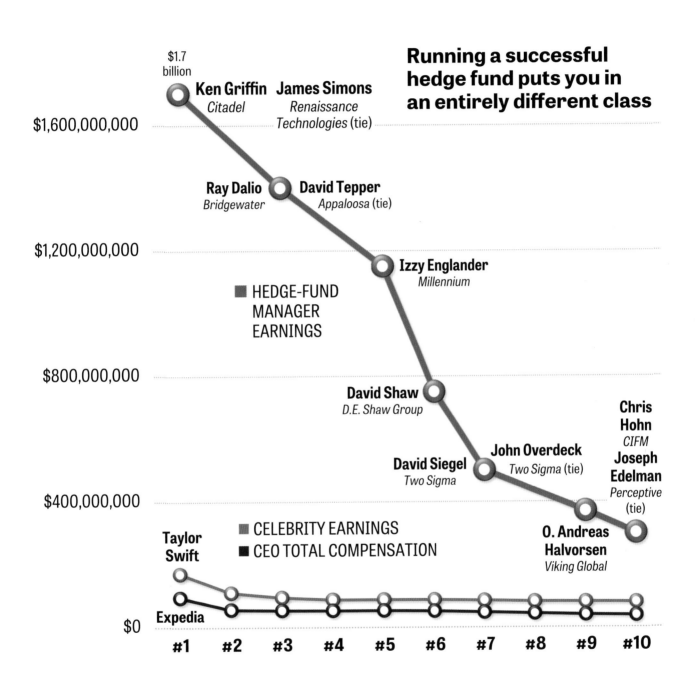

$1.7 billion

Ken Griffin
Citadel

James Simons
Renaissance Technologies (tie)

Running a successful hedge fund puts you in an entirely different class

$1,600,000,000

Ray Dalio
Bridgewater

David Tepper
Appaloosa (tie)

$1,200,000,000

Izzy Englander
Millennium

■ HEDGE-FUND MANAGER EARNINGS

$800,000,000

David Shaw
D.E. Shaw Group

Chris Hohn
CIFM

Joseph Edelman
Perceptive (tie)

John Overdeck
Two Sigma (tie)

David Siegel
Two Sigma

$400,000,000

■ CELEBRITY EARNINGS
■ CEO TOTAL COMPENSATION

Taylor Swift

O. Andreas Halvorsen
Viking Global

Expedia

$0

#1   #2   #3   #4   #5   #6   #7   #8   #9   #10

FIGURE 11-8
Source: Institutional Investor (hedge-fund manager earnings, May 10, 2016).[1228]
Hat-tip to Catherine Mulbrandon[1229]

If a crooked broker takes your money, don't count on getting it back

We've looked at the "long cons" of house funds, hedge funds, and fees that eat up your gains over time. But what if you're victimized by a "quick grab"—an outright looting of your account? Some unscrupulous brokers don't wait for fees to build up, preferring more direct forms of thievery.

Let's be clear. If you lost money just because the stock market went down, no one will give it back. You accept fluctuation—and risk—every time you invest.

But if you lost money because a broker steered your funds into his cousin's risky real-estate deal—or simply diverted a big chunk of your funds into his personal account—you **may** be able to get it back.

To recover money, you'll probably be forced to use binding arbitration. The agreement you sign with a broker prohibits you from suing as an individual. Nor can you usually join a class-action lawsuit—often the only way to win large judgments involving many victims.

Most arbitrations are run by Finra (the Financial Industry Regulatory Authority), a "self-regulatory" group run by banks and brokerage firms and overseen by the SEC.

The system isn't known for being consumer friendly. As William D. Cohen wrote in a 2016 article for the *New York Times*:[1230]

"Some 92 percent of the cases involving employee disputes and some 80 percent of the cases involving customer disputes are decided in favor of Wall Street banks. It just would not do for a Wall Street–controlled organization to be handing down rulings adverse to Wall Street's interests."

Even if the facts are with you, arbitration won't be speedy. The average case takes 14.8 months. The wait is more than 18 months if Finra's "Simplified Arbitration" panels (which deal with claims under $50,000) are excluded.[1231]

Arbitration also isn't cheap. Legal charges and filing fees can run into tens of thousands of dollars. What's more, arbitrators can rule that the losing party must pay the winning party's legal expenses.[1232]

You should always consult an attorney who specializes in this area before filing for arbitration. If your case is too weak to pursue, good legal counsel may help you recover some money anyway by negotiating a settlement with a broker without a formal hearing (Figure 11-9).

> **» KEY CONCEPT**
> ## arbitration is a long shot against fraud
> If you've been cheated by truly outrageous behavior, arbitration is a difficult process— but it can, in some cases, lead to a recovery.

An attorney who specializes in arbitration may help you recover from a financial scam

FIGURE 11-9

When a fraud is truly brazen, even Wall Street arbitrators sometimes recoil

Patricia Vannoy, a partner with Mattson Ricketts in Lincoln, Nebraska, and David Gaba, principal of Compass Law Group in Seattle, Washington, are two attorneys in this field. They've worked together on many successful complaints, like the following:

» LPL Financial held liable for broker. Ranked by 2015 revenue, LPL is the largest chain of independent broker/dealers in the US, employing more than 14,000 representatives.[1233]

In a signed plea bargain, a North Carolina rep agreed that he'd raised $1.4 million from 20 or so people, promising to protect their nest eggs in "safe investments."

The district's US Attorney proved that more than half of the money was, in reality, spent by the broker or used to make small "interest" payments to suspicious investors who wanted to see the promised 5% to 7% returns.[1234]

As a result, one 81-year-old widow represented by Vannoy and Gaba won more than $78,000 in restitution and penalties.

The broker was sentenced to jail time.[1235]

LPL, which had employed the rep, paid the restitution—but only after arguing that the claimant should "recover nothing."[1236]

» Citigroup forced to pay $137,000. One family filed for Finra arbitration after Citigroup Global Markets of New York City led the family's accounts to borrow money and trade risky options, causing $103,000 in losses. The arbitrator made the bank reimburse the claimants $82,400 (80% of the loss, on the theory that the family was 20% responsible) plus $54,933 for their legal costs.[1237]

» Schwab made to pay $95,000. A client reported that $63,925 had been unjustly transferred out of her 401(k) account. The arbitrator ordered Charles Schwab & Co. to pay the money back with 8% interest, plus $31,225 for her legal costs. The arbitrator also rejected a request to erase the award from the Schwab broker's record.[1238]

» TD Ameritrade ordered to pay $541,000. In another case of a broker borrowing money to trade options, $486,000 was granted to the appointee of her deceased father's trust, plus 8% interest and $62,958 for her legal costs. TD Ameri-trade was found to have "fostered" its broker's "negligence." The arbitrator refused to erase the case from the record.[1239]

Unfortunately, it's not just brokerage firms you need to watch out for. Your own employer may be charging high fees on the money in your retirement account.

One attorney, Jerome Schlichter, has extracted more than $300 million in class-action lawsuits against Boeing, Lockheed Martin, Caterpillar, and other large employers. Court rulings and voluntary settlements showed that these employers collectively overcharged their employees millions of dollars on 401(k) accounts.[1240]

> **» KEY CONCEPT**
> ## manage your own money
> No one will ever care as much about your savings as you do.

Despite the above successes, don't get optimistic about legal actions against a rogue Wall Street bank or an untrustworthy broker.

To avoid watching your nest egg shrivel—or having it stolen out from under you—your best bet is always to manage your own funds.

One journalist, John Rothchild, went undercover in the 1980s to investigate the training of new brokers at Prudential-Bache and Merrill Lynch—two of the largest brokerage firms at the time.

In his 1988 book, *A Fool and His Money*, he reported that most newly minted advisers had no financial expertise at all. Instead, they'd been selected for their skills in selling anything to anybody:

"There was a 250-pound ex–football player who used to sell insurance. There were a few ex–car dealers (one, Paul from Wichita, said that investments were just 'another vehicle'), a computer salesman or two, a rancher, a ballet dancer, a man who'd burned out on wheat futures, a 'syndicator' with nothing left to syndicate, plus some former schoolteachers."[1241]

The two building blocks on which informed investors make real money are:

1 · **Lower expenses to almost nothing.** This way, you'll keep 99% of your growth for yourself. (It's acceptable, of course, to pay reasonable fees that are a fraction of 1%.)

2 · **Reduce losses during bear-market crashes.** You'll retain almost all your gains and watch your savings grow over your entire lifetime.

"Being rich" means **you have enough money to buy everything you need, and you aren't afraid of losing it.**

By this definition, there are a lot of millionaires who aren't rich.

They are terrified of "wealth manager" ethics, or the way even an otherwise honest adviser might mismanage their money in a crash. They fear intolerable losses. They never really feel secure that their wealth will last.

You don't need to have those fears. Given the Index Investing Revolution and a few simple rules, you can manage your own wealth—no matter how large or small it may be—and enjoy your life instead of worrying about your money.

LIVINGSTON'S LAW OF CAVEAT EMPTOR
Beware of those in fancy clothes:
They charge high fees for things everyone knows.

12 There are no experts who can predict the future

"This is far and away the strongest global economy I've seen in my business lifetime."[1242]

HENRY PAULSON, US treasury secretary, July 2007, four months before the Great Recession began[1243]

Imagine you've assembled 1,000 of your best friends. They're milling about on an otherwise unused basketball court. You ask each person to flip a coin 10 times and keep track of how many times it comes up heads. Totally by chance, two of your 1,000 friends would likely see heads 10 times in a row.

Those two people would consider themselves lucky. But on Wall Street, when a fund manager beats the market five or 10 years in a row, he or she is treated like a genius. Camera crews descend on the lucky manager, seeking a victory speech and clamoring to hear about the brilliant strategy that made it possible.

Let's look for a minute at just one example:

Only two mutual funds came up heads five times in a row

Researchers for S&P Dow Jones Indices analyzed all 2,862 actively managed US stock mutual funds with at least a 12-month track record as of March 2010. The researchers then selected just the funds that had been in the top one-fourth of performance that year— 715 funds in all.[1244]

How many of these funds do you think **stayed** in the top one-fourth every year for four more years? **Just two.** That's only 0.28% of the original 715 first-year outperformers. This is illustrated in Figure 12-1.

It's quite likely two mutual funds out of 2,862 might stay in the top one-fourth of performance for five years in a row, just by random chance. Finding two such funds was simply the luck of the draw.

The S&P report didn't name the two lucky mutual funds, but the *New York Times* discovered they were Hodges Small Cap and AMG Southern-Sun Small Cap.[1245]

Sure enough, media like Yahoo Finance interviewed the managers of these two funds as though the study had demonstrated skill rather than luck. "In order to make big returns," Yahoo's article breathlessly assured its readers, "Hodges looks for businesses with large barriers to entry."[1246]

Out of 715 funds in the top quarter in 2010, only two stayed there five years— and they didn't last, either

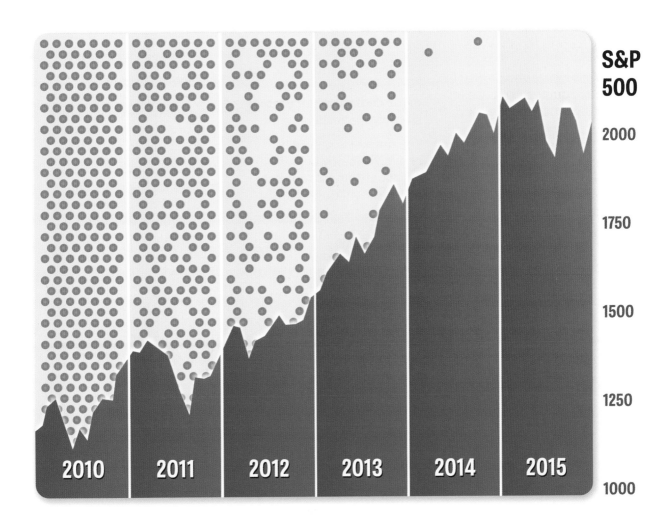

FIGURE 12-1 | Source: S&P Dow Jones Indices.[1247] Illustration by Pieter Tandjung

Next year's performance cannot be predicted, because no one is psychic

You might wonder whether those two mutual funds in Figure 12-1 repeated their top-quarter status the following year. Nope! They both sank into the **bottom half** of the rankings, according to the *Times*. You can't keep flipping heads forever.[1248]

There is little or no persistence of outperformance in the stock market among professional managers—or anyone else.

What are the chances that the most recent five-year performance of market-beating mutual funds will repeat in the following four years? Take the test in Figure 12-2.

Whether some funds do better than others is the result of random events. It's impossible to predict such things.

The market is moved by news. News—by definition—is whatever was **not** predicted.

Despite the fact that the S&P study shows mutual-fund outperformance usually does not persist, many investors continue to believe that someone, somewhere, can predict the future.

Figure 12-3 shows how poorly Wall Street's largest players can predict how much the S&P 500 will rise or fall in the coming 12 months.

As Bloomberg journalist Lu Wang reported in November 2017: "Data compiled by Bloomberg show that since 1999, Wall Street prognosticators have never once predicted a down year, putting the average annual [estimated] gain at 9 percent."[1249]

As Figure 12-3 reveals, the average Wall Street strategist's annual forecast was often way off—10 to 50 percentage points. That's **very** unreliable!

Market watcher Morgan Housel contrasts the strategists against the "Blind Forecaster." That mythical guru predicts every year that the index will rise 9%. The Blind Forecaster's formula achieved a closer fit to the actual S&P 500 gain than the average strategist's. You don't need high-priced advisers![1250]

FIGURE 12-2

Test your knowledge of persistence

Two mutual funds out of 2,862 were in the top one-fourth of performance for five 12-month periods in a row. What is the likelihood that the same two funds will remain in the top one-fourth for each of the next four years?

- ☐ **A** · There is a 25% chance.
- ☐ **B** · There is more than a 25% chance.
- ☐ **C** · There is less than a 25% chance.
- ☐ **D** · There is a 0.1% chance.
- ☐ **E** · It cannot be determined.

Your safest bet is "E." We have **no way** to determine whether any fund will be a top performer in the next four years.

» KEY CONCEPT
the future cannot be predicted
Don't bother acting on experts' guesses.

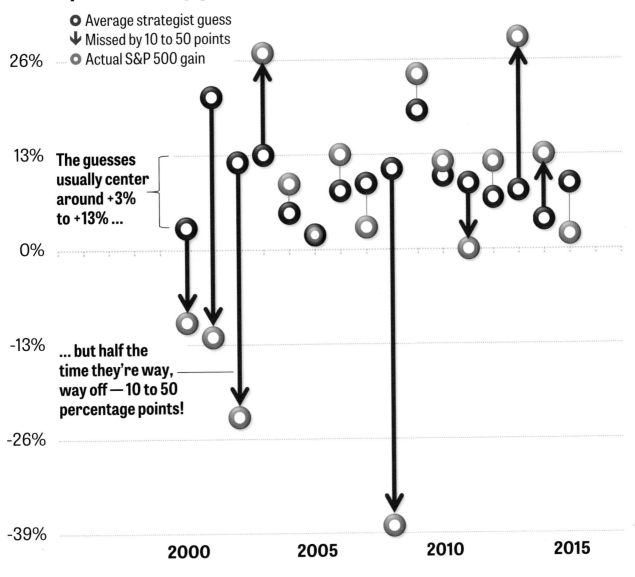

Wall Street bank strategists always predict an up year for the S&P 500

- ⊙ Average strategist guess
- ↓ Missed by 10 to 50 points
- ⊙ Actual S&P 500 gain

26%

13%

The guesses usually center around +3% to +13% ...

0%

... but half the time they're way, way off — 10 to 50 percentage points!

-13%

-26%

-39%

2000   2005   2010   2015

FIGURE 12-3 | Source: Birinyi Associates[1251]

Investors waste a lot of time in an endless search for Mr. Right

Birinyi Associates, a respected research and money-management firm, continuously tracks the one-year forecasts from 18 different financial institutions. These predictions are issued by some of the world's largest banks, including Bank of America, Citigroup, Deutsche Bank, Goldman Sachs, UBS, and others.[1252]

These giants, of course, can afford to hire the very best analysts, economists, and strategists. But, as we saw in Figure 12-3, their collective predictions about the S&P 500 are consistently wrong.

To attract client money, these big firms constantly tout the quality of their expertise. But their predictions are worthless, unable to alert you when a major market move is coming—even to warn you of a bear market that's already underway.

By the strategists' consensus, an up market was predicted for 2000. (Wall Street calls it a "consensus" to make it sound more impressive, but it's actually just an average.) As we know now, of course, 2000 was the first year of the dot-com crash.

The collapse of the Internet mania was obvious to everyone by the end of 2000, but the predictions the experts made for the following years—2001 and 2002—were even **worse.**

Every prediction was a "happy face." Every expert delivered the same sunny "buy stocks now" optimism—after all, that's what encourages people to hand over their money.

Analysts beamed forth this same garbage in 2000, 2001, and 2002. Experts predicted gains of 5%, 10%, or 20% in each of three dot-com crash years that destroyed investors' savings.[1253]

In reality, the S&P 500 dived even harder in 2001 and 2002 than it had in 2000.

These crushing failures apparently didn't teach anyone anything.

Expert predictions aren't much better when a bull market is underway. The strategists projected a gain of less than 10% for the S&P 500 as recently as 2013—a year in which the index actually rose 30%.

» KEY CONCEPT
no one has a crystal ball
Experts project the market with enormous confidence, but even the most expensive advisers can't predict the coming year.

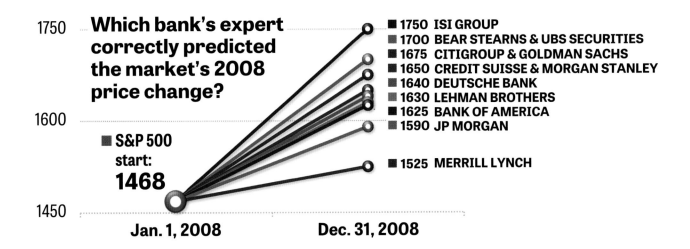

Which bank's expert correctly predicted the market's 2008 price change?

1750

1600

■ S&P 500
start:
1468

1450

Jan. 1, 2008　　　**Dec. 31, 2008**

■ 1750 **ISI GROUP**
■ 1700 **BEAR STEARNS & UBS SECURITIES**
■ 1675 **CITIGROUP & GOLDMAN SACHS**
■ 1650 **CREDIT SUISSE & MORGAN STANLEY**
■ 1640 **DEUTSCHE BANK**
■ 1630 **LEHMAN BROTHERS**
■ 1625 **BANK OF AMERICA**
■ 1590 **JP MORGAN**

■ 1525 **MERRILL LYNCH**

FIGURE 12-4 | Source: *Barron's*

There must be at least <u>one</u> expert who can predict next year's return

At this point, you may be thinking, "Those figures are just an average. Hidden within all that data, surely we must be able to find **one** true expert!"

At the end of December 2007, experts from 12 top financial institutions

predicted what the price of the S&P 500 would be at the end of 2008.

By late 2007, as you recall, America's Great Recession had already begun,[1254] the housing bubble had started to deflate, and two big mortgage-wracked hedge funds within Bear Stearns had collapsed.[1255]

Those were pretty good clues to the year to come, you'd think.

Figure 12-4 shows the predictions. Which expert correctly forecast what the S&P 500's price level would be one year later?

None of these superbanks guessed the S&P 500 would fall even one point

Figure 12-5 shows the experts' guesses along with the S&P 500's actual, horrendous 38.5% loss.

Not **one** of these experts predicted that the S&P 500 would fall even a single point!

The median prediction for 2008—made months, you recall, **after** the US housing bubble had started to burst—called for the S&P 500 to rise more than 10%.

An even more optimistic projection of an **11% gain** was made by the expert from Lehman Brothers. So much for insider knowledge!

An even more optimistic project or an 11% gain from Lehman Brothers.

In fact, the worst financial crisis since the Great Depression pushed the index down almost 40% in 2008. The experts missed the mark by nearly 50 percentage points.

Let's say there actually were a few superhero time travelers somewhere who genuinely could predict the market. Such near-magical powers would make these people extremely valuable. They'd be well paid by their deep-pocketed financial sponsors, who would ensure they stayed out of the limelight.

You wouldn't find these seers giving away their knowledge on a magazine panel, a blog, or a television program. Anyone who knows doesn't say, and anyone who says doesn't know.

Next Saturday morning, try the following experiment:

1 · Watch 30 minutes of cartoons on TV.

2 · Read the market commentary in the weekend edition of any newspaper or investing blog.

Both experiences will reveal exactly the same thing about what the market will do on Monday—**nothing!**

Tomorrow's market and next year's market cannot be predicted. Experts who exude confidence are just winging it. Hooray! You no longer have any need to shell out fat fees for predictions. Think of all the money you'll save!

Just remember that you're not psychic, either. We'll see in Chapters 14, 15, and 16 how you can defeat any belief you might harbor about having miraculous powers. That's the only mental change you need to run your portfolio in a sensible way.

LIVINGSTON'S LAW OF PSYCHIC ABILITIES

If you think the pros have a crystal ball,
You're all set up to take a fall.

» KEY CONCEPT

they're just guessing

Brokers work like palm readers and fortune-tellers: they tell you what you want to hear.

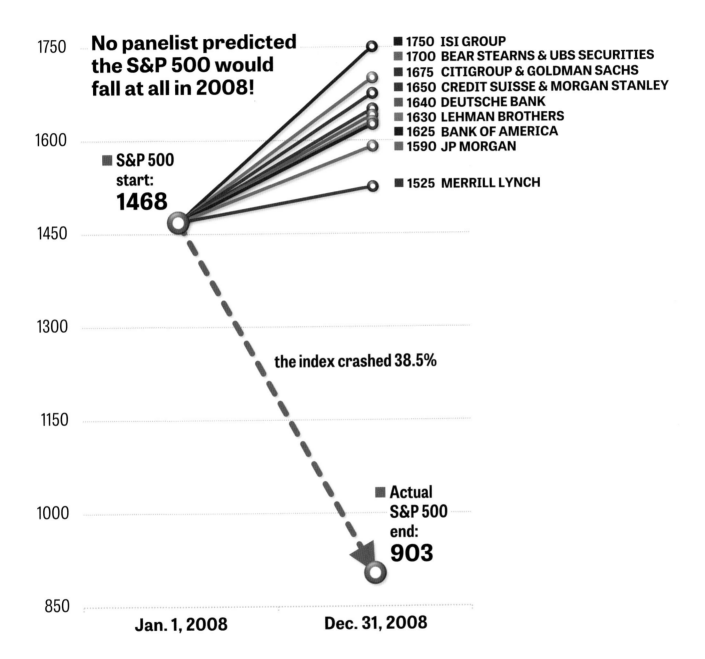

No panelist predicted the S&P 500 would fall at all in 2008!

- ■ 1750 ISI GROUP
- ■ 1700 BEAR STEARNS & UBS SECURITIES
- ■ 1675 CITIGROUP & GOLDMAN SACHS
- ■ 1650 CREDIT SUISSE & MORGAN STANLEY
- ■ 1640 DEUTSCHE BANK
- ■ 1630 LEHMAN BROTHERS
- ■ 1625 BANK OF AMERICA
- ■ 1590 JP MORGAN
- ■ 1525 MERRILL LYNCH

■ S&P 500 start: **1468**

the index crashed 38.5%

■ Actual S&P 500 end: **903**

Jan. 1, 2008

Dec. 31, 2008

FIGURE 12-5 | Source: *Barron's*

13 The 10-year projection exception: Bogle, Buffett, Shiller, *et al.*

"Individual investors only care about three periods of time: the last 30 years, today, and the next 30 years."

WALL STREET SAYING

As if in a dream, one lucky man succeeded in talking directly with God. "Lord," he asked, "what is a million years like to you?" In a deep, booming voice, God answered, "A million years to **you** is like a minute to **me**." The man continued, "Lord, what is a million dollars like to you?" "A million dollars to **you** is like a penny to **me**."

"Well," the man asked, his mortal desires coming to the fore, "can you give me a million dollars?"

"Sure!" God replied. "Can you wait a minute?"[1256]

Nothing good about investing happens fast. Investing is not about sudden gushers of money. It's a long game: a marathon, not a sprint.

Properly done—to paraphrase Nobel laureate Paul Samuelson—investing should be about as exciting as watching grass grow.[1257] The difference is that you're watching your **money** grow. That should be plenty of excitement!

But individual investors are impatient. It's hard to accept that the most useful information about the market isn't concerned with "now"; instead it involves long stretches of time.

Say you're retired, and you want your money to last 30 years. Surprisingly, the first 15 years are key to determining how much you can safely take from your nest egg each year.

As financial planner Michael Kitces explains, "the safe withdrawal rate for a 30-year retirement period has shown a whopping 0.91 correlation" with your rate of return over the first 15 years.[1258]

(See Chapter 22 on how to determine your own safe withdrawal rate.)

Figure 13-1 illustrates why the first decde or so is important.

Mr. Red retired at the beginning of 1972. He withdrew 5% yearly, adjusted for inflation, from a $1 million account.

Because the first 12 years, 1972 through 1983, had poor returns, Mr. Red's balance was depleted in 24 years. The strong second 12 years, from 1984 to 1995, came too late.

Ms. Blue retired at the beginning of 1984. She withdrew 5% yearly, adjusted for inflation, but started off with those strong returns in 1984 through 1995.

The graph simply flips the 12-year periods. Ms. Blue got the poor 1972 through 1983 returns second, when the weakness no longer bankrupted her.

Both retirees experienced the same two 12-year periods, but reversed. The first 12 years being bad or good made all the difference.

We estimate the market's return over the next 10 to 15 years so we know what we're facing.

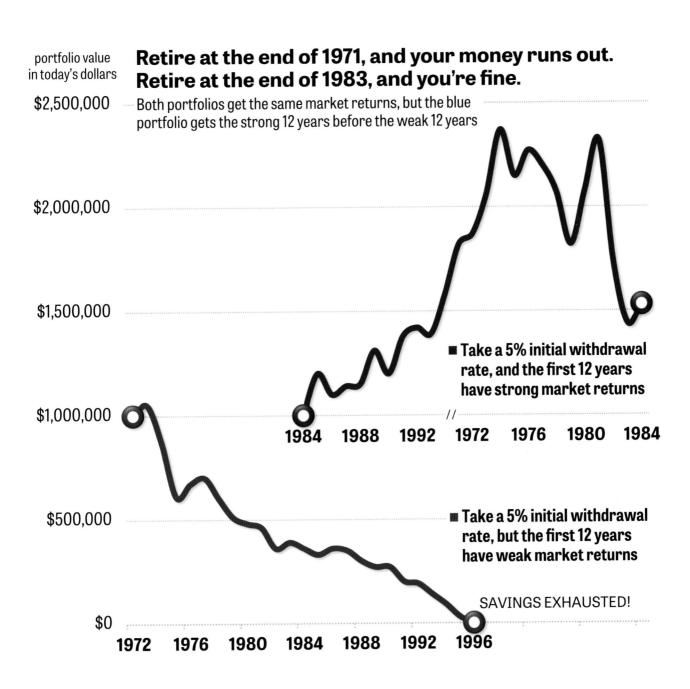

portfolio value in today's dollars

**Retire at the end of 1971, and your money runs out.
Retire at the end of 1983, and you're fine.**

Both portfolios get the same market returns, but the blue portfolio gets the strong 12 years before the weak 12 years

$2,500,000

$2,000,000

$1,500,000

$1,000,000

$500,000

$0

1984   1988   1992   1972   1976   1980   1984

■ Take a 5% initial withdrawal rate, and the first 12 years have strong market returns

■ Take a 5% initial withdrawal rate, but the first 12 years have weak market returns

SAVINGS EXHAUSTED!

1972   1976   1980   1984   1988   1992   1996

FIGURE 13-1 | Adapted from Blanchett, Finke, Pfau/Morningstar[1259]

Bogle's 10-year projections are fairly accurate, and he expects weak returns

You can't delay your life goals 15 years, hoping that you'll catch the first day of a bull market when you quit your job.

The examples we saw in Figure 13-1 show that, if you start your withdrawals at the beginning of a "bummer generation," stocks alone won't support you.

No expert can tell what will happen to stock prices one year in the future. But the market's expected return over the next 7 to 15 years **can** be roughly projected.

To get a long-term view, statisticians calculate how much the equity market is overpriced or underpriced. If stocks are bargains today, the return over the next decade should be good. But if stocks are richly priced, the expected return is low.

Figure 13-2 shows Vanguard founder Jack Bogle's formula for projecting the S&P 500's 10-year return. Called the Bogle Sources of Return Model (BSRM), it was first published in 1991 in the prestigious *Journal of Portfolio Management* (JPM).[1260]

After 25 years of actual returns, Bogle crowed about this model's accuracy in a 2015 JPM follow-up article with Michael Nolan Jr.[1261]

The predictions aren't precise enough to time the market. But the model is still impressive in helping you foresee a disappointing decade.

For buy-and-hold investors, Bogle's model predicts nearly the lowest S&P 500 return for any 10-year period in history.

"You're talking about a 4% nominal return on stocks," he told CNBC in a March 2017 interview.[1262]

Since nominal returns are not adjusted for inflation, that might mean real returns of only 1% or 2%. To get good results in **every** decade, you need asset-class choices other than just equities and bonds.

» TECH TALK

the stock market is not entirely random

The S&P 500's return over the next 10 years can be fairly accurately projected by Bogle and other statisticians. That's because the index is not perfectly random but wildly chaotic. What's the difference? There are three kinds of predictability:

» **Predictably random systems** include coin tosses:

a · It's impossible to predict the next toss, **but**

b · Multiple tosses will always approach a 50/50 outcome.

» **Predictably chaotic systems** include climate patterns:

a · Weather forecasters are 99% right about tomorrow's temperature, **but**

b · Their ten-day forecasts are worse than if you just consult an almanac.

» **Wildly chaotic systems** include stock markets:

a · It's impossible to predict tomorrow's prices, **but**

b · Next month's prices **are** slightly predictable using the momentum factor.

c · It's impossible to predict next year's return, **but**

d · The long-term return (7–15 years) **can** be estimated.

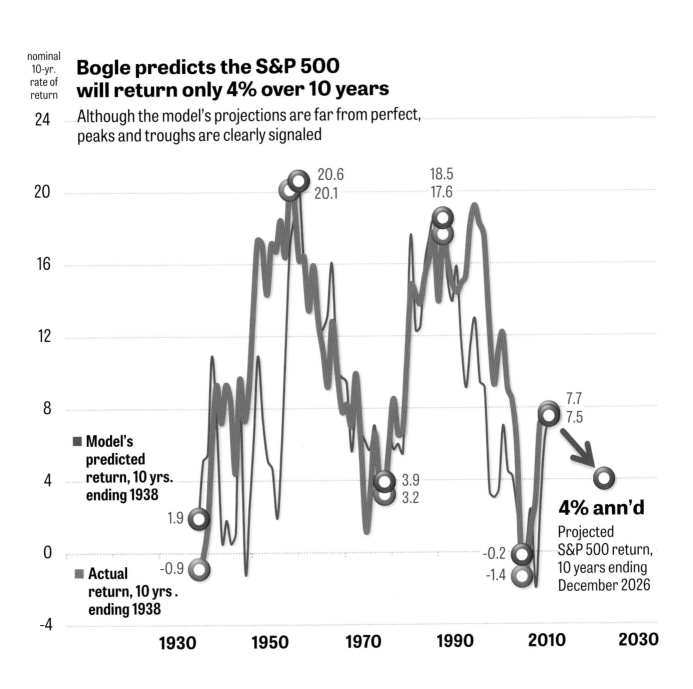

nominal
10-yr.
rate of
return

Bogle predicts the S&P 500 will return only 4% over 10 years

Although the model's projections are far from perfect, peaks and troughs are clearly signaled

24

20   20.6
     20.1

        18.5
        17.6

16

12

8   7.7
                                     7.5

■ Model's
  predicted
  return, 10 yrs.
  ending 1938   3.9   **4% ann'd**
4   3.2   Projected
  1.9   S&P 500 return,
                                  10 years ending
                                  December 2026
0   -0.2
  -0.9   -1.4
■ Actual
  return, 10 yrs.
  ending 1938

-4

1930   1950   1970   1990   2010   2030

FIGURE 13-2 | Source: "Occam's Razor Redux," Bogle & Nolan (2015)[1263]

Multiple formulas say US equities will be flat or down in the next decade

Experts like Warren Buffett and Robert Shiller estimate that the S&P 500 will deliver even weaker returns in the coming decade than Bogle projects. Four different forecasting methods are shown in Figure 13-3. Since 1954, each method has predicted the level of the S&P 500 a decade later relatively closely.

The four methods were calculated as of February 2018 by Stephen Jones, a New York–based financial and economic analyst.[1264] His estimates for real annualized returns are:

» **Shiller: +0.1% ann'd return**

Robert Shiller, a 2013 winner of the Nobel Prize in Economics, developed the Cyclically Adjusted Price/Earnings (CAPE) ratio.[1265] First, you adjust the past 10 years of corporate earnings for inflation. Second, you divide that by today's share prices. Economists constantly debate variations of this metric (also called P/E10).[1266]

» **Tobin: minus 0.7%**

The "Tobin's q" formula divides the market value of all US equities by the replacement cost of all the companies' assets.[1267] It was published by James Tobin and William Brainard in a 1976 paper.[1268]

» **Buffett: minus 5.3%**

Buffett didn't invent this formula, but he says it's "probably the best single measure of where valuations stand."[1269] Simply divide the S&P 500's market value by the US GDP. What you get is called MV/GDP.

» **Jones: minus 5.5%**

Jones believes America's aging workforce and 10-year GDP growth estimates must be taken into account. In a variation of Buffett's MV/GDP, Jones calculates a metric called the Demographically and Market-Adjusted (DAMA) Composite.

As shown in Figure 13-3, it's clear that DAMA has most closely predicted the S&P 500's return over the next 10 years.

What if the S&P 500's actual return comes in somewhere **between** these four forecasts? Say, a slightly negative real return over 10 years? To unfortunate buy-and-hold investors, that would be about as exciting as cold pizza and warm beer!

Don't try to use these projections to time the market. Even if we knew **for sure** that the market would fall at Jones's minus 5.5% rate, it wouldn't do so in a straight line.

The S&P 500's real total return could be:

» **1% ann'd** for five years;

» **Minus 11.58% ann'd** for another five.

That "bull market first, bear market second" scenario would produce a 10-year return of exactly the minus 5.5% projected by Jones.

Declines of 11.58% ann'd for five years would hand you a 46% drawdown, adjusted for inflation. Sound impossible? As we saw in Figure 1-7 in Chapter 1, the S&P 500 lost 56% in real dollars in just 17 months (2007–2009). Worse could happen.

» **KEY CONCEPT**

the S&P 500 won't give you much over the next decade

The stock market is expected to move sideways or down over the next 10 years. Make sure asset classes other than stocks are in your portfolio menu.

The S&P 500's real total return for the 10 years ending Feb. 2028 is projected to be +0.1% to −5.5%

You'll need asset classes other than stocks to make good gains

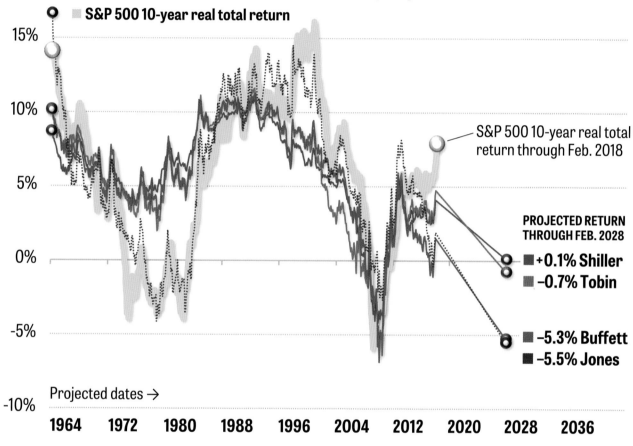

FIGURE 13-3 | Projections as of February 2018. Source: Stephen Jones [1270]

LIVINGSTON'S LAW OF CHOICE

Stocks can go down for years at a time;
Diversify now for your own peace of mind.

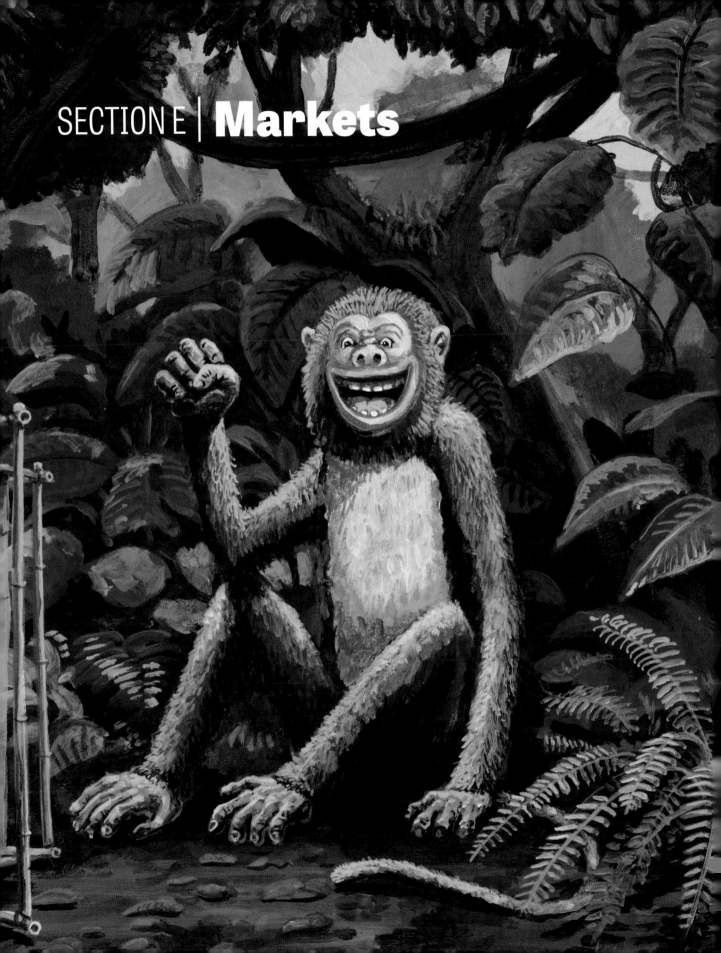

SECTION E | **Markets**

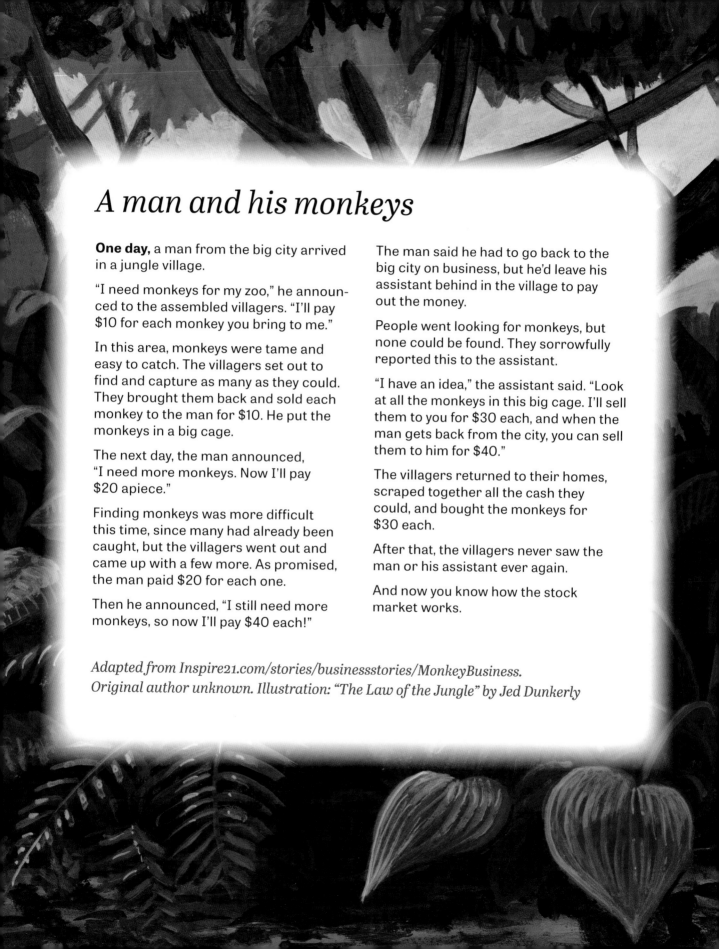

A man and his monkeys

One day, a man from the big city arrived in a jungle village.

"I need monkeys for my zoo," he announced to the assembled villagers. "I'll pay $10 for each monkey you bring to me."

In this area, monkeys were tame and easy to catch. The villagers set out to find and capture as many as they could. They brought them back and sold each monkey to the man for $10. He put the monkeys in a big cage.

The next day, the man announced, "I need more monkeys. Now I'll pay $20 apiece."

Finding monkeys was more difficult this time, since many had already been caught, but the villagers went out and came up with a few more. As promised, the man paid $20 for each one.

Then he announced, "I still need more monkeys, so now I'll pay $40 each!"

The man said he had to go back to the big city on business, but he'd leave his assistant behind in the village to pay out the money.

People went looking for monkeys, but none could be found. They sorrowfully reported this to the assistant.

"I have an idea," the assistant said. "Look at all the monkeys in this big cage. I'll sell them to you for $30 each, and when the man gets back from the city, you can sell them to him for $40."

The villagers returned to their homes, scraped together all the cash they could, and bought the monkeys for $30 each.

After that, the villagers never saw the man or his assistant ever again.

And now you know how the stock market works.

Adapted from Inspire21.com/stories/businessstories/MonkeyBusiness.
Original author unknown. Illustration: "The Law of the Jungle" by Jed Dunkerly

14 The biggest cause of disappointment is your brain on money

"Being without an opinion is so painful to human nature that most people will leap to a hasty opinion rather than undergo it."

WALTER BAGEHOT (1826–1877), British businessman[1271]

You probably think you're a pretty good investor. That, right there, is your biggest problem.

It turns out that the human mind is poorly suited to computing financial solutions.

Over thousands of years, our brains evolved a decision-making process aimed at keeping us alive. It makes us adept at the kind of split-second judgments that once meant the difference between catching dinner and becoming it. It's great for recognizing faces, making fight-versus-flight choices, and so on.

But as soon as numbers are thrown at your brain, it switches gears—at a cost to your portfolio.

Single-stimulus, single-response decision-making

Our minds evolved to handle situations that might be called one input, one output. For example:

» **Stimulus:** "I see a hungry tiger."

» **Response:** "I'll hide where it can't get me."

Over the years, this simple thought process has served us well. It's what worked long ago for your forebears —1,000 generations removed —helping them live, so they could pass their DNA along to you.

Market decisions aren't as easy as, "If A, I should do B." There's no single input. Instead, there are **millions.**

Scientists armed with brain-scanning equipment have shown that our minds make us overconfident when we're faced with financial data. Presented with numbers, we make poor decisions—all the while feeling convinced we know perfectly well what to do.

When we're calm and no money is at stake, we make financial decisions with our higher mind: the **prefrontal cortex.**

But when we've experienced a financial loss or are fearful of one, our higher brain steps aside. We revert instead to an older, lower mind called the **amygdala** or "reptilian brain" (Figure 14-1).

Ordinary individuals, compared with patients who had a damaged amygdala, demonstrated significant differences in risk-averse behavior, according to a 2010 study by researchers from the California Institute of Technology.[1272]

When you suffer a financial loss, control shifts from your higher mind to your lower mind

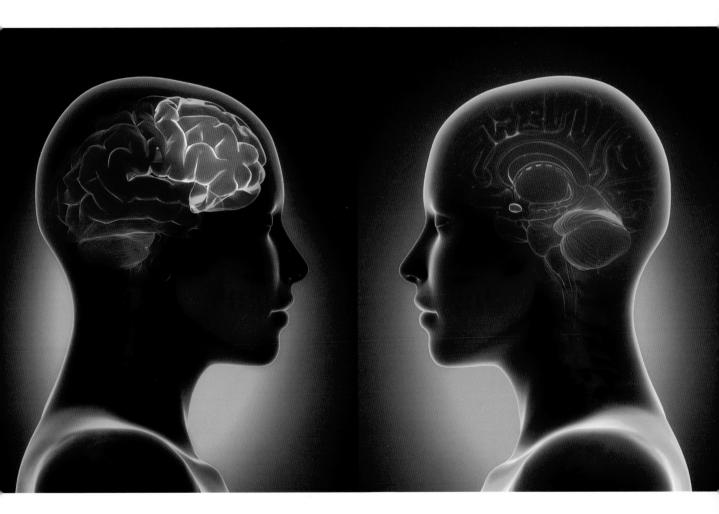

FIGURE 14-1 | The prefrontal cortex and the amygdala

Your risk profile is not a fixed number— your pain point plummets during crashes

If you've ever visited a wealth-management firm, the broker probably gave you a "risk profile" test. This is typically a series of questions designed to determine how much risk you're willing to take, on a scale from one (little risk) to nine (a lot of risk).

These tests are worthless. They're simply designed to make you feel like the broker understands you personally, while giving the firm a legal firewall when their strategies—loaded with risk—eventually cost you a bundle.

In reality, your tolerance for risk isn't measurable by a test taken during a calm office interview.

Figure 14-2 shows that your risk tolerance dives as the S&P 500 crashes. (The 2007 to 2009 bear market is used as an example.) Statisticians say your willingness to continue suffering has a "strong correlation" with the market as it falls. In plain English, we all tolerate more risk when things are going well than when they aren't.

For most investors, the concept of a "risk profile" from one to nine is nonsense. There aren't really different risk profiles among informed investors.

To illustrate this, let's look at another set of people who hope to avoid crashes: **skydivers.**

Do you think skydivers really fit the following three risk profiles?

» **Do "conservative" skydivers** pull the rip cord just one second after leaping out of the airplane?

» **Do "moderate" skydivers** pull the rip cord exactly halfway down a freefall?

» **Do "aggressive" skydivers** wait to pull the rip cord until the very last second?

Skydivers do none of these things. Instead, both skydivers and informed investors maintain a **margin of safety.**

Skydivers pull the rip cord after a reasonable amount of thrill but long before a random event might subject them to an intolerable loss (death).

Muscular Portfolios allow informed investors to avoid an intolerable loss even during the worst market crashes. That margin of safety allows them to ignore daily market gyrations and focus on things in life that really matter.

It's true that there are some very wealthy people whose investment style is ultra-conservative. These high-net-worth individuals can live off supersafe bonds that pay a small, predictable rate of interest, and want their principal to face no risk of loss at all.

Investors who are not so rich, however, **need** risk. Assets that fluctuate are what produce gains over time—which is probably what gives people the mistaken idea that higher risk always means higher gains. In truth, crashes that cut your life savings in half every decade or so are intolerable, no matter your "risk profile."

the behavioral pain point
Losses of more than 25% compel individuals to sell securities and switch to cash, harming their long-term performance.

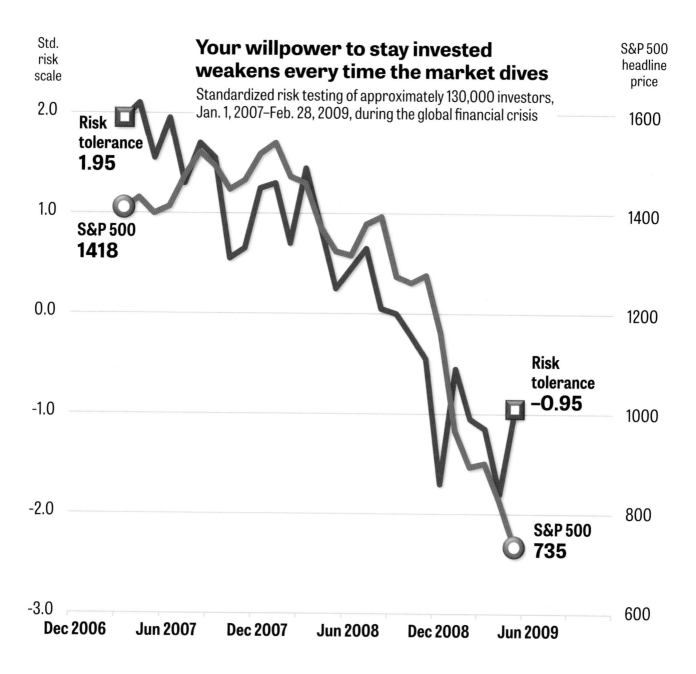

Your willpower to stay invested weakens every time the market dives

Standardized risk testing of approximately 130,000 investors, Jan. 1, 2007–Feb. 28, 2009, during the global financial crisis

Std. risk scale

2.0

Risk tolerance 1.95

1.0

S&P 500 1418

0.0

-1.0

Risk tolerance −0.95

-2.0

S&P 500 735

-3.0

Dec 2006   Jun 2007   Dec 2007   Jun 2008   Dec 2008   Jun 2009

S&P 500 headline price

1600

1400

1200

1000

800

600

FIGURE 14-2 | Source: Guillemette and Finke (2014), *Journal of Financial Planning*[1273]

The behavioral pain point appears to be around a 25% loss of capital

As Chapter 1 explained, losses that exceed a "pain point" activate investors' survival instincts, causing them to liquidate (essentially, a "flight to safety"). Well, what's the **exact** level of loss that causes this?

There will never be a precise answer that applies to every individual. We can only use a round number for the pain point:

» **A decline of more than 25% compels many investors to liquidate, causing a permanent loss of capital.**

How do we know for sure that many individuals bail out of the market, hurting their performance, after the market has dived more than 25%?

We know the average person lags the market by a lot. The Investment Company Institute (ICI) studies customer dollar flows into and out of stock-oriented mutual funds. For example, Russell Investments sponsors the Russell 3000, which holds most publicly traded American stocks. It analyzed ICI's data and concluded: "The average equity investor under-performed the Russell 3000 index by 2.2% annually" from 1984 through 2013.[1274]

This is called the **Behavior Gap,** and it's serious. Lagging by a mere 2.2 points per year may not sound so bad. But an investor with an annualized return of, say, 7.8% would amass **only half as much** in savings as an investor with a 10% return over a 34-year working career.

Charles Rotblut, vice president of the American Association of Individual Investors (AAII), periodically tests the behavioral pain point. Figure 14-3 is an example of two different investors. They both start with $100,000 in an S&P 500 index fund.

The armchair investor is a person who blissfully ignores the market until reading on December 31 of a given year that the S&P 500 lost over 20%. This person switches to a bond index fund (Vanguard's VWESX in Figure 14-3) and doesn't get back into the S&P 500 for 12 months.

From 2000 through 2017, this skittish investor suffered an annualized return of only 3.4%. Meanwhile, a buy-and-hold investor enjoyed a much greater 5.4% return. But the buy-and-hold person is largely a myth—most humans don't stay the course through such agonizing crashes as 2002 and 2008.

The difference between 3.4% and 5.4% is 2 percentage points. This almost matches what ICI found in actual dollar flows!

The $100,000 of the armchair investor gained only $83,000. Meanwhile, the S&P 500 tacked on nearly $158,000. In just 18 years, the market generated almost **twice the dollar gain** of the armchair investor.[1275]

The Behavior Gap has many explanations. Is everyone's pain point **exactly** 25%? Of course not. But the number is a danger zone that most portfolios violate.

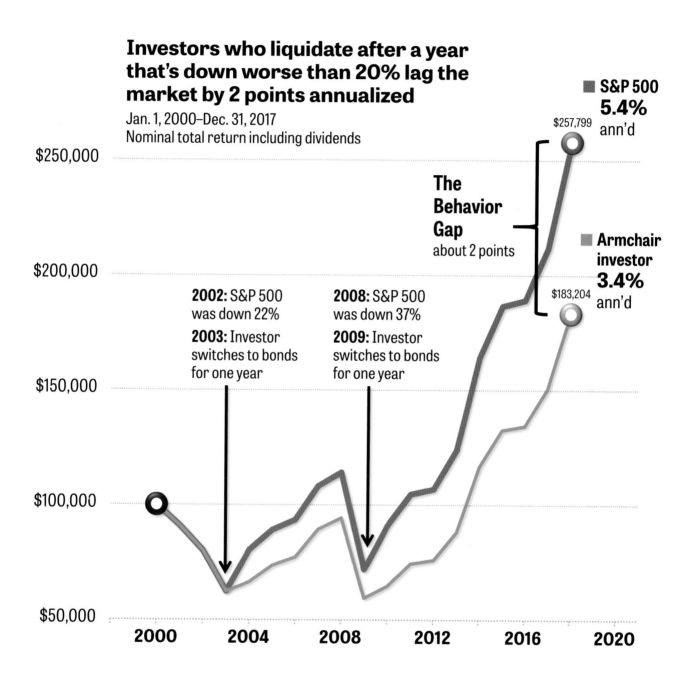

Investors who liquidate after a year that's down worse than 20% lag the market by 2 points annualized

Jan. 1, 2000–Dec. 31, 2017
Nominal total return including dividends

■ **S&P 500 5.4%** ann'd

$257,799

The Behavior Gap
about 2 points

■ **Armchair investor 3.4%** ann'd

$183,204

2002: S&P 500 was down 22%

2003: Investor switches to bonds for one year

2008: S&P 500 was down 37%

2009: Investor switches to bonds for one year

$250,000

$200,000

$150,000

$100,000

$50,000

2000   2004   2008   2012   2016   2020

FIGURE 14-3 | Adapted from Charles Rotblut/AAII Journal[1276]

If you liquidate during a bear market, you risk missing the bull-market bounce

Why is it so terrible for people to sell off their holdings near the bottom of a crash?

It's worse than the misfortune of merely selling at the end of a bear market. If you liquidate, you're likely to stay out of the market and miss the first year of the subsequent bull. That's when bull markets typically offer explosive gains, much greater than later stages of the bull.

Figure 14-4 shows the four stages that occur on average in a complete bear-bull market cycle:

» **A bear market** typically reduces an equity market 25% in about 26 months. The bear usually ends with a "capitulation low." At the bottom, there's widespread despair. Even the last optimistic holdouts dump all their stocks to stop the pain (at exactly the wrong moment).

» **The bounce** tends to be an explosive move off the bottom. (Individual recoveries, of course, may take any shape.) The bounce averages a 51% gain in 10 months. That's a phenomenal 61% annualized. You're not likely to see that rate of return again until years later in the **next** bull market.

» **The consolidation** is a time for the bull market to slowly digest its success. The average gain is a mere 11% over a long, drawn-out 33-month period.

» **The climax** completes the bear-bull market cycle. Indexes typically rise 27% in 14 months—a rate of 22.5% annualized. The final stage usually ends with a "climax top." In this period of public euphoria, even taxi drivers who usually don't play the market excitedly tell passengers which stocks they're speculating on.

As we saw in Charles Rotblut's thought experiment, average investors who throw in the towel wind up staying out of the market for at least 12 months—and often much longer.

The damage this "buy high, sell low" behavior does to your lifetime investing return is massive. Within 14 years (as we saw in Figure 14-3), the skittish player who liquidates has only **half** the dollar gain of a steady investor who stays the course.

Figure 14-4 is a composite of all continental EU stock exchanges for a 41-year period. The pattern applies equally well to the US stock market, so long as you keep in mind that the numbers are just averages. No actual historical returns are shown.

Free markets can and will do anything. Crashes and powerful bounces occur when you least expect them.

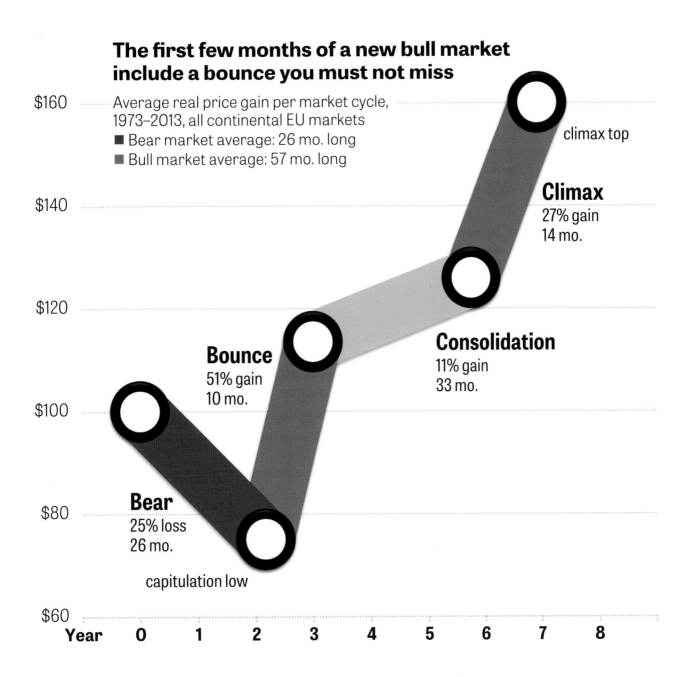

The first few months of a new bull market include a bounce you must not miss

Average real price gain per market cycle, 1973–2013, all continental EU markets
■ Bear market average: 26 mo. long
■ Bull market average: 57 mo. long

$160

$140

$120

$100

$80

$60

climax top

Climax
27% gain
14 mo.

Consolidation
11% gain
33 mo.

Bounce
51% gain
10 mo.

Bear
25% loss
26 mo.

capitulation low

Year   0   1   2   3   4   5   6   7   8

FIGURE 14-4 | Adapted from Goldman Sachs Global Investment Research[1277]

Your survival instinct is much stronger than your willpower—yes, yours

At this point, you might be saying, "That risk chart in Figure 14-2 doesn't apply to **me!** I'm tough. I can take more than half of my life savings vanishing."

This is like claiming your will is so strong that you can hold one hand in a pot of ice water and the other hand in a pot of boiling water. "On average, I'd be comfortable," you say.

It doesn't work like that. You couldn't hold your hand in boiling water for even one second. Your survival instinct would **force** you to pull your hand back, no matter how much willpower you think you have.

Watching your life savings decline 30%, 40%, or 50% triggers that instinct. Your brain says, "We can't take any more pain—let's liquidate **now** to prevent an even bigger decline."

As we've discussed before, selling near the bottom of a bear market locks in your losses. And that kills your lifetime rate of return.

The fact that your survival instinct is far more powerful than your will was demonstrated by Charles Darwin, the famous naturalist (Figure 14-5). Standing in the reptile house of the London Zoo, Darwin wrote in 1872:

"I put my face close to the thick glass-plate in front of a puff-adder in the Zoological Gardens, with the firm determination of not starting back if the snake struck at me; but as soon as the blow was struck, my resolution went for nothing, and I jumped a yard or two backwards with astonishing rapidity."[1278]

Darwin's automatic response to the lunging snake is caused by the same part of the brain that compels investors to lock in their losses during a crash: the amygdala. Shannon Cutts, citing research by Theodore George, MD, writes on PsychCentral:

"Darwin reacted as he did because there are two pathways in the brain—the pathway to the amygdala, which is the central 'threat processing unit' for the brain, and the pathway to the cortex, which is the central 'thought processing unit' for the brain. . . Because the survival instinct is just that— an instinct—we can't turn it off or overpower it or out-think it or otherwise divest ourselves of it."[1279]

When you throw in the towel, you don't feel like you're panicking. Your brain tells you you're doing the only logical thing to protect your family's life savings. Your survival instinct runs the show.

>> KEY CONCEPT

your survival instinct overpowers your will

Crashes of 30%, 40%, or 50% trigger the survival instinct, pushing investors to liquidate their holdings and lock in huge losses.

Even a scientist like Charles Darwin couldn't make his willpower overcome his survival instinct when a zoo snake lunged at the glass

FIGURE 14-5

Investors need discipline, which is something a lot of people don't have

What area of human activity produces more numbers than the stock market? One analysis program—AAII's Stock Investor Pro—contains about 2,200 data points on each of some 6,300 publicly traded companies. That makes the famously statistics-happy sport of baseball seem like the record book of a rock-paper-scissors tournament.

Each day generates yet another 2,200 data points for each company. You can find an infinite number of ways to multiply and divide all of those numbers: price/earnings ratios, growth rates, and all the other factoids you hear about on financial shows.

A now-famous experiment was conducted at Stanford University in 1970. Nursery school students aged four to six were shown a marshmallow on a plate. They were told they could eat the treat right away, or they could have **two treats** if they waited 15 minutes before eating the first one (Figure 14-6).

One little boy popped the marshmallow into his mouth before his teacher had even finished explaining the plan!

That young fellow might have been better off with a little more discipline. Follow-up studies 10 to 30 years later showed that the students with the patience to wait for the second marshmallow had achieved higher SAT scores, completed more years of education, and had lower obesity rates.[1280]

Individual investors need discipline to succeed, too.

Investors who try to beat the S&P 500 every year, and jump from one strategy to another, tend to badly underperform the market.

Do you have enough patience to judge a strategy's performance only over the long term—one complete market cycle? Do you have enough discipline to give your portfolio a tune-up for 15 minutes every month? If so, you can double your ending balance over the course of a working career compared with the average, jittery investor.

How your brain sabotages your investment success

As soon as the human mind is confronted with a glut of numbers, it switches gears. Your conscious mind remains completely unaware of the process. The result is bad financial decision-making.

Without knowing you personally, it's safe to say you have the following behavioral biases. We **all** have them. That's because we're human.

Some of the following examples are from John R. Nofsinger's book *The Psychology of Investing, 2nd Ed.,* a highly recommended educational resource.

You'll earn double the candy if you can just muster the patience of a five-year-old

FIGURE 14-6

The more data you have, the poorer the decisions you make

A fascinating experiment was performed by Joel Greenblatt, author of *The Little Book That Beats the Market.*

Gotham Asset Management, a financial investment service that Greenblatt cofounded, purchases stocks for customer accounts using strict screening criteria that his book calls "The Magic Formula."

The firm offers its clients "professionally managed accounts." In these holdings, each portfolio's position is automatically determined by Greenblatt's formula.

But, for a period of 24 months in 2009–2011, the firm's clients were also allowed to choose "self-managed accounts." These investors were given the formula's list but were free to pick which of the stocks they wished to buy or sell.

The cumulative two-year results of both groups (after expenses) and the S&P 500 are shown in Figure 14-7.

The "self-managed investors" were overconfident and decided to override the computerized formula. Their portfolios (up only 59.4%) had to settle for much poorer performance than the firm's own simple criteria had achieved (up 84.1%).

Greenblatt later wrote, "the people who 'self-managed' their accounts took a winning system and used their judgment to unintentionally eliminate all the outperformance and then some!"[1281]

The firm phased out its self-managed accounts on June 30, 2012.[1282]

In case after case, researchers have found that exposure to numbers makes your lower mind—your amygdala—quietly take control. The lower mind makes you overconfident and feeds you bad financial decisions. These judgments are communicated to your higher mind as being perfectly logical.

The human mind's overconfidence when faced with any significant amount of information probably evolved to help us out of tough pickles.

Imagine that your long-ago jungle ancestor found himself suddenly surrounded by **six** hungry tigers, not just one off in the distance. If your ancestor had just stood there, he'd have been eaten. He wouldn't have survived to pass down his DNA to you.

But a human who was filled with overconfidence in this situation might have run toward the smallest animal, screaming and waving his arms over his head. That's irrational. Who runs **toward** a hungry tiger? But the youngest cub might have been startled and bolted, giving your distant forebear a chance to jump to safety

People who overrode the computer suffered

Automatic-formula accounts	84.1%
S&P 500	62.7%
Self-managed accounts	59.4%

FIGURE 14-7
Source: Eyquem Investment Management[1283]

> ≫ KEY CONCEPT
> ## financial blindness
> Exposure to numbers makes your lower mind take control, feeding you bad financial decisions that your verbal center tells you are perfectly logical.

inside the crook of a tree. He would have survived, and his traits would have been passed down to future generations.

It's too bad our primitive behaviors don't produce good investment results.

Yale's William Goetzmann and Columbia's Nadav Peles asked two groups of investors how much their portfolios had outperformed or underperformed the overall market in the past year.

One group consisted of professional architects. Such people are highly educated college grads who are presumably very comfortable with numbers. The other group was drawn from a local chapter of the American Association of Individual Investors (AAII)—traders with years of experience.

The study's authors compared the investors' actual holdings with a benchmark's return. On average, the architects' imagined performance versus the market was 4.6 percentage points above reality. The recollection of the average AAII member was 5.1 points too high.

Selective recall of how great your performance has been is called **cognitive dissonance**. The study concluded, "even well informed investors tend to bias their perceptions regarding past performance."[1284]

Complex systems fail. In investing, simpler is better.

We tend to think we're superhuman, that the flaws we attribute to other people don't affect us.

One fine example of this was a hedge fund called Long-Term Capital Management. Founded in Connecticut in 1994, it boasted the Nobel Prize–winning economists Myron Scholes and Robert C. Merton, well-known traders like Salomon Brothers' John Meriwether, and many other notables. By early 1998, the fund had grown to an equity level of $4 billion.

None of these smart guys thought Russia would default on its bonds in August 1998. When it did, the fund plummeted so much that the Federal Reserve had to organize a consortium of financial institutions to take over 90% of the firm.

The banks injected $3.5 billion, stabilizing the firm and preventing a domino effect that could have bankrupted numerous other players.

All of the market experience and fancy titles in the world couldn't prevent the fund from losing nine-tenths of its value within four weeks.

To err is human, but to really mess things up requires Nobel laureates.

These professionals had biases and blind spots that contributed to their downfall. Behavioral biases affected them, and they affect you, too. Not one of us is exempt.

> **LIVINGSTON'S LAW OF UNSUITABILITY**
> *A mind is a terrible thing to trust.*
> *It turns our outperformance to dust.*

15 You don't need indicators that don't really indicate

"What the experts don't want you to know . . . is that prices are all that matter. Ideas count for nothing; opinions are distractions."

JASON KELLY, editor of The Kelly Letter[1285]

Whenever you go into a café or shop and see a Magic 8-Ball on the counter (Figure 15-1), you should give the thing a shake. Peer into its little crystal window to predict your future. This might give you valuable stock tips. For example, "SIGNS POINT TO YES" or "MY SOURCES SAY NO."

Perhaps Mattel Inc. will come out with a special Magic 8-Ball that shows "NINE PERCENT" every time. The only question you could ask would be, "What will be the S&P 500's price change this year?" As we saw in Chapter 12, a guess of 9% is more accurate than the projections of Wall Street's highest-paid gurus.

So many of the pundits' pronouncements turn out to be flat-out wrong! This leaves investors in a pickle. We know that we need a way to make decisions mechanically, not emotionally. But what approach should we use?

Many investors try to "figure out" the market. Surely, they think, there **must** be some secret formula that will predict which assets are going to go up the most.

This drives the popularity of "indicators." An indicator is a ratio of two or more market metrics.

Here's some bad news for the engineering-minded: The market cannot be reduced to a simple equation. It's a lot more complicated than that.

That doesn't stop people from trying. The more things you test, the more likely it is that one indicator or another will seem to work the best, completely by random chance.

As they say on Wall Street, "If you torture the data long enough, it will tell you what you want to hear."

Do you really think you can find a secret formula?

FIGURE 15-1

Researchers have learned a lot about indicators from lab rats

University biologists tell a story about how well we human beings judge random events:

~

The researchers wanted to see how quickly their lab rats could predict where some delicious cheese would be found in a maze with only two end points. A personal computer was used to generate the numbers 1 through 10 at random. The researchers decided to place the cheese on the left if the number came up 1 through 6, and on the right if 7, 8, 9, or 10.

After a few runs, the rats quickly learned that the cheese was on the left in 60% of the cases. So the rats started heading to the left every time.

The researchers then brought in a group of economics majors. The graduate students were given a complete history of where the cheese had been placed (but no explanation of how the positions were determined). The students were asked to figure out the formula and predict future positions.

The volunteers ran a series of computerized tests. They determined how many times in a row the cheese had been in the same spot, what happened next, and so forth. As a result, they all agreed that they'd discovered the formula. This is known as **backtesting.**

The researchers then brought out new cheese and let the lab rats look for it, using the PC to generate new random numbers, while the volunteers watched. The backtested formula predicted the location of the cheese only 52% of the time—essentially no better than chance!

Because the actual pattern was random, the old locations of the cheese revealed nothing about future locations, even though the data did contain recognizable patterns.

By simply turning left, the rodents had achieved a 60% accuracy rate. That beat the economics students' own 52% rate. Rats! So much for that college education . . .

~

This rat tale (Figure 15-2) has a great deal of relevance for investors. By approaching the cheese pattern in a complicated way, the economics students came up with a complicated indicator that didn't work.

In investing, simpler is better. Most indicators fail. An asset class's price, by contrast, always tells you something. Price is not an indicator, because it isn't the ratio of anything.

Lab rats predict the cheese's location in a maze more accurately than economics graduates

FIGURE 15-2

A good indicator, once uncovered, goes bad like milk in the fridge

One of the most disappointing stories in the investing world is the once-promising trading technique known as Bollinger Bands.

This short-term stock-picking method was first announced in 1983 by CNBC chief market analyst John Bollinger (when the channel was called the Financial News Network). After the system became popular among traders, the analyst published a book in 2001, *Bollinger on Bollinger Bands.* The volume zoomed around the world in at least 12 different translations.

The formula can be applied to almost any stock. The typical software draws a center line through a price chart, using the past 20 trading days' worth of data (Figure 15-3). Around the center line are two other lines that define a "high band" and a "low band."

Many technical software programs draw these charts. They're commonly configured so a stock's price will push through either the upper line or the lower line on one or two of every 20 market days. Traders interpret these events to construct "buy" and "sell" signals.

This formula produces an ever-flowing visual pattern that speculators find alluring, even hypnotic. It looks like it **must** work. It's so logical.

Unfortunately for short-term traders, Bollinger Bands fell victim to the "tragedy of the commons." The tragedy is that a public resource—such as an open field that cattle herders use—becomes "overgrazed" and eventually useless for anyone.[1286]

Three researchers from the Netherlands and New Zealand explored the formula, going back in history long before the battle of the bands began. The analysis covered the US, UK, Germany, Japan, Singapore, and eight other countries:

"Before the introduction of Bollinger Bands in 1983, the profitability was strong with high average returns in all countries. However, in the next subsample from 1983 to 2001, when Bollinger's book was published, the profitability of Bollinger Bands decreased by around 50% on average in all markets. In

the United States, there is no longer outperformance. After the book's publication, the profitability of Bollinger Bands further shrank with an average decline of 156% for all countries."[1287]

Larry Swedroe, director of research for the BAM Alliance, writes overviews of this and similar studies. He concludes that to persist, an investing formula must have "logical risk-based and/or behavioral-based explanations."[1288]

Muscular Portfolios are **less risky** than the market, so "greater risk" doesn't explain momentum's persistence. Instead, momentum takes advantage of human behavior. People tend to buy when the market is exciting and sell when the market is scary. This is unlikely to ever change.

> **» KEY CONCEPT**
> ## overgrazing
> Technical indicators usually stop working as soon as a lot of people start using them.

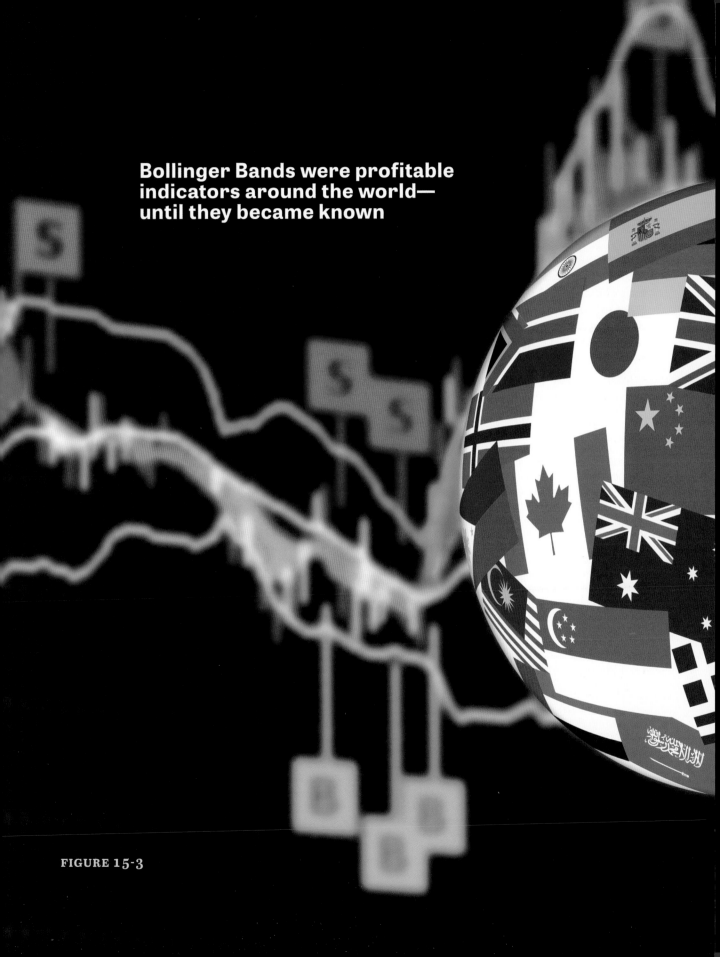

Bollinger Bands were profitable indicators around the world—until they became known

FIGURE 15-3

The lunar indicator is the most reliable—but you can't even make <u>that</u> profitable

Want to know one stock-market indicator that's actually reliable? Hope you're sitting down—it's the phase of the moon.

Numerous studies show that stock markets around the world—not just in the United States—go up more on the 14 days around the new moon and less on the 14 days around the full moon.

Unfortunately, you can't make profits trading on that fact. The reason why that's so gives us a big clue into the problem with indicators.

Ilia Dichev and Troy Janes studied stock indexes for the 100 years ending in 1999. They also examined 30 years of data from 24 other countries. The stronger lunar period produced "about double the returns" compared with the weaker period, they reported.[1289]

Similarly, three researchers analyzed in 2001 the returns of 48 countries. They found a difference of 3 to 5 percentage points in favor of the stronger periods.[1290]

When you think about it, lunar effects make sense. After all, it's well-known that more homicides are committed when the moon is full.[1291]

Why **wouldn't** the moon also affect people who wanted to make a killing in the market? (Figure 15-4.)

Surely you could make a profit with an edge like 3 to 5 points—couldn't you? Unfortunately for our indicator-seeking friends, **no.** There are many reasons why:

» **Say you bought stocks** on the first day of the strong lunar period. Then you sold the stocks and switched to cash on the first day of the weak period. You'd turn over your portfolio 200% every 29 days. That's more than 2,400% turnover per year. The transaction costs would eat you alive.

» **On the weaker days,** the stock market still goes up, on average. You'd miss a lot of gains on the days when your portfolio was in cash.

» **Add all that together** and you'd badly underperform whatever market index you were following.

Wealth manager Barry Ritholtz calls predictors that don't work "YAII." That stands for Yet Another Idiotic Indicator.[1292]

We may not be idiots, but if prices go up more during certain lunar cycles than others, the market is definitely driven by lunatics.

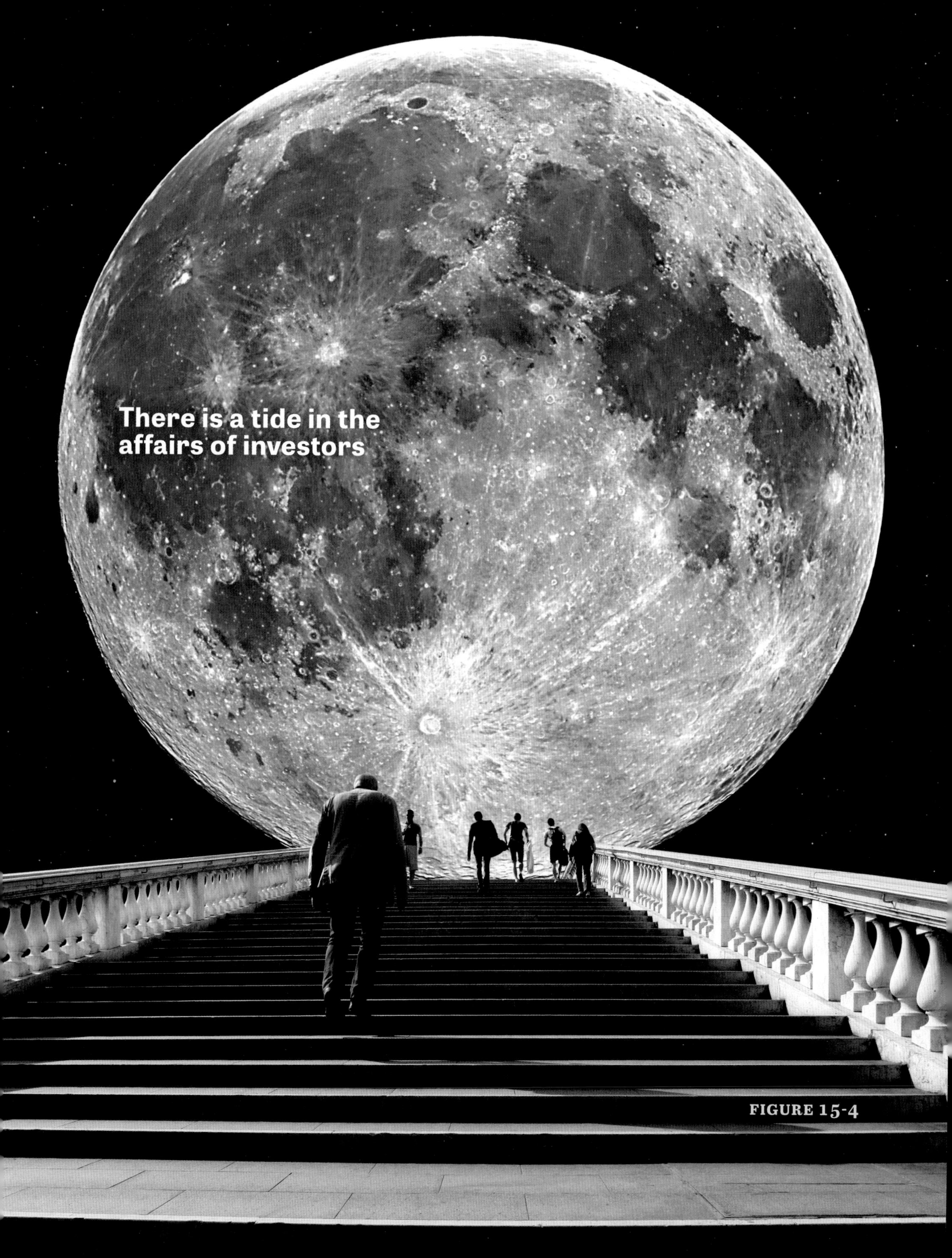

There is a tide in the affairs of investors

FIGURE 15-4

Why can't you find an indicator that always works?

The problems with market indicators can be illustrated with a pack of playing cards.

The deck contains 52 cards. How many unique ways of sorting the deck do you think there are? (Figure 15-5.)

If the deck is shuffled at random, the top card could be any one of the 52. The second card could be any of the other 51, because the top card already holds a position. The third card could be any of the other 50, and so on down to the last card.

There are this many possible outcomes:

52 × 51 × 50 . . . 3 × 2 × 1

Multiplying the possibilities like that results in a number called "52 factorial."

Let's translate 52 factorial into a number you could write out. It means there are more than **80 million quadrillion quadrillion quadrillion quadrillion** possible ways to shuffle a deck of cards. That's 80 followed by 66 zeros.

Want to see them all? At a rate of one deck per second, it would take longer than the age of the universe. Better start shuffling! [1293]

How does this relate to the stock market? Well—just to state the obvious—any stock exchange is a **lot** more complicated than a poker deck.

Instead of 52 cards, there are thousands of stocks, millions of lunatic investors, and on and on.

Now imagine that we back-test thousands of theories on all that market data. History is a sample of one. All of those backtests found a strategy that worked on that one history. But the same formula **won't** work in most of the possible futures.

How many different future stock markets are possible? It must be **way** more than 80 followed by 66 zeros.

And we wonder why the complex indicator that worked once doesn't work going forward! How in the world would we know which random future we're going to get?

A good example of a failed indicator is the famous Wall Street rhyme:

"Sell in May and go away, Don't come back till All Hallow's Day."

To follow this rule, you sell stocks on May 1 and buy on November 1.

It's certainly true that holding stocks in May through October was a terrible idea in the Great Depression. CXO Advisory analyzed 146 years of S&P returns. In 1931 through 1940—the depression—the index's average gain (including dividends) was **a loss of 2%** during the May-through-October period.

After that horrible decade, however, the index mostly rose in the warm months. But that old poem is still stuck in our brains. CXO concluded:

"Buying and holding stocks easily outperforms a 'Sell in May' market timing strategy." [1294]

> **» KEY CONCEPT**
> ## all indicators work until they don't
> When an indicator stops working, you won't know how long it won't work or which other indicator to use instead.

The stock market is infinitely more unpredictable than a mere pack of 52 cards

FIGURE 15-5

Some indicators work better than others in testing, but the difference is random

It's human nature to see a chart of the stock market and think, "There must be a secret formula—and **I can find it!**"

The truth is not so exciting.

Analysts have developed thousands of "indicators" to predict the market. Each indicator is a combination of two or more market metrics into a single reading that supposedly reveals when to buy and sell a hot security. These indicators form a body of art known as **technical analysis.**

Here's what actually happens:

» **An indicator worked great over the period of time that a researcher studied it.**

» **The indicator won't work in the future.**

One of the most exhaustive tests of stock market indicators is the 2007 book *Evidence-Based Technical Analysis* by David Aronson. He was a trader for Spear, Leeds & Kellogg before becoming an adjunct professor of technical analysis at Baruch College in New York City.[1295]

His book must be one of the most heroic scientific examinations of market indicators of all time. Aronson backtested 6,402 different technical-analysis rules. The study period was November 1980 through June 2005. That covered over 25 years, more than long enough to reveal a needle in the indicator haystack.

Of course, some rules did poorly and some did well. Aronson found that 320 of the 6,402 rules (5%) seemed to have performances that were statistically significant, using ordinary measures.

That's where the trouble begins. Ordinary trials for statistical significance fail to account for "data-mining bias" (Figure 15-6).

In short, when you test hundreds or thousands of investing strategies, by random chance some will look better than others.

Aronson corrected for this bias using two sophisticated tools called White's Reality Check and Monte Carlo Permutations.[1296]

After compensating for the noise from running thousands of trials, no formula stood out. The results fit an ordinary bell curve. In other words, the performances were random.

As Aronson put it:

"The performance of the best rule out of the 6,402 examined falls well within the range of ordinary sampling variability."[1297]

Computer runs showed that testing thousands of made-up, worthless rules would have revealed, by random chance, one that returned 11% annualized by buying and selling the market. But the best actual rule returned only 10.25%.

That one lucky rule wouldn't make you rich. Its success with past data simply wouldn't be repeated if you applied it to new market moves.

» **KEY CONCEPT**

data-mining bias

If you test hundreds or thousands of strategies, by random chance one will seem best, but it won't work in the future.

If you torture the data long enough, it will tell you what you want to hear

FIGURE 15-6

After testing almost 40,000 strategies, academics agree on price momentum

Aronson's experiment was truly monumental. But, to his credit, his book points out an even larger 2005 study. It tested 39,832 technical-analysis rules—six times more!

That study, by professors at Columbia University in New York and Academia Sinica in Taiwan, included rules even more complex than Aronson's.[1298]

Their 39,832 rules were run on additional indexes, not just the S&P 500 index that Aronson tested. The professors corrected for the data-mining bias of their thousands of tests.

Aronson dashed the hopes of millions of true believers in indicators by writing:

"The study showed that none of the rules produced statistically significant gains on either the Dow Jones Industrials or the S&P 500."[1299]

The larger Columbia/Sinica study did find some complex trading strategies that seemed to work on some markets, but nothing that a mere mortal could execute.

For most of us, complex indicators will remain a fantasy rather than a solution.

Despite Aronson's debunking of indicators that could be relied upon, his research did lead him to conclude that basic, ordinary price information can produce good performance (Figure 15-7).

He lists a handful of examples that work in all markets. Two of them are:

» **Price trends in industry groups and sectors persist long enough after detection by simple momentum indicators to earn excess returns.**

» **Stocks that have displayed prior relative strength and relative weakness continue to display above-average and below-average performance over horizons of 3 to 12 months.**[1300]

Using momentum alone, individual investors—devoting less than 15 minutes per month to the job—can do well in the market.

Speculators think simple rules are beneath them. Actually, the simpler the better. Let day traders spin their wheels on ever more complex schemes.

Price is not an indicator. An indicator is a ratio of two or more market metrics into a single reading.

An asset's price isn't a ratio of anything. The price is just the price.

The market price of an asset may not always match its "intrinsic value," but that doesn't matter.

Josh Brown, CEO of Ritholtz Wealth Management, explains that an asset's price is "the sum total of all investor fear and greed, both historical and real time."[1301] That doesn't mean the price is rational or efficient. An asset's price, however, is all informed investors need to know.

» KEY CONCEPT

you can't always get what you want, but price gets you what you need

Asset prices are the sum of all the greed and fear about a security by all the world's investors at that moment.

Out of all the factors, one stands far above the others

FIGURE 15-7

The Muscular Portfolios project aims to avoid data-mining bias

Data-mining bias is a strong temptation. Informed investors strive to avoid it.

This book did not backtest thousands of investing strategies and then select the few that floated to the top by random chance.

Instead, the book brings together the latest research on momentum. It shows how mere mortals can use it effectively on their portfolios.

The bad examples that were chosen consist of Lazy Portfolios that became popular in the 1990s (Chapter 3). The four model portfolios in the book are 21st-century strategies that have actual-money results covering a decade or more (Chapters 5 through 7 and 23). Full market cycles show what works.

To avoid data-mining bias, no attempt has been made to find the "very best" starter portfolio, the "very best" Muscular Portfolios, or the "very best" End Game Portfolio. The models in this book are time-tested and will work for you just fine—without being "optimized" by random chance.

To be sure, some determined analysts will be inspired to perform thousands of backtests. These computer runs will certainly suggest strategies that, in hindsight, seem "better."

But how will you know which data-mined strategies were ranked as number one by mere chance, signifying nothing? Would you bet your life savings?

The best strategy of all is KISS (Keep It Simple, Stupid).

There's no investing formula so simple that you can't mess it up. There's no investing strategy so perfect that you can't impose your own opinion over the strategy rules (Figure 15-8).

All we can do is resist these urges. Stay with the simplest strategy possible that actually does the job.

> **LIVINGSTON'S LAW OF INFALLIBILITY**
> *Indicators come and go.*
> *Price is all you need to know.*

'Birthdays are good for you!
Studies show that people who
have more of them live longer.'

FIGURE 15-8

16 Defeat behavioral biases and become your own investment adviser

"The stock market is the only place where, when they announce a sale, everyone runs out of the store."

PETER LYNCH, manager of the high-performing Fidelity Magellan Fund (1977 to 1990)[1302]

Right about now, it may occur to you: "Experts can't predict the future. And we can't trust our own opinions to make market decisions. What the heck is left?"

Muscular Portfolios are an example of "mechanical investing," a way to avoid predictions that fail us and opinions that deceive us.

The Muscular Portfolios investing strategy has a few core principles that underlie its practice.

Successful investors clearly identify their principles and keep them handy as a constant reminder—helping to stave off any irrational impulse by referring to them often. Figure 16-1 is a poster of the principles underlying Muscular Portfolios, namely:

**Principle 1.
Your Compounding Plan.**
By not removing your gains until you absolutely need to, your portfolio will eventually pay you more than you can earn by working.

**Principle 2.
Your Diversification Policy.**
Remaining 100% invested at all times in at least three asset classes from an expert-designed menu—including stocks, bonds, real estate, and commodities—will give you greater gains with smaller declines than a portfolio with only one asset class or a static asset allocation.

**Principle 3.
Your Momentum Rule.**
Holding only the strongest asset classes, defined as the ones with the best performance over the past 3 to 12 months, tends to improve a portfolio's gains and reduce its drawdowns.

> » KEY CONCEPT
> ## core principles of Muscular Portfolios
> Compounding, diversification, and momentum enable informed investors to match or surpass the S&P 500 during complete bear/bull market cycles.

The three core principles of Muscular Portfolios

Your Compounding Plan

By not removing your gains until you absolutely need to, your portfolio will eventually pay you more than you can earn by working at any job.

Your Momentum Rule

Holding the asset classes with the best performance over the past 3 to 12 months tends to improve a portfolio's gains and reduce its drawdowns.

Your Diversification Policy

Remaining 100% invested in at least three asset classes from an expert-designed menu gives you greater gains with smaller declines than a portfolio with only one asset class or a static asset allocation.

FIGURE 16-1

Pick one financial style—such as mechanical investing—and stick with it

There are dozens of styles of investing (Figure 16-2). Many of them—such as trading options or foreign currencies—demand your constant attention and require substantial computer savvy.

Most individual investors don't wish to stare at algorithms all day, however. For that reason, three of the simplest financial styles are most relevant to our discussion: active investing, passive investing, and mechanical investing.

What are the differences?

» A mechanical investor does not rely on "indicators" or try to guess which securities will go up. Instead, the investor relies on the clearest signal there is: an asset class's market price. A computer formula ranks each asset. Behavioral biases never color the rankings. Opinions are used only to choose restaurants and films, never to pick securities.

Muscular Portfolios are an example of mechanical investing. They work because computers are much better than our all-too-human brains at calculating an asset class's odds of performing well.

» An active investor picks assets using indicators. An indicator combines two or more market metrics—like a company's share price divided by its earnings—into a single signal. The signal supposedly indicates which securities to buy and sell. (Unfortunately, as we saw in the last chapter, such indicators are often wrong.)

To make matters worse, active investors often override their indicators and sometimes change their holdings several times per day or even per hour, driving up trading costs.

» A passive investor picks a fixed list of securities to hold in specific percentages. With a passive investing approach, you never change these percentages, except possibly to allocate more funds to bonds as you grow closer to retirement. To enforce the percentages specified for each asset, investors are usually told to rebalance their portfolios at the end of each year.

Passive investing is also called "strategic" or "static" asset allocation. This may sound familiar: Lazy Portfolios are an example of passive investing.

As we saw in Chapter 3, because a static portfolio never adapts to changing market conditions. passive investing exposes investors to huge losses during bear markets.

There's no overlap between mechanical, active, and passive investing. If you call yourself a mechanical investor, but allow your opinions to override your chosen computerized formula, you've just become an active investor. Don't make this mistake.

Mechanical investing is the most practical of many different styles of personal finance

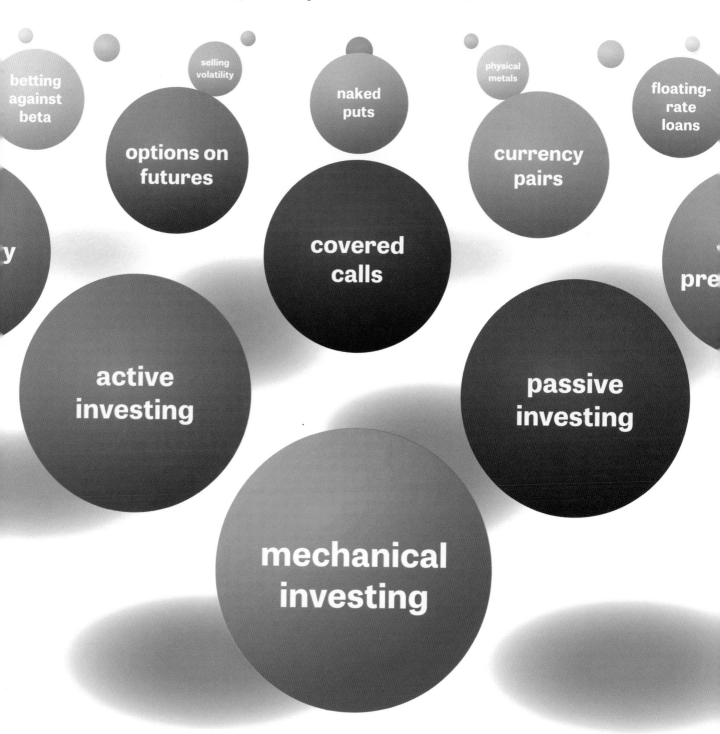

FIGURE 16-2 | Illustration by Pieter Tandjung

To earn a prize of $1 million, would you make guesses or use a supercomputer?

Following a simple computer formula liberates us from unreliable oracles and our own behavioral biases. Let's consider just two examples:

1 · How to beat a chess grandmaster

Imagine that you've been offered a prize of $1 million. All you have to do is play one round of chess and win. Oh, by the way, your opponent is a grandmaster and the undisputed winner of the most recent world championship.

The sponsors give you a choice: you can make your own moves, or accept whatever moves are recommended by the world's most powerful chess computer. Which would you pick?

Unless you're a moron, you'd choose the supercomputer, not your limited brainpower. It's widely known that IBM's Deep Blue defeated the world chess champion, Garry Kasparov, back in 1997. Computers have only gotten better since then.[1303] (Figure 16-3.)

2 · How to beat the trivia experts

Now imagine you've been chosen to compete on *Jeopardy*, the popular TV trivia quiz show. Playing against you will be the game's two all-time top scorers. Simply beat them both to claim your $1 million prize.

Again, you can come up with your own responses, or you can use ones that are fed to you by a supercomputer. Again, only an idiot would forego the computer—specifically, IBM's latest development, Watson. It famously beat Jeopardy's two human champions in 2011.[1304]

Follow a formula, not your opinion

People want to believe that with enough knowledge, they can overcome their behavioral biases and intuit the best investments all by themselves. But calculating financial probabilities is not a skill we were born with.

Researchers studied the trades of more than 238,000 anonymous investors who bought and sold index options over a six-year period. About 73% of the traders lost money. If they'd simply made guesses at random, on the other hand, half of them might have won.[1305]

Another study showed that only 2% to 3% of options traders demonstrate any genuine skill. The other 97% to 98% made **no** money or **lost** money, sometimes suffering enormous plunges.

Becoming a chess grandmaster, a *Jeopardy* whiz, or a legendary trader is super hard.

Learning to use Muscular Portfolios is easy. It frees you up to concentrate on something other than your investment account.

Wouldn't your time be better spent with your friends and loved ones rather than staring at computer screens all day to find some mythical "edge"?

» KEY CONCEPT
it's not how much you make, it's how much you keep
Flying high, and then losing half your life savings, is a terrible strategy.

It's best to let a computer pick your moves in complex games like chess and investing

FIGURE 16-3

You need both market volatility and a lot of patience to win long term

An earlier chapter discussed the *Hulbert Financial Digest*, which tracked the real-time performances of hundreds of investment newsletters beginning in 1980. Its editor, Mark Hulbert, says his very first digest covered 36 newsletters.

Only **three** of those 36 gurus (8%) beat the S&P 500 over the 34-year period from 1980 to 2014.

Did the three superior newsletters outperform every year? Absolutely not!

Hulbert discovered what we might call the "Long Night of the Portfolio." He says: "Each of the three winners lagged behind the S&P 500 in more than **half** of the five-year periods since 1980."

He wryly notes that it's "the rare investor who is willing to stick with a strategy after five years of market-lagging performance."[1306]

Informed investors are those rare souls. Armchair investors endlessly jump from one strategy that disappoints them to another. Informed investors are patient and disciplined.

The Vanguard Group repeated Hulbert's study, but it used the performance of actively managed US equity funds from 1998 through 2012.

In that 15-year period, only 18% of the funds (275 out of 1,540) both survived and outperformed their benchmark. Of those superior funds, virtually every one (97%) underperformed the benchmark in **at least 5 of the 15 years.**[1307]

Muscular Portfolios are designed never to lose more than 25%. To be sure, a drawdown of 25% in a crash can still be troubling. But your portfolio would be far outperforming the S&P 500, which would be down 30%, 40%, or 50%.

Such low, low drawdowns come with a trade-off. A Muscular Portfolio is unlikely to ever beat the S&P 500 in a roaring bull market.

A portfolio of ETFs representing three diverse asset classes—giving you a margin of safety—will **gently shadow** the S&P 500 when the index happens to be the strongest asset class.

Muscular Portfolios are designed to surpass the S&P 500 **only during bear markets.** Keeping losses small generates outperformance over the long term. Informed investors know enough to judge their portfolios **only** over complete bear/bull cycles.

The best investors in the long term are the minority who swear off S&P 500 envy. Betting your life savings on an overhyped and crash-prone index is a foolhardy risk. The goal is to watch your portfolio grow to meet your needs. Informed investors don't get jealous during bull markets. They patiently wait to see their balances top the index at the end of every bear market (Figure 16-4).

Patience turns investors' frowns upside down

FIGURE 16-4

Volatility is not risk—true financial risk is the likelihood of an intolerable loss

As Hulbert explains, all of the best-performing investment advisers lagged the S&P 500 for **five years in a row.** Not just that—the winners lagged the index in **half of all five-year periods.**

Despite these long runs of underperformance, the best advice delivered much better **long-term** performance than the S&P 500. Do you have the patience to wait out the soaring, Icarus-like flight of the S&P 500 during a bull market? If so, you'll be rewarded by avoiding the crash when Icarus falls to Earth every 10 years or so.

The volatility of stocks generates higher returns over time than so-called "risk-free" assets. Stocks over the past 100 years have generated a real total return of about 6.7% annualized, adjusted for inflation. Short-term Treasury bills have generated only about 2.7%. Volatile as-sets don't always produce higher returns, but there's no question that T-bills pay you less.

Volatility is not to be avoided. We now know how to construct asset-rotation portfolios. You tilt toward the ETFs that have good momentum and away from those that don't. Each ETF has volatility, but that's not an effective measure of risk.

Financial risk means **a portfolio's likelihood of subjecting you to an intolerable loss.** If a loss is intolerable, you don't tolerate it. After a bone-crushing drawdown, even some of the toughest investors can no longer take the pain. The loss compels them to liquidate near the bottom, stunting their performance.

Let's say you'd like to build a vacation home near the beach. Up for sale are two empty parcels of land. Which one should you construct your weekend getaway on?

One plot of land is right on the shoreline, offering immediate access to the beach. The other is on a hill, requiring a quarter-mile walk.

Does a beachfront house face a "risk" that the tide will go up and down? No! The tide is **guaranteed** to go up and down. Volatility is not risk. Normal high tides and low tides are not a concern.

But what if a major storm comes along every 10 years? The storm surge pounds the beach and bashes your shoreline house into kindling (Figure 16-5). The foundation is still there, but you've lost half your original investment. You must rebuild your beach house or throw in the towel on that piece of property.

Financial risk is this kind of intolerable loss. Avoid investment losses so great that they compel you to liquidate.

» KEY CONCEPT
volatility is not risk
Volatility is an opportunity for profit.

» KEY CONCEPT
risk is the likelihood of an intolerable loss
Investors don't tolerate the market's periodic crashes of 30%, 40%, and 50%— nor should they.

Build your financial house on higher ground

FIGURE 16-5

You can and should manage your own money, but a fee-only adviser might help

This chapter has discussed how to become your own financial adviser. However, being an informed investor doesn't mean you should **never** pay for expertise.

You may wish to hire qualified experts on the following subjects and many others that could never be covered by this or any other single book:

» **Tax planning**
» **Wills and trusts**
» **End-of-life directives**
» **College savings plans**
» **Loans/reverse mortgages**

In addition to the above professionals, you may find that an outside financial adviser can actually give you a much-needed perspective. That's especially true if you have a complicated situation.

If so, you can avoid some of the outrageous percentages that brokers lift from your savings if you select a **fee-only adviser.** These are financial planners who pledge not to accept sales commissions or kickbacks from mutual funds, insurance companies, or anyone else.

Fee-only advisers work solely for an hourly fee you pay. Ideally, that should make them serve your interests and not line their own pockets with kickbacks **plus** an annual percentage of your assets.

Don't confuse fee-only advisers with so-called **fee-based advisers.** The latter may charge you an hourly fee, but they can **also** quietly take commissions from investment choices they push. Talk about working both sides of the street!

Be cautious. You'd think that all advisers who claim to be "fee-only" really are. But an investigation published in 2013 by the *Wall Street Journal* revealed that as many as 11% who listed themselves as "fee-only" on the Certified Financial Planner (CFP) website were also able to receive commissions or kickbacks. That gives such advisers a conflict of interest.[1308]

The CFP board took action against six financial advisers in October 2017 for improperly calling themselves "fee-only," *WSJ* columnist Jason Zweig reported.[1309]

But don't start feeling too grateful. The CFP website describes these six "disciplinary actions" as mere letters of admonition, not suspensions.[1310]

Let's face it, you must do your own research.

Steven D. Lockshin—who was named the country's number one adviser in 2011 by *Barron's* magazine—has written an entire book on how to choose the right fee-only financial planner.

In *Get Wise to Your Advisor,* Lockshin points out that Registered Investment Advisers (RIAs) can legally say they are fee-only but still take commissions for steering your money into financial products with high expenses. All they must do is **disclose** the conflict of interest! Lockshin notes, "the disclosures are tucked into documents that are known for their mind-numbing legalese."[1311]

Lockshin was trained in the old Wall Street ways before starting his own firm, Convergent Wealth Advisors, in 1994. So he's familiar with the sales techniques that even skeptical consumers can fall for in a consultant's impressive-looking office.

how commission-driven salespeople get into your head

In *Get Wise to Your Advisor* Steven Lockshin describes the seduction process:

Effective salespeople know that a simple way to win over a potential client is to get him saying yes—or at least get the client nodding his head. I recall learning that if you can get a prospect to say "yes" seven times, then your likelihood of completing a sale goes up exponentially. Achieving that is simple: Just ask questions or make statements to which the only possible response is "yes" or "I agree." A nod of the head counts as a success.

Here's an idea of how such conversations typically go when advisors are doing the selling.

ADVISOR: I've been dealing with wealthy clients for many years. Most of these folks share some common goals. Rule #1 is that they want to be able to maintain their lifestyle no matter what.

POTENTIAL CLIENT: (nods head, thinking, Yep, that's me.)

ADVISOR: They want to minimize taxes . . .

POTENTIAL CLIENT: (Nodding head) Yep.

ADVISOR: And they want to protect their wealth so they can pass it on to their kids and/or charity, but not the government.

POTENTIAL CLIENT: (Nodding head) Exactly.

For those of you keeping score, that's three head nods in response to three statements. All the statements are aimed at the potential client's emotions, certainly not their intellect. (Is there any wealthy person who wants a less comfortable retirement, who wants to pay more taxes, who wants to leave everything to Uncle Sam? Well, there may be a few who want to disinherit their kids, but not very many.)

The questions are emotionally manipulative—and extremely effective. The potential client feels the advisor really "gets" him, and thanks to all that head-nodding, he's now in an agreeable frame of mind. After a few short platitudes about investment performance and client friendliness, the advisor typically has himself or herself a new client.

If you truly need outside expertise, hire a fee-only consultant. But before you make any decisions, read Lockshin's book—and, by the way, ask for five references.

LIVINGSTON'S LAW OF RISK

*You'll never know how much you care
Till half your savings are no longer there.*

SECTION F | **Implementation**

"My numbers indicate I can afford to quit working about six years after I die."

Illustration: "The Accountant" by Jed Dunkerley

17 Use bargain brokerages but watch out for hidden fees

"The average stock broker services his clients in the same way that Baby Face Nelson serviced banks."

WILLIAM BERNSTEIN, *The Investor's Manifesto* (2010)[1312]

The 21st century has blessed us with low-cost exchange-traded funds (ETFs). As we've seen in previous chapters, the ETFs in this book's model portfolios truly charge tiny fees.

If you use a 401(k) or other tax-deferral plan at work, you may not be able to control the fees you pay. But if you manage your own traditional IRA or Roth, you can guard your gains by keeping costs low.

Warning: Don't move your IRA to a different brokerage just to get "commission-free" ETFs. Such brokerages may actually charge you **higher** annual fees.

One example would be "12b-1" fees. You pay these hidden charges solely to subsidize a firm's marketing expenses. The haircut can be 0.25% to 1% per year. The Motley Fool's Dan Caplinger explains:

"Charles Schwab, TD AMERI-TRADE, and E*TRADE Financial generally charge a commission to buy mutual funds. But all of them offer their customers certain mutual funds at no transaction fee. If you look closely, you'll notice that in many cases, those no-transaction fee funds come with 12b-1 fees—and some of those 12b-1 fees help the fund companies pay brokers for listing their funds with no commission. So in other words, part of your fund fees are going to these brokers—even if you don't use them to buy your fund shares."[1313]

In addition, brokers may emphasize or even require their own house funds.

For example, Charles Schwab & Co. launched in 2015 a highly publicized "free" service called Intelligent Portfolios.

That sounds great. But in a May 25, 2015, cover story, *Barron's* writer Alexander Eule pointed out the problems:

"There's no free lunch, of course. Schwab's portfolios are costly in other ways. The firm mandates that all portfolios have at least 6% in cash at all times; its most conservative portfolios can have as much as 30%—an unusual construction for an investment portfolio."[1314]

The Investor Junkie website reports how that huge allocation to Schwab's own money-market funds makes profits for the firm but drags down your gains:

"Schwab will then either use that cash to invest or borrow out to others as a loan. For small portfolios (under $10,000), this drag on returns might not be so great, but it can be significant with larger accounts."[1315]

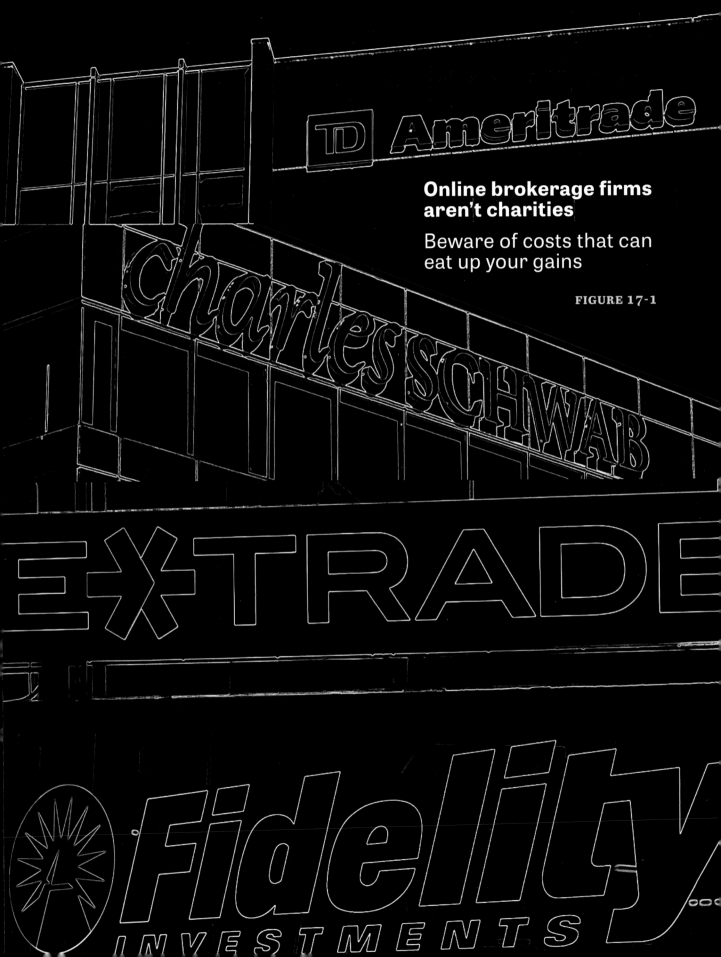

Online brokerage firms aren't charities

Beware of costs that can eat up your gains

FIGURE 17-1

Beware of trading restrictions and excessive add-on fees

Figure 17-2 is a partial list of firms that offer some or all of the ETFs in this book.

TD Ameritrade originally would have been in this list. However, TDA deleted all Vanguard ETFs and many iShares ETFs from its commission-free offerings in November 2017.[1316]

In 2015, writer Lewis Braham explained in *Barron's* how TDA and others ding you:[1317]

"Discount brokers like Schwab or Fidelity have gradually been boosting their charge for funds to be on their platforms, even if they have just one share class. Sometimes, the cost is as high as 0.4% of asset per year. Obviously, spending that much on distribution is detrimental for investors in the funds."

At this writing, TDA charges you 0.64% per year to hold PDBC, a commodity index ETF.[1318] The ETF sponsor's website shows that PDBC's annual fee is only 0.60%.[1319]

That extra 0.04 point would ding you $40 per year on a $100,000 position. That $40 is a **huge penalty** compared with the much smaller, one-time $6.95 commission you'd pay to buy or sell a "non-commission-free" ETF at TDA.

In addition, TDA charges a commission of $13.50 if you sell a "commission-free" ETF less than 31 days after you purchased it. That $13.50 is almost double TDA's usual $6.95 commission.

TDA considers Day 1 to be the day **after** you purchase the ETF. "Commission-free Day 31" is actually 32 days after.

The Vanguard Group is in Figure 17-2, but be aware that in March 2018, *Barron's* rated it "the highest-cost online broker." Barron's said Vanguard's own funds were cheap to trade, but anything else was costly.[1320]

In August 2018, Vanguard made the ETFs of several competitors commission-free, which is an improvement.

Best bargain brokerage for starter portfolios: Robinhood.com

If you have less than $10,000 to invest, and you're using a starter portfolio like the Baby Bear, the cheapest online brokerage firm is Robinhood.com. At this writing, its features are:

» **Trades cost $0** at Robinhood, and there are no monthly fees.

» **Robinhood *does* pass along** SEC fees of 2.31 cents per $1,000 sold and Finra fees of 1.19 cents per 100 shares sold.

Robinhood's many limitations may make you look elsewhere after your account has grown larger than $10,000:

» **As a start-up,** Robinhood lets you trade only through a smartphone app. There's no trading website, which would be a lot easier to use.

» **Robinhood doesn't support** IRA, custodial, joint, or trust accounts.

» **Robinhood doesn't offer** mutual funds—only equities and ETFs.

If those drawbacks don't bother you, Robinhood provides a way to invest as little as a few hundred dollars without seeing your balance eaten away by trading commissions.

How does Robinhood stay afloat? It makes its money on cash interest and margin accounts that collect monthly fees. It's no garage effort: Venture firms valued Robinhood at $5.6 billion in March 2018.

Brokerages with commission-free ETF trading (partial list)

	Folio with Unlimited Plan	robinhood	Vanguard
The Mama Bear			
VONE	YES	YES	YES
VIOO	YES	YES	YES
VEA	YES	YES	YES
VWO	YES	YES	YES
VNQ	YES	YES	YES
PDBC	YES	YES	no
IAU	YES	YES	no
VGLT	YES	YES	YES
SHV	YES	YES	no
The Papa Bear			
VTV	YES	YES	YES
VUG	YES	YES	YES
VIOV	YES	YES	YES
VIOG	YES	YES	YES
VEA	YES	YES	YES
VWO	YES	YES	YES
VNQ	YES	YES	YES
PDBC	YES	YES	no
IAU	YES	YES	no
EDV	YES	YES	YES
VGIT	YES	YES	YES
VCLT	YES	YES	YES
BNDX	YES	YES	YES
The Baby Bear			
VTI	YES	YES	YES
BND	YES	YES	YES

COLOR KEY

equities	hard assets	fixed income

FIGURE 17-2 | Data as of January 2018

Know when to place your trades to avoid high spreads during 'amateur hour'

An important focus of this book is to emphasize how you can keep trading costs low. This allows you to keep more of your money for yourself, rather than paying it to Wall Street professionals.

One of a kind expense that you can keep to a bare minimum using ETFs is known as a **bid-ask spread.** The stock exchanges rely on pros called **market makers** to facilitate the buying and selling of stocks, ETFs, and other tradable securities. The spread gives these market makers a profit margin.

If you **sell** a security, the **bid** price is the amount a market maker will pay, such as $49.99. The amount you'd pay to **buy,** is the **ask** price, such as $50.01.

The bid-ask spread is the difference between the two prices, divided by the ask price. The resulting percentage is also called the **round-trip spread** (the haircut when you sell a security and buy a different one). One-half of that is called the **one-way spread** (the cost when you make one transaction but not the other).

An ETF with a bid price of $49.99 and an ask price of $50.01 has a spread of two cents. In other words, you'd lose 0.04% if you sold that ETF and immediately bought it back.

Individual stocks can have bid-ask spreads that exceed 1%. This makes trading some equities a lot more expensive than trading most ETFs.

Figures 17-3 and 17-5 show that the most popular ETFs—the ones that are used in this book's model portfolios—have very reasonable bid-ask spreads.

The spreads average about 0.05% during the middle of the trading day. (See the black circle at 12:45 PM Eastern Time in Figure 17-3.)

Some ETFs have legitimately higher spreads. These include ETFs tracking long-term US Treasury bonds and commodities. Others have lower spreads, such as those tracking large-cap equities.

The spreads of ETFs and equities change all day. Notice that the spreads are much higher in the first 60 minutes, sometimes called "amateur hour." For example, at 9:45 AM, Vanguard's 30-year Treasury ETF (symbol: EDV) has an average spread of about 0.32%. By 10:30 AM, that drops to about 0.20% and remains low the rest of the day.

Why are spreads so high in the first hour? Market makers are allowed to charge unlimited spreads to match up any imbalance of buy-and-sell orders that arrived prior to 9:30 AM. Some slick traders profit off novices in the first hour, but don't assume you can play this game and win.

Don't place market orders before the market opens. You may be unpleasantly surprised when you learn the dollar amount of your trade. As one trader told the CNBC financial news network:

"Amateur hour is 9:30 to 10:30," said Michael Murphy, a hedge fund manager with Rosecliff Capital. "Smart money trades later in the day. Risk is definitely to the upside here."[1321]

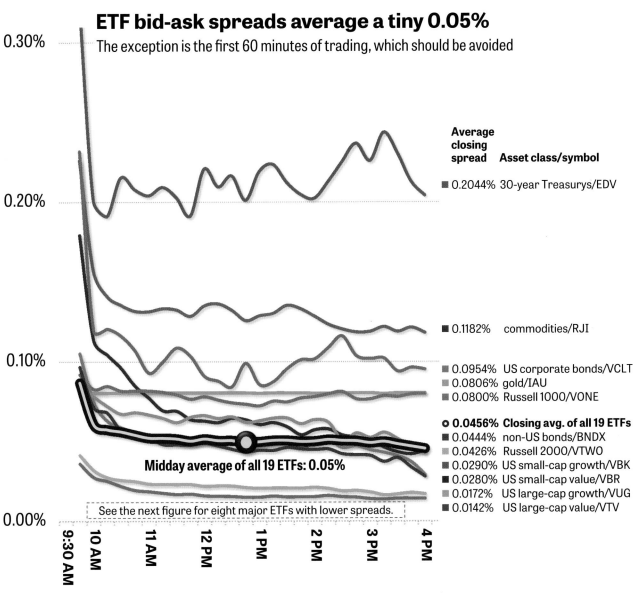

ETF bid-ask spreads average a tiny 0.05%

The exception is the first 60 minutes of trading, which should be avoided

0.30%

0.20%

0.10%

0.00%

Average closing spread   **Asset class/symbol**

0.2044%   30-year Treasurys/EDV

0.1182%   commodities/RJI

0.0954%   US corporate bonds/VCLT
0.0806%   gold/IAU
0.0800%   Russell 1000/VONE

0.0456%   Closing avg. of all 19 ETFs
0.0444%   non-US bonds/BNDX
0.0426%   Russell 2000/VTWO
0.0290%   US small-cap growth/VBK
0.0280%   US small-cap value/VBR
0.0172%   US large-cap growth/VUG
0.0142%   US large-cap value/VTV

Midday average of all 19 ETFs: 0.05%

See the next figure for eight major ETFs with lower spreads.

9:30 AM   10 AM   11 AM   12 PM   1 PM   2 PM   3 PM   4 PM

Market hours (New York time, corrected for Yahoo Finance 15-min. delay)

FIGURE 17-3 | Part 1 of 2 graphs. Source: Unpublished June 2014 study by John W. Gelm

Don't place market orders while the market is closed or in the first hour

If you want to sell one ETF and buy another, and you can wait until 10:30 AM Eastern—after "amateur hour" is safely past—doing so is likely to save you a little money.

If you're busy during the day, another way to avoid the first 60 minutes of trading is to establish an account at FolioInvesting.com, as explained later in this chapter. This online brokerage supports "window trades." These orders execute at 11 AM and 2 PM Eastern. You can place a window trade when the market is closed, and your trade occurs safely away from the market's opening or closing.

Check spreads at MuscularPortfolios.com

Price	Bid-ask spread
37.45	0.03%
97.74	0.06%

FIGURE 17-4

Other than the opening hour, don't worry about exact timing. Major ETFs incur very small spreads compared with some thinly traded stocks.

Figures 17-3 and 17-5 show that midday spreads range from only 0.20% for a 30-year Treasury ETF to a minuscule 0.009% for a money-market ETF.

However, one additional risk of buying and selling ETFs is that the market might be having a rare (but worrisome) **flash crash.**

A flash crash is a short-lived event that causes the prices of some stocks and ETFs to collapse. The prices revert to normal after a few minutes.

One of the first instances was on May 6, 2010. The Dow fell more than 600 points within five minutes. At the worst point, the index was down 9.2% from its opening price. But within 25 minutes, the market was trading normally again.[1322]

Another flash crash occurred on August 24, 2015. After some scary views, numerous individuals had placed "sell" orders over the weekend. At Monday's open, one ETF (symbol: SPLV) fell 46% within 15 minutes. It recovered by 10:30 AM. But many people who had placed a market order to sell that ETF at the open got an artificially low price.[1323]

During the crazy minutes of a flash crash, bid-ask spreads become very wide. Before you place a trade, defend yourself against these shocks by checking the ETF tables at MuscularPortfolios.com (see Figure 17-4).

If an ETF shows a spread greater than 1.0%, a flash crash may be occurring. If so, check back in an hour. If spreads have reverted below 1.0%, an orderly market has been restored. See the October 13, 2016, Muscular Portfolios Newsletter for details.[1324]

>> KEY CONCEPT

don't place market orders while the market is closed

Bid-ask spreads are highest in the first 60 minutes of each trading day, after which major ETFs boast very low spreads.

Many major ETFs have ultra-low spreads

Due to their liquidity, these funds are cheap to trade at almost all times

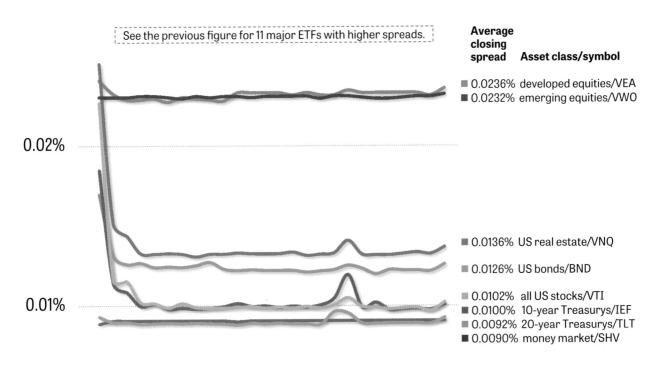

0.03%

See the previous figure for 11 major ETFs with higher spreads.

Average closing spread **Asset class/symbol**

- 0.0236% developed equities/VEA
- 0.0232% emerging equities/VWO

0.02%

- 0.0136% US real estate/VNQ
- 0.0126% US bonds/BND

0.01%

- 0.0102% all US stocks/VTI
- 0.0100% 10-year Treasurys/IEF
- 0.0092% 20-year Treasurys/TLT
- 0.0090% money market/SHV

0.00%

9:30 AM | 10 AM | 11 AM | 12 PM | 1 PM | 2 PM | 3 PM | 4 PM

Market hours (New York time, corrected for Yahoo Finance 15-min. delay)

FIGURE 17-5 | Part 2 of 2 graphs. Source: Unpublished June 2014 study by John W. Gelm

Best for Muscular Portfolios: FolioInvesting.com's low costs and powerful Web interface

The ideal online brokerage for Muscular Portfolios—and most portfolios, for that matter—is FolioInvesting.com. It has by far the easiest website to use. And it's one of the least expensive brokerages.

» Folio's Unlimited Plan might be your best value. For $30 per month or $290 per year, you can make as many trades of ETFs, mutual funds, and stocks as you need at no cost per trade.

» Folio's Basic Plan, by contrast, charges **no annual fee.** In that case, window trades cost only $4. There's a $15-per-quarter minimum fee that covers all of your subaccounts combined (taxable, IRA, Roth, etc.).

» If you make $15 to $29 worth of trades every three months, the Basic Plan is cheaper.

» If you make $30 worth of trades or more each quarter, choose the Unlimited Plan.

» Five trades per quarter, on average, are required to follow the Mama Bear or the Papa Bear (9 or 10 position changes per year, as explained in Chapter 19). If you own only one Folio subaccount—called a "folio"—making five trades per quarter at $4 each would cost you $20 using the Basic Plan.

» If you and your spouse have two IRAs, two Roths, and a taxable account, that's five subaccounts. (IRS regulations require that each person's tax-deferred funds are held separately.) Five trades per quarter multiplied by five subaccounts total 25 trades. That's $100 per quarter using the Basic Plan. It would be cheaper for you to select Folio's Unlimited Plan at $90 for three months ($72.50 per quarter, if paid annually).

» "Window trades" make these low prices possible. Folio's window trades occur at 11 AM and 2 PM Eastern Time every market day.

» When the market is closed, you can safely place a market order—thanks to the next morning's trading window. You can give Folio an order at night or before going to work, and the trade executes at 11 AM Eastern. That's well after "amateur hour"—the first 60 minutes, when high bid-ask spreads can cost you a lot.

» If you must trade this very second, Folio's immediate market orders are $10 each. (However, you should rarely need such speed.)

» Trading is super easy using Folio's website. It offers the most powerful interface on the Web to buy whatever you want (Figure 17-6). To allocate a new account for the first time, you simply enter each symbol and a comma, followed by your target percentage:

ABC, 34%
DEF, 33%
XYZ, 33%

You then select "Replace My Existing Folio" and click the Add button. The firm's computers automatically figure out for you (1) how many shares of your existing holdings to sell and (2) how many shares of your new choices to buy. Brokerage firms that require you to manually calculate dollar amounts or numbers of shares are obsolete.

» Folio's fractional shares make trading even more convenient. For example, you could purchase just $25 of Vanguard's small-cap value ETF (VIOV), which currently costs well over $100 per share.

Using the percentages you found at MuscularPortfolios.com, allocate your funds

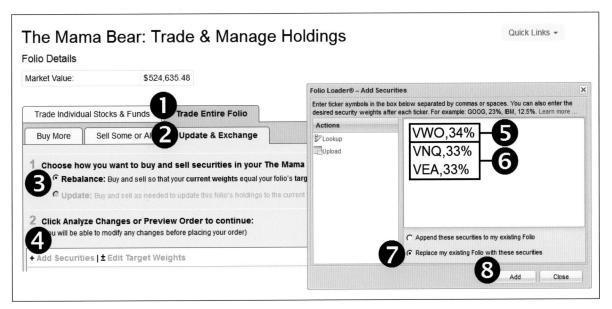

FIGURE 17-6

❶ Click the "Trade Entire Folio" tab. This tab gives you the low fees of a window trade, not a more-expensive market order.

❷ Click the "Update & Exchange" tab.

❸ Click the "Rebalance" button to assign new weights to the ETFs in your account.

❹ Click the "Add Securities" link. The Add Securities window opens, and the initial window becomes gray.

❺ Enter the symbol of the strongest ETF, a comma, and "34%." Press the Enter key at the end of the line.

❻ Enter the other two ETFs, a comma, and "33%." A one-point difference between ETFs is not significant.

❼ Select "Replace my existing Folio with these securities." This replaces any former allocation you had.

❽ Click the "Add" button to save your percentages.

Back on the Trade page, click the "Preview Order" button. On the Preview Order page, click "Place Order."

Getting started is the hardest step, but don't let it daunt you

Either a truly free brokerage, like Robinhood, or a low-cost Web-based brokerage like Folio can let you focus on your financial needs without worry.

If you don't have a brokerage account, the first step may seem daunting. If your account is larger than $10,000, you'll probably want the comfort of a brokerage with a sophisticated website and live telephone support. If you choose Folio, it's easy to (1) let a human help you through the process or (2) let the website guide you:

» Call Folio at 888-973-7890 or 703-245-5772 from 7 AM to midnight Eastern Time on weekdays (closed holidays) or 8 AM to 4 PM on weekends.

» Or visit FolioInvesting. com and click "Open New Account." The resulting Web page will help you transfer your account from your old bank or brokerage firm.

Don't contact your old brokerage firm and ask them to "push" your money to Folio. Instead, ask Folio for the forms to sign and let Folio "pull" the money.

Check one hour after trades to confirm order execution

Folio's window trades are very convenient. You can place an order at night, and Folio executes it the next day—well after "amateur hour" when bid-ask spreads are at their highest.

There's one catch, however. If market prices make big moves, Folio can't fill your order with your available funds. You should always check your order status 60 minutes after a window trade was to be executed.

If your order status says "Canceled," you'll have to resubmit the order. Fortunately, this happens rarely and it's easy to work around.

Simply redo the steps shown in Figure 17-8. Then click the "Modify Order" button on the Preview Order page. Buy a few dollars less of each ETF (Figure 17-7).

LIVINGSTON'S LAW OF BARGAIN BROKERAGES

Finding a firm where your orders can flow
Means using a broker that keeps your costs low.

» KEY CONCEPT

a bargain brokerage like Folio can help you at a tiny cost

No matter how self-reliant you are as a Web user, being able to call Folio's live human support to handle questions is reassuring.

Avoid paying commissions to buy or sell shares due to rounding errors

FIGURE 17-7

Folio makes it easy to buy 34%, 33%, or any percentage of any ETF. As shown in Figure 17-6, you simply type in the symbol and a percentage. Folio computes the number of shares for you.

If you pay a fee for each trade—as opposed to paying an annual fee for an Unlimited Account— you should avoid small trades due to rounding errors.

Say you're selling an "old" ETF and buying a "new" one. The old ETF represents 34% of your portfolio. You enter 0% to sell the old one and 34% to buy the new one. You enter the "Current Percentage" for other ETFs you're keeping. They shouldn't trade.

Folio's server may think you want to allocate **exactly** the "Current Percentage" to the ETFs you're keeping. If you see small buys or sells like this in your order:

❶ Click the "Modify Order" button.

❷ For the ETFs you're keeping, change the dollar amount to **$0.00.** Leave the "Buy" and "Sell" drop-downs the same. Don't change them to "None." Buying or selling $0.00 creates **no transaction at all**—so you don't pay $4 for each unnecessary trade.

18 Rebalance your portfolio without getting all obsessive about it

"It's difficult for intelligent people, especially in the world of finance, to admit that less is more and simple can be a far more effective framework than complex for the majority of investors. Some view this as an admission of ignorance. In fact, I view it as the ultimate sign of intelligence."

BEN CARLSON, *A Wealth of Common Sense*[1325]

At some point, every portfolio that contains multiple asset classes should be rebalanced to restore the original percentages.

Why? Because keeping your portfolio more-or-less balanced—without any one asset dominating—can improve your return almost one-half a percentage point every year.

Imagine the simplest possible allocation: the Baby Bear Portfolio. It starts out with 50% in a US stock ETF and 50% in a US bond ETF.

As time passes, stocks might rise to 70% of the portfolio, with only 30% in bonds. An imbalance like that harms diversification and worsens crashes.

To rebalance, you'd sell some of the stock ETF and use the cash to purchase some more of the bond ETF. That makes each asset class 50% of your portfolio again (Figure 18-1).

Numerous studies have looked at balanced portfolios with only two asset classes. The usual recommendation is to rebalance once a year,

but only if the assets are more than 5% off their ideal weight. For example, a Vanguard analysis concluded:

"Annual or semiannual monitoring, with rebalancing at 5% thresholds, is likely to produce a reasonable balance between risk control and cost minimization . . . Annual rebalancing is likely to be preferred when taxes or substantial time/costs are involved."[1326]

You can do even better with a Muscular Portfolio, using a slightly more sophisticated rebalancing method.

» KEY CONCEPT
conventional wisdom recommends rebalancing at 5% off target
Experts say 50/50 portfolios like the Baby Bear should be rebalanced each year if either of the two assets is more than 5% from equal weight.

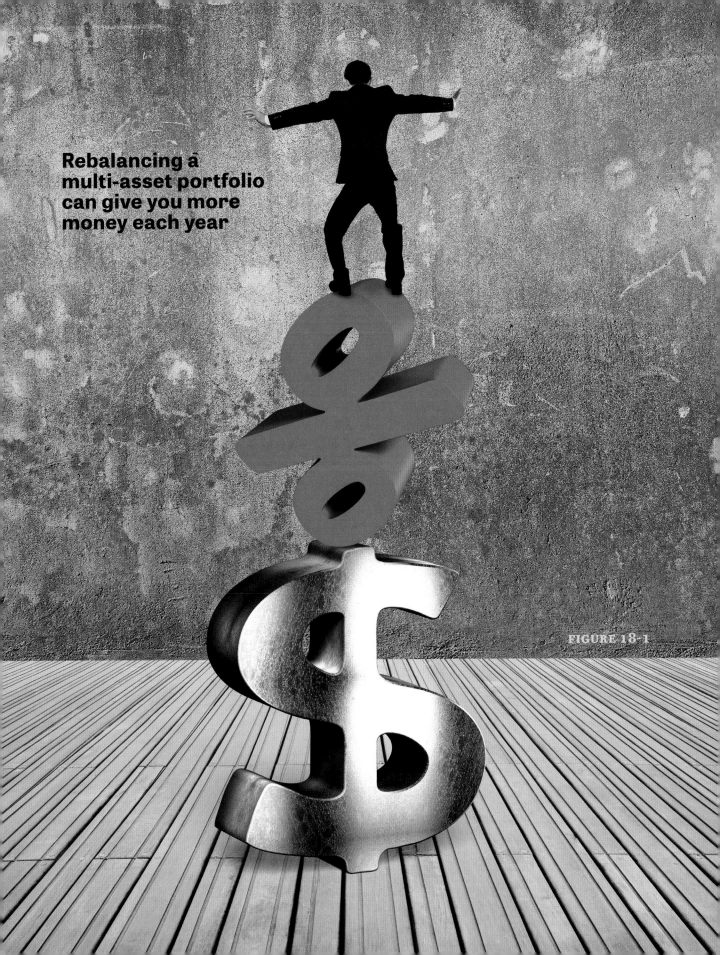

Rebalancing a multi-asset portfolio can give you more money each year

FIGURE 18-1

Rebalancing only when 20% off a target is best for Muscular Portfolios

The best rebalancing rule for a multi-asset portfolio was revealed in a 2008 study for the *Journal of Financial Planning*.[1327] The author showed that you should let your winners run until one asset is 20% off equal weight, not just 5%. The rules are:

1 · Check monthly. Compared with taking no action, rebalancing a multi-asset portfolio in any month when it's necessary improves your performance an annualized 0.40 percentage point. If you're really ambitious, checking twice a month offers an improvement of 0.45 point.

2 · Rebalance at 20%. Let's say your portfolio is worth $300,000. You start the year with $100,000 in each of three ETFs. Don't rebalance unless an ETF is over $120,000 or under $80,000.

3 · To reduce costs, just rebalance halfway. If an ETF is 20% higher than the ideal weight, you need only reduce the position to $110,000 from $120,000. Selling $10,000 of the asset instead of $20,000 cuts in half whatever bid-ask spread you'd pay. In a taxable account, this also reduces your capital gains tax.

Figure 18-2 shows how 20% **rebalancing bands** and 10% **tolerance bands** work. You simply sell some shares of the ETF that represents the largest percentage of your portfolio and use the cash to buy shares of the ETF that's the smallest.

Why wait for a 20% divergence when you could act on any 5% spread? CXO Advisory studied rebalancing a portfolio like the Mama Bear. Each of the portfolio's three ETFs started at a 33.3% allocation. The percentages were allowed to stray 5% (in other words, up to 35% or down to 32%).

These small differences had almost no effect:

"Deviations of a few percent from equal weights do not substantially change outcome. . . . These results indicate that it is safe to exercise judgment on whether to rebalance when portfolio weights deviate a few percent from equal."[1328]

In short, don't obsess about giving each of a Muscular Portfolio's ETFs the exact same dollar value every month. If each ETF is within 20% of its target—and you bring any wanderers within 10%—any differences in performance are probably too small to worry about.

LIVINGSTON'S LAW OF REBALANCING

If one of your assets is zooming away
Nudge it toward equal weight some day.

» KEY CONCEPT

use 20% tolerance for rebalancing

A Muscular Portfolio requires rebalancing only if one ETF is more than 20% off its ideal weight.

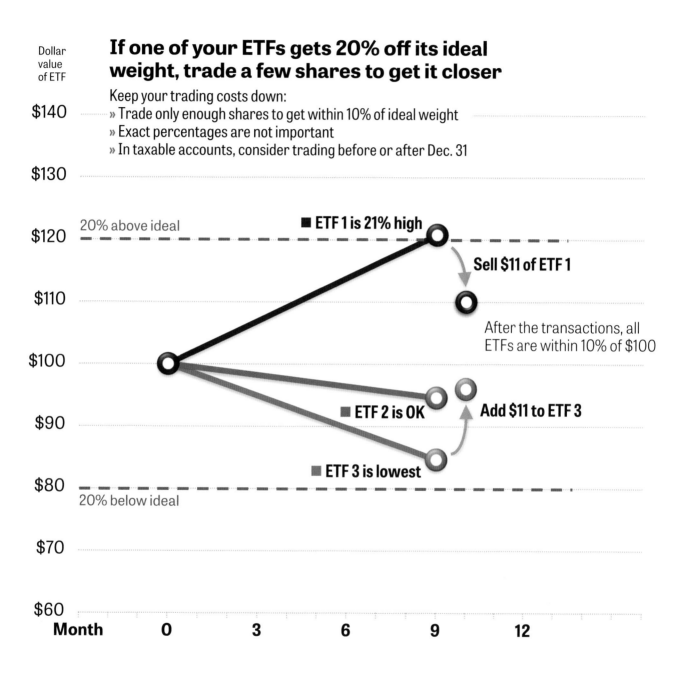

Dollar value of ETF

If one of your ETFs gets 20% off its ideal weight, trade a few shares to get it closer

Keep your trading costs down:
» Trade only enough shares to get within 10% of ideal weight
» Exact percentages are not important
» In taxable accounts, consider trading before or after Dec. 31

$140

$130

20% above ideal
$120 ■ ETF 1 is 21% high

Sell $11 of ETF 1

$110

After the transactions, all ETFs are within 10% of $100

$100

■ ETF 2 is OK   Add $11 to ETF 3

$90

■ ETF 3 is lowest

$80
20% below ideal

$70

$60
Month   0   3   6   9   12

FIGURE 18-2

19 Reduce the IRS tax bite with 401(k)s, IRAs, and Roths

"The best way to teach your kids about taxes is by eating 30% of their ice cream." [1329]

@BILLMURRAY, Twitter parodist (not the actor)

Most academic papers and books pretend taxes don't exist. The authors completely ignore the bite taxes can take out of your performance.

Books and whitepapers often say, "This study ignores trading commissions, bid-ask spreads, and taxes." But all of these are major hazards to your financial goals.

Such works are worse than useless. They're misleading! They can fool you right up until you wonder where your glorious gains got up and went.

As we saw in Chapter 11, "management" fees of 1%, 2%, or 3% can seriously transfer your life savings out of your pocket and into someone else's.

What do you think will happen to your return if you subtract 30% of your gains each year and send it to the IRS? You're right, it makes a big difference!

Paying taxes on your investment gains every year can cut your lifetime spendable money more than management fees, expense ratios, and everything else that drains your gains.

The IRS calls 401(k) plans and similar tax-deferred employer-sponsored programs **Qualified Plans.** By contrast, traditional IRAs, Roth IRAs, health savings accounts (HSAs), and others are called **individually managed plans.** Together, these two kinds of programs can save you big bucks on taxes.

This book uses **401(k)** as shorthand for all Qualified Plans, but the offerings vary wildly depending on whether you're self-employed or work for a corporation, government agency, or tax-exempt nonprofit.

This chapter shows you before-tax and after-tax returns for this book's Muscular Portfolios. Following that, you may be amazed to see the riot of tax-deferral programs the US government makes available to reduce your tax liability.

Never assume you can't lower your tax bite. Many people pay higher taxes than they actually should.

> » KEY CONCEPT
> ## Qualified Plans
> The IRS gives favorable tax treatment to programs such as the 401(k) for private employers, 457(b) for government agencies, and 403(b) for tax-exempt nonprofits.

Your biggest investing expense may be taxes, if you don't plan

FIGURE 19-1

The Papa Bear Portfolio can compete even in the highest tax bracket

The Papa Bear Portfolio is great in a taxable account for people in middle-class tax brackets (10% and 12%). For example, Figure 19-2 shows that the Papa Bear's annualized (ann'd) return of 16.2% was reduced less than 1 percentage point to 15.3% for filers in the 10% tax bracket, using 2018 tax rates.

However, the Papa Bear is also very attractive to people in the highest tax bracket. That includes people with taxable income over $600,000 for couples or $500,000 for singles. More than 50% of the Papa Bear's sales are long-term capital gains or gold gains. These are taxed at favorable rates of only 23.8% to 31.8%, rather than the much higher 40.8% rate on ordinary income.

In the highest tax bracket, including the 3.8% net investment income tax (new since 2013), the Papa Bear's annualized return drops to 10.7%. That's still above a buy-and-hold of the S&P 500 at 10.1% annualized.

What if the Papa Bear in a taxable account only **matches** the S&P 500 in future years? You would still enjoy the smooth ride and lack of crashes that the Papa Bear is known for.

S&P 500 vs. Papa Bear with no tax, low tax, or high tax	S&P 500 with no taxes	Papa with no taxes	Papa in lowest tax bracket	Papa in highest tax bracket
Annualized return	10.07%	16.22%	15.28%	10.73%
T-bill ann'd return	4.8%	4.8%	4.8%	4.8%
Ulcer Index	13.9%	7.4%	7.7%	10.3%
Martin ratio	0.38	1.53	1.36	0.57
Max. DD (including tax)	-50.95%	-25.48%	-25.48%	-26.65%
Round-trip trades/yr.	0.0	8.9	8.9	8.9
$100 becomes	$6,246	$64,913	$45,708	$8,086
Inflation annualized	3.98%	3.98%	3.98%	3.98%

All performance numbers reflect current trading costs and fees

COSTS

Round-trip trade cost	0.00%	0.10%	0.10%	0.10%
Annual mgmt. fees	0.05%	0.16%	0.16%	0.16%

TAX REPORT

Inflation-adj. dollars

PAPA BEAR TAXABLE GAINS	Total gain	Percent
(nominal start value: $100 on Jan. 1, 1973)		
Short-term capital gains	$83,880	49.86%
Long-term capital gains	75,738	45.02%
Gold gains	8,622	5.12%
SUM of all taxable investment gains	$168,240	100%

MARGINAL TAX RATES (including NIIT)	Lowest bracket	Highest bracket
Short-term capital gains	10.00%	40.80%
Long-term capital gains	0.00%	23.80%
Gold gains ("collectible" tax rate)	10.00%	31.80%

» KEY CONCEPT

Muscular Portfolios can be used in taxable accounts

The Papa Bear can excel even for households in the highest tax bracket.

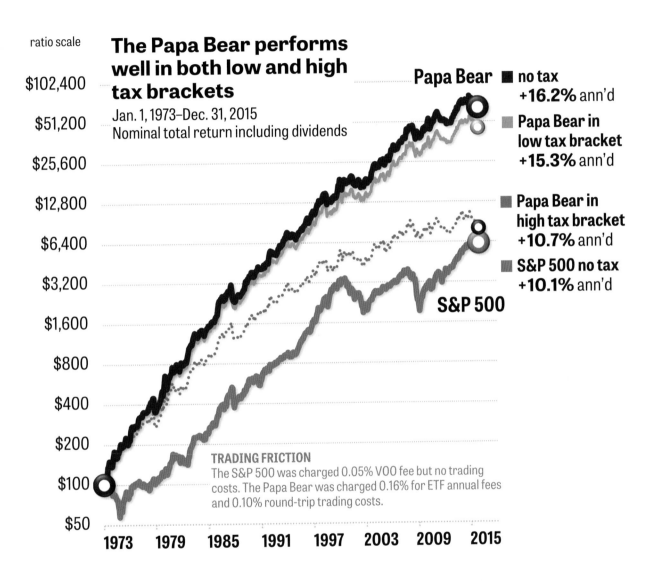

The Papa Bear performs well in both low and high tax brackets

Jan. 1, 1973–Dec. 31, 2015
Nominal total return including dividends

ratio scale

$102,400
$51,200
$25,600
$12,800
$6,400
$3,200
$1,600
$800
$400
$200
$100
$50

1973 1979 1985 1991 1997 2003 2009 2015

Papa Bear

■ no tax
+16.2% ann'd

■ Papa Bear in low tax bracket
+15.3% ann'd

■ Papa Bear in high tax bracket
+10.7% ann'd

■ S&P 500 no tax
+10.1% ann'd

S&P 500

TRADING FRICTION
The S&P 500 was charged 0.05% VOO fee but no trading costs. The Papa Bear was charged 0.16% for ETF annual fees and 0.10% round-trip trading costs.

FIGURE 19-2 | Source: Quant simulator

The Mama Bear incurs little tax for people with middle-class incomes

If this chapter teaches anything, it's the importance of moving as much money as you can each year from taxable accounts into tax-deferred accounts. Those include traditional IRAs, Roths, 401(k) plans, and other tax-privileged programs. These are described later in this chapter.

Figure 19-3 shows why this is so important. Over the last 43 years, the Mama Bear Portfolio would have risen at an annualized rate of return of 14.3% in a tax-deferred account.

For taxpayers in middle-class tax brackets—for example, couples with taxable income up to $77,000— that return would have been reduced by only 1 percentage point to 13.3% annualized using 2018 tax rates.

However, taxpayers in the highest tax bracket—taxable income over $600,000 for couples or $500,000 for singles—would have seen their rate of return cut more than 5 percentage points to 9.2% annualized. That would have eliminated the outperformance of the Mama Bear. A buy-and-hold of an S&P 500 tracking fund like VOO (which includes an annual fee of 0.05%) would have returned 10.1%.

S&P 500 vs. Mama Bear with no tax, low tax, or high tax	S&P 500 with no taxes	Mama with no taxes	Mama in lowest tax bracket	Mama in highest tax bracket
Annualized return	10.07%	14.32%	13.28%	9.16%
T-bill ann'd return	4.8%	4.8%	4.8%	4.8%
Ulcer Index	13.9%	4.8%	5.0%	7.6%
Martin ratio	0.38	1.98	1.68	0.57
Max. DD (including tax)	-50.95%	-18.17%	-18.17%	-24.51%
Round-trip trades/yr.	0.0	9.4	9.4	9.4
$100 becomes	$6,246	$31,876	$21,555	$4,366
Inflation annualized	3.98%	3.98%	3.98%	3.98%

All performance numbers reflect current trading costs and fees

COSTS

Round-trip trade cost	0.00%	0.10%	0.10%	0.10%
Annual mgmt. fees	0.05%	0.20%	0.20%	0.20%

TAX REPORT

Inflation-adj. dollars

MAMA BEAR TAXABLE GAINS (nominal start value: $100 on Jan. 1, 1973)	Total gain	Percent
Short-term capital gains	$33,009	61.16%
Long-term capital gains	16,986	31.47%
Gold gains	3,980	7.37%
SUM of all taxable investment gains	$53,974	100%

MARGINAL TAX RATES (including NIIT)	Lowest bracket	Highest bracket
Short-term capital gains	10.00%	40.80%
Long-term capital gains	0.00%	23.80%
Gold gains ("collectible" tax rate)	10.00%	31.80%

To keep all of your Mama Bear gains, maximize your use of tax-deferred accounts. But even if you only have taxable accounts, the Mama Bear is still preferable, because it avoids the S&P 500's intolerable 30% to 50% crashes every 10 years or so.

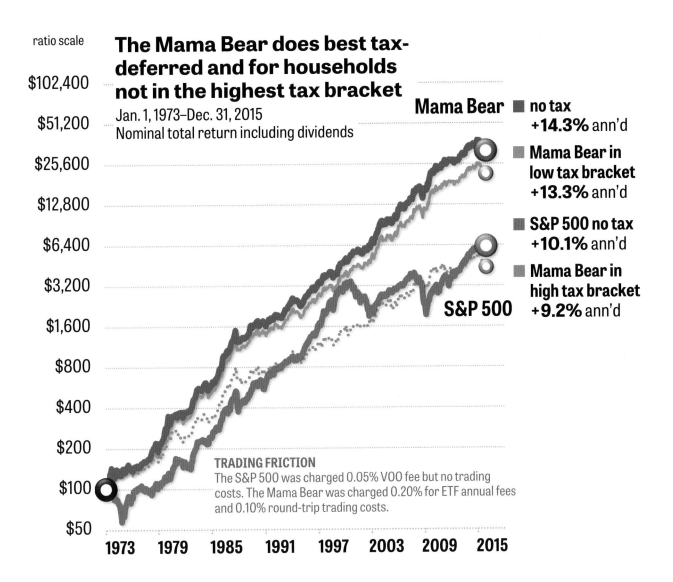

The Mama Bear does best tax-deferred and for households not in the highest tax bracket

Jan. 1, 1973–Dec. 31, 2015
Nominal total return including dividends

ratio scale

$102,400

$51,200

$25,600

$12,800

$6,400

$3,200

$1,600

$800

$400

$200

$100

$50

Mama Bear

■ no tax
+14.3% ann'd

■ Mama Bear in low tax bracket
+13.3% ann'd

■ S&P 500 no tax
+10.1% ann'd

■ Mama Bear in high tax bracket
+9.2% ann'd

S&P 500

TRADING FRICTION
The S&P 500 was charged 0.05% VOO fee but no trading costs. The Mama Bear was charged 0.20% for ETF annual fees and 0.10% round-trip trading costs.

1973   1979   1985   1991   1997   2003   2009   2015

FIGURE 19-3 | Source: Quant simulator

Reduce taxes and keep more money with 401(k)s, IRAs, and Roths

Benjamin Franklin wrote in 1789, "In this world, nothing can be said to be certain, except death and taxes."[1330]

Well, we still face death. But the US government does a lot to reduce or completely eliminate taxes on your investment gains—if you know the drill.

The ways Americans shelter their returns from tax seem to be limited only by the imagination. And informed investors are **very** imaginative.

In Chapter 21, we'll see that a small shift from one account to another can make big differences in the taxation of Social Security benefits.

In this chapter, we examine how to:

1 · **Maximize tax breaks for your savings plans** and

2 · **Minimize your lifetime tax bite.**

Important: Every taxpayer has a different situation. If you earn more than a minimal income, be sure to consult a tax professional.

The types of plans summarized in Figure 19-4 are explained in detail later in this chapter. There are four guidelines:

1 · **In high-tax years**—when your tax bracket is greater than 12%—make tax-deductible deposits to **before-tax accounts.** You can usually deduct these contributions on your tax return if you have self-employment or wage income that year.

2 · **In low-tax years**—when your tax bracket is 12% or lower—consider making after-tax contributions directly into a Roth. Contributions taxed 12% or less can save you money over time, as explained later in this chapter. Roth gains and allowable withdrawals are never taxed.

3 · **Every year,** make tax-deductible contributions to a health savings account (HSA), if you qualify. You must have a high-deductible health insurance policy, and you must save receipts for all unreimbursed health bills. But, as we'll see, an HSA is both a "stealth IRA" and a "super Roth."

4 · **Every year** from about age 55 through 69, make taxable conversions from **before-tax accounts** to a Roth. Research that's described in this chapter shows that paying tax on conversions before age 70 can give you significantly more money over your lifetime.

People don't seem to "get" Roths. Americans have $11.8 trillion in 401(k)s and traditional IRAs, but only $660 billion in Roths. Let's fix that.[1331]

How to play the Game of Life Savings

Preserve your gains by making IRA-to-Roth conversions over time.

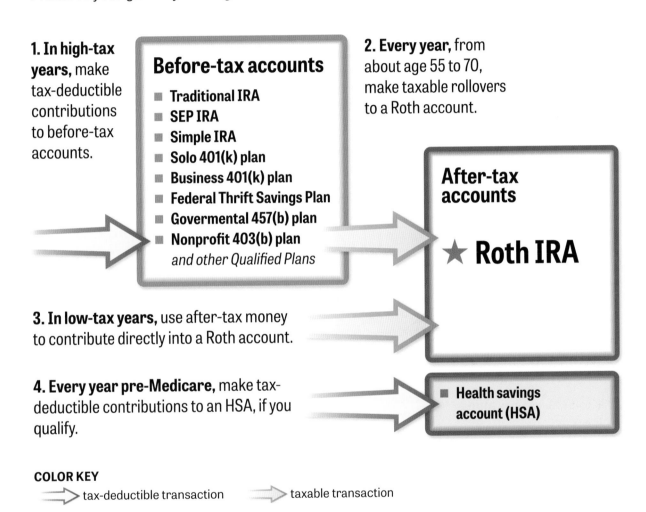

1. In high-tax years, make tax-deductible contributions to before-tax accounts.

Before-tax accounts

- **Traditional IRA**
- **SEP IRA**
- **Simple IRA**
- **Solo 401(k) plan**
- **Business 401(k) plan**
- **Federal Thrift Savings Plan**
- **Govermental 457(b) plan**
- **Nonprofit 403(b) plan**
  and other Qualified Plans

2. Every year, from about age 55 to 70, make taxable rollovers to a Roth account.

After-tax accounts

★ **Roth IRA**

3. In low-tax years, use after-tax money to contribute directly into a Roth account.

4. Every year pre-Medicare, make tax-deductible contributions to an HSA, if you qualify.

- **Health savings account (HSA)**

COLOR KEY

⇒ tax-deductible transaction   ⇒ taxable transaction

FIGURE 19-4 | Illustration by Pieter Tandjung

Get tax deductions with a traditional IRA and then tax-free income from a Roth

The Roth IRA is a tax shelter established by Congress in 1997—more than two decades after the traditional IRA was first authorized back in 1974.[1332]

With a traditional IRA, you receive a full deduction on your tax return in the year of your deposit, up to certain limits. You pay no tax on that income that year and no tax on any gains your investments earn. Taxes are due only when you finally make withdrawals from the account, years in the future (Figure 19-5).

Of course, the US Treasury wants to get some tax dollars eventually. You must take a percentage called a required minimum distribution (RMD) from your IRA after age 70½. You pay ordinary income tax rates—at marginal rates of 10% to 37%—on the money you remove. You don't get the lower long-term capital-gains tax rate of 0% to 20%. It doesn't matter whether you've held an IRA for more than 12 months.

A Roth is more interesting. With a Roth, your money is taxed when it goes in but not when you take it out. Like a traditional IRA, your gains grow tax-free—a tax break that compounds.

Two features make a Roth better than an IRA:

1 · You can remove any of your contributions from a Roth at any time, with no penalty or tax.

2 · You can remove any capital gains from your Roth with no penalty or tax as soon as you're over 59½ and you are **seasoned.**

What does "seasoned" mean? It means your Roth account has existed for at least **five tax years** starting on January 1 of the first contribution year.

For example, say you open a Roth account by making an initial contribution on April 15, 2022. You tell your brokerage firm to record the contribution for tax year 2021, not 2022. Your five-year "seasoning clock" therefore started ticking on January 1, 2021—15½ months **before** you made the actual deposit.

The result is that you can remove any of your Roth **gains** without tax or penalty on January 1, 2025, if you're over 59½ at that time.

On January 1, 2025, your Roth is in its fifth tax year. But January 1, 2025, is only 3 years and 8½ months after you opened the account on April 15, 2022.

Don't wait until the last minute to start a Roth. A brokerage firm may take several business days to open a new account.

It makes sense to fund your first Roth as soon as possible, even if it's just $100. But be sure to do so before you turn 55½. You want to be seasoned by the time you're 59½, enabling you to remove your gains tax-free.

A conversion from an IRA, a Qualified Plan, or a designated Roth (described later in this chapter) into a new Roth **also** starts your seasoning clock. If you happen to have two or more Roths, the **oldest** one determines whether you are seasoned.

Caution: So-called designated Roths each have their own, separate five-tax-year seasoning clock.[1333]

See "To Roth or Not to Roth" at Kitces.com.[1334]

Eventually moving your money from a 401(k) to an IRA or a Roth is the goal

FIGURE 19-5

Don't underestimate the Roth; one entrepreneur saved $95 million, tax free

As we've seen, the most attractive feature of a Roth is that any of your gains can be removed without penalty or tax after you turn 59½. This no-tax aspect of Roths has drawn the interest of business people who are able to control the timing of their withdrawals.

There are stories of some company founders putting millions of early-stage shares into Roths. Shares may be worth only a fraction of a penny before a company gets going. But if the firm is ever acquired or goes public, the shares can suddenly trade for hundreds of times more.

If the gain occurred within a Roth, it's **never taxed** when withdrawn.

These tales are not merely idle rumors. The facts are detailed in official financial reports that company executives are required to file with the US Securities & Exchange Commission (SEC).

Deborah Jacobs, a finance columnist for *Forbes* magazine, reports that the former chairman of the review site Yelp.com, Max Levchin, used just such a technique (Figure 19-6). SEC filings show that Levchin sold 3.1 million Yelp shares that had been inside a Roth in 2010, according to Jacobs. The SEC also showed that the Roth still held 3.9 million as-yet-unsold Yelp shares in 2012.[1335]

Based on the prices of the shares then, this all adds up to $95 million—maybe more, if other startups are involved, too. The gain will never be taxed, assuming Levchin waits until he's 59½ to withdraw the profits. That's the way to Max out your Roth!

Tax-free gains on this scale require a special plan sponsor called a "self-directed IRA custodian." That trick is described at the end of this chapter.

Max Levchin, as chairman of Yelp, sheltered 7 million shares from taxation

FIGURE 19-6

The US subsidizes wealth-building accounts more than all discretionary social spending combined

The federal government devotes more subsidies to various wealth-building tax shelters than it spends on the discretionary budgets of every social agency combined.

Figure 19-7 shows that the US devotes $620 billion in **tax expenditures** (subsidies) to wealth-building activities.

These subsidies in the 2014 budget exceeded the entire $581 billion military budget.[1336] And they far exceeded the $464 billion spent on all discretionary social programs, such as Housing and Urban Development, Veterans Affairs, and others.[1337] (Social Security, Medicare, and other entitlements are mandatory, not discretionary.) A former member of George W. Bush's Council of Economic Advisors has called the subsidies "spending in disguise."[1338]

The top 20% of households enjoy about 74% of the government's subsidy dollars for IRAs, Qualified Plans, and other programs, according to Prosperity Now (formerly CED).[1339]

You may agree or disagree with these government priorities. Either way, you're leaving a lot of money on the table unless you use every tax shelter you can.

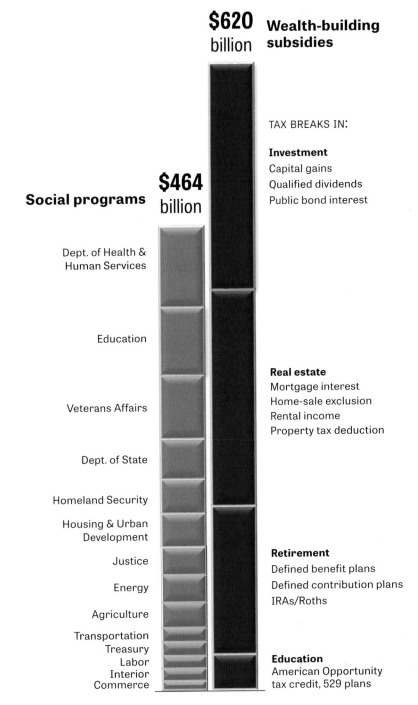

$620 billion — Wealth-building subsidies

TAX BREAKS IN:

Investment
Capital gains
Qualified dividends
Public bond interest

Real estate
Mortgage interest
Home-sale exclusion
Rental income
Property tax deduction

Retirement
Defined benefit plans
Defined contribution plans
IRAs/Roths

Education
American Opportunity
tax credit, 529 plans

$464 billion — Social programs

Dept. of Health & Human Services
Education
Veterans Affairs
Dept. of State
Homeland Security
Housing & Urban Development
Justice
Energy
Agriculture
Transportation
Treasury
Labor
Interior
Commerce

FIGURE 19-7 | Sources: Prosperity Now,[1340] *New York Times*[1341]

Understand which tax bracket you're in to see how much you can save

A crucial factor in building up your nest egg is how much you shelter your earnings and gains from tax.

Figure 19-8 shows (in yellow) a big benefit of sheltering as much income as possible into Roths, HSAs, and other nontaxable sources of income. If you shelter your savings and keep your taxable income under $77,400 for couples ($38,700 for singles), your long-term capital gains in taxable accounts are taxed at 0%. That's **the golden zero.** This one tax break can really increase your spendable income.

A much different situation applies to ordinary taxable incomes over $600,000 for couples ($500,000 for singles). Any additional capital gains in their taxable accounts can be taxed as much as 40.8%. (That's the 37% marginal tax rate plus the 3.8% net investment income tax.)

Informed investors use two primary methods to reduce taxes on their gains:

» Reduce taxable income through deductions. The lower your taxable income, the lower the rate you'll pay on your investment gains. This is an area where paying for a good tax preparer can be well worth it. Figure 19-9 lists just a few tax-reducing options—there are many others.

» Max out tax-deferred accounts. Income that you contribute to a company-sponsored savings plan like a 401(k) or into your own traditional IRA can be deducted from this year's income.

If you don't qualify for one of these plans, you may be able to contribute dollars into a Roth IRA instead. Roth contributions reap no tax deductions. The big benefit is that you pay no tax on gains you withdraw after you are

59½ and "seasoned" (you've had any Roth for at least five tax years).

You can exploit some combinations of 401(k), IRA, and Roth for higher gains with lower taxes:

» Contribute to a 401(k) or an IRA in your high-earning years, and then

» Convert your 401(k) or IRA dollars into Roth dollars in years when your earnings are low. The conversion is taxable, but you're in a low bracket. How to do this is explained later in this chapter.

You **never** pay the marginal rate on your entire income, as we'll see in Figure 19-9. You pay the lowest rate on your "first dollar." Higher rates are only charged on dollars in higher brackets.

Use the 'golden zero'—a 0% tax rate on long-term capital gains for average earners

Taxable income, single filers		Taxable income, joint filers		Marginal rate, short-term capital gains	Marginal rate, long-term capital gains
$ 0 –	9,525	$ 0 –	19,050	10%	**0%**
$ 9,526 –	38,700	$ 19,051 –	77,400	12	**0%**
$ 38,701 –	82,500	$ 77,401 –	165,000	22	15%
$ 82,501 –	157,500	$ 165,001 –	315,000	24	15
$ 157,501 –	200,000	$ 315,001 –	400,000	32	15
$ 200,001 –	500,000	$ 400,001 –	600,000	35	15
$ 500,001 +		$ 600,001 +		37	20

» **Long-term capital gains** (sales that are at least 12 months and 1 day after purchase, as well as qualified dividends) incur **no tax** for households who arrange their "taxable income" to stay under $77,400 for couples, $38,700 for singles.

» **Above those income levels,** long-term capital gains are taxed at only 15% to 20%—lower tax rates than short-term gains.

» **In taxable accounts, short-term** capital gains (sales of securities 12 months or less after purchase) are taxed 10% to 37%, just like ordinary income.

» **In tax-deferred accounts,** such as traditional IRAs, sales incur no tax, but withdrawals incur short-term capital gains tax rates (just as ordinary income does).

NIIT and AMT for high earners

» Above a MAGI (modified adjusted gross income) of $200,000 single, $250,000 joint, you pay an additional 3.8% net investment income tax on capital gains and other investment income.

» Alternative minimum tax (AMT) may also be due for certain high earners.

FIGURE 19-8
2018 tax rates. Sources: Tax Foundation (tax brackets);[1342] IRS (net investment income tax)[1343]

About 47% of Americans pay no federal income tax and needn't worry about it

A campaign issue in the 2012 US presidential election was the fact that about 47% of Americans make so little money that they don't have to pay any federal income tax. The joke is that the other 53% are using various shelters to reduce the bite but haven't **quite** achieved a zero income tax rate yet.

Figure 19-9 shows one of these near-zero taxpayers. Even with a luxurious gross income of $150,000, a highly compensated worker can pay an "effective" tax rate of only 1.65%. That's far from the 24% marginal rate, which is a sort of "mythical" rate.

On the other end of the spectrum, many moderate-income households owe no income tax despite holding one or more full-time jobs. To be sure, they may pay a substantial amount in Social Security taxes, Medicare taxes, state sales taxes, local property taxes, and other levies. But moderate earners may be able to avoid paying income tax on wages or even on capital gains.

As Figure 19-8 showed, couples with taxable income as high as $77,400 (and single filers up to $38,700) pay **no income tax at all** on long-term capital gains.

As we saw on page 262, more than 50% of the Papa Bear Portfolio's dollar profits are long-term capital gains and gold gains, both of which are taxed at preferential rates. These tax-advantaged gains make Muscular Portfolios relatively tax-efficient.

By contrast, people who pay no federal income tax may be able to avoid tax on both short-term **and** long-term capital gains in their savings accounts.

Here's how one person arrived at an income tax liability of zero (this example uses 2018 rates):

» **Dana is a working parent with one child.** Let's assume the local, state, and federal minimum wage levels in the area are all the same: $7.25 per hour. Working a 40-hour-per-week job, Dana earns a gross income of $15,080 per year.[1344]

» **The IRS standard deduction** for a head of household in 2018 was $18,000.

» **The earned income tax credit (EITC)** for a person in Dana's situation was $3,461.[1345]

» **The child tax credit** for Dana was $2,000.[1346]

The $18,000 deduction and $5,461 of credits equaled more than Dana's $15,080 gross income. Dana owes **no income tax.** The EITC and child tax credit are "refundable" (payable), so Dana received from the IRS a cash payment of $5,461.

Finally, say Dana has a small, taxable brokerage account. It could realize up to $2,920 of short- or long-term capital gains and **incur no income tax.** Also, capital gains like these wouldn't reduce Dana's tax credits.

Even people with long work histories can sometimes find themselves in low-tax situations. For example, an entrepreneur starting a new business might have no profit in the first year. That would put him or her in the lowest tax bracket.

No one actually pays the marginal tax rate

For this single, highly compensated worker, the mythical **marginal rate is 24%.**
But $150,000 of gross income requires paying only an **effective rate of 1.65%.**

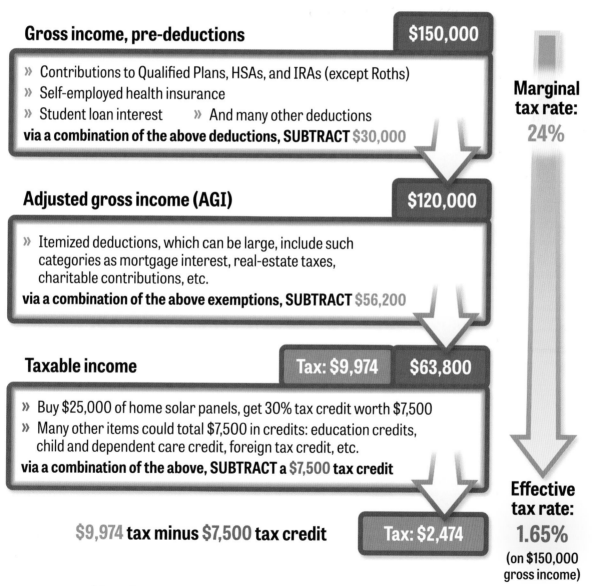

Gross income, pre-deductions   **$150,000**

» Contributions to Qualified Plans, HSAs, and IRAs (except Roths)
» Self-employed health insurance
» Student loan interest   » And many other deductions
via a combination of the above deductions, SUBTRACT $30,000

Adjusted gross income (AGI)   **$120,000**

» Itemized deductions, which can be large, include such
  categories as mortgage interest, real-estate taxes,
  charitable contributions, etc.
via a combination of the above exemptions, SUBTRACT $56,200

Taxable income   Tax: $9,974   **$63,800**

» Buy $25,000 of home solar panels, get 30% tax credit worth $7,500
» Many other items could total $7,500 in credits: education credits,
  child and dependent care credit, foreign tax credit, etc.
via a combination of the above, SUBTRACT a $7,500 **tax credit**

$9,974 **tax minus** $7,500 **tax credit**   Tax: $2,474

Marginal tax rate:
24%

Effective tax rate:
1.65%
(on $150,000 gross income)

FIGURE 19-9 | Based on 2018 tax rates. Source: Denise Olivier.[1347]
Adapted from Bonnie Lee, Fox Business. Illustration by Pieter Tandjung

Don't miss the saver's credit, which can put 2,000 bucks in your pocket

One little-known tax credit actually **pays** you up to $1,000 if you're single, and $2,000 if you're married—just for contributing to your own savings plan.

The so-called saver's credit was authorized by Congress in 2001. But only 12% of taxpayers who are eligible to get the money actually claim it on their tax returns.[1348]

The maximum adjusted gross income (AGI) to qualify in 2018 was $31,500 for single filers and $63,000 for joint filers.[1349] But remember the facts we saw in Figure 19-9. Even if a couple's gross income is over $100,000, deductions and exemptions might push the AGI down into saver's credit territory.

Examples of the credit amounts you could receive are in Figure 19-10. Let's look at some details:

» Singles can get a credit up to $1,000 for contributions up to $2,000.

» Married couples can get a credit up to $2,000 for contributions up to $4,000.

» Pretax contributions to Qualified Plans and traditional IRAs count, in addition to after-tax contributions to Roths. You can deduct Qualified Plan and IRA contributions from your reported income **and then subtract an additional credit** up to $2,000 from whatever tax you owe.

» You must lower your claimed contribution by any withdrawals you made in the past two tax years (and in the current year up to your filing deadline). Say you contributed $3,000 to a plan last year but withdrew $1,250 two years ago. Your contribution last year is considered to be only $1,750.

» You must be over 18 and must not have been a full-time student in five or more months of the year.

» If you were claimed as a dependent on someone else's tax return, you're not eligible for the saver's credit.

» You won't get a check from the IRS. The credit reduces the tax you pay but doesn't push it below zero. Even so, if the credit reduces your tax bite, it's still free money for you (Figure 19-11).

If you're eligible for the credit, it might cover your tax preparer's bill to fill out your entire return!

Saver's credit for filers with AGI under $63,500 (couples) or $31,500 (singles)

Joint filers' AGI	Example	Credit
$ 0 – 38,000	50% of $4,000	$ 2,000
$ 38,001 – 41,000	20% of $4,000	$ 800
$ 41,001 – 63,000	10% of $4,000	$ 400

Single filer's AGI	Example	Credit
$ 0 – 19,000	50% of $2,000	$ 1,000
$ 19,001 – 20,500	20% of $2,000	$ 400
$ 20,501 – 31,500	10% of $2,000	$ 200

FIGURE 19-10 | 2018 rates

Only 12% of eligible households claim this credit on their tax returns

FIGURE 19-11

Understand the alphabet soup of tax shelters to take maximum advantage

There are hundreds of money-saving breaks hidden away in the US tax code. There are four major types of programs for:

a · Employees of private companies, as well as individuals who are self-employed;

b · Employees of federal, state, and local government agencies, including the military;

c · Employees of tax-exempt nonprofits—schools, hospitals, and the like; and

d · Anyone who qualifies to contribute to individually managed IRAs, Roths, and HSAs.

To be sure, no chart can possibly explain every detail of every tax shelter. The IRS has published literally thousands of pages of regulations on tax-deferred savings accounts alone (Figure 19-12).

But you can get a bird's-eye view in Figures 19-13 through 19-16 of how to max out every possible tax-sheltered dollar. The following rules apply to most programs:

» Don't defer more than the maximum. If you qualify for several plans, the 2018 rules generally allowed you to contribute across all of them no more than $18,500 per year under age 50; $24,500 afterward. (What a coincidence! At 50, $24,050 is how much you must save each year—plus inflation, tax-deferred—to amass $1 million in today's dollars by 70. See Chapter 8.)

» Many plans count toward the max. The IRS sums your contributions to Qualified Plans such as 401(k), 403(b), Simple IRA, and Simple 401(k) accounts. The total you contribute—not counting employer contributions—must remain under your maximum for the year.

» IRAs and Roths have a combined maximum, too. The same way company-based savings plans must keep your deposits below the combined max, individually managed accounts must, too. If you have no access to a company-sponsored plan, your total contributions each year into IRAs and Roths could not exceed $5,500 ($6,500 after age 50) in 2018.[1350]

» Some plans do NOT count toward your maximum. For instance, nonprofits can sponsor a 403(b) **and** a 457(b). Employees can contribute the max to **each** plan. It's double the tax shelter.

» Health savings accounts don't push the limit. No matter how much you add to any other plan, you can contribute to an HSA every year (until you enroll in Medicare).

» You're taxed if you over-contribute. If you deposit more than the annual max, the excess amount may be taxed every year it stays in your account **and** perhaps taxed again when withdrawn. Not good.[1351]

» Rollovers have no limit. You can **roll over** (move) an unlimited amount from an employer-sponsored plan into an IRA or a Roth.

» Your pay represents a ceiling. No matter how high your combined max may be, you usually can't contribute more than your taxable income that year (salary, wages, self-employment income, etc.).

All those letters and numbers add up to serious money in your pocket

FIGURE 19-12

Qualified Plans present opportunities for employees and the self-employed

The IRS uses the term "Qualified Plan" for many different kinds of employer-sponsored tax-deferred savings accounts. To make things even more confusing, accounts for various types of employers use different numbers and names:

» **401(k) plans** are usually operated by for-profit corporations.

» **SIMPLE 401(k) plans and SEP IRAs** are typically set up by small businesses.

» **Solo 401(k) plans**—also known as Individual 401(k)s —are used when spouses or a sole owner run a very small company with no employees.

» **401(a) plans** are profit-sharing or money-purchase programs funded by for-profit employers.

» **The Thrift Savings Plan (TSP)** is for federal government employees, including those in the military.

» **457(b) plans** are either governmental (state/local agencies) or tax-exempt (nonprofits, schools, etc.).

» **403(b) plans** are another type of tax-deferral program that tax-exempt nonprofits can set up.

All of the above, plus several variations, are referred to as Qualified Plans.

Self-employed people should compare whether a SEP IRA or a so-called Individual or Solo 401(k) allows them to shelter more money. Free estimates are provided at **SEPIRA.com/calculator .html.**[1352]

Figure 19-13 outlines some types of Qualified Plans that are available to self-employed individuals and employees of private businesses. Consult your company's personnel department or your tax preparer to determine which programs you qualify for and what your contribution limit may be each year.

The language of specific Qualified Plans may or may not allow after-tax shelters called "designated Roths." If they **are** permitted, they're called:

» **Designated 401(k) Roths** in private business (Figure 19-13);

» **Designated 457(b) Roths** in government (Figure 19-14);

» **Designated 403(b) Roths** in nonprofits (Figure 19-15).

Funds you hold within a Qualified Plan can usually roll over only to a designated Roth within that same employer. (This is called an in-plan rollover.) Rollovers to a designated Roth are taxable, but no tax is due on qualifying Roth withdrawals. Ask your personnel department whether rollovers from a Qualified Plan to a designated Roth are permitted.

» **Qualified Plans may restrict** the securities you can buy within each plan. These constraints can harm the return that would be possible with the unlimited selection available to individually managed plans, such as HSAs, IRAs, and Roths. See "Many employers provide a 'bad' 401(k), which you might be able to fix" later in this chapter.

» **Traditional pension plans** covered 38% of American workers in 1979 but only 14% by 2011.[1353]

If you have a pension plan, contributions are funded by your employer and you receive a defined benefit amount for life at retirement age.

There are many regulations and variations that affect Qualified Plans. Figure 19-13 only scratches the surface. This is an area where professional advice from your company's human resources group or your tax preparer is essential.

If you're employed by a PRIVATE COMPANY

Account type	Max contrib. under 50	Max contrib. 50 or over	Maximum employer match	No-penalty withdrawals*
401(k) plan or designated 401(k) Roth	$18,500	$24,500	Up to the lesser of $55,000 (including employee contrib.) or 100% of compensation	After age 59½
Safe harbor 401(k) Match is required, formula may vary	$18,500	$24,500	Example: employer matches employee contributions up to 4% to 6% of compensation	After age 59½
Solo 401(k) plan or Roth Solo 401(k) For spouses or sole owners with no employees	$18,500	$24,500	Company may add money up to a total of $55,000 ($61,000 age 50 or over)	After age 59½. *For Roth Solo 401(k) rules, see Roth IRA*
SIMPLE IRA or SIMPLE 401(k)	$12,500	$15,500	1% to 3% of compensation	After age 59½
Simplified Employee Pension SEP IRA for employees or self-employed individuals	Employer or self-employed contributions only	Employer or self-employed contributions only	Employer or SE individual contribution up to the lesser of $55,000 or 25% of compensation	After age 59½
401(a) plan Money-purchase or profit-sharing plans	Primarily funded by employer	Primarily funded by employer	Employer contribution up to the lesser of $55,000 or 100% of compensation	After age 59½
Pension plan Defined-benefit plans	Primarily funded by employer	Primarily funded by employer	Employer contribution varies	After age 59½

Not shown: Archer medical savings accounts (MSAs), flexible spending arrangements (FSAs), health reimbursement arrangements (HRAs), mass transit and parking benefits, and others with lower limits.
*At any age, plans may allow withdrawals without penalty for certain hardships, such as disability.

FIGURE 19-13 | Only a partial list. 2018 limits. Many details not shown. Limitations on totals may apply if you're eligible for multiple accounts. Source: irs.gov

Government agencies offer plans that may have a small match or none at all

Figure 19-14 shows plans that may be available to you if you're an employee of a federal, state, or local government agency or the US military.

» Government savings plans are different from the plans of most private companies. Notably, government agencies often cover employees with traditional pension plans **plus** allow employees to contribute some of their salaries into a qualified plan.

» Matching contributions are available to federal civilian employees in the Thrift Savings Plan (TSP), but matches are usually not offered to employees of state and local governments or the US military.

» The Thrift Savings Plan (TSP) is unique to federal government agencies, including the US military. Perhaps TSP's most compelling feature is that the US government automatically pays 1% of an employee's paycheck into that person's TSP account whether or not the employee makes **any contributions at all.**

If a worker **does** contribute, the government matches the contributions dollar for dollar, up to 3% of pay (for a total of a 4% match). Employees hired before August 2010 receive a match up to 5% (a total of 6%). Members of the military, however, do not receive any match. Both civilian and military employees qualify for pension benefits, though, in addition to their TSP accounts.

The downside of TSP is that its investment choices are severely limited. Mutual funds representing only five asset classes are offered, plus five "L" (lifecycle) funds. The L funds are target-date funds. They hold aggressive to conservative allocations of the five basic funds, roughly determined by a participant's age.

The limited menu gives TSP the reputation of a "bad 401(k)" among Qualified Plans. See "Many employers provide a 'bad' 401(k), which you might be able to fix" later in this chapter.

On a positive note, all of TSP's investment choices have exceptionally low annual fees. As of 2015, the expense ratio for each of the 10 funds was only 0.029%—lower than any Vanguard ETF that's available to the general public.

» 457(b) plans are sponsored by state and local agencies, not the federal government. Confusingly, nonprofits can also sponsor accounts called 457(b) plans, which have different features (Figure 19-15).

Unlike the federal government's Thrift Savings Plan, state and local 457(b) plans usually don't match employee contributions.

As if to compensate for the lack of a match, employees of state and local agencies may be allowed to contribute more during each of the final three years before the plan's "normal retirement age." That limit is twice as much as the under-50 limit.

» The Dept. of Defense (DoD) Savings Deposit Pro-gram allows soldiers serving in combat zones to deposit several thousand dollars per tour of duty. The military doesn't offer a match but does pay a generous 10% rate of interest.

If you're employed by a GOVERNMENT AGENCY

Account type	Max contrib. under 50	Max contrib. 50 or over	Maximum employer match	No-penalty withdrawals*
Thrift Savings Plan (TSP) or Roth TSP For employees of federal agencies and the military	$18,500	$24,500	1% automatic contribution plus up to 5% agency match	After age 59½
457(b) plan or designated 457(b) Roth For employees of state and local governments	$18,500	$24,500 *or up to $37,000 in final 3 yrs.*	Few state or local agencies match contributions	At any time, if leaving the job or retiring
DoD Savings Deposit Program (SDP) For military personnel deployed in combat zones	$10,000 *per tour*	$10,000 *per tour*	No match, but DoD pays 10% interest (gains on which are taxable)	At tour end or for emergency

*At any age, plans may allow withdrawals without penalty for certain hardships, such as disability.

FIGURE 19-14 | Only a partial list. 2018 limits. Many details not shown. Limitations on totals may apply if you're eligible for multiple accounts. Source: irs.gov

Tax-exempt nonprofits can offer plans businesses and governments can't

Many nongovernmental nonprofit organizations—essentially **all** tax-exempt corporations except churches—are able to sponsor pretax accounts unlike those that any other employer can offer.

These nonprofits, such as tax-exempt hospitals, universities, and schools, can help highly compensated executives defer taxation on **up to 100% of their pay.** The account balances of nonprofit 457(f) plans can accept **unlimited contributions.** The sheltered dollars are never taxed until they're withdrawn after an executive leaves the organization. At that time, he or she will probably be in a lower tax bracket. Figure 19-15 shows these and other plans for nonprofits.

Not only is a 457(f) the richest and most favorable tax shelter available from any employer, it gets better. Tax-exempt non-profits can also sponsor what are called 403(b) plans. Highly compensated employees of tax exempts can contribute the max to **both** programs. By contrast, employees of businesses and government agencies are limited to a single combined maximum across all of their qualified plans.

Here's how these plans work:

» **457(f) plans** are usually reserved for top university or hospital executives. A compensation level of $120,000 or more per year is often mentioned as a lower limit. As a result, 457(f) plans are called "top hat" plans by the US Department of Labor.[1354]

Federal tax rules specifically prohibit employees who receive only middle-class compensation from participating in a nonprofit's 457(f) plan.

According to a report posted at IRS.gov, "Typical 457(f) plans are used as a means of placing 'golden handcuffs' on executives," such as requiring a new executive to remain for a number of years.[1355]

After the new executive is on board, the plan may receive contributions from the employer, the executive, or both. The dollar amount is unlimited. The contributions are tax-deductible and may grow in the account tax free until withdrawals begin after the executive has left the organization.

» **457(b) plans** are variations on this theme, which are also limited to highly compensated executives. However, a nonprofit 457(b) plan can accept contributions only from the employee, not the employer.

An employee's tax-deductible contribution has a specific limit under age 50. The limit becomes $6,000 higher at age 50. It may become **double** the under-50 limit in the final three years before the plan's "normal retirement age."

» **403(b) plans** are open to employees of all salary levels. These plans are similar to private 401(k) plans. Unlike nonprofit 457(b) plans, 403(b) plans have no special "final three years" provision. However, in addition to employee contributions, the tax-exempt employer may also contribute.

» **You may contribute to both a 457 and a 403(b)** without the deposits counting against the limit for Qualified Plans. A highly compensated employee can shelter a total of $55,000 in a 403(b), including employer contributions, plus any amounts that went tax deferred into a 457.

If you're employed by a TAX-EXEMPT NONPROFIT

Account type	Max contrib. under 50	Max contrib. 50 or over	Maximum employer match	No-penalty withdrawals*
403(b) plan or designated 403(b) Roth	$18,500	$24,500	Up to $55,000, employer and employee combined	After age 59½
Safe harbor 403(b) Match is required, formulas vary	$18,500	$24,500	Example formula: employer matches employee contributions up to 4% to 6% of compensation	After age 59½
457(b) plan Only for managers and highly compensated executives	$18,500	$24,500 or up to $37,000 in final 3 years	None	At any time, if leaving the job
457(f) plan Only for managers and highly compensated executives	No limit, up to 100% of compensation	No limit, up to 100% of compensation	Employer and/or employee may contribute a total of up to 100% of compensation	At any time, if leaving the job. *Most Roth conversions prohibited.*
Supplemental executive retirement plan (SERP) Top executives only, formulas vary	Primarily funded by employer	Primarily funded by employer	Example formula: employer may buy $100,000 per year of cash-value life insurance to fund payouts	No payouts until employment ends. *Most Roth conversions prohibited.*

*At any age, plans may allow withdrawals without penalty for certain hardships, such as disability.

FIGURE 19-15 | Only a partial list. 2018 limits. Many details not shown. Limitations on totals may apply if you're eligible for multiple accounts. Source: irs.gov

Contribute to an individually managed plan if no Qualified Plan is available to you

Figure 19-16 summarizes individually managed plans, including traditional IRAs, Roth IRAs, health savings accounts, and school savings plans.

» Traditional IRA (individual retirement account). You can always make a contribution to a traditional IRA up to your annual limit. A Qualified Plan at your employer doesn't stop you from making an IRA contribution.

However, you cannot **deduct** an IRA contribution if you are an "active participant" in a Qualified Plan. Such plans include the 401(k) for corporate employees, 457(b) for government employees, and 403(b) for employees of tax-exempt nonprofits.

» Roth IRA. Contributions to Roth IRAs are not deductible. Roths, however, have other benefits: (1) gains in a Roth are tax-free; (2) withdrawals are never forced, like the required minimum distributions that start at 70½ from traditional IRAs; (3) withdrawals of principal are tax-free at any time; and (4) withdrawals of gains are tax-free after the owner is 59½ **and** you are "seasoned."

You are "seasoned" if your oldest Roth account is at least in its fifth tax year.

The IRS seasoning clock was explained earlier in this chapter. You may be able to withdraw your Roth gains tax-free as soon as 3 years and 8½ months after you opened your first Roth.

You can contribute to a Roth as long as you live, if you have earned income in a given year. IRAs and HSAs prohibit deposits after the ages shown in Figure 19-16.

» Health savings account (HSA). The HSA subsidy, which first became available in 2004, is sometimes called a "stealth IRA" or a "super Roth." That's because (1) HSA tax deductibility is superior to that of a traditional IRA, and (2) HSA tax-free withdrawal rules are better than those of a Roth:

1. HSA deposits are tax-deductible. Anyone with earned income can deduct HSA deposits up to maximum contribution. You aren't disqualified from an HSA if you have access to other types of savings plans. **Advantage: HSA over IRA.**

2. HSAs allow tax-free withdrawals. HSA funds may be withdrawn without tax or penalty at any age. However, the withdrawals must be no more than the receipts you saved for unreimbursed health expenses since the day you opened the HSA. By contrast: (a) traditional IRAs impose tax on **all** withdrawals, and (b) Roths impose tax **and** a 10% penalty on withdrawals of gains unless the owner is over 59½ and "seasoned." **Advantage: HSA over IRA and Roth.**

» Savings plans for students and the disabled are complex beasts. The 50 states operate widely different programs called 529 (for college and K–12) and 529 ABLE (for the disabled). In addition, the US government allows tax-free growth in "Coverdell ESAs" (Education Savings Accounts) and "custodial accounts" (Uniform Gifts to Minors Act/Uniform Transfers to Minors Act).

All of these plans allow tax-free withdrawals for qualified expenses. Entire books attempt to make sense of these programs. Compare 529 plans yourself at Saving For College,[1356] College Savings,[1357] and Fidelity.[1358] To find states that run 529 ABLE plans, see AbleNRC.org.[1359]

If your account is MANAGED BY YOU

Account type	Max contrib. under 50	Max contrib. 50 or over	Maximum employer match	No-penalty withdrawals*
Traditional IRA Full deduction may be allowed if your modified adjusted gross income (MAGI) is under $61,000 single, $98,000 joint. Nondeductible deposits allowed up to the max contribution at any income level. *Contributions are prohibited after 70½.*	$5,500	$6,500	None	After age 59½
Roth IRA Full contribution is allowed if your modified adjusted gross income (MAGI) is under $116,000 single, $183,000 joint. *Contributions are permitted at any age.*	$5,500	$6,500	None	Take **deposits** at any time, **gains** if owner is 59½ and "seasoned" (see text)
Health savings account ("stealth IRA") Full deduction at any level of income. Requires insurance with minimum $1,350 deductible. *HSA contributions are prohibited after you enroll in Medicare.*	$3,450 *54 or under*	$4,450 *55 or over*	None	No penalty or tax for withdrawals up to unreimbursed health bills
College and K–12 savings plans • 529 prepaid tuition or savings plan • Custodial account (UGMA/UTMA) • Coverdell Education Savings Account *Deposits may be state tax-deductible.*	529 and custodial: $15,000** Coverdell: $2,000	529 and custodial: $15,000** Coverdell: $2,000	None	For qualified educational expenses and 529 transfers to 529 ABLE accounts
Savings for the disabled (529 ABLE) For those who were blind or disabled prior to age 26. See AbleNRC.org for conditions and eligible states.	$15,000	$15,000	None	For qualified living needs

*At any age, plans may allow withdrawals without penalty for certain hardships, such as disability.
**Contributions above $15,000 per year per person can be made to 529 plans and custodial accounts but may incur gift tax.

FIGURE 19-16 | Only a partial list. 2018 limits. Many details not shown. Limitations on totals may apply if you're eligible for multiple accounts. Source: irs.gov

Increase your lifelong assets by making timely IRA-to-Roth conversions

During your working years, try to contribute as much as possible into pretax accounts, as shown in Figures 19-13 through 19-16. That income is **tax-deferred.**

The downside of getting a tax break **going in** is the tax bite you face years later when your dollars **come out.** After age 70½, you'll be forced to take a required minimum distribution (RMD) each year—a specific percentage calculated on the sum of your IRAs and Qualified Plans.[1360]

RMDs force you to withdraw 3.65% to 14.93% from your pretax balance, rising every year after age 70½ (see Chapter 21). IRA and 401(k) withdrawals are always taxed as ordinary income, **not as long-term capital gains.** Your withdrawn dollars go into taxable accounts, where future realized gains are reduced by taxes each year.

For better results, make **IRA-to-Roth conversions.** To do so, you ask your plan sponsor to transfer funds to a Roth from a tax-deferred account. (Don't withdraw the money and move it yourself.)

To maximize your gain, think in two life stages:

» During your highest-earning years, such as age 25 to 55, contribute as many dollars as possible into tax-deferred IRA and 401(k) accounts.

» During low-earning years, such as 55 to 70, make Roth conversions. Ask your tax preparer how much you can convert each December without pushing you above the 12% tax bracket.

Roth conversions are treated as taxable income. But you can end up with far more spendable money, compared with paying tax on mandatory RMDs **and** Social Security after age 70½.

Figure 19-17 shows the improvement. It's based on the following example by Judith Ward, VP of T. Rowe Price Investment Services:

» Dick and Jane have saved $630,000 during their married life. Their IRAs hold $500,000, and a taxable account holds $130,000.

» The IRAs grow at a real rate of 6%. But the taxable account, after paying tax, grows only 4.32%. (This assumes the account pays 28% tax.)

» Dick and Jane continue to contribute $6,500 to their IRAs each year, adjusted for inflation, until they quit their jobs at age 65.

» If they make no Roth conversions, their balance would grow by age 95 to $4.42 million in today's dollars. (Assume the couple has other income and is preserving their savings accounts for heirs.) After 70½, they must take RMDs. They pay tax on the withdrawals and also on realized gains thereafter. Over 40 years, they lose $660,000 to taxes.

» If they start converting at 55—transferring $40,000 each year until 70—their accounts would grow by age 95 to $5.23 million in today's dollars. That's an additional $810,000 the couple could leave to heirs or spend themselves. They lost only $342,000 to taxes.

» If they start at age 60, the couple would wind up with $4.83 million. Even converting for just five years, age 65 to 70, they'd have $4.59 million. Whether saving it or spending it, they'd enjoy hundreds of thousands more dollars, compared with making no conversions at all.[1361]

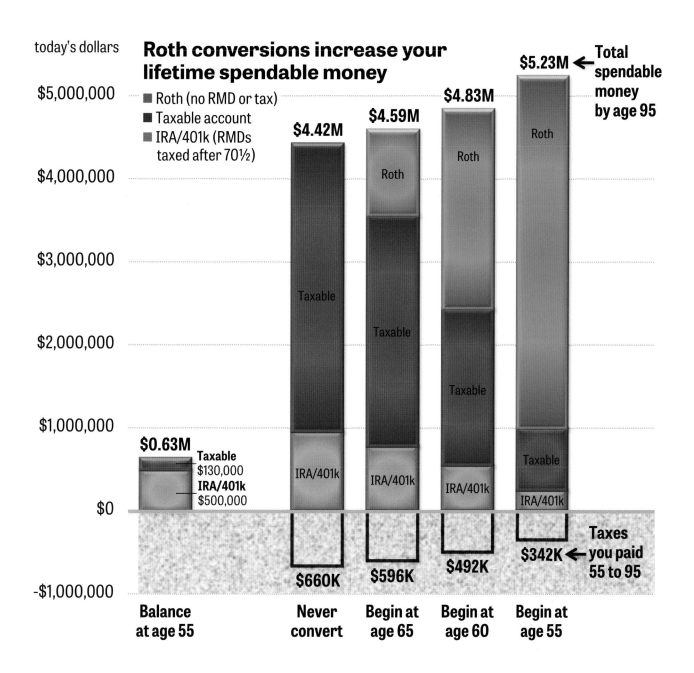

FIGURE 19-17 | Source: Judith Ward, VP of T. Rowe Price Investment Services[1362]

The Conversion Game's goal is to change before-tax dollars into after-tax dollars

We've seen that IRA-to-Roth conversions before age 70½ can help you leave a bigger legacy for your heirs or enjoy more spending money during your retirement.

Figure 19-18 shows a few of the many paths in the Conversion Game. The object of the game is to get as many of your pretax dollars as possible into Roths in the upper-right quadrant of the diagram before age 70½, when IRA RMDs must begin.

No chart can cover every regulation. Consult your personnel department or tax preparer for details that fit your particular situation.

You might ask, "When I make Roth conversions, how can I pay the least tax on the dollars I convert?"

Imagine the following situations. They could make your taxable income very low or even negative—an ideal time for a Roth conversion:

» **Live off taxable and Roth accounts until 70.** You might save enough to quit your job at 55, 60, or 65. To get the maximum Social Security benefit, you decide not to claim it before 70. You live for a few years off your taxable and Roth accounts; withdrawals don't count as income. This puts you in a low tax bracket, and a rollover each year might incur little or no tax.

» **Bear markets.** If your portfolio realizes a loss in a given year, you can subtract the loss from your income. This may give you a low effective tax rate. See "tax-loss harvesting" later in this chapter for details.

» **Back to school.** If you skip work for a few years to earn a degree, your taxable income will be small.

» **World travel.** Any long break without pay can put you in a very low tax bracket for that year.

» **First year(s) of a startup.** If you're an entrepreneur, the founding of a new business means you may be working harder than ever but receiving little income while you build a base of customers.

» **Unemployment.** If you're laid off and spend a significant part of a calendar year looking for work, your income may be low enough that a Roth rollover would incur a small or zero tax liability.

Even if you earn a great salary until you're 70 and your marginal rate is 28% every year, that doesn't mean a conversion actually **costs** you 28%. In Figure 19-7, we saw several ways to reduce the tax bite.

A tax expert with the online brokerage firm Betterment has estimated the haircut on a $100,000 conversion for someone in a high-tax state like New York. In the 28% tax bracket, the move would cost you only $17,250 (17.25%) in federal and state income taxes after all deductions— not $28,000 (28%).[1363]

Remember, a single filer is eligible for a standard deduction of $12,000. Couples enjoy twice that amount. And both single and joint filers may be able to deduct even more using itemized deductions and tax credits.[1364]

Say your deductions pushed you into a 15% tax bracket. If so, the same $100,000 rollover would cost you just $9,750 or 9.75%—**way** below 28%.[1365]

The lower your effective tax rate—after maxing out deductions, exemptions, and credits—the better the numbers in Figure 19-17 get for Roth conversions.

How to play the Conversion Game

(1) In high-earning years, make tax-deferred deposits to **before-tax accounts.**
(2) In years when you're in a low tax bracket, do conversions into **after-tax accounts.**

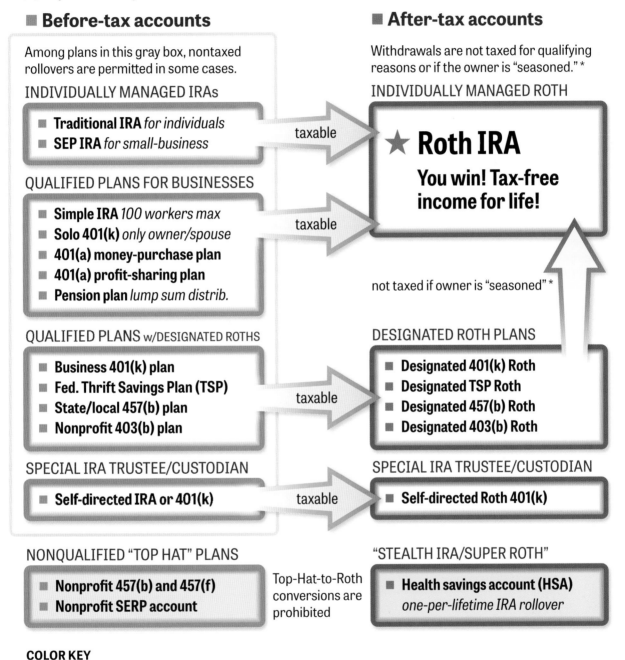

■ **Before-tax accounts**

Among plans in this gray box, nontaxed rollovers are permitted in some cases.

INDIVIDUALLY MANAGED IRAs

- **Traditional IRA** *for individuals*
- **SEP IRA** *for small-business*

taxable

QUALIFIED PLANS FOR BUSINESSES

- **Simple IRA** *100 workers max*
- **Solo 401(k)** *only owner/spouse*
- **401(a) money-purchase plan**
- **401(a) profit-sharing plan**
- **Pension plan** *lump sum distrib.*

taxable

QUALIFIED PLANS w/DESIGNATED ROTHS

- **Business 401(k) plan**
- **Fed. Thrift Savings Plan (TSP)**
- **State/local 457(b) plan**
- **Nonprofit 403(b) plan**

taxable

SPECIAL IRA TRUSTEE/CUSTODIAN

- **Self-directed IRA or 401(k)**

taxable

NONQUALIFIED "TOP HAT" PLANS

- **Nonprofit 457(b) and 457(f)**
- **Nonprofit SERP account**

Top-Hat-to-Roth conversions are prohibited

■ **After-tax accounts**

Withdrawals are not taxed for qualifying reasons or if the owner is "seasoned." *

INDIVIDUALLY MANAGED ROTH

★ **Roth IRA**
You win! Tax-free income for life!

*not taxed if owner is "seasoned" * *

DESIGNATED ROTH PLANS

- **Designated 401(k) Roth**
- **Designated TSP Roth**
- **Designated 457(b) Roth**
- **Designated 403(b) Roth**

SPECIAL IRA TRUSTEE/CUSTODIAN

- **Self-directed Roth 401(k)**

"STEALTH IRA/SUPER ROTH"

- **Health savings account (HSA)**
  one-per-lifetime IRA rollover

COLOR KEY

➡ taxable transaction   ➡ nontaxed transaction

* "Seasoned" means you are over 59½ **and** you've had any Roth for five tax years.
FIGURE 19-18 | Illustration by Pieter Tandjung

How to tell whether or not you have a 'good' 401(k) plan

By now, it should be obvious that you want to move every dollar you can into tax-deferred accounts. Even better, people with good jobs can contribute to Qualified Plans during high-earning years and gradually convert those dollars into IRAs and Roths in low-earning years.

The American payroll deduction system is a scandal. Many employers choose whichever 401(k) plan sponsor pays the largest kickbacks. That usually isn't the best provider from the employees' point of view.

The average employed couple with a median income will pay $155,000 during their working years to 401(k) fees and expenses, according to a study by Demos, a research organization. That eats up one-third of the couple's investing returns.[1366]

Well-managed companies sponsor Qualified Plans with low fees and excellent benefits. You should look for:

» **A high company match.** An employer match of up to 6% of your pay is the gold standard, if you can get it, says consulting firm Aon Hewitt.[1367]

» **Low fees.** On average, plans with over 10,000 participants charge 0.43% in annual fees. For plans with fewer than under 100 enrollees, it's a much higher rate of 1.29%. Lower fees are better.[1368]

» **A full set of asset classes.** A plan doesn't need exactly the same ETFs as the Mama Bear or Papa Bear. You can substitute a similar ETF or mutual fund. See Appendix A for a complete set of ETF substitution tables. However, many 401(k) plans don't offer a wide variety of asset classes to choose from.

» **A brokerage window.** If your plan lets you buy securities through a brokerage, you can choose any low-cost mutual fund or ETF, not just a handpicked few.

» **Designated Roths.** Only 42% of plans support in-plan rollovers to a Roth 401(k) or similar, but it's a provision worth asking your company for.[1369]

Two websites that allow you to see how your company rates are BrightScope and My Plan IQ. Figure 19-19 shows that United Parcel Service's "BrightScope Rating" was 90 in 2018.

BrightScope.com rates 401(k) plans, helping you learn how the company you work for stacks up

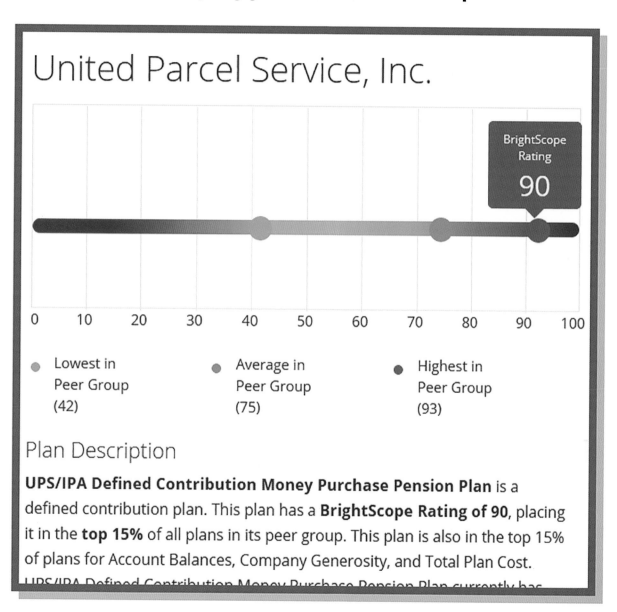

United Parcel Service, Inc.

BrightScope Rating

90

| 0 | 10 | 20 | 30 | 40 | 50 | 60 | 70 | 80 | 90 | 100 |

- Lowest in Peer Group (42)
- Average in Peer Group (75)
- Highest in Peer Group (93)

Plan Description

UPS/IPA Defined Contribution Money Purchase Pension Plan is a defined contribution plan. This plan has a **BrightScope Rating of 90**, placing it in the **top 15%** of all plans in its peer group. This plan is also in the top 15% of plans for Account Balances, Company Generosity, and Total Plan Cost.

UPS/IPA Defined Contribution Money Purchase Pension Plan currently has

FIGURE 19-19 | Source: BrightScope[1370]

Many employers provide a 'bad' 401(k), which you might be able to fix

Even if a corporation is a "good citizen" in many ways, its employee payroll deduction plan might stink. One common response by the affected employees is to handle it the good ol' American Way: they sue.

More than a dozen major class-action lawsuits have been filed in recent years, all alleging excessive or hidden fees.[1371]

The targets of the lawsuits have agreed to pay settlements in the majority of cases. For example, Ameriprise Financial paid $27.5 million and Lockheed Martin paid $62 million. Both companies also pledged to improve their 401(k) policies.[1372]

If you find that your employer's plan is loaded with high costs, your first response shouldn't be, "I'll see you in court."

Instead, try one of these easier approaches:

» Just ask. A step-by-step guide to persuading your company to switch 401(k) providers is available free from ConsumerReports .org.[1373]

» Max the match. Be sure to contribute each year the amount of dollars your employer will match. Even if the company only increases your $1,000 to $1,500, and the provider charges an outrageous 5% annual fee, the result is still a 42% one-year return. That's far better than any portfolio strategy offers. When you change jobs, roll your 401(k) balance into an IRA or a Roth, where you pay little or no management fee.

» Use low-cost funds. Some of your provider's flashy equity offerings may charge high fees, while its boring old bond funds would cost you only 0.5% per year. Keep your money in the lowest-cost funds. If you get any corporate match at all, even a tiny 1% bond return would be fine if you also get that 42% one-year gain.

One example of an inadequate set of investment options is the Federal Employee Thrift Savings Plan (TSP). This is the primary tax-deferred program for the US government's 5 million workers.[1374]

Figure 19-20 shows that My Plan IQ gives TSP only 40 points on a scale of 100. That's partly because employees can choose from only five funds. They're called S, C, I, G, and F (as well as cash and a few target-date options, which are just different blends of the five main funds):

» S   **US small caps**
» C   **US large caps**
» I   **Non-US large caps**
» G   **5–10 year Treasurys**
» F   **Other bonds**

In TSP's defense, each investment choice is a low-cost Vanguard fund, averaging a tiny 0.2% fee. Also, TSP matches employees' contributions up to 5%.

With only a few asset classes, TSP supports little diversification. But My Plan IQ shows how employees can improve their returns by adding momentum—even to a menu of choices that's this constricted—as Figure 19-21 reveals.

My Plan IQ gives Federal Employee TSP a low score of 40 because the plan offers only a few funds

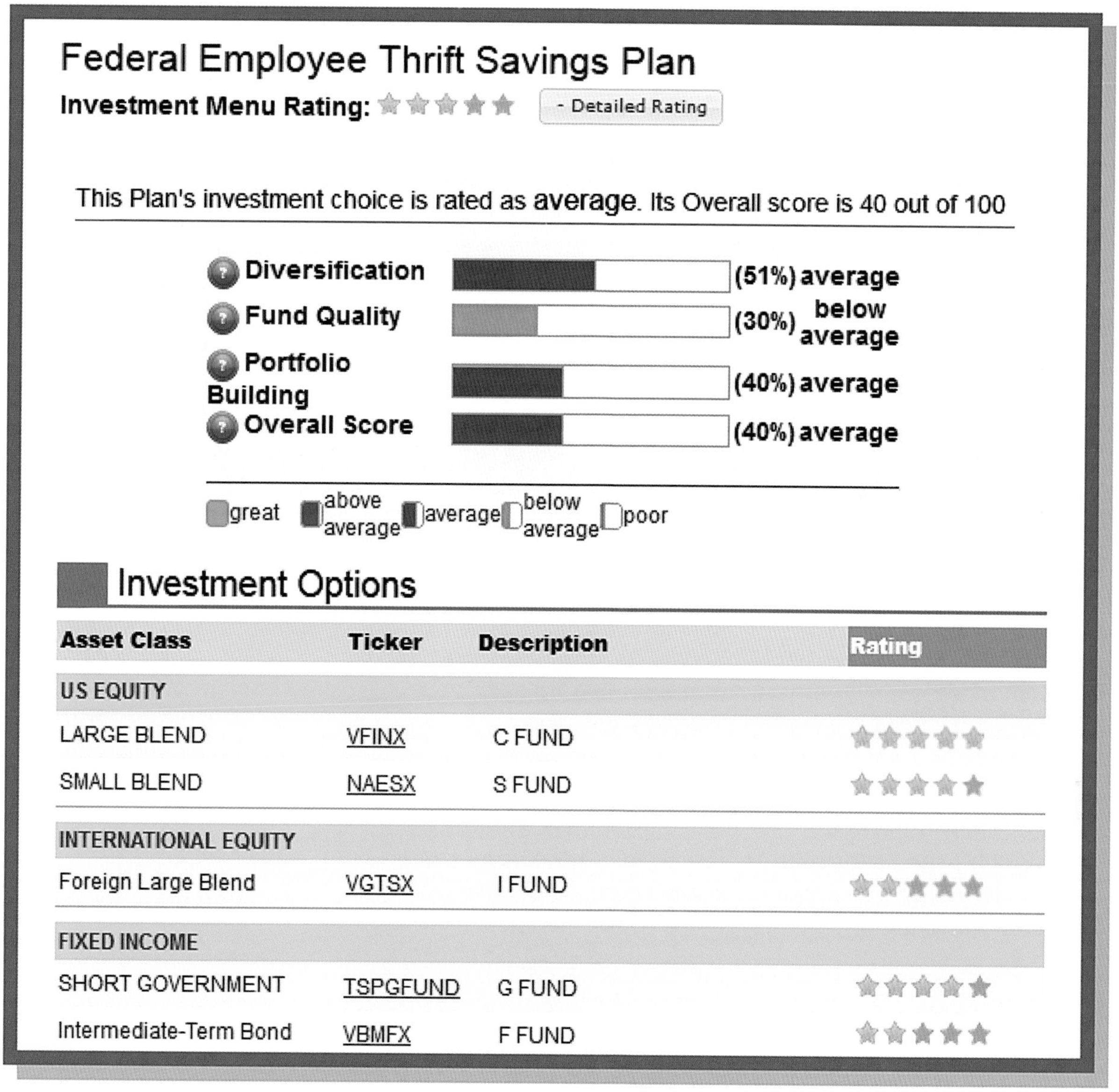

Federal Employee Thrift Savings Plan

Investment Menu Rating: ☆☆☆☆☆ [- Detailed Rating]

This Plan's investment choice is rated as **average**. Its Overall score is 40 out of 100

⊙ **Diversification**	▓▓▓▓▓░░░░░	(51%) average
⊙ **Fund Quality**	▓▓▓░░░░░░░	(30%) below average
⊙ **Portfolio Building**	▓▓▓▓░░░░░░	(40%) average
⊙ **Overall Score**	▓▓▓▓░░░░░░	(40%) average

☐ great ▪ above average ☐ average ☐ below average ☐ poor

Investment Options

Asset Class	Ticker	Description	Rating
US EQUITY			
LARGE BLEND	VFINX	C FUND	★★★★★
SMALL BLEND	NAESX	S FUND	★★★★★
INTERNATIONAL EQUITY			
Foreign Large Blend	VGTSX	I FUND	★★★★★
FIXED INCOME			
SHORT GOVERNMENT	TSPGFUND	G FUND	★★★★★
Intermediate-Term Bond	VBMFX	F FUND	★★★★★

FIGURE 19-20 | Source: My Plan IQ [1375]

Over the past 17 years, momentum made the Federal Employee TSP actually enjoyable

You might not succeed in reforming a corporate savings plan that has high fees, but you might improve one that's stuck with only a small menu of choices:

» Use an inside-outside strategy. Buy those funds that are **inside** the plan, but diversify by buying funds that are **outside** the plan, in your IRA or Roth account.

» Use the Momentum Rule. Using mechanical investing, hold each month the three plan assets that have the best momentum.

As we saw in Chapter 3, My Plan IQ has tracked many portfolio strategies in real time for almost two decades. Lazy Portfolios—strategies with allocations that never change—enjoyed improved performances, usually with smaller losses, when a simple Momentum Rule was applied.

Figure 19-21 shows how the momentum version of the TSP portfolio outperformed a Lazy TSP (holding an equal weight of each fund). The momentum version delivered improved returns **without subjecting the investor to losses anywhere near bear-market pain.**

The momentum portfolio actually gained 10% while TSP lost 19% in 2001–2002. Other momentum-version losses were 3% and 9%— not even corrections.

Over the 17-year period, the S&P 500 returned 6.4% (not shown). That was a slight improvement over the momentum portfolio (limited to TSP's asset classes). But the S&P 500 subjected people to intolerable crashes, such as –51% in 2007–2009. Many investors liquidate after that much pain.

My Plan IQ's results are not backtests. The site posts the numbers **live** for each portfolio as they occur.

The site has not "optimized" a different rule for each portfolio it monitors. The site automatically applies the same Momentum Rule to every strategy My Plan IQ tracks.

My Plan IQ's formula is very simple. The site averages each asset class's total return over the past 1, 3, 6, and 12 months and the most recent week to determine momentum. (The Papa Bear Portfolio uses a similar rule but dispenses with the one-month and one-week calculations.)

In normal times, My Plan IQ allocates 60% to TSP's equity funds and 40% to its bond funds. But when stocks exhibit poor momentum, the site mechanically increases the allocation to TSP's fixed-income offerings.

My Plan IQ publishes its monthly Momentum Rule al-locations for the TSP portfolio under the name "Federal Employee Thrift Savings Plan Tactical Asset Allocation Moderate."[1376]

At no charge, any visitor may see the percentages the Momentum Rule determines, with a delay of 1½ months. To get the allocations as they occur requires a basic subscription for $19.95 per month or $199.95 per year.[1377]

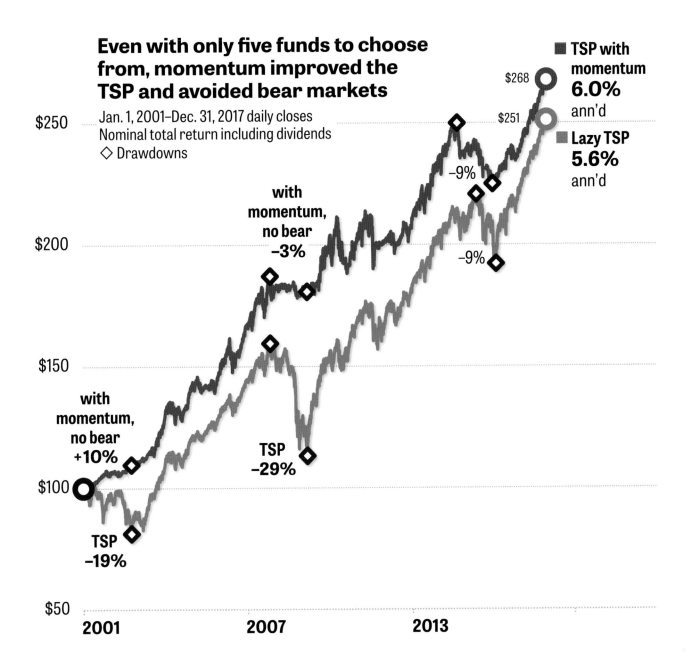

Even with only five funds to choose from, momentum improved the TSP and avoided bear markets

Jan. 1, 2001–Dec. 31, 2017 daily closes
Nominal total return including dividends
◇ Drawdowns

$268 ■ TSP with momentum **6.0%** ann'd

$251 ■ Lazy TSP **5.6%** ann'd

with momentum, no bear **−3%**

−9%

−9%

with momentum, no bear **+10%**

TSP **−29%**

TSP **−19%**

$250
$200
$150
$100
$50

2001
2007
2013

FIGURE 19-21 | Source: My Plan IQ

Use a backdoor Roth and other legal tricks to defer taxes on your gains

No investing book can possibly reveal to you every tax break. If you have a healthy income, be sure to consult a professional. Good tax preparers can often save you more money than their fees set you back (Figure 19-22).

» Use a backdoor Roth. You can't make a contribution directly into a Roth if:

(1) You contributed the annual limit to a qualified plan, IRA, or Roth, or

(2) Your income is higher than the Roth cutoff amount.

In that case, you can make a **backdoor Roth** contribution. The Vanguard Group says more than 20,000 of its account holders made backdoor Roth transactions in 2013.[1378]

You first make a nondeductible IRA contribution, which is possible at any income level. You then make an IRA-to-Roth conversion, which has no transaction limit. For details, see "Backdoor Roth: A Step by Step Guide."[1379]

» Use a mega backdoor. A backdoor Roth has a traditional IRA contribution limit. (In 2018, that was $5,500 or, for those over 50, $6,500.)

A mega backdoor can move up to $36,500 per year into the shelter of a Roth. See the Mad Fientist's "Mega Backdoor Roth."[1380]

The easiest way to use a mega backdoor is to work for an employer whose qualified plan permits after-tax contributions and Roth rollovers. Only about 40% of plans enable this, according to Vanguard.[1381]

If your employer's qualified plan doesn't have the enabling language, and you have at least some self-employment income, you can use a mega backdoor by setting up a solo 401(k). You must choose a service provider that supports this, as described by The Finance Buff.[1382]

» Make the Roth conversion. Be aware of new IRS regulations on Roth conversions from Qualified Plans, as described by Fairmark. com.[1383]

» Cut your taxes via "asset location." If all of your money is in tax-deferred accounts, great! But what if some is tax-deferred and some is taxable?

In that case, you can save on taxes by placing securities that enjoy preferential tax treatment—such as tax-free municipal bonds—in taxable accounts.

State Street Global Advisors reports that "tax smart" investment location could give you 17% more after-tax money over a 20-year period.[1384]

» Sequence your withdrawals. After you quit your job, you may own three kinds of accounts: before-tax (such as an IRA), after-tax (Roth), and taxable.

Taking withdrawals in the ideal order can increase your spendable income 5% to 137% over less-effective methods, according to a 2017 paper by James S. Welch Jr. in the *Journal of Financial Planning*.[1385]

He's programmed ORP, a free Optimal Retirement Planner. It's the best tool available, but you may need a tax preparer to dig up some of the numbers it requires.[1386]

You can get the most money into the safety of a Roth through the back door

FIGURE 19-22

Tax-loss and tax-gain harvesting can save you money with few side effects

As we've just seen, strategies like backdoor Roths and optimal withdrawal sequences can maximize your spendable money. But don't forget that withdrawing the maximum can affect your heirs.

For example, if you exhaust a taxable account, it eliminates the tax break known as "step up." When your loved ones inherit a taxable account, its cost basis "steps up" to its value on the date of your death. Assets can be passed to heirs tax free up to $11.18 million per person ($22.36 million per couple), based on 2018 tax rates. The limits increase each year for inflation.[1387]

Inheriting a traditional IRA, by contrast, means the heirs —whether a spouse or someone else—must begin taking required minimum distributions (RMDs), as Chapter 21 describes. The heirs pay no income tax on the inherited IRA balance, but they must pay tax on each RMD. (It's better to bequeath a Roth: heirs pay no tax on the balance **or** on withdrawals.)[1388]

Here's a strategy with no ill effects on your heirs: **tax harvesting.** Unlike withdrawals, this creates more money for everyone:

» **Tax-loss harvesting** means selling securities prior to Dec. 31 if they've declined. You can deduct the loss from that year's taxable capital gains and $3,000 from your ordinary income every year until the carryforward is exhausted. See Appendix A for more detailed rules.

Michael Kitces, director of wealth management for Pinnacle Advisory Group, provides two excellent articles on "Tax-Loss Harvesting"[1389] and "How Not to Calculate Tax Alpha."[1390] The latter explains how some robo-advisers exaggerate the benefits of tax-loss harvesting by 10 times.

» **Tax-gain harvesting** means selling some securities this year and some the following year to reduce the tax bite.

In Figure 19-23, a taxable account grows 10% a year. Realizing gains of $26,000 in Year 1 and another $26,000 in Year 2 would incur 0% tax on long-term capital gains for a couple in the 12% tax bracket. But if they waited until Year 2 to sell, their $54,600 compounded gain would incur tax. (With tax-gain harvesting, a security you sell can immediately be repurchased without penalty.)

Caution: Even though long-term capital gains incur no income tax for filers in the 10% and 12% tax brackets, the gains are included in your adjusted gross income (AGI). In a series of articles, Kitces notes that many programs consider your AGI:

» **Your Social Security** might become taxable (see Chapter 21).[1391]

» **The 3.8% net investment income tax** might be triggered.[1392]

» **Affordable Care Act (ACA) tax credits** may phase out as your AGI rises.[1393]

» **Your exemption** from the alternative minimum tax may be lost.[1394]

Other experts note that a higher AGI can affect other programs:

» **Medicare Part B and D** premiums may rise, according to Kiplinger.com.[1395]

» **Property tax exemptions** may be lost, based on state regulations revealed by HouseLogic.com.[1396]

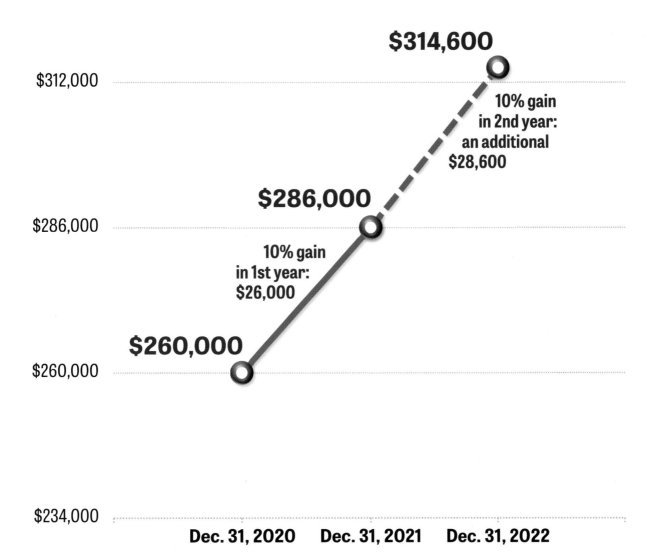

TAX-GAIN HARVESTING

If the couple sells $26,000 in the 1st year, they pay <u>no tax</u> on long-term gains in their tax bracket.

$314,600

$312,000

10% gain
in 2nd year:
an additional
$28,600

$286,000

$286,000

10% gain
in 1st year:
$26,000

$260,000

$260,000

$234,000

Dec. 31, 2020   Dec. 31, 2021   Dec. 31, 2022

FIGURE 19-23

When planning to shelter millions from tax, a 'self-directed custodian' is needed

If you're an entrepreneur, don't think you can just start a business, issue yourself penny shares via your 401(k), and roll over millions of dollars into any old Roth IRA. You'll need an attorney who's experienced and clever (but not **too** clever).

In the *Forbes* article mentioned earlier in this chapter, Deborah Jacobs reported that Max Levchin of Yelp, Peter Thiel of PayPal, and other millionaire entrepreneurs had used a special **self-directed IRA custodian:** Pensco Trust Co. According to Jacobs, Thiel had at least $31.5 million in such a Roth (Figure 19-24).[1397]

These flush IRAs came to public attention in a 2012 *Wall Street Journal* article.[1398]

The next day, Pensco stated it had more than 250 accounts with $1 million to $100 million, plus three over $100 million.[1399]

The NuWire Investor news site lists 37 other custodians, conveniently sorted by assets under management.[1400]

You might ask, "Aren't all IRAs self-directed?" The answer is, "No." A traditional IRA is considered to be an **individually managed IRA.**

A **self-directed IRA** is a different animal. Most traditional IRA sponsors will allow your account to hold only publicly traded stocks, mutual funds, exchange-traded funds, and similar "vanilla" securities. Self-directed IRAs, which are available only from a self-directed IRA custodian, can also hold real estate, gold bullion, even entire businesses such as limited liability companies (LLCs).

You should never consider a self-directed IRA without expert legal advice. These accounts have strict legal requirements, which some millionaires seem to have worked around:

» Ordinarily, you can deposit into a Roth IRA only $5,500 per year ($6,500 for those 50 and up).

» If your IRA holds real estate, such as a house, you and your immediate family members cannot stay in that house, even for a single night. That's prohibited as **self-dealing.**

» Your IRA typically cannot purchase shares of a company that you own or control, another example of self-dealing.

How did entrepreneurs like Levchin and Thiel get around the $5,500 limitation? *Forbes* writer Jacobs speculates that they may have collected numerous penny shares of stock through a startup's 401(k) plan. A rollover from the 401(k) to a Roth IRA could have been done at a later time. A 401(k)-to-Roth rollover can involve an unlimited number of dollars.

And what about the self-dealing rule? Experts say the IRS may allow an IRA to own shares in a person's company, so long as the IRA owner doesn't hold enough shares to have **voting control.**[1401]

For cautions about self-directed IRAs, see FoxBusiness.com,[1402] MarketWatch.com,[1403] and Fool.com.[1404]

LIVINGSTON'S LAW OF TAX SHELTERS

Our tax system has one little flaw:
It consists of more loopholes than law.

A self-directed IRA can hold real estate and other alternative assets most brokerages won't

507

FIGURE 19-24

20 Don't step on virtual land mines along the road of life

"Much has been written about panics and manias . . . but one thing is certain, that at particular times a great deal of stupid people have a great deal of stupid money."

WALTER BAGEHOT, British journalist and businessman, in *Literary Studies* (1879)[1405]

The investor's challenge is illustrated by a classic of science fiction—*Space Cadet* by award-winning author Robert A. Heinlein. Imagine the scene (Figure 20-1):

Years in the future, humans are exploring the solar system. Many students apply for positions in the prestigious Interplanetary Patrol, but only the very best will be accepted.

To determine the most qualified cadets, each applicant is subjected to a series of tests. One ambitious young pilot is brought into a room with a video-game console, festooned with buttons and lights. The screen states:

"Press START to begin as soon as you have read these instructions. The object of the exercise is to score points. In order to score a point, press the left button when the red light is ON, but do not press the button if the green light is also ON."

The instructions continue in this same vein, scrolling off the screen.

After reading the rules for several minutes, the cadet walks away from the console and approaches the officer in charge.

"Excuse me, sir," says the candidate. "According to the instructions, it's impossible to score any points."

"Fine," the officer replies. "Proceed to the next room."

"But what about the test?"

"You passed."

Before you invest, you must first understand some sneaky tricks Wall Street might throw at you. Don't play games you can't win. For some reason, brokerages usually emphasize all of their blinking lights and forget to mention how the game really works.

» KEY CONCEPT
don't play in the Street
Playing games you can't win, or thinking you're some trading genius, is a big mistake.

Some Wall Street games are rigged against you

FIGURE 20-1

You don't need to pay your hard-earned money to robo-advisers

Robo-advisers were a fad that started around 2010, when the global financial crisis was fresh in the minds of shell-shocked investors.

The idea is that a 100% computerized system—a robo-adviser—would accept your savings and invest it in a variety of ETFs. You would never be entirely invested in the S&P 500 or, at the other extreme, entirely sitting in low-yielding cash.

The problem is that robo-advisers typically restrict people's savings to a Lazy Portfolio of one kind or another. They use a formula from the 1970s rather than adopting the scientific findings of the 21st century on diversification and momentum.

As we saw in Chapter 3, Lazy Portfolios crash almost as horribly as the S&P 500 itself, with no additional gain to show for it. As soon as the next severe bear market comes along, people who trusted robo-advisers will be wondering where so much of their money went.

For this service, robo-advisers take annual fees of 0.25%, 0.50%, or more. You can do better for free—just give a Muscular Portfolio a 15-minute tune-up once a month and keep all the robo-fees for yourself.

After the fad peaked, most robo-advisers either closed down or were folded into corporate acquirers. Michael Kitces, director of wealth planning for Pinnacle Advisory Group, described in 2017 how "captured" robo-advisers became a way for fund sponsors to push their house funds:

"BlackRock decided to acquire FutureAdvisor to distribute their iShares ETFs,

"Invesco bought Jemstep to distribute PowerShares ETFs, and

"WisdomTree invested heavily into AdvisorEngine to distribute WisdomTree ETFs . . . turning the robo-advisor into a distribution channel." [1406]

Because of the above problems and others, robo-advisers found it hard to get people to hand over their money. Robos have to spend up to $1,000 just to acquire a single new customer, according to Alessandra Malito of *Investment News*.[1407]

With expenses like that, certified financial analyst Michael Wong of Morningstar estimated it would be difficult for robos "to earn any profit for an account worth around $100,000."[1408] Most of the clients they're attracting are much smaller.

At this writing, the largest remaining 2010-era robo-firms are Wealthfront and Betterment. (The latter's average client account size in 2016 was only $27,000.)[1409]

Wealthfront recently added a feature called Advanced Indexing—a small step toward asset rotation. But the company's own backtests show that its strategy lost **more than 50%** in the 2007–2009 bear market! That's far worse than investors would or should tolerate.[1410]

Wealthfront and Betterment had booked between them only $15.5 billion in assets under management by 2017. One hybrid competitor, Vanguard's Personal Advisor, had attracted over four times that in just two years.[1411]

Unfortunately, Personal Advisor charges a 0.30% fee, has a $50,000 minimum, and permits only Vanguard funds in what are essentially Lazy Portfolios.[1412]

Avoid robo-fees. The person who cares most about your money will always be you—not a computer (Figure 20-2).

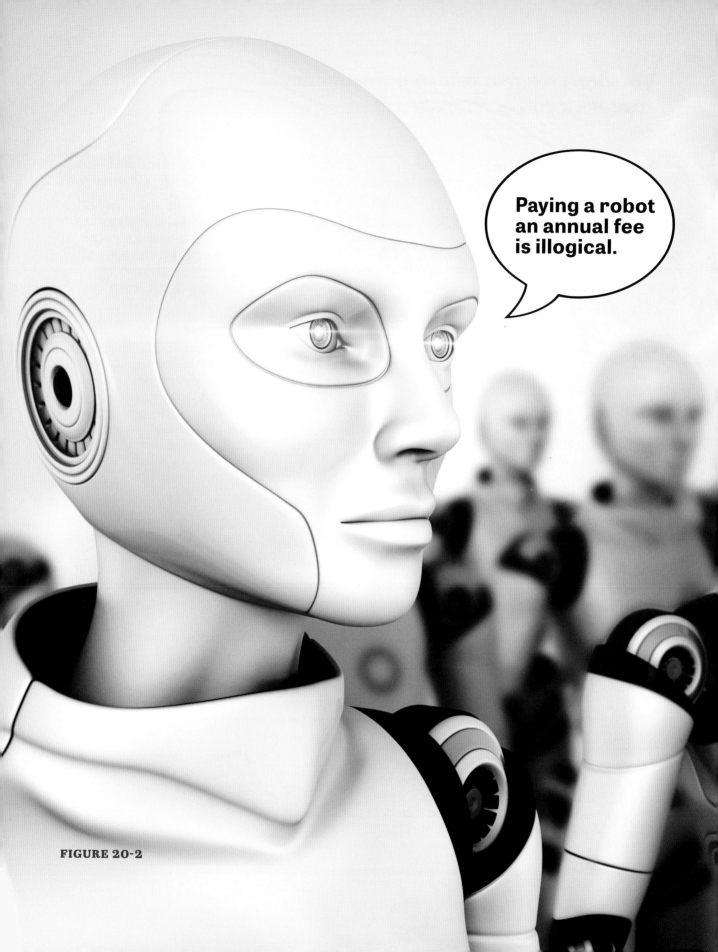

FIGURE 20-2

You don't need to fear high-frequency traders if you don't trade often

"High-frequency trading" (HFT) is conducted by financial tricksters. They pay the New York Stock Exchange, Nasdaq, and other exchanges to hook cables directly into the market's central computers (Figure 20-3).

This speed advantage lets the "freeks" see incoming transactions from institutions and other investors a fraction of a second ahead of time. The freeks' computers buy and sell before the slower orders get processed. This skims a little bit of money out of each investor's orders.

Michael Lewis's 2014 book *Flash Boys* estimated that this trick costs investors an average of 0.07% per trade. That's 7 cents per $100 you buy or sell. It's not much on a single trade. But applied to the $225 billion daily volume of the entire US stock market, it means the freeks were collectively siphoning off $160 million of profits **per day.**[1413]

Big Wall Street banks established private exchanges called "dark pools" to try to avoid the HFT shops. *Flash Boys* revealed that about 30% of all trades were occurring off the exchanges—mostly in dark pools—by mid-2011.[1414]

Fortunately, the freeks are fading. The revenue of HFT firms from US equity trading was $7.2 billion in 2009 but only $0.9 billion in 2017.[1415]

To keep your money away from freeks, get off their time scale! Trade only once a month or less, as a Muscular Portfolio does. Until HFT is banned, losing a few pennies per trade is just an irritation rather than a serious concern.

No news is good news, they say

One of the best ways to avoid the temptation to trade is to eliminate the "fog machine." Michael Stokes of the Financial Coaching Group describes the dumbing-down effect of market chatter in the following way:

"Psychologist Paul Andreassen of Harvard studied the link between the news media and investing. Andreassen found that the group of investors that had access to the news earned less than half as much per share traded as the group that received no news."[1416]

You should turn off and completely ignore the following sources of noise about the market:

» Newspaper and magazine articles;

» Television and radio programs;

» Internet blogs and tweets.

The past performance of investment advisers does not predict their future performance. This is especially true over short periods such as 1, 3, and 5 years. Yet numerous mainstream outlets routinely publish articles about "the analyst of the year" or even "the analyst of the quarter"! The sooner you make yourself ignore all this, the better.

High-frequency firms pay the exchanges for direct access

FIGURE 20-3

You don't need target-date funds to dictate your asset allocation

Target-date funds supposedly protect you from a new Great Depression.

Say you were planning to quit your job on March 9, 2009, after the global financial crisis. At that point, the S&P 500 was down more than 50%. If you held all stock, half your savings would be gone. You might have to work several more years to rebuild your account balance (Figure 20-4).

Target-date funds start out with a high percentage of equities. They shift a little to bonds each year. Vanguard Target Retirement 2065, for example, launched in 2017 with 90% in stocks and only 10% in bonds.[1417]

Protection against crashes is a noble goal, but target-date funds are poor solutions.

Target-date funds can force you to hold equities all the way to the bottom of crashes. In other years, they overload you with bonds when stocks are soaring.

At this writing, target-date funds offer nothing but Lazy Portfolios. That's an obsolete economic theory from the 1970s. The designers of target-date funds seem to be unaware of the scientific findings of the 21st century.

The average 2010 target-date fund crashed 30% in calendar year 2008 alone. Some collapsed as much as 41%—far beyond investors' behavioral pain point. For this **lack** of protection, the average target-date fund charges an outrageous 0.96% annual fee.[1418]

By contrast, Muscular Portfolios automatically tilt you toward an appropriate percentage of asset classes—whichever ones are in uptrends.

Endure less strife with your loved ones

No wealth-management strategy is worth a hill of beans if it causes arguments between you and your family members.

Imagine you're suddenly responsible for managing your elderly mother's $1 million brokerage account. Your parent has lost the capacity to make financial decisions.

You're grieving over your mother's condition. Do you want to add a battle with your spouse and your brothers and sisters every time they hear some "development" in the market? That could turn your sorrow into a living hell.

Mechanical investing can save you from hell. Using an asset-rotation approach—including the very stable End Game Portfolio described in Chapter 23, if appropriate for your situation—the rules are completely specified in advance. Directions are posted on the Web by a computer every day. There are no news reports to evaluate, no rumors to react to. Every buy and sell complies with simple directions based on 21st-century financial principles.

Target-date funds are not the best way to get where you need to go

FIGURE 20-4

You don't need so-called smart-beta products for superior returns

"Smart beta" ETFs are a new quirk in financial products. The term is said to have arisen in 2009 from Towers Watson, an advisory firm based in London.[1419]

What is smart beta? The meaning is elusive. In a 2013 ETF.com interview with two financial experts, one said it's "not smart" and "not beta." Clear as mud![1420]

Beta is the degree to which a security goes up and down compared to how much an index like the S&P 500 goes up and down. Beta is explained more fully in the Bonus Chapter.

The **smart** part is a reaction to the makeup of the S&P 500 itself. The index holds companies in proportion to their **market capitalization,** which is their share price multiplied by the number of outstanding shares. That fact makes the S&P 500 **cap-weighted.**

Say Company A's market cap is $100 billion and Company B's is $200 billion. The S&P 500 will allocate twice as many dollars to B as it does to A.

This makes a lot of sense if you're a mutual fund that tracks an index. Imagine a day in which A's price doesn't change but B's goes up 10%. B's market cap is now $220 billion.

The mutual fund wouldn't have to buy or sell any shares (which costs money). The change in price by itself means the fund still holds A and B in proportion to their market capitalization. For example, the fund might now own $100,000 of A and $220,000 of B.

The knock on cap weighting is that the S&P 500, over time, holds more and more dollars in glamorous companies whose prices have gone up and up. This may fill the index with "Icarus stocks" that are too close to the sun. These high-flying companies may also explain why the S&P 500 is so prone to crashes.

Smart-beta ETFs weight their holdings in any way **other** than cap weighting:

» **Equal weighting**—for instance, buying $1 million worth of 500 different stocks;

» **Value tilt**—buying companies with low prices compared to their earning power;

» **Small-cap tilt**—buying companies smaller than a market cap of $2 billion.

The problem is that each approach often **performs worse** than the broad market and **crashes harder** than a cap-weighted index.

Figure 20-5 shows RSP, a popular smart-beta ETF. The fund has held an equal weight of the S&P 500 from its inception on April 30, 2003. The graph starts at that point, indexing both RSP and the S&P 500 (SPY) to 100 on July 19, 2007. RSP hit an all-time high on that date near the end of the 2003–2007 bull market.

RSP outperformed SPY in that run-up, but the sucker punch was devastating. In the 2007–2009 bear market, SPY crashed "only" 55% but RSP lost a heart-stopping 60%. That's far beyond most people's pain points. Many investors liquidated, doing huge damage to their portfolios.

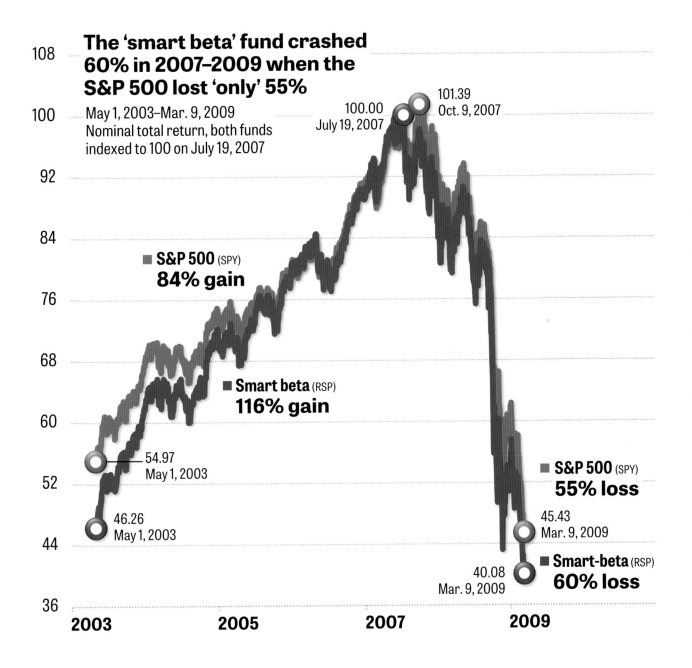

The 'smart beta' fund crashed 60% in 2007–2009 when the S&P 500 lost 'only' 55%

May 1, 2003–Mar. 9, 2009
Nominal total return, both funds indexed to 100 on July 19, 2007

100.00
July 19, 2007

101.39
Oct. 9, 2007

■ S&P 500 (SPY)
84% gain

■ Smart beta (RSP)
116% gain

54.97
May 1, 2003

46.26
May 1, 2003

■ S&P 500 (SPY)
55% loss

45.43
Mar. 9, 2009

40.08
Mar. 9, 2009

■ Smart-beta (RSP)
60% loss

FIGURE 20-5 | Source: Yahoo Finance

In case you think currency trading sounds hot, it's not a great alternative

You might think you can make more money than a Muscular Portfolio by getting out of dollars. Why not bet on the euro, or the yen, or some other currency? Anything besides boring old greenbacks!

There's a market for this kind of thinking. It's called "trading currency pairs." The concept is simple. You bet that the euro will go up versus the US dollar. Or the yen against the British pound, or any combination of other currencies.

This provides a great example of the advantages of mechanical investing, which we saw in Chapter 16. Faithfully following a predetermined formula—the way a chess supercomputer beats a grandmaster—is better than using one's own opinions to "play" a market that is actually playing you.

Trading currencies involves picking one currency over another. When the euro goes up against the yen, the yen goes down against the euro. Simple! Just flipping a coin to choose which side of the bet to take should give you 50/50 odds of winning (minus transaction costs).

It doesn't really work out that way. A 2014 study by the European Central Bank showed that over 70% of retail traders of currency lose money.[1421]

Figure 20-6 tells the sad story. Almost 73% of the foreign-exchange trading accounts at IBFX/TradeStation—a major broker/dealer at the time—lost money in the first quarter of 2016.

Coda: After the numbers in Figure 20-6 were released by the National Futures Association, the regulatory agency banned IBFX for "capital deficiencies"[1422] and FXCM for "deceptive and abusive execution activities."[1423]

Most currency traders lose money

Brokerage	Losing traders
IBFX/TradeStation	72.9%
FXCM	72.0%
Gain Capital	71.0%
OANDA	65.5%
Interactive Brkrs.	56.0%

FIGURE 20-6
Source: National Futures Association, first quarter 2016

Our opinions deceive us about which way currencies will go

FIGURE 20-7

Stay far away from strange creations, such as leveraged and inverse ETFs

The ETF revolution has a dark side. Andreas Clenow of ACIES Asset Management of Switzerland gives us a searing analysis of new ETF-like products he calls "veritable financial landmines":[1424]

"The real problem is that as ETFs gained a nice reputation for being a safe and prudent investment vehicle, the business started relabeling any junk as ETFs."

The products Clenow particularly rails against are "inverse" ETFs, which supposedly go up when the market goes down, and "leveraged" ETFs, which magnify your losses using debt:

"If an ETF is marketed as Short S&P 500, you'd think it's a pretty straightforward instrument. If the index goes down ten percent, you gain ten percent. No. Doesn't work like that."

ETFs that are inverse or leveraged (also called levered) rebalance or "reset" their dollar value every night. This is disclosed in each security's prospectus, but few people read such documents.

The reset removes a little from your account each night. In the business, this is known as "value decay," among the printable things it's been called.

As a result of value decay, leveraged and inverse ETFs almost never deliver exactly the 2X or negative 1X performances they put in their names.

The Short S&P 500 inverse fund that Clenow mentioned gives us an example. In 40 weeks from September 2008 to June 2009, the S&P 500 index ETF (SPY) lost 26% of its value. Was the inverse ETF **up** 26%? Absolutely not!

Because of the value decay, the inverse ETF was **down** more than 7%. Even if you perfectly guessed the direction of the market—which is unlikely—you would have lost money with the inverse ETF.

EFTs that are leveraged 2X have even worse problems. Figure 20-8 shows an example.

The MSCI Emerging Markets Index holds stocks in fast-growing countries, such as Brazil and India. An iShares index fund, EEM, has tracked the index since 2003. Inverse (–1X) and leveraged (–2X) ETFs based on it came out in November 2007.

The next eight years were rough for emerging-market stocks. EEM lost 27%, including dividends.

You'd think the –1X ETF would be **up** 27%, wouldn't you? And the double-short –2X ETF should be up twice that: 54%, right?

In fact, both of these exotic vehicles **lost** big time: down 55% and 93%. The problem is that leveraged products move erratically in noisy markets.

To be sure, you can find time periods when leveraged ETFs look OK. The sponsors emphasize that these products operate as expected for only one day, not longer. But even then, the risks are enormous. These ETFs throw around terms like 1X and 2X, but you can't rely on them. Keep your distance.

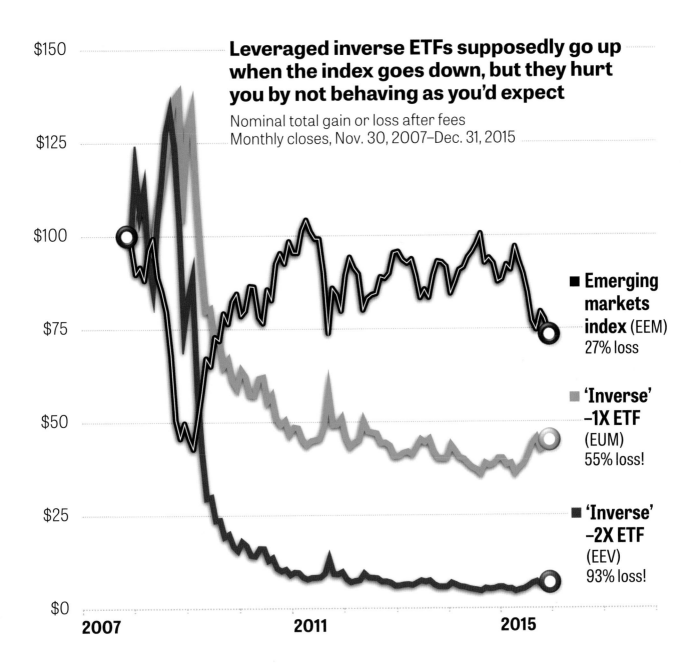

Leveraged inverse ETFs supposedly go up when the index goes down, but they hurt you by not behaving as you'd expect

Nominal total gain or loss after fees
Monthly closes, Nov. 30, 2007–Dec. 31, 2015

■ **Emerging markets index** (EEM) 27% loss

■ **'Inverse' –1X ETF** (EUM) 55% loss!

■ **'Inverse' –2X ETF** (EEV) 93% loss!

FIGURE 20-8 | Data source: Yahoo Finance

The best way to invest in your favorite social causes may surprise you

Some companies do bad things. They pollute, they mistreat their employees, and worse. This spawned **ESG ETFs.** These funds buy stock in corporations that have certain **environmental, social, or governance** policies (Figure 20-9).

Some companies' poor behaviors have indeed been changed through well-publicized boycotts of their **products.** Unfortunately, it's hard to affect a firm's policies by divesting from its **stock.**

Imagine that you and 1,000 friends all sell your shares of company XYZ one day. This drives the stock price down $1.

Supercomputers around the world notice that company XYZ is now a "better value." Traders buy the cheap shares, making a profit. Did you reform the company? No.

Sad to say, if you really want only ESG ETFs, no book can tell you which ones you'd prefer. Some social ETFs oppose "alternative lifestyles."[1425] Others support "LGBT employment equality."[1426]

It might shock you to learn that Vanguard's "social-responsibility" European Stock Fund owns British American Tobacco and Royal Dutch Shell, according to *Forbes*.[1427] Finally, many ESG ETFs charge fees more than double those of broad-market ETFs.[1428]

You might do your cause more good by using plain-vanilla ETFs and donating the money you save on fees to **shareholder activism** groups. These include the Interfaith Center on Corporate Responsibility (ICCR),[1429] As You Sow,[1430] and Ceres.[1431]

You don't need to phase in your money—put it right to work

If you're just now starting a Muscular Portfolio, what's the best way to begin?

Say you inherit $120,000. Should you invest immediately in the top three ETFs of a Muscular Portfolio? Or should you **cost-average** your dollars, investing $10,000 a month over 12 months, with the remainder sitting in cash?

Fortunately, the Vanguard Group has studied this question. Researchers examined every overlapping 12-month period as far back as good records go.

The answer? **Immediately investing** your lump sum into a balanced portfolio made you richer two-thirds of the time. Phasing in over 12 months was better in fewer than one-third of the cases.[1432]

It made no significant difference whether the tested market was the United States (back to 1926), the United Kingdom (back to 1976), or Australia (back to 1984). Immediate investment won out.

> **LIVINGSTON'S LAW OF UNWINNABLE GAMES**
>
> *Wall Street is bad at explaining the rules*
> *Because there's more profit in dealing with fools.*

Donating directly to a cause precisely targets your support

FIGURE 20-9

A **2224% ROI** Over the La

3 Years of Churn and Pun

Grandma's

$600 Money

$73,845 In J

OW to Tu

5,000 Int

4.88 Millio

(In Just 3.5 Years!)

a Fortune...
On $5,000
or Less!

ouncing The Incr   t Sin,

Today

Market into an

Monthly Pr

66%

ide, see if y

Money

**IF I Promised To Show You a Way
You Could Potentially Turn $10,000
Into an Annual Income of $368,446**

How You

Gain...

Anu Da   Every Expert with

**Huge, Fast Gains of 100%...500%...
Even 1415% in 6 Days!!!**

Comn

$400

For Earning

84.7% Return

On the Entire Account

n Just 30 Days

thing A Little $400

You Could Easily Turn

$20,000 Into $186,250

Tho Spi

NOW—You Too Can Tar

608.3% Annual Return

Ripped from today's headlines

If you have a little nest egg, you probably receive ads like these: "You can make
50% a year, 100%—even more!"

If you've learned anything from this book,
you know you can throw these come-ons
into the trash.

The world's best investors are billion-dollar
university endowment managers. In a
17-year period, their annualized returns
averaged 8.4%. The highest was 12.3%.
Even the slowest-growing college—

Cornell, with a 6.8% return—beat the
S&P 500's mere 5.5%. (Worse, the index
crashed 36% one year.)

A *Journal of Wealth Management* article
showed that individual investors could
have done roughly the same, 10.7% annualized, using just four index funds and a
simple asset-rotation rule.[1433] If you're
willing to commit 15 minutes a month, you
can do as well or better with a Muscular
Portfolio—and ignore the mailers.

Ivy League endowment funds, July 1, 1998–June 30, 2015	17-year annualized return	Maximum 1-year drawdown
Yale	12.3%	−24.6%
Princeton	11.8	−23.5
Duke	11.7	−24.3
Stanford	11.6	−25.9
MIT	11.2	−17.1
Columbia	9.7	−16.1
Harvard	9.7	−27.3
Average of 97 endowments over $1 billion	8.4	−20.5
Penn	7.3	−19.0
Cornell	6.8	−26.0
S&P 500	5.5	−35.9

Source: Douglas Roberts, *Journal of Wealth Management*, Fall 2017

Collage by Jed Dunkerley of actual mass mailers

21 Maximize your Social Security benefits and avoid the Tax Torpedo

"An obscure tax that hit a handful of affluent retirees in 1984 hits 30 percent of retirees today."

SCOTT BURNS (2015), syndicated columnist[1434]

Congress, in its infernal wisdom, has placed an explosive device underneath you after you quit working. It's called the "Tax Torpedo." It subjects up to 85% of your Social Security (SS) to taxation.

The tax on SS benefits began in 1983 and was increased in 1993. But Congress never adjusted the income levels for inflation. Only 3% of SS recipients were taxed in 1983, but 30% are bitten today. The reach grows wider by the year. All this agony for a tax that generates only 4% of SS revenues.[1435]

The good news: You can reduce or eliminate the Tax Torpedo. However, it takes a bit of planning.

Required minimum distributions are the key. RMDs begin the year you turn 70½. They count as taxable income, which can push you into Tax Torpedo territory. RMDs force you to withdraw a percentage of your combined IRA and Qualified Plan bal-ances (Figure 21-1). You don't have to spend the money, but you must pay tax on it.

The fix is to convert as many dollars as possible out of traditional IRAs and Qualified Plans like 401(k)s **before** you turn 70½. Convert the funds into after-tax dollars, such as Roths and health savings accounts, which are exempt from RMDs.

To minimize taxes, make small conversions in high-earning years and larger ones in low-earning years (e.g., when you're in the 10% or 12% tax bracket).

Caution: RMDs and conversions push up your household's modified adjusted gross income (MAGI). If you're over 65, a MAGI above about $85,000 might cost you a surcharge of hundreds of dollars for Medicare Part B premiums. A high MAGI also affects your eligibility for other federal and local benefit programs. For details, see Medicare's "Part B Costs"[1436] and Michael Kitces's "RMD Rules"[1437] and "Strategies to Minimize or Delay RMDs."[1438]

It's best to think about the conversion process years **before** you're hit with a significant tax bill.

If your annual income after age 70½ will be $125,000 or more, there may be **no way** to prevent 85% of your Social Security from being taxed. If so, simply skip this chapter and go on to the next.

But if your income will be $50,000 to $125,000, small shifts in your account balances can mean big reductions in the tax you must pay.

> **» KEY CONCEPT**
> ## avoid the Tax Torpedo
> Maximizing Roths and HSAs during your working career can eliminate taxes on your future Social Security benefits.

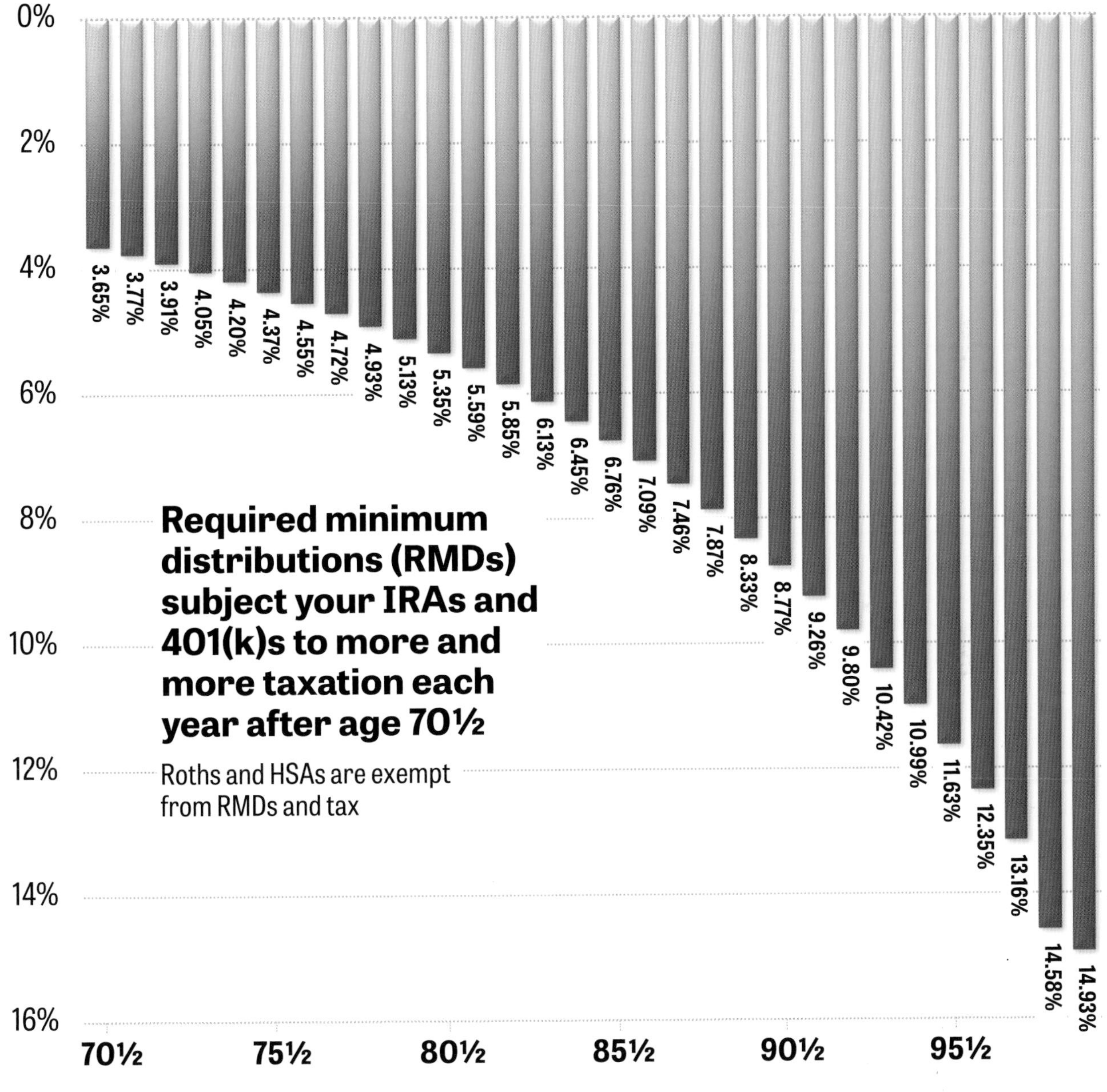
0%
2%
4%
6%
8%
10%
12%
14%
16%
3.65%
3.77%
3.91%
4.05%
4.20%
4.37%
4.55%
4.72%
4.93%
5.13%
5.35%
5.59%
5.85%
6.13%
6.45%
6.76%
7.09%
7.46%
7.87%
8.33%
8.77%
9.26%
9.80%
10.42%
10.99%
11.63%
12.35%
13.16%
14.58%
14.93%
Required minimum distributions (RMDs) subject your IRAs and 401(k)s to more and more taxation each year after age 70½
Roths and HSAs are exempt from RMDs and tax
70½
75½
80½
85½
90½
95½

FIGURE 21-1 | Source: IRS Publication 915[1439] Note: Different percentages apply to married couples whose ages are more than 10 years apart; see Table 2 of IRS Publication 590-B.[1440] For an RMD estimate, use the T. Rowe Price RMD Calculator[1441]

Distributions can make 85% of your Social Security benefits taxable

Figure 21-2 shows how required minimum distributions can cause Social Security benefits to become taxable for a single taxpayer. The numbers for a married couple are described in Figure 21-3.

» Meet our single filer. This taxpayer worked for 40 years as a high-tech manager before retiring at 70. We'll call him Bill (for the tax bill he must pay).

» High contributions to SS. Bill's job earnings have always been close to the ceiling at which wages are fully taxed for Social Security(SS). As a result, he'll receive a healthy $40,000 per year when he starts claiming SS at 70. (The maximum benefit at age 70 was $44,376 per year in 2018.)[1442]

» Before-tax dollars. During his career, Bill has maintained a traditional IRA and enjoyed generous company matches in his 401(k) Qualified Plans. By retirement, he's amassed $1.35 million total in these before-tax accounts.

» No IRA-to-Roth conversions. Bill never converted any of his before-tax dollars into after-tax dollars. (As described in Figure 19-17 of Chapter 19, IRA-to-Roth conversions during working years are taxed but can be profitable in the long run.)

» Required minimum distributions (RMDs). Bill must withdraw 3.65% of the total balances of his IRAs and Qualified Plans in the year that he turns 70½. If he doesn't, the IRS imposes a catastrophic 50% tax on the amount that wasn't withdrawn.

» 3.65% RMD of $1.35 million is $49,275. Bill's RMD at 70½ is taxable as ordinary income. Every year, the percentage that he must withdraw and pay tax on rises. The percentage is 3.77% at 71½, 3.91% at 72½, and so on, as we saw in Figure 21-1.

» RMDs slash his otherwise tax-free benefits. "Provisional income" (PI) determines whether or not your SS benefit is taxed. PI includes one-half of your benefit, plus 100% of most other types of income. PI includes withdrawals from before-tax accounts but **not** from after-tax accounts. In Bill's case, $20,000 plus $49,275 is $69,275. That's higher than the IRS's $34,000 PI test for singles. In this example, 85% or $34,000 of Bill's SS benefit becomes taxable.

» Deductions reduce only part of the pain. Bill's adjusted gross income is the RMD, $49,275, plus the $34,000 taxable portion of his SS. The sum is his AGI: $83,275. He subtracts the standard deduction of $13,000 for singles over 65. This leaves taxable income of $69,675. Bill has no other income or deductions.

» Tax eats $11,653 of Bill's spending money. In his golden years, the $11,653 bite from his taxable income cuts Bill's spending by about one-sixth. His original $89,275 annual budget is reduced to only $77,622.

» Using Roths, he'd have 15% more to spend. Before he turned 70, Bill could have gradually converted some of his before-tax dollars into Roths, as described in Chapter 19. He would have enjoyed 15% more dollars to live on each year. Roths and health savings accounts (HSAs) are not forced to take RMDs. Also, rule-compliant withdrawals from Roths and HSAs are tax-free and aren't counted as PI.

The Tax Torpedo for singles

Using Roths and avoiding RMDs, this single filer enjoys 15% more spending money

$1,350,000 portfolio in
BEFORE-TAX accounts

Budget		Provisional Income test:
annual Social Security benefit 85% TAXABLE	**$40,000** ┄┄┄▶	**+$20,000** (half of SS)
required minimum distributions (RMDs) from IRAs and Qualified Plans **100% TAXABLE** Included in Provisional Income test? YES	**+49,275** ┄┄┄▶	**+ 49,275** (RMD income) ――――――――――――― **$69,275** total **Prov. Income**
tax on Social Security and RMDs	**−11,653**	Total Provisional Income is greater than the **$34,000** test for singles. In this case, 85% of the single's Social Security benefit is subject to income tax.
annual spending money	**$77,622**	

$1,350,000 portfolio in
AFTER-TAX accounts

Budget		Provisional Income test:
annual Social Security benefit NOT TAXABLE	**$40,000** ┄┄┄▶	**+$20,000** (half of SS)
withdrawals from after-tax accounts from Roths and HSAs NOT TAXABLE Included in Provisional Income test? NO	**+49,275** ┄┄┄▶	**+ 0** (after-tax income) ――――――――――――― **$20,000** total **Prov. Income**
no tax on SS or after-tax withdrawals	**0**	Total Provisional Income is less than the **$34,000** test for singles. Therefore, none of the single's Social Security benefit is subject to income tax.
annual spending money	**$89,275**	

15% more money to spend each year

FIGURE 21-2 | 2018 tax rates

Many couples pay tax on their SS benefits because of the "provisional income" test

Figure 21-3 shows how the tax situation can differ for married couples filing jointly, compared with the example in Figure 21-2 for single filers.

» **A working couple with long careers.** Unlike Bill, the well-paid manager in the previous example, our joint filers—we'll call them Dick and Jane—have always earned only average wages. (The median US household income was $58,829 in December 2017.)[1443]

» **Middling SS contributions and benefits.** Dick and Jane are two people rather than one, obviously. But their middle-income payroll history gives them each a Social Security benefit of just $20,000 for a combined $40,000, the same as Bill, the single person. (The average retired worker received a Social Security benefit of $15,486 in 2018.)[1444]

» **Respectable before-tax savings.** Despite their moderate earnings, Dick and Jane have saved with enthusiasm during their 40 working years. Including the wise investing of a small inheritance many years ago, by age 70 they've accumulated $1.6 million in their various before-tax accounts. That includes traditional IRAs and Qualified Plans where they worked.

» **No conversions to after-tax accounts.** Just like Bill, neither Dick nor Jane carried out any IRA-to-Roth conversions during their working years.

» **Required minimum distributions (RMDs).** Since they're both 70½, Dick and Jane are forced by law to withdraw 3.65% of their $1.6 million combined before-tax dollars this year. The percentage rises each year, as we saw in Figure 21-1.

» **The 3.65% RMD of $1.6 million is $58,400.** Dick and Jane's RMDs at 70½ are taxable as ordinary income. What's worse, their $58,400 RMD is enough to make 85% of their SS benefits taxable.

» **RMDs slash their "tax-free" Social Security checks.** On their tax return, Dick and Jane must use the provisional income (PI) test for couples. Their PI is above the $44,000 test. In this case, 85% or $34,000 of their $40,000 SS benefit becomes taxable.

» **Joint deductions are some help.** Dick and Jane's adjusted gross income is the $58,400 RMD plus the $34,000 taxable portion of their SS. The sum is their AGI: $92,400. They subtract a standard deduction of $26,600 for couples over 65. This leaves taxable income of $65,800. They have no other income or deductions.

» **Tax eats $7,827 of the couple's spending money.** In their golden years, the $7,827 bite from their taxable income cuts Dick and Jane's spending by about one-tenth. Their original $98,400 annual budget is reduced to only $90,573.

» **Using Roths, they'd have 8.6% more to spend.** Before turning 70, Dick and Jane could have gradually converted some of their before-tax dollars into Roths, as described in Chapter 19. The couple would have enjoyed 8.6% more dollars to live on each year. Roths and HSAs are not forced to take RMDs. Also, rule-compliant withdrawals from Roths and HSAs are tax-free and aren't counted as PI.

The Tax Torpedo for couples

Using Roths and avoiding RMDs, these two married people enjoy 8.6% more spending money

$1,600,000 portfolio in
BEFORE-TAX accounts

Budget		Provisional Income test:
annual Social Security benefit 85% TAXABLE	**$40,000**	+$20,000 (half of SS)
required minimum distributions (RMDs) from IRAs and Qualified Plans 100% TAXABLE Included in Provisional Income test? YES	**+58,400**	+ 58,400 (RMD income)
		$78,400 total **Prov. Income**
tax on Social Security and RMDs	**−7,827**	Total Provisional Income is greater than the **$44,000** test for couples. In this case, 85% of the couple's Social Security benefit is subject to income tax.
annual spending money	**$90,573**	

$1,600,000 portfolio in
AFTER-TAX accounts

Budget		Provisional Income test:
annual Social Security benefit NOT TAXABLE	**$40,000**	+$20,000 (half of SS)
withdrawals from after-tax accounts from Roths and HSAs NOT TAXABLE Included in Provisional Income test? NO	**+58,400**	+ 0 (after-tax income)
		$20,000 total **Prov. Income**
no tax on SS or after-tax withdrawals	**0**	Total Provisional Income is less than the **$44,000** test for couples. Therefore, none of the couple's Social Security benefit is subject to income tax.
annual spending money	**$98,400**	

8.6% more money to spend each year

FIGURE 21-3 | 2018 tax rates

No example can possibly match your personal tax situation

No single chapter of any book can predict the interactions between your income and all of the deductions, exemptions, and tax credits you may have.

You'll need to sit down with your tax software or your tax preparer. Your before-tax and after-tax balances all affect the taxation of your Social Security benefits.

Figure 21-4 shows a partial list of income and expenses that may figure into the calculation of your provisional income. Knowing what counts is half the battle. For specifics, see IRS Publications 915[1445] and 590-B.[1446]

You may be able to test your alternatives using a free website named CalcXML.com. You'll need 15 different income and expense numbers. A tax preparer may be necessary to dig up this data for you.

If that's not too daunting, you can also estimate the tax bite using CalcXML's Social Security Benefit Tax Calculator.[1447]

Unfortunately, one thing that can't be estimated by any Web service is the amount your Social Security benefits might be taxed by your state or local area. There are simply too many different jurisdictions charging various rates.

See Figure 21-5 for the 13 states that tax Social Security benefits. Contact your local tax bureau to see whether any local taxes apply.

How to figure your provisional income

DO include in provisional income:

» Only one-half of your Social Security benefits

» 100% of the taxable lines in your Form 1040 "income" section, **plus**

» Add tax-exempt interest (for instance, municipal bonds)

» Add ordinarily disregarded foreign income

» Add adoption tax benefits

Do NOT include in provisional income:

» Qualifying withdrawals from Roth, HSA, and taxable accounts

» Qualified dividends (from stocks you've owned for 60 days)

Subtract from provisional income:

» Alimony you paid

» Educator expenses

» Moving expenses

» Penalties on early withdrawals from savings

» Withdrawals from after-tax accounts

» All other lines in your Form 1040 "adjusted gross income" section

Exceptions: Add back into provisional income:

» Tuition and fees deduction

» Student-loan interest deduction

» Domestic production activities deduction

FIGURE 21-4 | Source: IRS.gov Publication 915

Benefits are taxed not just by the IRS, but also by 13 states

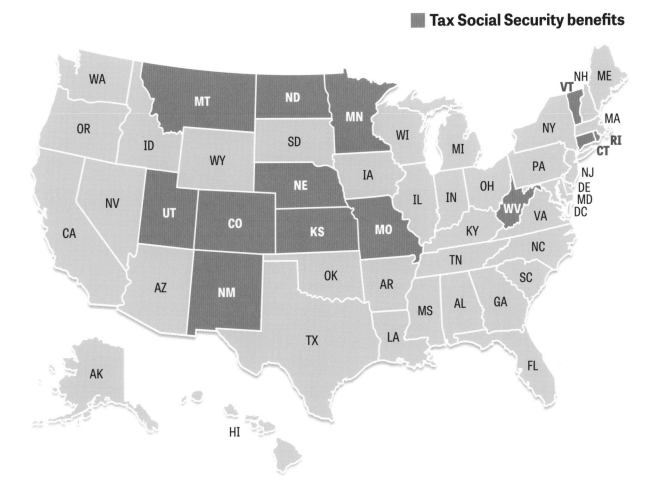

■ Tax Social Security benefits

FIGURE 21-5
Source: Kiplinger.com as of Jan. 1, 2018.[1448] Illustration by Pieter Tandjung

---

LIVINGSTON'S LAW OF SOCIAL SECURITY
Planning long before you turn seventy
Can ensure you'll end up with plenty.

22 Find a safe withdrawal rate to last you the rest of your life

"The elements of good trading are: (1) cutting losses, (2) cutting losses, and (3) cutting losses. If you can follow these three rules, you may have a chance."

ED SEYKOTA (2016), famous commodities trader[1449]

Here's the bad news:
Let's say, for the sake of discussion, that you really can expect a 10% rate of return. After all, both the Baby Bear Portfolio and the S&P 500 delivered approximately that much over the past four decades. That **doesn't** mean you can quit your job, withdraw 10% each year from your tax-free Roth account, and expect the balance to support you for the next 30 years (Figure 22-1).

You can **never** withdraw each year as much as **any** portfolio's annualized rate of return. If you did, the withdrawals you made during bear markets could exhaust your account and leave you broke.

Statisticians have said for many years that you can withdraw only about 4% in the first year after you quit your job. Each year after that, you would increase your initial withdrawal amount solely for inflation.

Here's the good news:
The 4% "safe withdrawal rate" (SWR) has been challenged as too low by numerous experts.

Michael Kitces, director of wealth planning for Pinnacle Advisory Group, writes: "Over 2/3rds of the time, the retiree finishes the 30-year time horizon still having more-than-double their starting principal."[1450] The 4% rule can make you starve yourself for no good reason!

To solve the puzzle scientifically, Kitces published an amazingly comprehensive literature review of 32 academic studies. His review, titled "20 Years of Safe Withdrawal Rate Research," reveals a firm set of rules.[1451]

The proper initial withdrawal rate for you may actually be 5%, 6%, or 7%.

Instead of initially withdrawing only 4% of your wealth annually, how'd you like a secure income that's 1.5 times as much: a rate of 6%? Read on.

Figures 22-2 and 22-3 contain a graphical road map and the same information as a checklist—greatly simplified. For full details, read Kitces's literature review.

Take out an amount that's just right and you'll go far

FIGURE 22-1

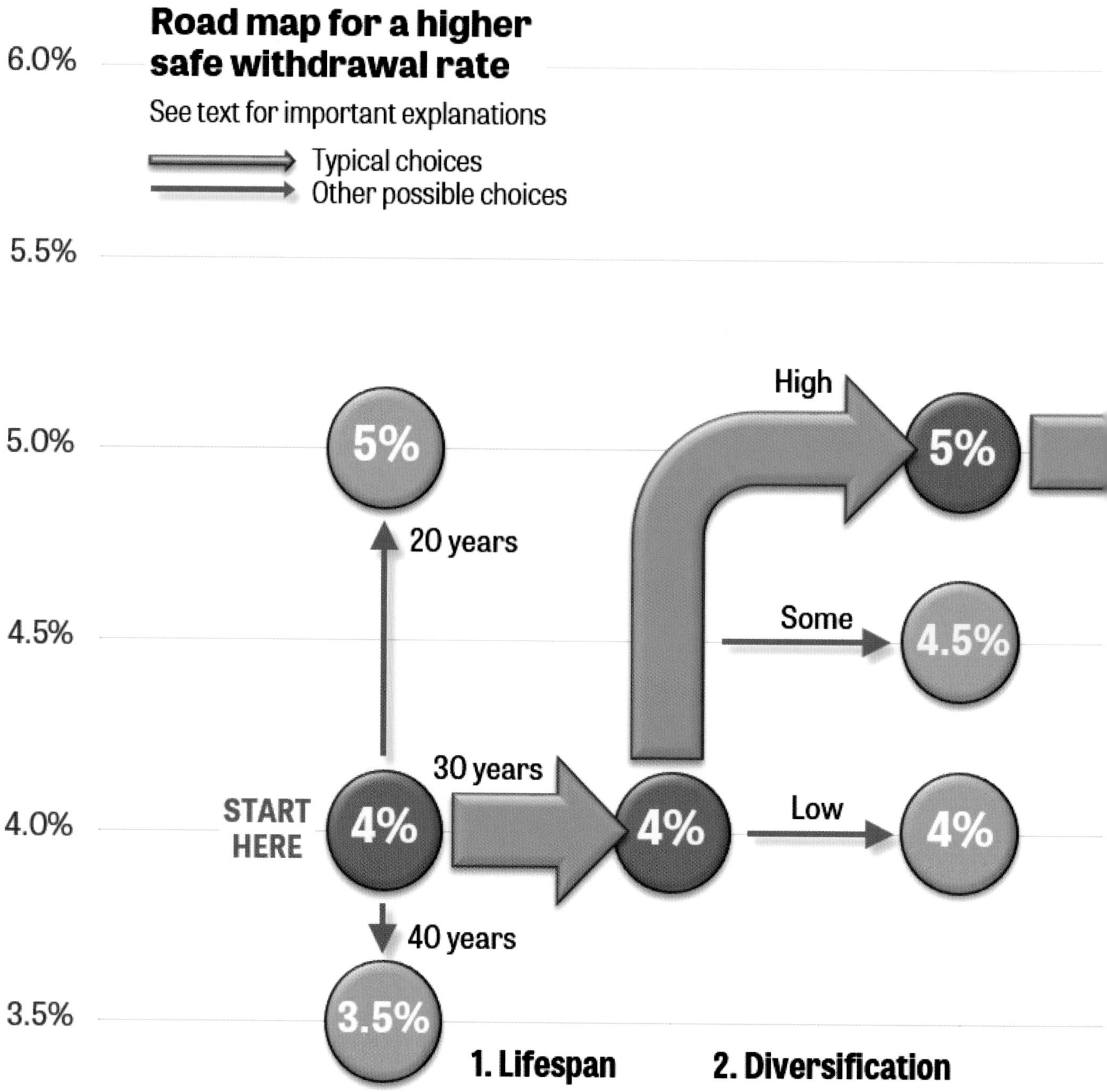

Road map for a higher safe withdrawal rate

See text for important explanations

⟹ Typical choices
→ Other possible choices

6.0%

5.5%

5.0% 5%

4.5% 4.5%

4.0% START HERE 4% 30 years 4% Low 4%

3.5% 3.5%

20 years

High 5%

Some

40 years

1. Lifespan   2. Diversification

FIGURE 22-2 | Adapted from "20 Years of Safe Withdrawal Rate Research"[1452]

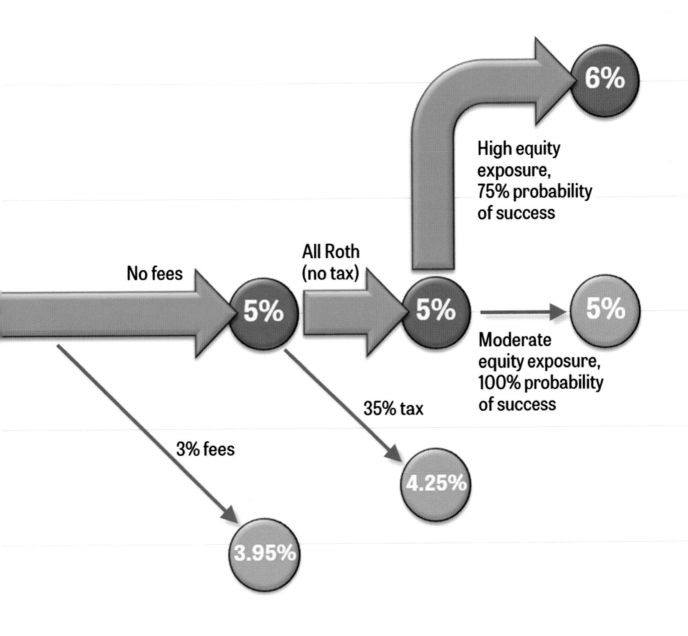

No fees

5%

All Roth
(no tax)

5%

High equity
exposure,
75% probability
of success

6%

Moderate
equity exposure,
100% probability
of success

5%

3% fees

3.95%

35% tax

4.25%

3. Management fees   **4. Taxation**   **5. Risk tolerance**

Five rules help you determine the safe withdrawal rate for a Muscular Portfolio

Use Figure 22-2 as a road map and Figure 22-3 as a checklist. Both show the same five choices that a Muscular Portfolios investor must make.

The following five decision rules apply to both the road map and the checklist. The summary below is explained in much more detail in "20 Years of Safe Withdrawal Rate Research."[1453] Four additional rules—less relevant for Muscular Portfolios—are described later in this chapter for completeness.

1 · Lifespan rule

Imagine a male and female nonsmoking couple in average health. They're both 65. There's a 37% chance that after 30 years, at least one person will still be alive. There's only a 3% chance of that after 40 years. Smokers have half those percentages.

Use the calculator at LongevityIllustrator.org to compute your odds (single or couple). Then select 20, 30, or 40 years as the desired lifespan of your portfolio—not your personal expected lifespan.

2 · Diversification rule

People have a behavioral bias to purchase only stocks and bonds from their own country. It's called "home bias." Kitces's review shows that global asset classes, "especially the inclusion of commodities and real estate," support higher withdrawal rates. Muscular Portfolios automatically tilt toward global asset classes at the right times, so these portfolios are considered to have high diversification.

3 · Management fee rule

Add up your ETF annual fees and any management fees you pay to wealth managers. If the answer is, "almost nothing for ETFs, absolutely nothing for brokers," great! You don't have to reduce your safe withdrawal rate. As the review explains, "The safe withdrawal rate goes down 0.35% for every 1% of expenses." Management fees don't reduce your SWR on a one-for-one basis, but every dollar you keep for yourself does help.

4 · Taxation rule

Other than qualifying Roth withdrawals, you must pay tax on withdrawals from IRAs and realized gains within taxable accounts. If you use funds **outside** those accounts to pay your tax bills, your SWR is unchanged. What if you have no income **other** than your savings accounts to pay taxes? You can withdraw the same SWR, but assume you'll have 0.25 point less spendable money in a low tax bracket like 12%. You'll have 0.5 point less in the 24% bracket and 0.75 point less in the 35% bracket.

5 · Risk-tolerance rule

Can you tolerate a 75% equity exposure? Muscular Portfolios can hold up to 100% equities in bull markets. That adds 0.5 point to your SWR.

Add another 0.5 point if you're willing to accept a 25% chance that you must take a cutback in your withdrawals after a market crash. Muscular Portfolios are designed to avoid crashing in bear markets, so you're unlikely to need to cut back.

> **» KEY CONCEPT**
> ## use evidence-based rules to determine your personal safe withdrawal rate
> The 4% baseline can adapt to your situation.

Use this checklist to determine the highest SWR for a Muscular Portfolio

	Typical choice	Initial value
Baseline safe withdrawal rate (START HERE)		**4%**
1. Lifespan of portfolio rule a. If you assume your portfolio must last 30 years, add 0 points. b. If you expect you'll need it for only 20 years, add 1 point. c. If you retire young and need it for 40 years, subtract 0.5 point.	a	+0%
2. Diversification rule (REITs, commodities, and non-US assets) a. If your portfolio's use of diverse assets is high, add 1 point. b. If your portfolio uses some diverse assets, add 0.5 point. c. Home-bias portfolio (US stocks and bonds only), add 0 points.	a	+1%
3. Management fee rule a. If you pay no adviser fees from your portfolio, add 0 points. b. For each 1% of fees paid from your portfolio, subtract 0.35 point.	a	+0%
4. Taxation rule (depends on your tax bracket) a. If all your savings are in tax-free Roth accounts, add 0 points. b. For each 12% of tax on your accounts' gains, subtract 0.25 point.	a	+0%
5. Risk-tolerance rule a. For aggressive portfolios with at least 75% equities, add 0.5 point. b. If you accept a 25% chance of a need to cut spending, add 0.5 point. c. With 50% US equities and a zero chance of cutbacks, add 0 points	a & b	+1%
Total initial safe withdrawal rate		**6%**

For additional rules that are less relevant to Muscular Portfolios, see text.

FIGURE 22-3 | Adapted from "20 Years of Safe Withdrawal Rate Research"[1454]

Four additional rules are less relevant to Muscular Portfolio users

The review by Kitces (Figure 22-4) describes four more rules. They're less likely to affect your SWR decision, but consider them now—just in case.[1455]

6 · Market-valuation rule

The US stock market's valuation can be considered "high" when Shiller's CAPE ratio is above 20, "moderate" at 12 to 20, and "low" below 12. (CAPE, also called Shiller P/E10, was explained in Chapter 13.)

Kitces says, "Increase safe withdrawal rate by 0.5% in moderate/average valuation environments, and 1.0% in favorable low valuation environments."

Muscular Portfolios automatically tilt toward assets in uptrends and away from assets in the basement. Asset rotation isn't affected by today's CAPE ratio.

7 · Legacy rule

Some investors wish to leave a legacy to heirs or charities. A 4% initial SWR supports this goal. As the review states: "In a whopping 96% of the cases the client's **entire** starting principal remains!"

But if you want a 100% likelihood of your original balance to be available at your death, subtract 0.2 point from the SWR you calculated in Figure 22-3. That seems like a small adjustment. But as Kitces notes, a 0.2-point bite out of a baseline of 4% "represents a spending cut of nearly 5% of the starting amount, per year, for life."

8 · Glide-path rule

Various researchers recommend a "glide path." This means raising or lowering your equity exposure as you age. However, the review says various glide paths have a "limited apparent benefit in terms of allowing for a higher initial withdrawal rate."

9 · Annuity rule

If your expected lifespan is long, an annuity may be wise. You pay a lump sum to a financial institution, which agrees to pay you a monthly income for life.

However, Kitces found that this "may not necessarily lead to a higher initial withdrawal rate."

> **» TECH TALK**
>
> ## no extra points for Muscular Portfolios
>
> Some academic papers say a momentum portfolio could support a safe withdrawal rate as high as 10.2%.[1456]
>
> This book makes no such claim. A Muscular Portfolio's return might be high or it might be low. Consider it gravy if your portfolio **does** gain more than the market over a complete bear-bull market cycle.
>
> Your best approach is to adapt your withdrawal rate if your portfolio falls or soars much more than the S&P 500. Simply reevaluate your withdrawal rate after the end of every bear market. (A 20% rise in the S&P 500's nominal price level confirms a new bull, allowing you to determine the last bear's end.)
>
> Calculate what your portfolio's balance was on the last day of the bear. Revise your withdrawal rate, if need be. (For example, your desired portfolio lifespan might then be only 20 years rather than 30.) And enjoy the new bull market!

The rules in this chapter are simplified. In particular, it's not really known how all of the checklist items in Figures 22-2 and 22-3 will work together.

Kitces sums up near the end of his paper by emphasizing that there are a **lot** of variables:

"The first and most significant is that many of the factors discussed here were evaluated in separate research studies, and it is not necessarily clear whether they are precisely additive."

That's why this book takes a conservative approach. Don't give yourself bonus points just because a Muscular Portfolio might or might not have a higher rate of return than other investing strategies.

To fully inform yourself, it's worth your time to read Kitces's full 14-page review.[1457]

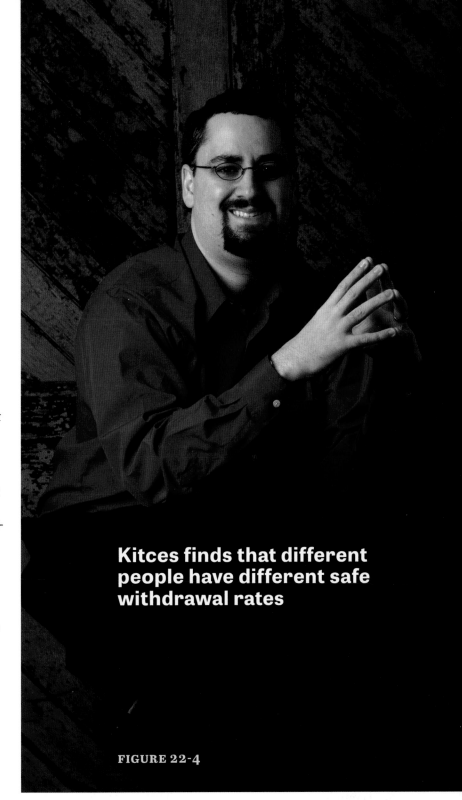

Kitces finds that different people have different safe withdrawal rates

FIGURE 22-4

Work, save, budget, and eventually you'll cover all your expenses

How did we wind up with such confusing rules for something as simple as a "safe withdrawal rate"? The answer is that one size doesn't fit all.

The 4% withdrawal rule was estimated in 1994 by William P. Bengen, a registered investment adviser in San Diego, Calif. It was designed to protect you against a new Great Depression beginning around the time you quit working.

Bengen assumed that a person aged 60 to 65 would a 50/50 split of US stocks and intermediate-term Treasurys. He wrote: "A first-year withdrawal of 4 percent . . . followed by inflation-adjusted withdrawals in subsequent years, should be safe." He said the 4% rate assumes "a minimum requirement of 30 years of portfolio longevity."[1458]

In truth, the 4% rule was never intended to be an absolute mandate for every individual. Bengen met with his investing clients every year and tailored their withdrawal rates to their particular situations.

But the mainstream media rarely acknowledged this tailoring. Instead, article after article proclaimed 4% as the "safe withdrawal rate" —not just a baseline—regardless of your financial condition.

If you're depending on your own funds, save every penny you can. Work as many years as possible. Maximize your use of tax-deferred plans like 401(k)s, IRAs, and Roths. Postpone taking Social Security until you really need it.

Fortunately, you may not require as much money to live on as you thought. Figure 22-5 shows that some major expenses actually go down as we age:

» **Transportation and housing spending** drops 40% for people 75 and over—a time when you're likely to travel less and live in a smaller home.

» **Fewer payments** into savings plans and the Social Security Administration (SSA) are a big deal. People 75 and over spend only one-eighth as much on contributions to savings and SSA as people 45–54.

» **Health care spending** is about $1,000 per year higher for those 65 and up, on average, than it is for the 45–54 age group. Medicare and Medicaid programs for seniors keep some health costs down.

Use this chapter's formulas with caution. If your gains are good, consider yourself lucky.

Ultimately, your safe withdrawal rate comes down to a bet you make with your life. Only you can decide how much to budget and take out.

LIVINGSTON'S LAW OF WITHDRAWALS

If you raise your take over four percent
The extra money will seem heaven-sent.

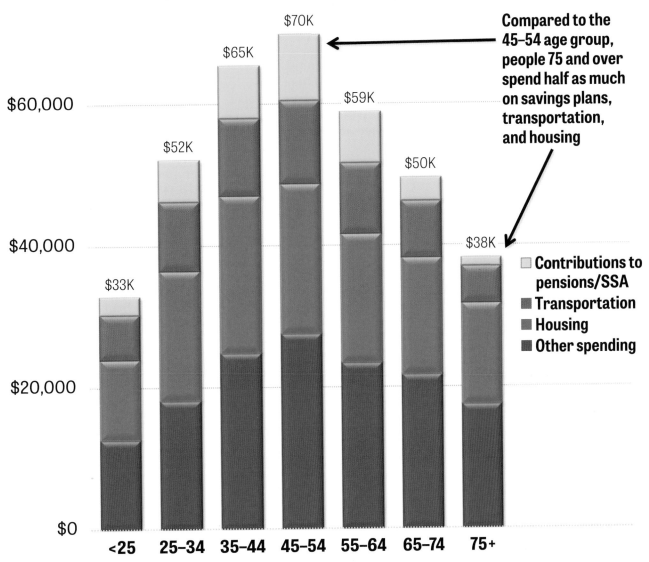

After age 55, Americans spend about $1,000 less each year

$70K

$65K

Compared to the 45–54 age group, people 75 and over spend half as much on savings plans, transportation, and housing

$52K

$59K

$60,000

$50K

$40,000

$38K

Contributions to pensions/SSA

Transportation

$33K

Housing

Other spending

$20,000

$0

<25 25–34 35–44 45–54 55–64 65–74 75+

FIGURE 22-5 | Source: "Consumer Expenditures in 2015," Table 5, Bureau of Labor Statistics[1459]

23 The End Game Portfolio gives you a smooth ride with special bond ETFs

"The bonds of matrimony are like any other bonds—
they mature slowly."

PETER DE VRIES (1910–1993), author of *The Tunnel of Love*[1460]

The day may come when you've worked hard, saved like crazy, and taken full advantage of Muscular Portfolios. Your brokerage accounts contain more money than you'll ever need. Hooray, you've won the investing game!

If you've won the game, why keep playing?

If you've accumulated $5 million or more, you should consider the End Game Portfolio. This strategy involves placing 80% of your investment dollars into bond ETFs that provide you with all the monthly interest you need to live. You keep the other 20% of your dollars in a Muscular Portfolio to provide growth.

Why not switch to a portfolio of 100% bonds? The reason is that the principal amount of your bonds would never grow. If you started out with $5 million in bonds, you'd still have $5 million ten years later—no growth to help you face inflation.

By contrast, keeping 20% of your portfolio in the Mama Bear or Papa Bear would give you growth. Once a year, if the Muscular Portfolio has grown to more than 20% of your holdings, you simply sell some ETF shares and purchase a bond ETF, increasing your fixed-income principal.

Figure 23-1 shows that the End Game would have fallen only 12.4% at the worst point of the 2007–2009 financial crisis. Its maximum drawdown in 43 years was 13.9% from September 1979 through March 1980.

Other drawdowns during the 43-year simulation were so small they're hardly visible at the scale of Figure 23-1:

Mar.–Aug. '74	–7.2%
Sept.–Oct. '87	–4.9%
Nov. '93–Nov. '94	–7.0%
May–July '02	–2.0%

The 100% bond portfolio we saw in Figure 9-6 had a maximum drawdown of more than 20% in 1980 and took over two years to recover. A 20/80 mix is more stable.

Fortunately for investors, you no longer need to buy individual bonds from a stockbroker. You can now get bonds from hundreds of different issuers with a single purchase of a **defined-maturity bond ETF.** DM ETFs are available from almost any online brokerage.

Defined-maturity ETFs combine the predictable income of individual bonds with the promise that 100% of your principal will be returned to you on a specific maturity date—no matter what happened to interest rates in the meantime.

> » KEY CONCEPT
> ## defined-maturity bond ETFs
> DM ETFs give you hundreds of bonds with a single purchase and provide the certainty of a specific maturity date.

ratio scale

The End Game with 80% bonds and 20% Mama Bear offers the smallest possible drawdowns

Jan. 1, 1973–Dec. 31, 2015
Nominal total return including dividends

$6,400

$3,200

$1,600

$800

$400

$200

$100

$50

2007–2009 crash

$6,293

$6,010

■ End Game +10.1% ann'd

■ S&P 500 +10.0% ann'd

S&P 500 maximum drawdown: –51%

End Game maximum drawdown: only –12.4%

TRADING FRICTION
The two portfolios were charged the current ETF annual fees and round-trip trading costs described in Chapter 1 (S&P 500 and Mama Bear) and Chapter 8 (bonds).

1973   1979   1985   1991   1997   2003   2009   2015

FIGURE 23-1 | Source: Quant simulator

Reduce interest-rate effects on your portfolio by 'laddering' your bonds

If your nest egg is large, you can stop playing the equity game! Would an allocation of 80% of your portfolio to DM bond ETFs produce enough interest to support your lifestyle? If so, use the End Game and enjoy a smooth ride for the rest of your life.

It's reasonable to ask: "Wouldn't an 80% allocation to bonds expose me to a lot of interest-rate risk?" It's well-known that bonds lose market value when interest rates go up, as we'll see later in this chapter.

The answer to the question is called a **bond ladder**. With this strategy, you stagger your assets so a few of your bonds mature each year (Figure 23-2).

You simply hold each DM ETF to its maturity date, when it returns your principal. On that date, you buy a new DM ETF.

If interest rates rise between the time you bought a DM ETF and the date it matures, the new DM ETF you purchase will yield a higher interest rate, paying you more money. If not, the Muscular Portfolio in your account will provide some growth to compensate.

Studies show two benefits of holding a bond ladder:

1 · Interest-rate hikes don't affect the market price of your portfolio as much; and

2 · Your long-term return can be slightly higher.

For example, a bond ladder typically outperforms a **bullet strategy**—a portfolio of bonds with the same long maturity, such as 8 to 12 years. The improvement was about 0.2% annualized over a 20-year period analyzed by Thornburg Investment Management.[1461]

MarketWatch's Mark Hulbert shows another benefit of bond ladders. He studied the 17 years from 1965 through 1982, when Treasury yields almost tripled. The S&P 500 had an annualized total return of 5.9%. A bond ladder of Treasurys with a constant maturity of five years delivered an almost identical return of 5.8%.[1462]

There are two ways to convert a Muscular Portfolio to an End Game Portfolio:

» Immediate switchover. You could sell 80% of a Muscular Portfolio in a single day, and then buy equal amounts of DM ETFs maturing in 1, 2, 3, 4, 5, 6, and 7 years. **Disadvantage:** The bond ETFs with the shortest maturities would pay you low interest rates.

» Gradual switchover. It's better to shift one-ninth (about 11½%) of your Muscular Portfolio into bonds each year. If you start seven years before you quit your last job, all of your DM ETFs will pay you the higher interest rates offered by longer-term bonds (seven-year maturities).

Allocating 80% to bond ETFs and 20% to a Muscular Portfolio gives you income and growth

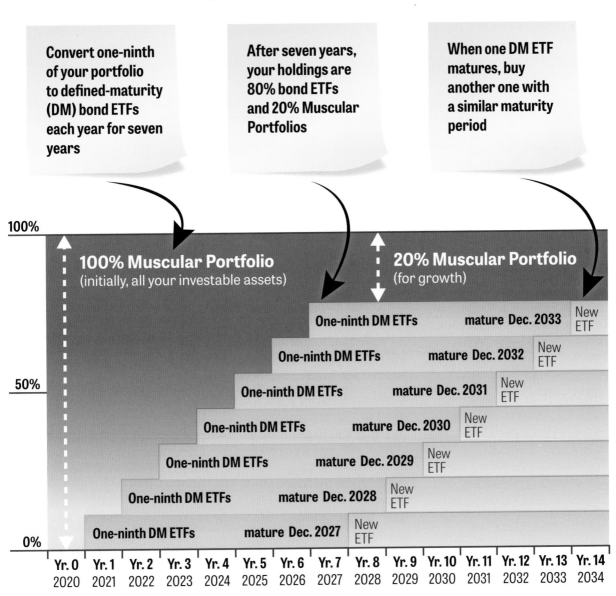

Convert one-ninth of your portfolio to defined-maturity (DM) bond ETFs each year for seven years

After seven years, your holdings are 80% bond ETFs and 20% Muscular Portfolios

When one DM ETF matures, buy another one with a similar maturity period

FIGURE 23-2 | Illustration by Pieter Tandjung

Defined-maturity ETFs have big advantages over ordinary bond funds

Let's say you've saved enough to live off the End Game Portfolio (plus any Social Security or other income you may have).

You might be tempted to sock 80% of your assets into a single fund. You might select the Vanguard Long-Term Corporate Bond ETF (VCLT). After all, it's in the Papa Bear menu and holds US bonds with respectable, investment-grade (IG) credit ratings of AAA, AA, A, or BBB.

However, defined-maturity bond ETFs have advantages. Ordinary bond funds fall in price when interest rates rise and might take years to recover.

A benefit of defined-maturity bond ETFs is that they have, ahem, defined maturity dates, like individual bonds. On the maturity date, 100% of your principal will be returned, assuming no issuer defaults. (Investment-grade companies almost never default, as explained later in this chapter.)

You can totally ignore the day-to-day value of an End Game Portfolio. Check it only once a year. If your Muscular Portfolio has grown above 20% of your holdings, sell a few shares and buy new DM bond ETFs. Bliss!

Why does the market price of a bond fall when interest rates rise? (See Figure 23-3.)

1 · You purchase $100 in bonds. Say you pay $100 to buy a one-year note. It offers you 3% in interest payments that year.

2 · Rates suddenly rise. The next day, issuers start offering a yield of 3.09% on new one-year notes.

3 · Your market price is now $97. You'd get about $97, not $100, if you sold today.

4 · Now $97 buys what $100 used to. Buyers would pay you only $97 to get the $3 annual interest from your note. They'd get a 3.09% yield. That's the same yield as paying $100 to get $3.09 from a new note.

With DM bond ETFs, changes in interest rates don't concern you one bit. But with ordinary bond ETFs, you must worry about differences in **types** of bonds.

If interest rates rose one percentage point, the prices of individual bonds would drop as follows:

- » **30-yr. Treasurys**   −17.6%
- » **10-yr. Treasurys**   −8.3%
- » **IG corp. bonds**   −7.0%
- » **Municipal bonds**   −6.1%
- » **High-yield bonds**   −4.1%

Treasury bonds are the **most sensitive** to interest-rate hikes. That's because government bonds have little default risk. Almost all of their risk comes from interest rates rising.

High-yield bonds, also called junk bonds, have credit ratings of BB, B, CCC, or lower. They're the **least sensitive** to interest-rate hikes. Almost all their fluctuation in price is due to junk bonds' higher probability of default. (The above statistics were calculated by JPMorgan as of Jan. 31, 2018.)[1463]

With DM bond ETFs, you don't have to worry about any of this. You can ignore interest-rate changes and live your life.

The market prices of bonds fall when interest rates rise

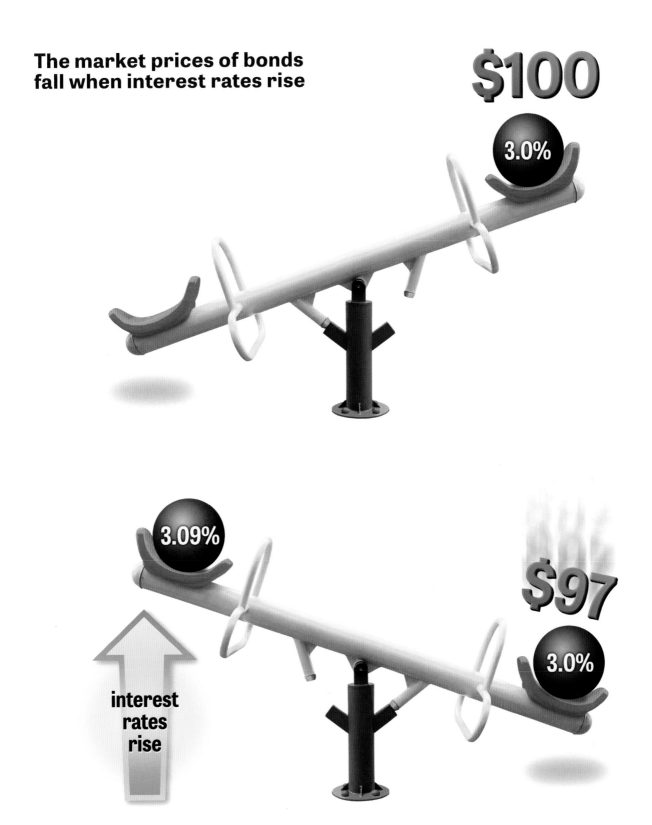

FIGURE 23-3 | Illustration by Pieter Tandjung

How to choose DM ETFs for your income or savings goals

In many ways, buying individual bonds is not like buying shares of stock.

Shares of every company in the S&P 500 trade thousands of times a day. Bonds are different. There are more than 150,000 individual bonds in the US market, Dave Nadig of ETFdb.com estimates. But only a few thousand of them change hands even **once a day.**

Imagine you wanted to buy a bond from a well-known company like Krispy Kreme. You might have to wait **four days** before some owner of Krispy Kreme bonds happened to put any units on the market, Nadig says.[1464]

Defined-maturity bond ETFs eliminate the need to buy individual bonds. DM bond ETFs trade constantly while the market is open. And they give you the security of holding hundreds of different issuers with a single purchase.

But **which** DM bond ETF should you buy?

A partial listing from the two largest sponsors of DM ETFs is shown in Figure 23-4. For current yields, see the Web pages of Invesco[1465] and

iShares.[1466] (In April 2018, Invesco acquired the ETFs formerly owned by Guggenheim and lowered their annual fees.)

» Invesco sponsors both investment-grade and high-yield DM ETFs. The junk-bond ETFs offer higher interest, but some issuers could default in a recession. More about that later in this chapter.

» iShares sponsors ETFs holding investment-grade bonds or municipal bonds. The munis are tax-free, even from the alternative minimum tax (AMT). Ask your tax preparer whether low-yielding munis are worthwhile in your tax bracket.

For short-term goals—such as amassing a down payment to buy a house—choose the DM ETF that matures just before you'll need the money.

For retirement income, choose whichever fund has the highest yield within your time horizon. As Figure 23-4 shows, Invesco's December

2025 investment-grade DM ETF (BSJO) offered an SEC-standardized yield of 3.04%.

Note: Defined-maturity bond ETFs can trade at a slight premium or discount to the net asset value (NAV) of the underlying bonds. In December 2017, for example, the Invesco funds shown in Figure 23-4 closed at a 0.1 percentage point premium above NAV, on average.

This tiny difference shouldn't upset you. A 0.1 point premium on a five-year DM ETF would reduce your yield 0.02 point per year—pretty much a rounding error.

If tiny slippage like this does concern you, simply check the premium or discount of each DM ETF at the Invesco and iShares websites, which update daily.

Defined-maturity bond ETFs usually offer higher yields if you select longer maturity dates

Guggenheim bond ETFs	Maturity	Symbol	Fee	Standardized yield after fees
Investment-grade corporate bonds	Dec 2019	BSCJ	0.24%	2.04%
	Dec 2020	BSCK	0.24%	2.23%
	Dec 2021	BSCL	0.24%	2.42%
	Dec 2022	BSCM	0.24%	2.62%
	Dec 2023	BSCN	0.24%	2.75%
	Dec 2024	BSCO	0.24%	2.92%
	Dec 2025	BSCP	0.24%	3.04%
High-yield corporate bonds	Dec 2019	BSJJ	0.44%	3.85%
	Dec 2020	BSJK	0.44%	4.33%
	Dec 2021	BSJL	0.44%	4.55%
	Dec 2022	BSJM	0.44%	4.60%
	Dec 2023	BSJN	0.44%	4.76%
	Dec 2024	BSJO	0.42%	4.58%
	Dec 2025	BSJP	0.42%	5.27%

iShares bond ETFs	Maturity	Symbol	Fee	Standardized yield after fees
Investment-grade corporate bonds	Dec 2019	IBDK	0.10%	2.21%
	Dec 2020	IBDL	0.10%	2.38%
	Dec 2021	IBDM	0.10%	2.60%
	Dec 2022	IBDN	0.10%	2.81%
	Dec 2023	IBDO	0.10%	3.00%
	Dec 2024	IBDP	0.10%	3.18%
	Dec 2025	IBDQ	0.10%	3.30%
Tax-free and AMT-free municipal bonds	Sep 2019	IBMH	0.18%	1.41%
	Sep 2020	IBMI	0.18%	1.50%
	Dec 2021	IBMJ	0.18%	1.58%
	Dec 2022	IBMK	0.18%	1.65%
	Dec 2023	IBML	0.18%	1.86%

FIGURE 23-4 | Yield as of January 2018. Sources: Invesco[1467] and iShares[1468]

BB-rated high-yield bonds hold up well in recessions; B-rated and lower fade fast

It's hard not to notice that the high-yield bonds in Figure 23-4 offer better interest rates than investment-grade bonds—currently about 2 points more per year. Could that justify the additional risk of default?

The Muscular Portfolios in this book never include junk bonds but still offer strong returns. However, many investors seek yield. Even institutional manager Morningstar recommends that individual investors who follow the firm's Bucket Portfolio (as described in Chapter 1) allocate 5% to a junk-bond ETF.

If you choose high-yield bonds for your portfolio, be aware of the losses you may experience.

A **default**, as S&P defines it,[1469] could be as mild as a six-day payout delay or as awful as a company going bankrupt and giving bondholders a total loss. On average, investors ultimately recovered about 40% of their principal after corporate credit defaults, according to a 2017 study by economists at Stanford University.[1470]

During business expansions, few corporate bonds of any kind default. But in a recession, a fair number of junk bonds delay their payouts—or worse.

Figure 23-5 graphs the Great Recession. In 2009, the default rates (in declining rating order) were:

- » **AAA to BBB:** almost 0%
- » **BB:** only 1.04%
- » **B:** 10.77%
- » **CCC/CC/C:** 49.46%

Figure 23-6 shows the default rates in tabular form. (Plus and minus ratings, such as A+, A, and A–, are combined in the table.)

Invesco's junk ETFs center on BB-rated issues. For example, the majority of dollars in BSJO, maturing December 2024, are in bonds rated BB, BBB, or ultra-safe cash:

- » **Cash:** 19%
- » **BBB:** 2%
- » **BB:** 48%
- » **B:** 28%
- » **CCC/CC/C:** 3%

BSJO owns bonds from household names like Hanes, Hilton, and Sprint, but famous brands still have risk.

What if you bought $10,000 of BSJO on Jan. 1, 2019, and a severe recession struck before maturity in 2024? BSJO is well diversified, holding 133 different bonds, but let's say 30% of them defaulted. At maturity, when your $10,000 was supposed to be returned, it would be worth only $8,200: a decline of 18%. That's because you recovered only 40% of the face value of the defaulted bonds.

Yes, BSJO gave you a high 4.58% yield. But your cash flow after six years would be 5% fewer dollars than if you'd held BSCO, the corresponding investment-grade ETF, with its smaller 2.92% yield.

> **LIVINGSTON'S LAW OF THE END GAME**
> *If you save like crazy or achieve a little fame,*
> *There comes a point when you don't need stocks pain.*

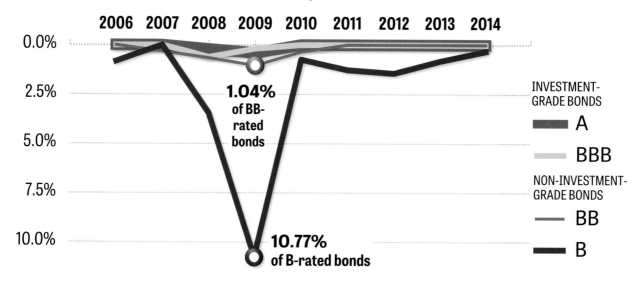

In 2009, few BB's defaulted, but a lot of B's did

1.04%
of BB-rated bonds

10.77%
of B-rated bonds

INVESTMENT-GRADE BONDS
A
BBB

NON-INVESTMENT-GRADE BONDS
BB
B

FIGURE 23-5 | Source: S&P[1471]

Almost half of CCC/CC/C bonds defaulted in 2009

Year	Investment-grade bonds				Non-investment grade		
	AAA	AA	A	BBB	BB	B	CCC/CC/C
2006	0%	0%	0%	0%	0%	0.82%	13.33%
2007	0%	0%	0%	0%	0.32%	0%	15.24%
2008	0%	0.44%	0.21%	0.61%	0.66%	3.45%	27.00%
2009	0%	0%	0.40%	0.19%	1.04%	10.77%	49.46%
2010	0%	0%	0%	0%	0.36%	0.74%	22.73%
2011	0%	0%	0%	0%	0%	1.27%	16.42%
2012	0%	0%	0%	0%	0%	1.44%	27.33%
2013	0%	0%	0%	0%	0%	0.82%	24.18%
2014	0%	0%	0%	0%	0%	0.33%	17.03%

Default rate 0.01% to 0.99% ▪ 1% to 9.99% ▪ 10% to 40% ▪ Above 40%

FIGURE 23-6 | Source: S&P[1472]

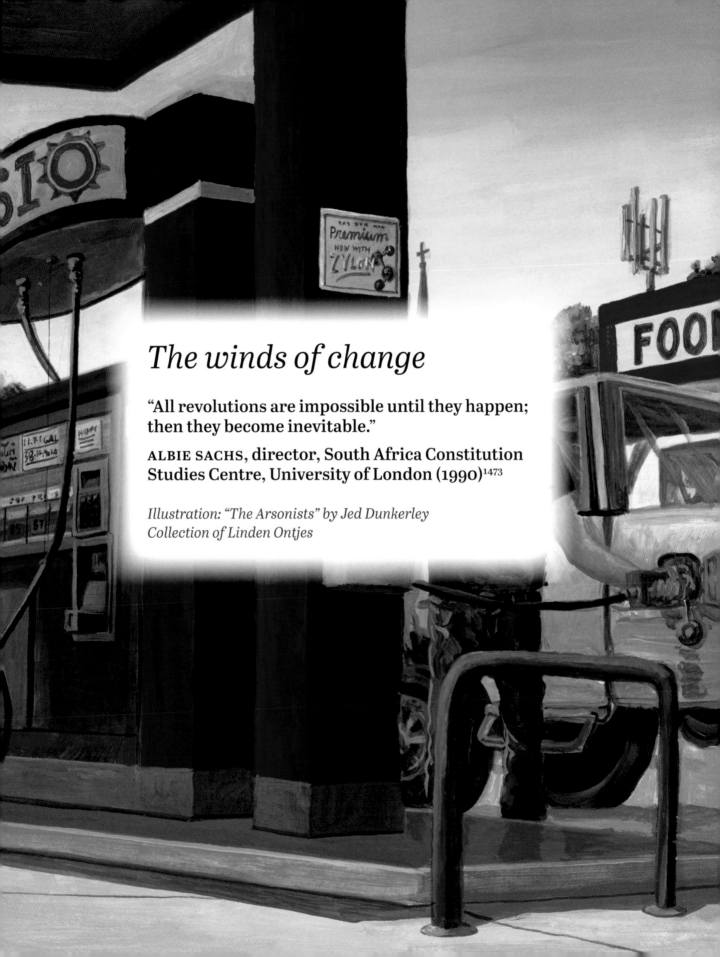

The winds of change

"All revolutions are impossible until they happen;
then they become inevitable."

ALBIE SACHS, director, South Africa Constitution
Studies Centre, University of London (1990)[1473]

Illustration: "The Arsonists" by Jed Dunkerley
Collection of Linden Ontjes

The Dynamic Portfolio Model: An Index Investing Revolution

"The generally accepted view is that markets are always right . . . I believe that market prices are always wrong in the sense that they present a biased view of the future."

GEORGE SOROS, American billionaire, in *The Alchemy of Finance* (1994)[1474]

They say a true magician never reveals how a magic trick works (Figure BC-1). If that's so, this chapter won't please the Wall Street Magicians Club—the people who saw your money in half.

Raising your return while lowering your loss—once thought impossible—is now simple, if you know the secret.

About half of scientific literature is overturned within 45 years

In a raucous 2012 book, *The Half-Life of Facts,* Harvard mathematician Samuel Arbesman explains how quickly new findings push the old ones aside. Half of typical medical research papers are refuted within 45 years.[1475]

"A lot of medical students are taught that everything they learn is going to be obsolete soon after they graduate," Arbesman says.[1476]

In his book, Arbesman quotes a well-known physician saying: "It takes 50 years to get a wrong idea out of medicine, and 100 years a right one into medicine."[1477]

Falsehoods that people refuse to give up are called "zombie ideas."[1478]

If a theory happens to cover the stock market, it's likely to become a zombie idea even more quickly than findings in medicine.

As Arbesman told *The Economist,* "One thing we have seen is that the social sciences have a much faster rate of decay than the physical sciences."[1479]

John Maynard Keynes quipped that otherwise-sensible people "are usually the slaves of some defunct economist."[1480]

Figure BC-2 reveals old theories about the market that gained wide acceptance but were rendered obsolete within just a few years—not that the victims ever stopped believing in them.

> **» KEY CONCEPT**
> ## zombie ideas
> Economic myths—such as, "to get more gain, you must take more risk"—eat into our brains long after the original theories have been disproven.

THE MAGIC TRICK

Raising your returns while lowering your losses requires the latest research findings

FIGURE BC-1

Fads and fashions come and go in finance just like, well, the fashion industry

Let's go behind the curtain, where the models hang out.

No, this isn't a fashion runway. We're in the halls of academe. Finance professors and trading pros are hunched over their spreadsheet models, guessing what the market may do given this stimulus or that.

Figure BC-2 shows which market models are still useful and which fell under the weight of criticism.

We honor every contribution. There's no shame in proposing a theory that's replaced by a better one in a few years. Without experimentation, science couldn't progress.

the Dynamic Portfolio Model

Megatrends in the 21st century have converged to form the Dynamic Portfolio Model: remain 100% invested at all times in the three asset classes with the strongest momentum.

Models that lost their usefulness

» **Modern Portfolio Theory (MPT)**

» **The "efficient frontier" theorem**

» **The Capital Asset Pricing Model (CAPM)**

» **The Efficient Markets Hypothesis (EMH)**

» **Arbitrage Pricing Theory (APT)**

» **Lazy Portfolios,** aka "static asset allocations" (SAA)

Four economic breakthroughs

» **Behavioral finance** reveals that people underreact and overreact when making decisions about money.

» **Asset allocation theory** shows that a portfolio's asset-class mix makes a bigger difference in its volatility than any individual securities you could select.

» **The four-factor model** by Fama, French, and Carhart demonstrates momentum as the strongest of four market factors that predict returns.

» **Muscular Portfolios,** aka "global tactical asset allocation" (GTAA), were defined in a 2006 whitepaper by Mebane Faber. Numerous studies by other researchers have confirmed the same principles.

The Dynamic Portfolio Model (DPM) is a synthesis of these seminal findings. DPM is the foundation of Muscular Portfolios. These portfolios are currently the best investment strategies individuals can easily manage by themselves without paying fees to anyone.

Will Muscular Portfolios ever be debunked? Perhaps. A hundred years from now, we might be using Teleportation Portfolios and beaming up our gains.

But today, Muscular Portfolios combine the best aspects of behavioral finance, asset allocation, and the four-factor model.

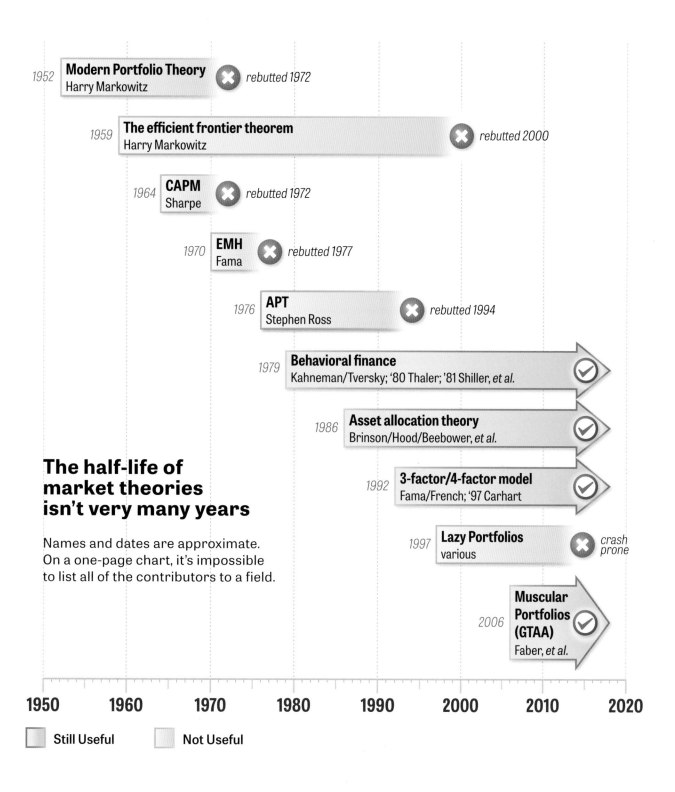

1952 **Modern Portfolio Theory**
Harry Markowitz
❌ *rebutted 1972*

1959 **The efficient frontier theorem**
Harry Markowitz
❌ *rebutted 2000*

1964 **CAPM**
Sharpe
❌ *rebutted 1972*

1970 **EMH**
Fama
❌ *rebutted 1977*

1976 **APT**
Stephen Ross
❌ *rebutted 1994*

1979 **Behavioral finance**
Kahneman/Tversky; '80 Thaler; '81 Shiller, *et al.*
✓

1986 **Asset allocation theory**
Brinson/Hood/Beebower, *et al.*
✓

1992 **3-factor/4-factor model**
Fama/French; '97 Carhart
✓

1997 **Lazy Portfolios**
various
❌ *crash prone*

2006 **Muscular Portfolios (GTAA)**
Faber, *et al.*
✓

The half-life of market theories isn't very many years

Names and dates are approximate. On a one-page chart, it's impossible to list all of the contributors to a field.

1950 1960 1970 1980 1990 2000 2010 2020

▯ Still Useful   ▯ Not Useful

FIGURE BC-2 | Adapted from Scott Welch/Fortigent[1481] and others

Modern Portfolio Theory (1952) was rebutted in 1972

One of the 20th century's strongest influences on investing was a 1952 paper in the *Journal of Finance* by Harry Markowitz.[1482] At that point, he was a graduate student at the University of Chicago.

In the mid-1900s, investors usually thought "stocks are risky" and "bonds are safe." Markowitz's breakthrough showed mathematically that combining two risky assets can make a portfolio **less risky** than either asset individually.

This became known as Modern Portfolio Theory (MPT). Markowitz despised the term, which never appeared in his paper. In fact, in his 1959 book *Portfolio Selection,* he said derisively of the name MPT, "There's nothing modern about it."[1483]

Respecting his wishes, MPT should correctly be called Markowitz Portfolio Theory, the name used in the rest of this chapter.

Markowitz defended his dissertation in 1955. The well-known University of Chicago professor Milton Friedman initially opposed granting the student a Ph.D. As Markowitz tells the story, the objection Friedman put forth was "portfolio theory is not economics"![1484]

Despite early skepticism, Markowitz Portfolio Theory became gospel. The idea states that every possible combination of risk assets defines a **hyperbola** (the curve in Figure BC-3).

In his 1952 paper, Markowitz said "a straight line that is tangent" to the curve was the "efficient line."[1485] Later called the "efficient frontier," this line starts at the risk-free rate (T-bills). The slope—also known as the "capital allocation line"[1486]—intersects the curve at a "tangency portfolio." You could add cash or leverage to this ideal portfolio. Each such combination "on the efficient frontier" would have the highest return for a given level of volatility.

But many follow-up studies found that MPT's assumptions don't work in actual financial markets.[1487] For instance, the idea that mere volatility equals risk was refuted in 1972 by the economists Michael Jensen, Fischer Black, and Myron Scholes.[1488]

Perhaps the strongest case against MPT today is that even Markowitz himself doesn't use it.

As we saw in Chapter 7, the 80-year-old Nobel Laureate, now a consultant to wealth-management firms, was asked how he allocated his personal money.[1489]

He feared being 100% in bonds during a stock boom or 100% in stocks during a crash. So he chose to hold 50% bonds and 50% stocks at all times (like the Baby Bear Portfolio).[1490]

We can do better than that today. While respecting Markowitz's insights, we don't have to follow his thesis.

> **» KEY CONCEPT**
> ## MPT never really worked
> Markowitz Portfolio Theory does not predict the best asset allocation in actual securities markets.

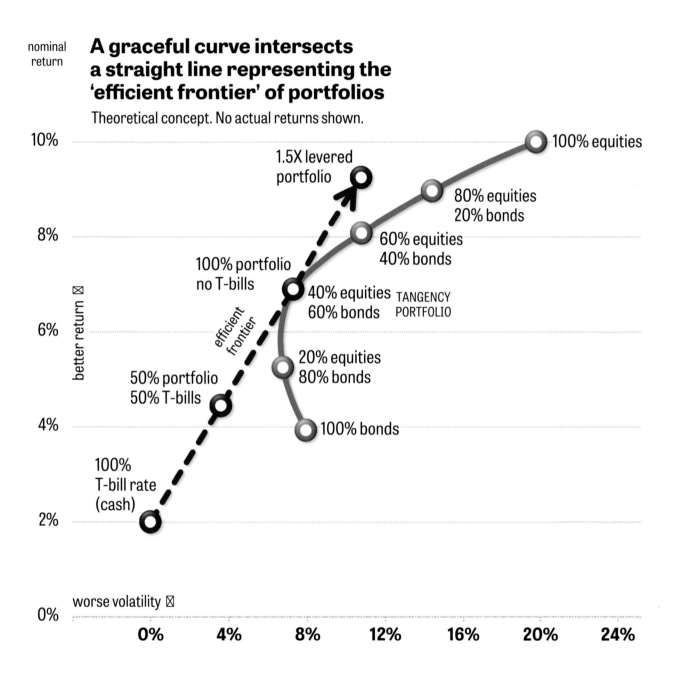

A graceful curve intersects a straight line representing the 'efficient frontier' of portfolios

Theoretical concept. No actual returns shown.

nominal return

10%

1.5X levered portfolio

100% equities

8%

80% equities 20% bonds

100% portfolio no T-bills

60% equities 40% bonds

better return ⊠

40% equities 60% bonds   TANGENCY PORTFOLIO

efficient frontier

6%

50% portfolio 50% T-bills

20% equities 80% bonds

4%

100% bonds

100% T-bill rate (cash)

2%

worse volatility ⊠

0%

0%   4%   8%   12%   16%   20%   24%

FIGURE BC-3

The efficient frontier (1959) was rebutted in 2000

The upward-pointing line that came to be known as "the efficient frontier" was assumed to optimize all possible combinations of stocks, bonds, cash, and leverage. If you were ultra-conservative, you might choose 20% stocks and 30% bonds, with 50% in T-bills to reduce volatility.

Over the years, various financial gurus expanded the efficient-frontier concept. A lot more than two "risk assets" were tossed into the mix. Index mutual funds, pioneered by the Vanguard Group, arose for real-estate investment trusts (REITs), emerging markets, and other assets. Combinations could be plotted on graphs.

The joke is that the various allocations of these assets formed a beautiful, upward-sloping "efficient frontier" only in the data that Markowitz could access in 1952. For periods as long as whole decades, the hyperbola turns against you with a fury.

There were no personal computers back in the day. Markowitz had only slide rules, desktop-sized adding machines, and printed books of data to help him. Those elegant curves and lines must have looked great to him as a reward for his long nights of crunching numbers by hand.

The hard, cold facts were revealed by many researchers. Perhaps none wrote as wittily as William Bernstein, a former medical doctor who is now a wealth manager and author of several investing works. In a 2000 book, *The Intelligent Asset Allocator,* Bernstein said he and a colleague examined 800 different portfolio allocations involving seven distinct asset classes over a 27-year period (1970–1996). The result:

"Had you calculated the efficient frontier for the first half of the whole period (1970–1983) and used it to determine your portfolio for the second half of the period (1984–1996), you'd have gotten your head handed to you. The efficient-frontier portfolio . . . for the first half would have tanked in the second half."[1491]

Figure BC-4 illustrates that an efficient frontier from **one** time period can be catastrophic if followed in the **next** period. (The decade 2000 to 2009 is just the most recent example.) For simplicity, the graph is limited to only two asset classes: five-year Treasury bonds and US large-cap stocks, held in various combinations with no T-bills. Imagine the complexity of including **every** asset class.

In *The Intelligent Asset Allocator,* Bernstein sums up the problem with the efficient frontier:

"It's a little like trying to generate electrical power by placing a battery and a lightning rod at the last place you saw lightning strike. It isn't likely to strike there again. In other words, next year's efficient frontier will be nowhere near last year's. Anybody who tells you that their portfolio recommendations are 'on the efficient frontier' also talks to Elvis and frolics with the Easter Bunny."

» KEY CONCEPT

there is no efficient frontier
Past efficient frontiers don't predict future efficient frontiers.

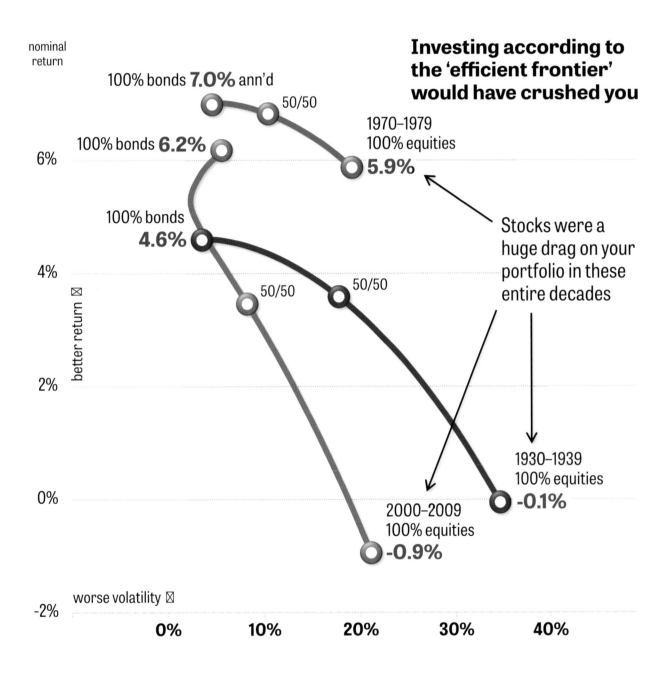

Investing according to the 'efficient frontier' would have crushed you

nominal return

100% bonds **7.0%** ann'd

50/50

1970–1979
100% equities
5.9%

6%

100% bonds **6.2%**

100% bonds
4.6%

Stocks were a
huge drag on your
portfolio in these
entire decades

4%

better return ⊠

50/50

50/50

2%

0%

1930–1939
100% equities
-0.1%

2000–2009
100% equities
-0.9%

worse volatility ⊠

-2%

0%   10%   20%   30%   40%

FIGURE BC-4 | Data source: Dan Sotiroff/The Personal Finance Engineer[1492]

The Capital Asset Pricing Model (1964) was rebutted in 1972

Markowitz Portfolio Theory (MPT) said past returns and volatility predict which combination of securities and cash would produce the best risk/return ratio in the future. The ideal combinations were called the efficient frontier.

This left open the question of why some stocks rose in price more than others. In a 1964 paper in the *Journal of Finance*, Bill Sharpe (Figure BC-5), then an associate professor at the University of Washington, proposed an answer.

He theorized that the prices of stocks adjust "to account for differences in their risk." An investor, in this view, "may obtain a higher expected rate of return on his holdings only by incurring additional risk."[1493]

Thus was born what became known as the **Capital Asset Pricing Model** or **CAPM**. This "high risk equals high gain" metric was soon labeled **beta.**

The idea that beta explains different stocks' returns was called "the single-factor model." The economics profession adopted as truth the idea that only by taking on greater risk (beta) could an investor achieve greater returns.

Before long, several experts had revealed that CAPM was wrong. It was first rebutted in a 1972 book, when Jensen, Black, and Scholes tested the CAPM theory against 35 years of market data and found it lacking.[1494]

They wrote: "We therefore concluded that the traditional form of the asset pricing model is not consistent with the data."[1495]

In 1982, Yale University professor Burton Malkiel wrote:

"It became clear that beta could not be used to guarantee investors a predictable performance over periods of a few months or even a year. And even over some longer periods of time—when the market has produced a positive rate of return—investors have actually been penalized for taking on more risk. . . . past betas for individual stocks are relatively poor predictors of future betas."[1496]

Ten years later, finance professors Eugene Fama and Kenneth French forcefully demolished the whole basis of CAPM.

After studying thousands of stocks over five decades, Fama and French published "The Cross-Section of Expected Stock Returns." It hit like a bombshell: "In short, our tests do not support the most basic prediction . . . that average stock returns are positively related to market betas."[1497]

In an interview that year with Eric Berg of the *New York Times*, Fama minced no words:

"The fact is, beta as the sole variable in explaining returns on stocks is dead."[1498]

As Travis Morien, an Australian financial adviser, wrote: "This was like the Pope announcing that there is no God."[1499]

Bill Sharpe, 2010

FIGURE BC-5

The Sharpe and Sortino ratios were refuted by Sortino himself

Data providers often try to rate portfolios. Let's say two strategies had the same gain. The portfolio with less fluctuation (deviation) over time is said to have a better "risk-adjusted performance."

The **Sharpe ratio** was developed by the same Bill Sharpe who proposed CAPM. The ratio's Achilles' heel is that the formula assumes mere deviation equals the risk of an intolerable loss.

A well-known challenger to the Sharpe ratio is the **Sortino ratio**. It was first defined in the *Journal of Risk Management* in 1981 by Frank Sortino, a former finance professor at San Francisco State University.[1500]

The Sortino ratio counts only the deviation of **losses.** Unlike the Sharpe ratio, Sortino doesn't penalize a portfolio for gains, which investors actually like.

However, both the Sharpe and Sortino ratios have been rejected by Frank Sortino himself.

For his 2009 book, *The Sortino Framework for Constructing Portfolios,* he tested both the Sharpe and Sortino ratios. He used both to rate hundreds of mutual funds across more than two decades.

His finding? Neither the Sharpe ratio **nor** the Sortino ratio was useful! For example, they weren't much better

than chance at estimating which funds with top performance in one period would remain there in the next.[1501]

Sortino wrote in a 2012 blog post: "There was a time that I believed the Sortino Ratio was the best way to measure performance. When the evidence began to accumulate in the 1990s that I was wrong, I wrote a paper pointing out the flaw and posted it on my website."[1502]

In his book, Sortino proposed a new metric: Desired Target Return alpha (DTR-α). However, few data providers have adopted it.

The Sharpe ratio has been rendered obsolete by the Martin ratio

The Martin Ratio, introduced in 1989, stands out as a replacement for the Sharpe and Sortino ratios. The Martin ratio measures the **depth** of all losses—not just a single, maximum drawdown—and the **length of time** investors suffered them. That's how actual investors experience the pain of bear markets.

Figure BC-6 graphs three very different outcomes: (1) a gradual rise, (2) a crash, and (3) a depression. All three get the **same score** from the Sharpe and Sortino ratios. They are misleading as gauges of risk-adjusted performance.

» The orange line is the S&P 500. Buy-and-hold investors in SPY—the largest index ETF that tracks the S&P 500—watched 55% of their life savings vanish during the 2007–2009 crash.

» The blue line is a Diverse Portfolio. This theoretical portfolio has exactly the same end value as SPY. The daily returns of the index have been re-sorted in random order. The Diverse Portfolio's maximum daily drawdown was a mere 29%.

» The red line is a Depression Portfolio. This portfolio also has exactly the same daily returns as SPY, re-sorted. In this case, most of the bad days occurred first and most of the good days last. The Depression Portfolio lost 78% of the investor's money before recovering.

The three portfolios all ended up in the same place: $100,000 became $112,000 over 5½ years. **Any** return series **always** produces the same ending value, regardless of how you re-sort the gains and losses. (The exception is a 100% loss, which cannot be recovered from.)

What causes the identical rankings? Economists say the Sharpe and Sortino ratios are "path-insensitive."

In the 1989 book *The Investor's Guide to Fidelity Funds,* Peter Martin and Byron McCann defined true risk: **the likelihood of intolerable losses.**[1503] (Fun fact: McCann was once a student of Bill Sharpe's.)[1504]

It's the depth and length of a portfolio's drawdowns—not its mere deviation—that drive investors to liquidate. Martin and McCann compute these drawdowns as a number called the Ulcer Index (UI). The UI determines the Martin ratio, correctly giving better scores to portfolios with smaller losses (in this case, 0.12, 0.07, and 0.02).[1505]

Data providers are moving toward the Martin ratio and away from Sharpe:

» AAII scores more than 60 investing strategies using the Ulcer Index rather than deviation or Sharpe ratio.[1506]

» The Motley Fool's Mechanical Investing forum routinely ranks portfolios by UI and Martin ratio (also known as the Ulcer Performance Index or UPI).[1507]

» Formula Research calls the Ulcer Index "perhaps the most fully realized statistical portrait of risk there is."[1508]

The Sharpe ratio is useless, assigning the same score to horribly different portfolios

	Sharpe ratio	Martin ratio
■ Diverse portfolio	.07	.12
■ S&P 500	.07	.07
■ Depression portfolio	.07	.02

Oct. 9, 2007–Mar. 20, 2013 daily closes
Nominal total return
◇ = Max. drawdown between two closes

portfolio value

$160,000

$140,000

$120,000

$100,000

$80,000

$60,000

$40,000

$20,000

2007   2008   2009   2010   2011   2012   2013

■ Diverse portfolio ◇ −29%

$112K

■ S&P 500
−55% max. drawdown

■ Depression portfolio −78%

FIGURE BC-6 | Adapted from TangoTools.com/ui/ui.htm[1509]

Mere deviation should never be used to evaluate the risk of a portfolio

Old economic theories assume stock market returns will behave like the famous "bell curve." For example, the average height of an adult male in the US is 5 feet 10 inches. Let's say you brought together every male. If you could distribute the shorter ones on the left and the taller ones on the right, the result would look from above like a bell curve.[1510]

The problem is that stock markets do not follow a bell curve (something economists call a **normal distribution**).

Look at the leftmost column of Figure BC-7. Over the years, **10 times as many** individual stocks suffer huge underperformance of market indexes than a bell curve predicts.

What's true for individual stocks is even more true for the market as a whole.

How often would a bell curve predict that the Dow Jones Industrial Average will fall 3.9% or worse in a single day? It would say, "Only seven days every 82 years."

In reality, the Dow fell more than 3.9% on 151 days (1928–2010). Those collapses occur **20 times more often** than

a normal distribution predicts.[1511]

So what! Who cares if markets crash far more often than predicted?

It matters a lot, if you want your life savings to grow.

Rather than a normal distribution, markets follow what's been called a **free-market distribution** or a **capitalism distribution**. There are a few big winners and a lot of big losers.

Figure BC-7 illustrates this with green and red columns. The red columns represent the US stocks that underperformed the Russell 3000 index, which includes 98% of the US equity market. The green columns represent the US stocks that rose **more** than the index.

About 64% of the stocks underperformed the index. If you trained 3,000 dart-throwing monkeys to each pick a stock at random, the market would beat 64% of them, not 50%—a popular misconception.

In a normal distribution, half of the companies would outperform the index and half underperform. But that's not the reality of Wall Street.

"Simply picking a stock out of a hat means you have a 64% chance of underperforming a basic index fund," comments Mebane Faber, CEO and chief investment officer of Cambria Investment Management, "and roughly a 40% chance of losing money!"[1512]

To see how lopsided the market is—not at all like a bell curve—look at the rightmost 4% of US stocks in Figure BC-7. "The best-performing four percent of listed companies explain the net gain for the entire U.S. stock market" from 1926 through 2016, according to Hendrik Bessembinder of Arizona State. The losses and weak gains of the other 96% of stocks added up to no more than you would have received from T-bills.

This is why individual stock-picking is nearly impossible. Could you pinpoint in advance the 4% of stocks that will outperform all the others combined? No, you couldn't. Virtually no one can.

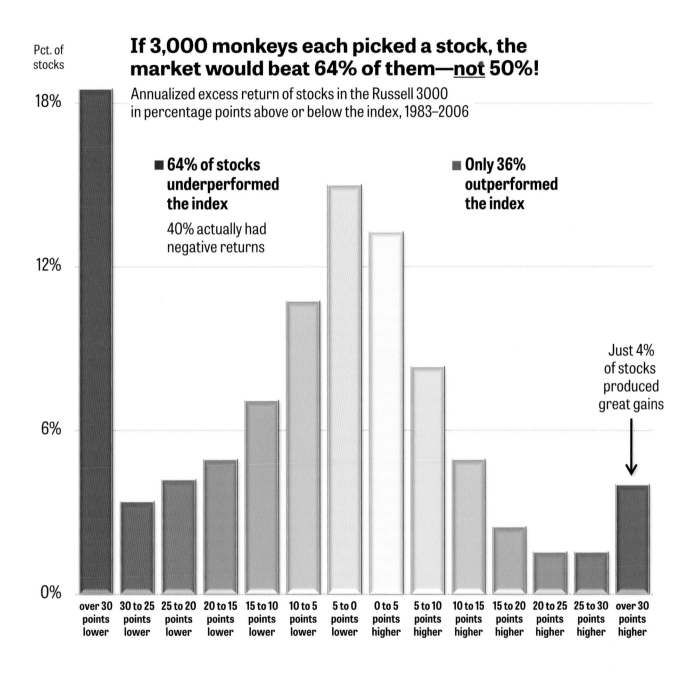

Pct. of stocks

If 3,000 monkeys each picked a stock, the market would beat 64% of them—<u>not</u> 50%!

Annualized excess return of stocks in the Russell 3000 in percentage points above or below the index, 1983–2006

■ **64% of stocks underperformed the index**

40% actually had negative returns

■ **Only 36% outperformed the index**

Just 4% of stocks produced great gains

18%													
12%													
6%													
0%													

over 30 points lower | 30 to 25 points lower | 25 to 20 points lower | 20 to 15 points lower | 15 to 10 points lower | 10 to 5 points lower | 5 to 0 points lower | 0 to 5 points higher | 5 to 10 points higher | 10 to 15 points higher | 15 to 20 points higher | 20 to 25 points higher | 25 to 30 points higher | over 30 points higher

FIGURE BC-7 | Source: "The Capitalism Distribution," Crittenden and Wilcox (2012)[1513]

The Efficient Markets Hypothesis (1970) was refuted in 1977

The efficient Markets Hypothesis (EMH) burst forth upon the economics community in a May 1970 article published by the *Journal of Finance*. The author, Eugene Fama of the University of Chicago, proposed that "security prices at any time 'fully reflect' all available information."[1514]

The implication of this theory was that nothing about the past gave any hint of what might happen to an asset's price in the future. If security prices instantly moved to the "right" level as new information came out, no one could profit from informed research about companies' plans or prospects.

Fama himself acknowledged in his article that some aspects of his theory made it "so general that it has no empirically testable implications."

Cases that didn't support the theory were considered "anomalies": situations that would be explained by further discoveries at some later time.

Ultimately, however, EMH lost its appeal. The *Journal of Finance* published a counterpoint in June 1977 by Sanjoy Basu of McMaster University. Basu showed that stocks with low prices compared to their earnings—low P/E ratios—had higher returns than predicted. This was the academic genesis of "value" investing and the beginning of the end of EMH.[1515]

The new field of behavioral economics also killed the Efficient Markets Hypothesis. Because of behavioral bias, actual investors wildly overreact and underreact to new information. Robert Shiller proved in 1979 that interest rates are more volatile than mere data explains.[1516] And he followed this up in 1981 by showing that stock prices vary far more than is justified.[1517]

Shiller famously summed up the EMH criticisms in a 1984 essay for the Brookings Institution:[1518]

"This argument for the efficient markets hypothesis represents one of the most remarkable errors in the history of economic thought. It is remarkable in the immediacy of its logical error and in the sweep and implications of its conclusion."

Obviously, asset prices **do** respond to new information, but calling the market "fully efficient" is a stretch (Figure BC-8).

"I'd be a bum on the street with a tin cup if markets were always efficient," according to master investor Warren Buffett.[1519]

Describing the theory, Buffett told his company's shareholders in a 1988 letter: "Naturally the disservice done students and gullible investment professionals who have swallowed EMT has been an extraordinary service to us and other followers of Graham. . . . In any sort of contest—financial, mental, or physical—it's an enormous advantage to have opponents who have been taught that it's useless to even try."[1520]

You don't need complex formulas when a very simple rule will do

FIGURE BC-8

Arbitrage Pricing Theory (1976) was rebutted in 1994

After the 1972 Jensen/Black/Scholes critique of CAPM, other theories of market behavior arose.

The most important of these, and one that became widely accepted, was the Arbitrage Pricing Theory (APT). It stated that broad economic forces, such as inflation and investor confidence, explained stock performance. Papers in 1976 and later by Wharton School's Stephen Ross[1521] and UCLA's Richard Roll[1522] stated that there were three, four, five, or more factors, rather than just beta.

APT was alluring to academics as a theory that explained everything. Unfortunately, economists could never agree on which three, four, or five factors actually explained **anything** about the stock market. Worse, whichever factors were tested failed to produce the desired results.

The edifice of APT began to collapse when studies showed that economic factors didn't predict markets. In 1994, a paper by Concordia University's Lawrence Kryzanowski and two other researchers[1523] found that economic forces were so correlated that they couldn't independently explain stock returns.[1524]

A 2014 review by Jamal Munshi of the whole sorry affair concluded that "research fads often subvert the orderly accumulation of knowledge."

"In the end," Munshi wrote, "it turned out that what APT had to offer was nothing more than complexity for the sake of complexity."[1525]

In investing, simpler is better

As we saw in Chapter 1, the supersimple Baby Bear Portfolio—50% stocks, 50% bonds—performs as well as a 100% stock portfolio. Yet the Baby Bear's easy two-asset strategy has **less volatility** and **smaller drawdowns** than the S&P 500.

The truth is that that investors earn good returns by **lowering** risk, not increasing it. It's only a small step beyond the Baby Bear to see that the Mama Bear and the Papa Bear achieve **better** returns than the S&P 500—measured over complete bear/bull market cycles—while lowering risk.

>> KEY CONCEPT
risk is not always rewarded
Individual investors don't have to take a greater risk of loss to achieve a higher return.

The Nobel Committee gives disputed theories more credit than they deserve

Despite the many rebuttals of MPT and CAPM, the Nobel Prize in Economics was awarded in 1990 to Markowitz, Sharpe, and others.[1526]

Soon, MPT and CAPM were "absolutely standard in the security market," according to a news release by Stanford University, where Sharpe had taught finance. The elegant formulas became required reading at business schools around the world.[1527]

The wrongheadedness of this widespread fawning led to a backlash. The bestselling author of *The Black Swan*, Nassim Taleb of New York University, railed against the heavily publicized awards that had been granted:

"The Nobel Committee could have tested the Sharpe and Markowitz models—they work like quack remedies sold on the Internet—but nobody in Stockholm seems to have thought of it. Nor did the committee come to us practitioners to ask us our opinions; instead it relied on an academic vetting process that, in some disciplines, can be corrupt all the way to the marrow."[1528]

Taleb went so far as to threaten to sue the sponsors of the economics prize. He claimed they'd given legitimacy to bogus investing principles that caused the 2008 financial crisis. "No one would have taken Markowitz seriously without the Nobel stamp," Taleb told Bloomberg News in a 2010 interview.[1529]

>> TECH TALK

the Nobel Prize in Economics isn't an original Nobel

NYU's Nassim Taleb isn't the only one who's considered suing the Nobel Committee. Swedish attorney Peter Nobel—the great-grandnephew of the prize's founder—charged that the sponsors of the economics prize were misusing his family's name.

The economics award is not one of the five $1.1 million honors—the Nobel Prizes in Chemistry, Literature, Medicine, Peace, and Physics—that were endowed by Alfred Nobel in his 1895 will. Instead, the economics committee was created much later (1969) by the Swedish National Bank and is funded out of the bank's coffers.[1530]

From 1978 to 1990, the award was advertised—against the wishes of many Nobel family members—as the Alfred Nobel Memorial Prize in Economic Sciences. Under pressure, the official name was changed in 1991 to "The Swedish National Bank Prize in Economic Sciences in Memory of Alfred Nobel."

That doesn't have quite the same ring as "Nobel Prize," so the official name is widely ignored by the mainstream press (as well as in this book.)

When Friedrich Hayek won the award in 1974, he joined other critics by questioning (in his acceptance speech, no less) whether it should even exist: "The Nobel Prize confers on an individual an authority which in economics no man ought to possess."[1531]

Out of chaos comes order: the Fama-French-Carhart 4-factor model

With the demolition in 1992 of the idea that higher volatility (beta) led to greater returns, Fama and French and many other researchers started proposing other variables (Figure BC-9).

At first, asset traits that were associated with higher returns were called "anomalies" (abnormalities) that would later be explained away.

But evidence built that markets were not perfectly efficient. Eventually, what were formerly labeled anomalies became known as "market factors" or simply "factors."

It's impossible to understand the huge mental U-turn that economists have taken on momentum and other effects without a wee bit of history:

In their 1992 article that had debunked CAPM, Fama and French first proposed a "three-factor model."

Academic proof of a fourth factor—momentum—came less than one year later in March 1993.

Two UCLA professors, Narasimhan Jegadeesh and Sheridan Titman, showed mathematically that US securities that had performed well in the past 3 to 12 months tend to continue to do well for the next few months.[1532]

In 1997, Mark Carhart, then of the University of Southern California (Figure BC-10), proposed a "4-factor model." The fourth factor, of course, was momentum.[1533]

The four factors were:

» **Market.** Stocks in the US, over long periods, generate returns about 8.4 percentage points better than Treasury bills. This factor is called the "equity risk premium."

» **Small cap (the size factor).** The smallest 5% or 10% of stocks by market cap were thought to have better long-term returns than larger companies.

» **Price to book (the value factor).** Stocks with the lowest ratio of price-to-book value (P/B) were thought to outperform more richly priced companies. Other ratios include P/E[1534] and TEV/EBITDA, as documented by Wesley Gray and Jack Vogel.[1535]

» **Momentum.** Asset classes with good returns in the past 3 to 12 months tend to perform well for the next few months.

Over the years, problems have emerged with the small-cap and value premiums. For one thing, they are notably smaller than the market premium.

Small-cap and value portfolios outperformed by only 3.4 and 5.0 percentage points, respectively—much less than the equity risk premium of 8.4 points.[1536] (The premiums interact in complex ways. You can't just add these three factors to get a return of 16.8 percentage points over T-bills, as we'll see.)

Today, various researchers constantly announce new "factors." Fama and French dissected some of these in a 2014 paper, analyzing a "five-factor model" and even a "six-factor model." The economists concluded:

"All models that do not include a momentum factor fare poorly."[1537]

This debate will never end—nor should it. Science evolves in fits and starts.

**Eugene Fama and
Kenneth French,
2005**

FIGURE BC-9

**Mark Carhart,
2011**

FIGURE BC-10

There is no Santa Claus: The small-cap factor probably doesn't actually exist

This is like trying to explain that the stork doesn't really bring babies, but here goes.

The idea that small-cap stocks outperform large caps may have arisen from nothing but a statistical error made by data providers decades ago.

The size factor was famously "discovered" in two 1981 *Journal of Financial Economics* articles. One was by Northwestern University's Rolf Banz,[1538] the other by University of Chicago graduate student Marc Reinganum.[1539] (The study was partially funded by the Center for Research in Security Prices or CRSP.)

Two Ph.Ds employed by Research Associates—Jason Hsu and Vitali Kalesnik—examined in 2014 the widely held myth that small caps outperform large caps. As they explain it, stocks that went bankrupt or were delisted for other reasons were left out of the CRSP database. This caused a fatal "survivorship bias":

"The small-cap anomaly has not been observed in the United States since the early 1980s and does not exist outside the US dataset. . . . Apparently, missing returns for delisted stocks in the CRSP database created a systematic bias in the computed returns for small stocks, which are more likely to face delisting. When this bias is adjusted for, the small-cap anomaly is no longer observed . . ."[1540]

Hsu and Kalesnik pointed to an academic study called "The Delisting Bias in CRSP's Nasdaq Data and Its Implications for the Size Effect." Its authors, Tyler Shumway and Vince Warther, stated:

"After correcting for the delisting bias, there is no evidence that there ever was a size effect on Nasdaq."[1541]

Columbia's Andrew Ang—then a consultant to the World Bank, IMF, and others—explains in his 2014 book *Asset Management* how the so-called size effect vanished almost as soon as it was discovered:

"Since the mid-1980s there has been no premium for small stocks, adjusted for market exposure. . . . Fama and French (2012) also find no size premiums in a comprehensive international dataset over recent periods."[1542]

Even if a size effect could be detected statistically, you wouldn't be able to buy such small stocks without the price moving away from you. Horowitz, Loughran, and Savin of Notre Dame and the University of Iowa found in 2000 that eliminating micro-cap stocks under $5 million disposed of any size effect whatsoever.[1543]

In the 2012 edition of *What Works on Wall Street,* money manager James O'Shaughnessy says stocks under a market cap of $25 million are:

"impossible to buy and . . . therefore shunned by mutual funds and individual investors alike."[1544]

Figure BC-11 shows that small US companies outperform large companies only about half the time—not exactly a sure thing.

Small caps outperformed in only 50.24% of the months from January 1980 through December 2014, according to figures from Index Fund Advisors (IFA), an index provider. When expanded to every rolling 120-month period (overlapping 10-year periods) small caps outperformed only 50.83% of the time.

Small caps outperformed in certain rolling 5-year and 20-year periods. The outperformance of small caps rose as high as 57.62% and 58.51%, respectively.

But do you want to pin your hopes on a size effect that comes and goes in different decades?

If so the Papa Bear tilts your portfolio toward small caps when they're in fashion and large caps when they're hot.

But the momentum factor is both larger and more dependable than the small-cap factor.

Large caps beat small caps about half the time

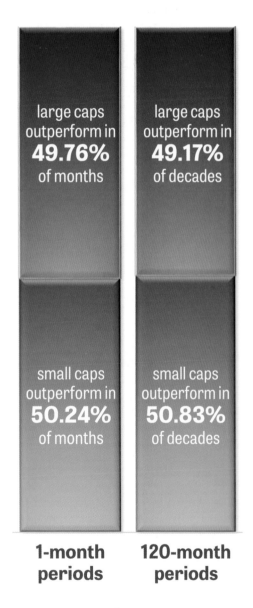

large caps outperform in
49.76%
of months

large caps outperform in
49.17%
of decades

small caps outperform in
50.24%
of months

small caps outperform in
50.83%
of decades

1-month periods

120-month periods

FIGURE BC-11 | Data: IFA.com[1545]

There's no tooth fairy, either: The value factor disappears for years at a time

The previous paragraphs may have loosened your belief in the widely held misconception that small-cap stocks always outperform large-cap stocks.

If you're not yet in tears over the loss of a cherished belief, let's now take a hard look at another sacred cow. This is the idea that "value" stocks always outperform "growth" stocks.

A company is considered a **value stock** if its share price is low compared to the company's **book value**. A company's book value is equal to the net assets on the company's books.

By contrast, a **growth stock** is one with a high price-to-book ratio. (Many other definitions compete to be the "best" value formula.)

Growth stocks are also called **glamour stocks.** In theory, people will pay a higher share price for companies that have an exciting story.

Over long periods of time—generations—it's certainly true that value stocks rise in price more than growth stocks.

But unless you're Rip Van Winkle, you don't go to sleep for whole generations. Humans experience time minute by minute. There's no reason you should endure several years of underperformance just to preserve a "value" belief system.

Figure BC-12 illustrates the 25-year period 1993 through 2017. More than half of the time, growth stocks outperfomed value stocks, when measured by the total return of monthly closes. The months when value stocks underperformed growth stocks is shown in the graph as orange columns falling below the 0% line. Value stocks and growth stocks generated almost exactly the same over the 25 years: approximately 9.6%. (The graph uses the returns of actual Vanguard index funds, which automatically subtract their annual fees.)

As Ang explained in his book *Asset Management:*

"The risk of the value strategy is that although value outperforms over the long run, value stocks can underperform growth stocks during certain periods. . . .

"The bad times for value do not always line up with bad times for the economy. Certainly value did badly during the late 1970s and early 1980s when the economy was in and out of recession. We had a recession in the early 1990s when value also did badly, and the financial crisis in 2008 was unambiguously a bad time when value strategies posted losses. But the bull market of the late 1990s? The economy was booming, but value got killed."[1546]

So the small-cap factor may be an illusion, and the value factor disappears for longer than people can tolerate. As a result, this book concentrates on momentum, by far the most reliable factor.

Stocks that merely have a good value may disappoint you. Most people want securities that are a good value **and are going up in price.** That's what the Momentum Rule does for the Mama Bear and Papa Bear Portfolios.

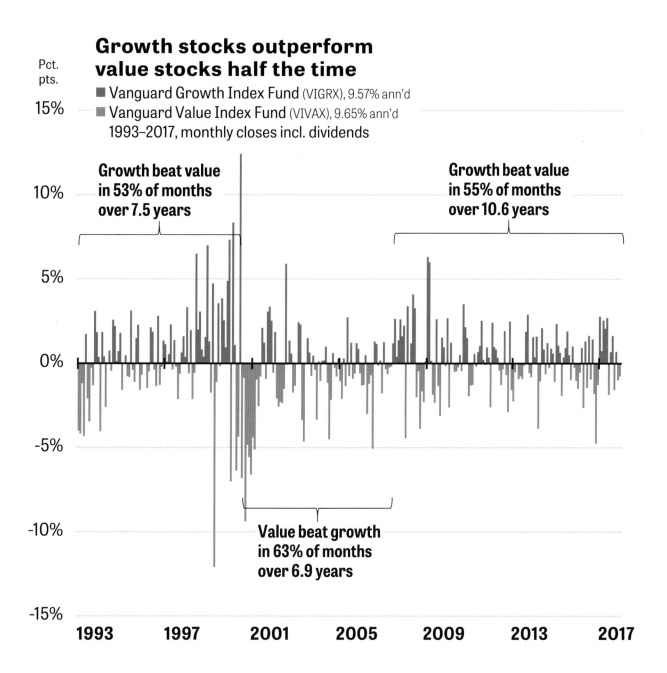

Growth stocks outperform value stocks half the time

Pct. pts.

■ Vanguard Growth Index Fund (VIGRX), 9.57% ann'd
■ Vanguard Value Index Fund (VIVAX), 9.65% ann'd
1993–2017, monthly closes incl. dividends

Growth beat value in 53% of months over 7.5 years

Growth beat value in 55% of months over 10.6 years

Value beat growth in 63% of months over 6.9 years

15%

10%

5%

0%

-5%

-10%

-15%

1993   1997   2001   2005   2009   2013   2017

FIGURE BC-12 | Data source: Yahoo Finance

Who will replace the old theories? Mandelbrot says the market is fractal

The most devastating debunker of old economics was a French-speaking math genius named Benoît Mandelbrot (1924-2010), who became Sterling Professor of Mathematics at Yale University.

Mandelbrot's signature discovery was fractal mathematics. A surprisingly simple formula can lead to patterns that repeat in ever smaller and larger scale. (An example is shown in the upper-left corner of Figure BC-13.)

Fractals, which were unknown before Mandelbrot described them in 1975, are responsible for an infinity of patterns in nature.

In his 2006 book, *The (Mis)behavior of Markets*, Mandelbrot provides a practical illustration: the border between Spain and Portugal has infinite roughness. The length is shorter if you measure it with a yardstick than if you examine it with a 12-inch ruler.

"Spanish authorities reckoned their border with Portugal to be 987 kilometers long, whereas the plucky Portuguese counted 1,214 kilometers ... So how long is it? A useless question, as we have seen."[1547]

Most of his book shreds what's left of tired old economic theories. Like many other writers, he blames simplistic assumptions of "normal distributions" for almost sinking the Western banking system during the global financial crisis. The October 2008 edition of his book skewers misleading software apps that try to predict a bank's Value at Risk (VaR):

"Let us say volatility is 10 percent. Then, with a few more [keyboard] strokes, you get your answer: There is only a 5 percent chance that your portfolio will fall by more than 12 percent. Forget about it.

"The flaw should be obvious by now. The potental loss is far, far greater than 12 percent ... There is no limit to how bad it could get for the bank. Its own bankruptcy is the least of the worries; it will default on its obligations to other banks—and so the final damage could be greater than its own capital."

Optimistic bets based on VaR led to Lehman Brothers' sudden collapse in late 2008. A cascade of falling dominoes required enormous sums of taxpayer money to keep many other banks alive.

Mandelbrot determined that free markets are fractals. Anyone who's read a stock chart will find this example familiar:

"Without the identifying legends, one cannot tell if a price chart covers eighteen minutes, eighteen months, or eighteen years. This will be expressed by saying that markets scale. Even the financial press scales: There are annual reviews, quarterly bulletins, monthly newsletters, weekly magazines, daily newspapers, and tick-by-tick electronic newswires and Internet services."

TED CONFERENCE, 2010

**Mandelbrot saw
the true patterns
of the market**

FIGURE BC-13

'Volatility clustering' reveals one predictable aspect of the market

Fortunately for us, Mandelbrot didn't just criticize sloppy economic thinking. He actually showed how to reduce the risk that crashes will devastate an individual investor's portfolio.

A major plank of what he called the multifractal model is the discovery of "volatility clustering."

Contrary to the so-called random walk idea—the theory that no past market behavior predicts anything—Mandelbrot showed that **prices** may not be predictable, but **extreme price changes are:**

"Markets are turbulent, deceptive, prone to bubbles, infested by false trends. It may well be that you cannot forecast prices. But evaluating risk is another matter. . . .

"The data overwhelmingly show that the magnitude of price changes depends on those of the past, and that the bell curve is nonsense. Speaking mathematically, markets can exhibit dependence without correlation."

What did Mandelbrot mean by **dependence without correlation?**

Dependence: Figures BC-14 and BC-15 show one-day moves over 3% in the S&P 500. Dependence means any move that's greater than 3% tends to be quickly followed by more such **wild days**.

Without correlation: A wild day does not predict whether the next one will be **down** or **up.** There's no correlation (prediction of direction).

Moves greater than 3%—either down or up—usually cluster during market corrections and bear markets.

In Figures BC-14 and BC-15, boxes outline every correction and bear market from 1997 through 2014. The majority of wild days occur during these periods.

Some sales-hungry stockbrokers exhort individual investors to remain fully exposed to the stock market at all times. If you missed the 10 biggest up days in the past two decades, these salespeople say, it would have cut your annualized return down to 6.1% from 9.85%.[1548]

The joke is that no one can miss out on just the 10 best days—or the worst, for that matter.

Certified financial planner Paul Gire recently published an analysis of the "10 best days" claim. He found that the best days hug the worst days so closely that cherry-picking them is hardly possible. Pushing the ten-days refrain "could be construed as an ethical violation" of SEC rules, Gire writes.[1549]

Don't try to time the market! An up day is not a "buy." A down day is not a "sell." Look at the 2000–2002 bear market in Figure BC-14. This brutal dot-com crash began with **eight** big up days in a row. After the 8th green square, the S&P 500—already over 10% down—sank another 40%. Don't try to time the market!

Instead, use momentum—the antidote to volatility.

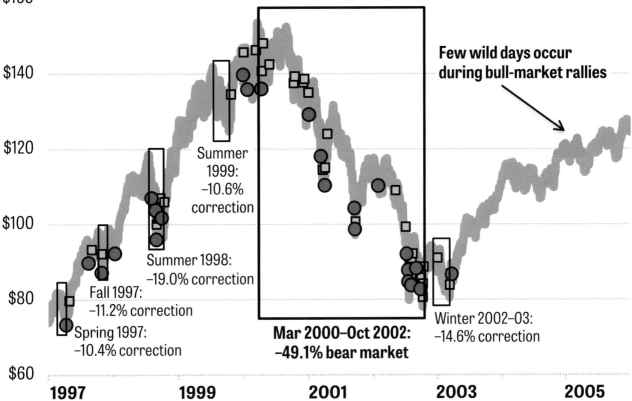

VOLATILITY CLUSTERING, 1997–2005

Most wild days—closing more than 3% down or up—occur during bear markets and corrections

- S&P 500 daily headline price (SPY)
- □ Day up more than 3%
- ● Day down more than 3%

Few wild days occur during bull-market rallies

Summer 1999: –10.6% correction

Summer 1998: –19.0% correction

Fall 1997: –11.2% correction

Spring 1997: –10.4% correction

Mar 2000–Oct 2002: –49.1% bear market

Winter 2002–03: –14.6% correction

$200
$180
$160
$140
$120
$100
$80
$60

1997   1999   2001   2003   2005

FIGURE BC-14 | Part 1 of 2 figures. Data source: Yahoo Finance

The Momentum Rule tilts your portfolio toward less volatile asset classes

As Mandelbrot emphasized several times in his writings, the direction of a wild day **does not predict** the future direction of the market. All a wild day **does** predict is a likelihood of more wild days to come. Those days could be up or down.

The most reliable method to tune up your asset allocation is momentum. The Momentum Rule doesn't predict volatility clusters or even which specific assets will do the best in the months to come. All the rule does is tilt your portfolio away from assets that have poor momentum. Those assets are the most likely to fall.

Figure BC-15 is the second half of the previous figure and shows the years 2006 through 2014. This period is another good illustration of the way wild 3% moves tend to cluster within and close to corrections and bear markets.

In Figure BC-15, the prevalence of volatile days in bad times becomes obvious in the 2007–2009 bear market. More than 50 wild days, most of them gut-wrenching losses, hit investors in less than 1½

years. But there were no corrections or 3%+ days in the bull-market rally of 2012, 2013, or 2014.

Ironically, Mandelbrot was the faculty adviser for a young Eugene Fama. Mandelbrot describes what the student wrote in his doctoral thesis:

"Whatever the stock index, whatever the country, whatever the security, prices only rarely follow the predicted normal pattern. . . . Big price changes were far more common than the standard model allowed. Large changes, of more than five standard deviations from the average, happened two thousand times more often then expected. Under Gaussian rules, you should have encountered such drama only once every seven thousand years; in fact, the data showed, it happened once every three or four years." [1550]

We'll leave the old behind and focus on the horizon ahead, with this parting shot from *The (Mis)behavior of Markets*:

"You cannot beat the market, says the standard market doctrine. Granted. But you can sidestep its worst punches." [1551]

» TECH TALK

old theories predict too few crashes

Plenty of evidence is provided by the crashes that investors were subject to in 2000–2002 and 2007–2009 by the S&P 500 and Lazy Portfolios. Traditional economic theories fail to accurately project the losses a strategy will suffer. This is because the obsolete models assume that asset prices follow a bell curve or "normal distribution."

The bell curve is also called a "Gaussian distribution," after Carl Friedrich Gauss, a German mathematician who published the method in 1809. [1552] Mandelbrot proved that asset prices actually follow a "Levy distribution," after the French statistician Paul Levy (1886–1971). [1553]

All of the above is a fancy way of saying, "The market crashes way more often than a bell curve predicts."

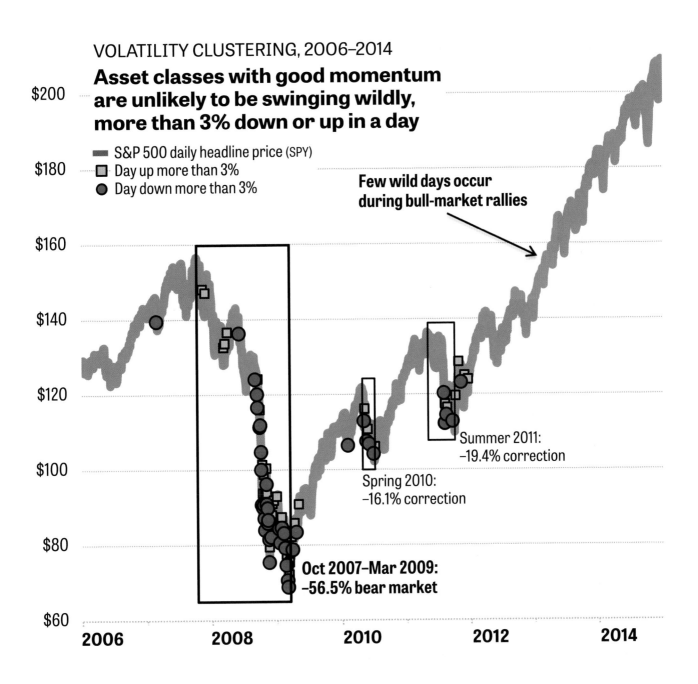

VOLATILITY CLUSTERING, 2006–2014

Asset classes with good momentum are unlikely to be swinging wildly, more than 3% down or up in a day

- ▬ S&P 500 daily headline price (SPY)
- ☐ Day up more than 3%
- ⬤ Day down more than 3%

Few wild days occur during bull-market rallies

Summer 2011: –19.4% correction

Spring 2010: –16.1% correction

Oct 2007–Mar 2009: –56.5% bear market

FIGURE BC-15 | Part 2 of 2 figures. Data source: Yahoo Finance

The future belongs to the Nobel Prize winners of the 21st century, not the 20th

The 2003 Nobel Prize in Economics went to Robert Engle III and Clive Granger (Figure BC-16) for their joint work to advance Mandelbrot's thinking. The selection committee particularly cited their "classic and remarkably influential paper."[1554]

The two economists developed mathematical formulas showing the importance of trends and ways to predict volatility. Software built on these principles was called ARCH.

Despite these advances, investors are far more familiar with the names Markowitz and Sharpe than they are with Engle and Granger. Fortunately, the names themselves are not as important as whether individual investors can use the new concepts to help their nest eggs grow.

Adam Butler and Michael Philbrick of ReSolve Asset Management have repeatedly documented the failures of Markowitz Portfolio Theory.

In their four-part series, "Dynamic Asset Allocation for Practitioners," the authors point out two big errors:

Error #1. Assuming that returns and correlations over the past four or more decades should determine your static allocation for all time, and

Error #2. Assuming that you can sell short the assets with the poorest momentum.[1555]

In fact, they say, you do very well if you follow two different principles:

Principle #1. Only the returns and correlations over the past 3 to 12 months are relevant when forming portfolios for the coming month; and

Principle #2. Shorting is prohibited. Assets with poor momentum can suddenly shoot up, causing short sellers unlimited losses.

Muscular Portfolios use both of the above two principles. These strategies use the returns over the past 3 to 12 months, and Muscular Portfolios never short any asset.

One paper made a splash in 2011 by claiming to have discovered "momentum crashes." The authors complained about the fact that traders were shorting stocks with poor momentum,

» KEY CONCEPT
shorting is prohibited
There are no such things as "momentum crashes," which are more accurately called "shorting crashes."

betting they would always go down. These speculators would sometimes lose a great deal of money.[1556]

Stocks with poor momentum can rise sharply in the "bounce" at the beginning of a bull market. This happens so fast that traders who short these stocks can wipe out big-time.

Don't short securities. As Larry Swedroe of the BAM Alliance writes: "Long-only momentum strategies are not subject to such deep crashes."[1557]

THE NOBEL PRIZE

Engle and Granger, 2003

FIGURE BC-16

Dynamic asset rotation reflects a 21st-century philosophy of investing

One of the pioneers of asset rotation is Smart Portfolios LLC. Run by former managers of Prudential Securities, Reign Capital Management, and elsewhere, it uses Engle and Granger's principles. Its Dynamic Portfolio Optimization (DPO) software picks ETFs to minimize risk while retaining gains.

Smart Portfolios' CEO, Bryce James, was profiled in the 2012 book *Winning with ETF Strategies* by Max Isaacman. James is quoted as saying:

"Current information is far more valuable than the average price of the previous 40 years. The DPO model utilizes the historical averages as a placeholder, but implements advanced mathematics to guide current allocation decisions."

James says using decades-old data to choose assets is like reading the *Farmer's Almanac* to predict today's weather. It's much better to allocate your portfolio using the most recent data, such as the past 12 months. This is like having Doppler radar (the kind that weather forecasters point to on TV).

Figure BC-17 illustrates how the best asset allocation is not a fixed line on a two-dimensional plane. Instead, as market conditions change and assets gain and lose momentum, the optimum mix moves along a three-dimensional surface. The best portfolios tilt toward those assets that have the best odds on this curved opportunity set.

Smart Portfolios does not accept new accounts for money management, but it does offer a website called PortfolioMason.com. For a monthly fee—ranging at this writing from $75 to $300 per month with a 15-day free trial—hardcore number crunchers can test their own theories against market conditions going back several decades.

Figure BC-18 outlines the old MPT way of thinking and the scientific principles behind the new Dynamic Portfolio Model (DPM).

Don't worry if some of the jargon isn't familiar. It's already built into Muscular Portfolios—no math required. The differences between MPT and DPM will be the subject of academic papers for decades to come.

Fortunately, most individual investors don't need software as complex as Portfolio Mason or theories like volatility clusters. Simply use a Muscular Portfolio, which automatically adapts to whatever the market throws at you.

LIVINGSTON'S LAW OF THEORIES

*Out with the old, in with the new
Roses are red, violets are blue.*

The best asset allocation lies on a 3-D surface, not a 2-D line

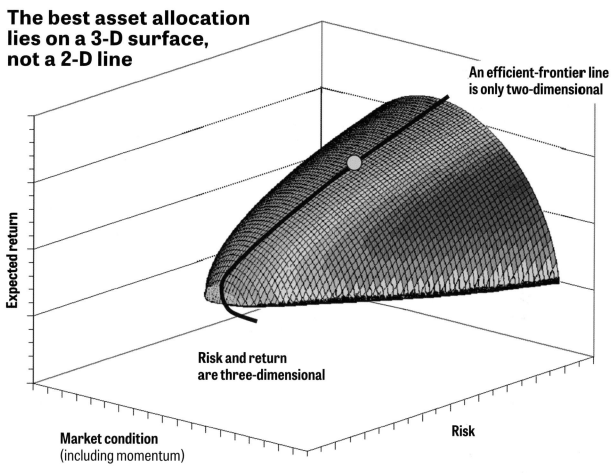

An efficient-frontier line is only two-dimensional

Expected return

Risk and return are three-dimensional

Market condition
(including momentum)

Risk

FIGURE BC-17 | Source: Smart Portfolios LLC

Differences between 20th-century theories and the 21st-century model

	Markowitz Portfolio Theory/ neoclassical finance	Dynamic Portfolio Model/ the Index Investing Revolution
Market fits a bell curve	Yes—normal distribution	No—free-market distribution (fat tails)
Risk varies over time	No—risk is static	Yes—volatility clusters and ARCH/ GARCH
Correlation measure	Pearson's r (linear correlation)	Copula (nonlinear correlation)
Market factors	None—the market is efficient	Momentum and others

FIGURE BC-18

You're perfectly qualified to be your own portfolio manager—free

If this book were written as a murder mystery, right now you'd be expecting the hero to unmask the culprit. Who killed your portfolio's performance?

The answer is that **you** killed your performance. Does any of the following sound familiar?

» Buying high and selling low. You got into equities when the market was exciting and got out when the market was scary. This hurt your performance terribly.

» Overconfidence. You thought you could discover a "secret formula" that thousands of trading pros around the world weren't already exploiting.

» Individual security selection. You convinced yourself you could use your opinions to pick stocks that would soar.

» Believing well-dressed experts. You paid advisers large fees for results that were worse than mediocre.

» Loading up on risk. You sought lottery-like wins and cranked up the riskiness of your holdings, thinking this would somehow capture more gains.

» Ultraconservatism (the reverse of risk-seeking). Once you'd been burned, you pulled your funds out of growth assets and let your money earn little or nothing sitting in cash.

Despite our behavioral blind spots, ordinary individuals **can** make good decisions.

In the 2015 book *Superforecasting,* Wharton professor Philip Tetlock tested how well 20,000 average people could predict various outcomes after only a few minutes of simple training.[1558]

Jason Zweig wrote in the *Wall Street Journal* that the forecasts of Tetlock's amateurs "were more accurate more often, and the confidence they had in their forecasts—as measured by the odds they set on being right—was more accurately tuned."[1559]

The best 2% of amateurs were then teamed up. These average people's predictions were 35% to 60% better than those of the most-respected experts at four major institutions.[1560]

You don't need complex mathematical formulas, the intricate schemes that have failed investors over the years. The simpler the investing approach, the better it works.

Muscular Portfolios don't even require you to do any math (Figure AW-1). The rankings are done for you every market day, free of charge, at:

MuscularPortfolios.com

You are perfectly capable of being your own investment adviser without paying a fee to anyone. The only requirement is that you tune out opinions about the market—especially your own.

Mechanical investing, in which you faithfully follow a Muscular Portfolio, is the way to stop your opinions from driving you into one losing investment strategy after another.

Live long and prosper!

Muscular Portfolios require no math. Let the computer do the work—while you enjoy life

FIGURE AW-1

Use ETF substitution tables to fix wash sales and bad 401(k)s

The substitution tables in this appendix can help you buy securities that avoid the IRS's "wash sale" rule and correct a "bad" 401(k) plan.

Avoiding the "wash sale" rule

If you happen to sell a security at a loss, you can normally deduct that loss from:

» Any capital gains you received that year, or

» Your ordinary income, up to $3,000 that year and up to $3,000 in future years until you've exhausted the loss carryforward.

An exception occurs if you buy a very similar security within 30 days before or after the sale. You **cannot** deduct the loss in that tax year if you bought what the IRS calls a "substantially identical" security.

To make the loss deductible, buy a fund that tracks the same asset class but that your brokerage firm will not report to the IRS as "substantially identical." Contact your brokerage firm to confirm this.

How to correct a "bad" 401(k)

What if your 401(k) or other Qualified Plan doesn't offer **any** of the ETFs that match the Muscular Portfolios in this book? Use the tables in this appendix to look for similar mutual funds and ETFs that your plan **may** offer.

What if your Qualified Plan offers **none** of the ETFs or mutual funds listed in this appendix? In that case, you'll have to do a little searching to discover comparable funds that **are** available to you.

Let's say you want to find ETFs correlated with Vanguard's VTI (which tracks all US stocks). Enter the following line in any browser and scroll to the bottom of the resulting ETFScreen.com page:

ETFScreen.com/price-chart.php?s=VTI

For ETFs that track other asset classes, use ETFdb.com to look for funds by category:

ETFdb.com/etfdb-categories

Caution: You may find ETFs with a "perfect correlation." A website may display that as 1.0 or 100%. But a **high correlation** doesn't ensure that two funds will have the **same performance.**

Always check that two funds from different providers have similar returns. To do so, chart the longest period that both funds have been available.

For instance, you can reveal **big differences** among four "global bond" ETFs using StockCharts.com's free PerfCharts feature. Enter the following address in a browser, all on one line:

StockCharts.com/freecharts/perf.php?IUSB,BNDX,IGOV,BWX&n=702&O=011000

Baby Bear Portfolio substitution funds

If your 401(k) does not offer the same ETFs as this book

Asset class	Vanguard ETFs		Vanguard Investor Shares*		Vanguard Admiral Shares*		Other low-cost ETFs	
	Baby Bear ETF	Annual fee	Mutual fund	Annual fee	Mutual fund	Annual fee	Low-cost ETF	Annual fee
All US stocks	VTI	0.04%	VTSMX	0.15%	VTSAX	0.04%	IWV	0.20%
All US bonds	BND	0.05%	VBMFX	0.15%	VBTLX	0.05%	AGG	0.05%
Minimum investment	none		$3,000		$10,000		none	

COLOR KEY

equities	fixed-income

FIGURE A-1

*Vanguard's "Investor Shares" require a minimum investment of $3,000; "Admiral Shares" require $10,000. Fees current as of March 2018 but subject to change at any time

How to use the ETF substitution tables in this appendix

» **The ETFs used by the model portfolios** in this book are in the first column.

» **If an ETF in the first column is not available,** look toward the right. You may be able to buy a Vanguard "Investor Shares" or "Admiral Shares" mutual fund that tracks the same index.

» **If none of those funds are available,** look to the rightmost column for low-cost ETFs from other providers that you may be able to buy.

» **Vanguard currently doesn't offer any funds** for some important asset classes, such as commodities, gold, and money-market funds. In those cases, the substitution tables in this appendix show equivalent ETFs from other low-cost sponsors.

» **If your 401(k) doesn't have any ETFs,** use the techniques described above to find an equivalent mutual fund and purchase that one instead. Then ask your 401(k) sponsor or brokerage firm to add to your plan the same ETFs that are used by Muscular Portfolios.

Mama Bear Portfolio substitution funds

If your 401(k) does not offer the same ETFs as this book

Asset class	Vanguard and others' ETFs		Vanguard Investor Shares*		Vanguard Admiral Shares*		Other low-cost ETFs	
	Mama Bear ETF	Annual fee	Mutual fund	Annual fee	Mutual fund	Annual fee	Low-cost ETF	Annual fee
US large-cap stocks	VONE	0.12%	VLACX	0.18%	VLCAX	0.06%	IWB	0.15%
US small-cap stocks	VIOO	0.15%	NAESX	0.18%	VWMAX	0.06%	IJR	0.07%
Developed-market stocks	VEA	0.07%	VDVIX	0.17%	VTMGX	0.07%	IEFA	0.08%
Emerging-market stocks	VWO	0.14%	VEIEX	0.32%	VEMAX	0.14%	IEMG	0.14%
US REITs	VNQ	0.12%	VGSIX	0.26%	VGSLX	0.12%	RWR	0.25%
Commodities	PDBC^	0.59%	none^		none^		GSG†	0.75%
Gold	IAU^	0.25%	none^		none^		GLD	0.40%
US Treasurys, 10–25 yrs.	VGLT	0.07%	VUSTX	0.20%	VLGSX	0.07%	TLT	0.15%
Cash (money market)	SHV‡	0.15%	VMMXX	0.16%	VMRXX#	0.10%	BIL	0.14%
Minimum investment	*none*		*$3,000*		*$10,000*		*none*	

COLOR KEY

equities	hard assets	fixed-income

FIGURE A-2

*Vanguard's "Investor Shares" require a minimum investment of $3,000; "Admiral Shares" require $10,000.

^PowerShares PDBC and iShares IAU are low-cost ETFs chosen because Vanguard offers no commodity or gold funds.

†GSG, an iShares commodity ETF, sends investors an IRS Form K-1, which can complicate your tax filing.

‡SHV is an iShares ETF that holds T-bills maturing in 1 to 12 months. Vanguard does not offer a money-market ETF.

#At this writing, VMRXX, a Vanguard Admiral Shares money-market mutual fund, requires a minimum investment of $5 million.

Fees current as of March 2018 but subject to change at any time

Papa Bear Portfolio substitution funds

If your 401(k) does not offer the same ETFs as this book

Asset class	Vanguard and others' ETFs		Vanguard Investor Shares*		Vanguard Admiral Shares*		Other low-cost ETFs	
	Papa Bear ETF	Annual fee	Mutual fund	Annual fee	Mutual fund	Annual fee	Low-cost ETF	Annual fee
US large-cap value stocks	VTV	0.06%	VIVAX	0.18%	VVIAX	0.06%	IVE	0.18%
US large-cap growth stocks	VUG	0.06%	VIGRX	0.18%	VIGAX	0.06%	IVW	0.18%
US small-cap value stocks	VIOV	0.20%	VISVX	0.19%	VSIAX	0.07%	IJS	0.25%
US small-cap growth stocks	VIOG	0.20%	VISGX	0.19%	VSGAX	0.07%	IJT	0.25%
Developed-market stocks	VEA	0.07%	VDVIX	0.17%	VTMGX	0.07%	IEFA	0.08%
Emerging-market stocks	VWO	0.14%	VEIEX	0.32%	VEMAX	0.14%	IEMG	0.14%
US REITs	VNQ	0.12%	VGSIX	0.26%	VGSLX	0.12%	RWR	0.25%
Commodities	PDBC^	0.59%	none^		none^		GSG†	0.75%
Gold	IAU^	0.25%	none^		none^		GLD	0.40%
US Treasurys, 30-year	EDV	0.07%	VUSTX	0.20%	VLGSX	0.07%	ZROZ	0.15%
US Treasurys, 10-year	VGIT	0.07%	VFITX	0.20%	VSIGX	0.07%	IEF	0.15%
US inv.-grade corp. bonds	VCLT	0.07%	VWESX	0.22%	VLTCX‡	0.07%	CLY	0.20%
Non-US bonds	BNDX	0.11%	VTIBX	0.13%	VTABX	0.11%	IUSB#	0.06%
Minimum investment	*none*		*$3,000*		*$10,000*		*none*	

COLOR KEY

equities	hard assets	fixed-income

FIGURE A-3

*Vanguard's "Investor Shares" require a minimum investment of $3,000; "Admiral Shares" require $10,000.

^PowerShares PDBC and iShares IAU are low-cost ETFs chosen because Vanguard offers no commodity or gold funds.

†GSG, an iShares commodity ETF, sends investors an IRS Form K-1, which can complicate your tax filing.

‡VLTCX, a Vanguard corporate bond mutual fund, charges a 1% purchase fee as well as a $10,000 minimum.

#IUSB, an iShares ETF, tracks a USD-denominated bond index of US and non-US issuers, not the same index as BNDX.

Fees current as of March 2018 but subject to change at any time

Find the best ETFs, even without MuscularPortfolios.com

As we saw in Chapter 4, it's easy to find out which ETFs to hold each month. Simply visit the Web page of the Mama Bear or Papa Bear:

MuscularPortfolios.com/mama-bear

MuscularPortfolios.com/papa-bear

But what if MuscularPortfolios.com is temporarily out of service? There are umpteen reasons why a server might be down at times (power outage, plague of locusts, whatever).

The good news is that the portfolios in this book are fully disclosed and based purely on ETF prices, not indicators. That means you can use zillions of free Internet sites to find out which ETFs to hold.

The best website for data on exchange-traded funds is ETFScreen.com. The site covers virtually every ETF and a whole lot more.

To get started, visit ETFScreen.com. Click Register in the main menu to create a free account. The site does not sell your personal information. Then take the following steps (keyed to the numbered circles in Figure B-1):

1 · Once you're signed in, pull down the **My Pages** menu and select **New Portfolio.**

2 · In the **Enter Symbols** area, type the ETFs for the Mama Bear menu from Chapter 5 (shown in Figure B-1) or the Papa Bear menu from Chapter 6.

3 · In the **Define View/Layout** area, click the last box. Change the selection in that box to one of the following two options.

» For the Mama Bear Portfolio, select:

Total Return, 5-months

» For the Papa Bear Portfolio, select:

Total Return, 3, 6, 12-mo average

Click the hyphens in the last box and select **desc** (descending) as the sort. This makes the best ETFs appear atop the list.

4 · In the **Save** area, enter the new portfolio name: **Mama Bear** or **Papa Bear.** Click the Save Changes button.

On the main menu, pull down **My Pages,** select **Portfolios,** and then select the name of your portfolio. You can choose to see the rankings based on current prices (delayed 20 minutes) or recent closing prices. Hold the first three ETFs in the list.

ETFScreen.com supports a great array of functions for users who select Premium Access ($15.95 per month at this writing).

For premium users, the site's **Tools** menu reveals correlations between different ETFs, monthly seasonality effects, and many technical-analysis options.

For customer support, registered users can access ETFScreen's contact page.[156]

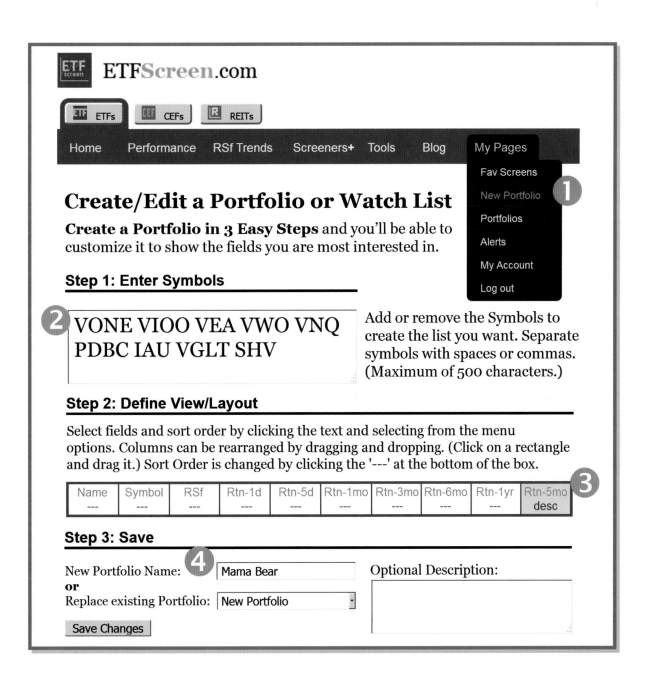

FIGURE B-1 | Use ETFScreen.com to get picks for the Mama Bear or Papa Bear

Many free websites can be used to find the right ETFs each month

You can employ almost any market-data site to find the picks. The following example uses StockCharts.com.

Unlike ETFScreen, StockCharts' "PerfCharts" do not show current prices. They show yesterday's closing prices until after today's market has settled. This shouldn't matter, since the momentum rankings of ETFs remain the same for days or weeks.

The ETFs for the Mama Bear Portfolio

First enter the following address into any Web browser (all on one line). Then take steps 1, 2, and 3 below (keyed to the numbered circles in Figure B-2):

stockcharts.com/freecharts/perf.php? VONE,VIOO,VEA,VWO,VNQ,PDBC,IAU, VGLT,SHV&n=106&O=111000

1 · Make sure the date range shows **106 days** to provide each ETF's five-month total return (105 trading days). If it doesn't, double-click the date range, enter **106,** and press Enter.

2 · Make sure the Columns button is on, displaying the Histogram Chart. This shows the top three ETFs more clearly than the default Line Chart.

3 · Note the three ETFs with the highest five-month return. Hold those ETFs.

The ETFs for the Papa Bear Portfolio

Using StockCharts to get the picks for the Papa Bear requires more steps than the Mama Bear. StockCharts allows no more than 10 symbols in a PerfChart, but the Papa Bear menu includes 13 symbols.

Enter the following address into any Web browser (all on one line) to see the first 9 of 13 ETFs in the Papa Bear menu. Then take steps 1, 2, and 3 below:

stockcharts.com/freecharts/perf.php? VTV,VUG,VIOV,VIOG,VEA,VWO,VNQ,PDBC, IAU&n=64&O=111000

1 · Make sure the date range shows **64 days** to provide each ETF's three-month total return (63 trading days). If it doesn't, double-click the date range, enter **64,** and press Enter.

2 · Make sure the Columns button is on, displaying the Histogram Chart. This shows the top ETFs more clearly than the default Line Chart.

3 · Write down each ETF's three-month total returns.

Double-click **64 days,** type **127** to display six months, and press Enter. Write down each ETF's returns. Then repeat this using **253** to display 12 months. Write down each ETF's returns.

Enter the following Web address (all on one line) to see the last 4 of 13 ETFs. Repeat all of the above steps:

stockcharts.com/freecharts/perf.php? EDV,VGIT,VCLT,BNDX&n=64&O=111000

Average the returns for each ETF. Hold the top three ETFs.

For questions about StockCharts, use the website's support center.[1562]

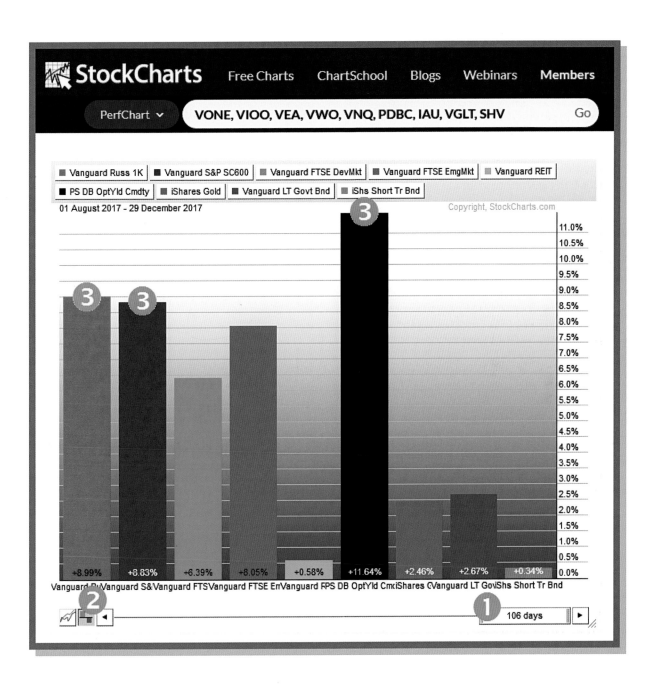

FIGURE B-2 | Use StockCharts.com to get picks for the Mama Bear or Papa Bear

Appendix C

The static asset allocations of major Lazy Portfolios

A Lazy Portfolio typically holds five or more asset classes in unchanging percentages. Such strategies usually rebalance to the original percentages annually. A Lazy Portfolio is also called a "strategic" or "static asset allocation" (SAA) strategy.

Lazy Portfolios lag behind the S&P 500 during bull markets but crash almost as badly during bear markets. Chapter 3 shows that the S&P 500 and all Lazy Portfolios are examples of "downer portfolios"—strategies that lose 30% or more every few years. These losses compel people to liquidate their assets, harming their performances.

This book primarily uses Lazy Portfolio definitions determined by MyPlanIQ.com. That site tracks in real time thousands of investing strategies, including a few specifically labeled Lazy Portfolios. The site uses the returns from actual index mutual funds, which automatically subtract their annual fees.

Figures C-1 and C-2 show the asset allocations of 10 Lazy Portfolios, as described in Chapter 3. For details, see the footnote after each portfolio name.

My Plan IQ tracks each Lazy Portfolio using the asset classes that were originally publicized, even if an author made little-noticed changes at a later time. Here are some notes:

» The Coward's Portfolio was announced in 1996 by William Bernstein. (Despite Bernstein's preferred name, MarketWatch.com calls it the "Smart Money Portfolio," because it once appeared in *Smart Money* magazine.)

The portfolio allocates 45% to US stocks and REITs, 15% to non-US equities, and 40% to short-term bonds. The 40% bond portion is best represented by Vanguard's VBISX bond fund, according to My Plan IQ[1563] and Bogleheads.org.[1564]

Figure C-1 therefore allocates 28% to short-term Treasurys and 12% to investment-grade corporate bonds, all with maturities of one to five years—the same as VBISX.

» The Unconventional Success Portfolio was specified by David Swensen in 2005. His book, *Unconventional Success,* said the portfolio's fixed-income allocation should be equally split between TIPS (Treasury Inflation-Protected Securities) and "long-term, default-free Treasury bonds."[1565]

The word "long-term" means Treasury bonds with maturities of 20 to 30 years, such as Vanguard's VUSTX. However, an email by Swensen to followers one year later suggested they use "the weighted average duration" of Treasurys with maturities of 1–3, 7–10, and 20–30 years,[1566] such as VFITX.

My Plan IQ tracks the original definition in the 2005 book, which was widely read. The book's definition performed better than the email's definition. Quant simulations show that long-term Treasurys slightly outperformed "the weighted average duration" of Treasurys in the 43-year period 1973–2015.

Portfolio name	Bucket	Coffee-house	Coward's	Family	Gone Fishin'
See footnote	1567	1568	1569	1570	1571
Author	Christine Benz	Bill Schultheis	William Bernstein	Ted Aronson	Alexander Green
All US stocks	13.33%			5%	15%
Large-cap stocks	28.67%	10%	15%	15%	
Large-cap growth					
Large-cap value		10%	10%		
Mid-cap stocks				10%	
Small-cap stocks		10%	5%		15%
Small-cap growth				5%	
Small-cap value		10%	10%	5%	
All non-US stocks	13.33%	10%			
Non-US value stocks					
Developed-markets					
European stocks			5%	5%	10%
Asia-Pacific stocks			5%	15%	10%
Emerging-markets			5%	10%	10%
US REITs		10%	5%		5%
Commodities	5%				
Prec. metals (incl. gold)					5%
Natural resources					
All US bonds (govt. & corp.)		40%			
Treasurys, long-term				10%	
Treasurys, medium.-term	11%				
Treasurys, short-term	8%		28%		
Treasurys, infl. prot. (TIPS)	6.67%			15%	10%
Corp. inv.-grade bonds	9%				
Corp. short-term IG bonds			12%		10%
Corp. high-yield bonds	5%			5%	10%
Non-US bonds					

COLOR KEY

equities	hard assets	fixed-income

FIGURE C-1
Lazy Portfolio static asset allocations. Sources: Morningstar (Bucket), My Plan IQ (others)

Portfolio name	Ideal	Nano	7Twelve	Ultimate	Unconven.
See footnote	1572	1573	1574	1575	1576
Author	Frank Armstrong	John Wasik	Craig Israelsen	Paul Merriman	David Swensen
All US stocks		20%			30%
Large-cap stocks	6.25%		8.33%	6%	
Large-cap growth					
Large-cap value	9.25%			6%	
Mid-cap stocks			8.33%		
Small-cap stocks			8.33%	6%	
Small-cap growth	6.25%				
Small-cap value	9.25%			6%	
All non-US stocks	31%	20%			
Non-US value stocks				12%	
Developed-markets			8.33%	12%	15%
European stocks					
Asia-Pacific stocks					
Emerging-markets			8.33%	6%	5%
US REITs	8%	20%	8.33%	6%	20%
Commodities			8.33%		
Prec. metals (incl. gold)					
Natural resources			8.33%		
All US bonds (govt. & corp.)			8.33%		
Treasurys, long-term					15%
Treasurys, medium-term				20%	
Treasurys, short-term			8.33%	12%	
Treasurys, infl. prot. (TIPS)		20%	8.33%	8%	15%
Corp. inv.-grade bonds		20%			
Corp. short-term IG bonds	30%				
Corp. high-yield bonds					
Non-US bonds			8.33%		

COLOR KEY

equities	hard assets	fixed-income

FIGURE C-2

Lazy Portfolio static asset allocations. Source: My Plan IQ

Notes

Every footnote links to a longer document with more details.

» Enter **bri.li/1000** into any browser to see an example.
» Enter **bri.li/1001** to see the first footnote in this book.
» Enter **bri.li/1200** to see the 200th footnote, and so forth.

To preview the destination, add a hyphen (-) to the end, like this: **bri.li/1000-**

The 2nd edition of this book will use tiny links that begin with "2," etc.

All of the footnotes in the 1st edition are clickable at **MuscularPortfolios.com/1e**.

1001 bri.li/1001 or www.barrons.com/articles/whats-next-for-etfs-1510976833
1002 bri.li/1002 or ssrn.com/abstract=94143
1003 bri.li/1003 or fic.wharton.upenn.edu/fic/papers/06/p0614.htm
1004 bri.li/1004 or www.ebri.org/publications/benfaq/index.cfm?fa=retfaq14
1005 bri.li/1005 or works.bepress.com/brooke_harrington/5/
1006 bri.li/1006 or www.aeaweb.org/articles.php?doi=10.1257/jel.52.1.5
1007 bri.li/1007 or www.theatlantic.com/international/archive/2014/05/the-danger-of-financial-ignorance-do-you-understand-money/361851/
1008 bri.li/1008 or www.americanfunds.com/individual/planning/market-fluctuations/past-market-declines.html
1009 bri.li/1009 or baldwinclarke.com/wp-content/uploads/2016/01/JPMorgan-Slide-14-Bear-Markets-and-Subsequent-Bull-Runs-cut-768x557.jpg
1010 bri.li/1010 or am.jpmorgan.com/us/en/asset-management/gim/adv/insights/guide-to-the-markets/viewer
1011 bri.li/1011 or www.advisorperspectives.com/dshort/updates/Four-Totally-Bad-Bears.php
1012 bri.li/1012 or www.advisorperspectives.com/dshort/updates/Four-Totally-Bad-Bears.php
1013 bri.li/1013 or en.wikipedia.org/wiki/The_Intelligent_Investor
1014 bri.li/1014 or books.google.com/books?id=klYquu4H1wAC&pg=PR12&ved=0CDAQ6AEwAA#v=onepage&q&f=false
1015 bri.li/1015 or stockcharts.com/freecharts/perf.php?VUSTX,VFINX&l=309&r=4148&O=011000
1016 bri.li/1016 or www.aaii.com/journal/article/trading-more-frequently-leads-to-worse-returns
1017 bri.li/1017 or www.marketwatch.com/story/timing-this-market-is-guaranteed-to-make-you-a-loser-2014-08-08/print
1018 bri.li/1018 or www.aaii.com/journal/article/trading-more-frequently-leads-to-worse-returns
1019 bri.li/1019 or www.forbes.com/sites/billharris/2012/12/10/want-to-boost-investment-returns-start-with-tax-management
1020 bri.li/1020 or www.etf.com/etf-education-center/21017-why-are-etfs-so-tax-efficient.html
1021 bri.li/1021 or finance.yahoo.com/news/etfs-capital-gains-distributions-remain-120000409.html
1022 bri.li/1022 or www.fool.com/investing/mutual-funds/2010/11/11/the-true-cost-of-12b-1-fees.aspx
1023 bri.li/1023 or www.ici.org/pdf/2015_factbook.pdf
1024 bri.li/1024 or reuters.com/article/us-money-etf-401k/etfs-are-hot-everywhere-but-workplace-retirement-plans-idUSKCN1AV1J1
1025 bri.li/1025 or www.ici.org/pdf/2015_factbook.pdf
1026 bri.li/1026 or www.seeitmarket.com/what-are-etf-and-mutual-fund-flows-trends-telling-investors-now-14449
1027 bri.li/1027 or books.google.com/books?id=bOcEAAAAQAAJ&pg=RA1-PA81&dq=%22cut+short+your+losses+let+your+profits+run+on%22&hl
        =en&sa=X&ved=0ahUKEwjWs_-7xfXPAhXJqVQKHYWVDVYQ6AEILjAD#v=onepage&q=%22cut%20short%20your%20losses%20let%20
        your%20profits%20run%20on%22&f=false
1028 bri.li/1028 or onlinelibrary.wiley.com/enhanced/doi/10.1111/0022-1082.00072/
1029 bri.li/1029 or onlinelibrary.wiley.com/doi/10.1111/j.1540-6261.1993.tb04702.x/full
1030 bri.li/1030 or www.imca.org/sites/default/files/current-issues/JIC/JIC151_MultiStyleGlobalInvesting.pdf
1031 bri.li/1031 or onlinelibrary.wiley.com/doi/10.1111/j.1540-6261.1970.tb00518.x/full
1032 bri.li/1032 or books.google.com/books?id=kAtba1WxkKkC&pg=PA129&lpg=PA129&dq=%22failure+of+the+efficient+markets+mod
        el+is+thus+so+dramatic%22&source=bl&ots=YhB_veCNIN&sig=tMv7IZM_sUPErqIzN9bC6tcHnjQ&hl=en&sa=X&ved=2ahUKEwj-9O_
        Fj8jcAhWOITQIHbmKAa8Q6AEwAnoECAEQAQ#v=onepage&q=%22failure%20of%20the%20efficient%20markets%20model%20is%20
        thus%20so%20dramatic%22&f=false
1033 bri.li/1033 or news.yale.edu/2011/02/17/shiller-paper-cited-one-century-s-top-economic-articles

1034 bri.li/1034 or www.jstor.org/stable/2327804

1035 bri.li/1035 or www.researchgate.net/publication/4769783_Dissecting_Anomalies

1036 bri.li/1036 or SSRN.com/abstract=1720139

1037 bri.li/1037 or p.feedblitz.com/t3.asp?/332386/4534930/0/www.paecon.net/PAEReview/issue66/GuerrienGun66.pdf

1038 bri.li/1038 or nobelprize.org/nobel_prizes/economic-sciences/laureates/2002/press.html

1039 bri.li/1039 or nobelprize.org/nobel_prizes/economic-sciences/laureates/2017/press.html

1040 bri.li/1040 or books.google.com/books?id=TA7Q27RWljOC&printsec=frontcover&dq=%22thinking+fast+and+slow%22+kahneman&hl=en&sa=X
            &ved=0ahUKEwjBg8eXx-TWAhVLjFQKHZJ6ASIQ6AEIJzAA#v=onepage&q=chapter%201&f=false

1041 bri.li/1041 or advisorperspectives.com/newsletters12/Daniel_Kahneman_on_the_Two_Kinds_of_Thinking.php

1042 bri.li/1042 or ritholtz.com/2017/05/181576/

1043 bri.li/1043 or johncbogle.com/wordpress/wp-content/uploads/2011/09/NMS-9-12-12.pdf

1044 bri.li/1044 or stockcharts.com/freecharts/perf.php?EDV,SPY&l=261&r=374&O=011000

1045 bri.li/1045 or www.morningstar.com/cover/videocenter.aspx?id=718639

1046 bri.li/1046 or jpm.iijournals.com/content/42/1/119

1047 bri.li/1047 or https://en.wikipedia.org/wiki/Index_fund#Origins

1048 bri.li/1048 or https://news.morningstar.com/articlenet/article.aspx?id=638885

1049 bri.li/1049 or bri.li/morning

1050 bri.li/1050 or www.researchaffiliates.com/en_us/publications/articles/488_if_factor_returns_are_predictable_why_is_there_an_investor_return_gap.html

1051 bri.li/1051 or fortune.com/2016/05/11/warren-buffett-hedge-fund-bet/

1052 bri.li/1052 or blogs.cfainstitute.org/investor/2015/02/12/betting-with-buffett-seven-lean-years-later/

1053 bri.li/1053 or www.fool.com/investing/2018/01/03/warren-buffett-just-officially-won-his-million-dol.aspx

1054 bri.li/1054 or pensionpartners.com/the-hedge-fund-myth/

1055 bri.li/1055 or www.aaii.com/n/theaaiistory

1056 bri.li/1056 or calpers.ca.gov/page/about/organization

1057 bri.li/1057 or www.calpers.ca.gov/docs/total-fund-investment-policy.pdf

1058 bri.li/1058 or blogs.wsj.com/moneybeat/2016/08/19/this-is-radical-three-new-etf-ideas-that-actually-make-sense/

1059 bri.li/1059 or www.etf.com/etf-education-center/21021-who-are-authorized-participants.html

1060 bri.li/1060 or blogs.wsj.com/moneybeat/2016/08/19/this-is-radical-three-new-etf-ideas-that-actually-make-sense/

1061 bri.li/1061 or www.icap.com/~/media/Files/I/Icap-Corp/documents/October%202016%20Monthly%20Summary.pdf

1062 bri.li/1062 or books.google.com/books?id=dcNMZTnEz6UC&pg=PA5&lpg=PA5&dq=%22don%E2%80%99t+speculate+unless+you+can+make+it+a+
            full-time+job%22+baruch&source=bl&ots=Z_W_IkY8EO&sig=6AUAQw429_1t9lTOCoH86uEL4YY&hl=en&sa=X&ei=a9ZsVZWKPIawy
            QSqrYP4Cw&ved=0CFEQ6AEwCA#v=onepage&q=%22don%E2%80%99t%20speculate%20unless%20you%20can%20make%20it%20
            a%20full-time%20job%22%20baruch&f=false

1063 bri.li/1063 or books.google.com/books?id=DCqFYOrGyegC&printsec=frontcover&dq=%22fooled+by+randomness%22&hl=en&sa=X&ved=0a
            hUKEwi79oepq4_LAhVGwGMKHT9rDLsQ6AEIJjAA#v=onepage&q=%22fooled%20by%20randomness%22&f=false

1064 bri.li/1064 or ssrn.com/abstract=806246

1065 bri.li/1065 or blogs.wsj.com/moneybeat/2018/03/02/is-warren-buffett-too-big-to-beat-the-market/

1066 bri.li/1066 or https://www.cxoadvisory.com/2758/individual-gurus/warren-buffett/

1067 bri.li/1067 or books.google.com/books?id=veBdeTGxA4AC&pg=PA340&dq=%22standard+%26+poor%27s+index+committee%22&hl=en&sa=X
            &ved=0ahUKEwiGx4jA7tbPAhUKrlQKHfKEBtoQ6AEIOTAF#v=onepage&q=%22standard%20%26%20poor%27s%20index%20commit
            tee%22&f=false

1068 bri.li/1068 or app.box.com/s/3b5d4rd059pepg5bgtlr

1069 bri.li/1069 or books.google.com/books?id=JStv2T6nL74C&pg=PA158&lpg=PA158&dq=Mark+Hulbert+constructed+a+hypothetical+portfolio+
            made+up+of+each+year%27s+top-performing+newsletter+portfolio+12+months&source=bl&ots=RRf67Azr3v&sig=yR8n34bqqqX
            Owd8wPACMN3VxwQg&hl=en&sa=X&ved=0CCIQ6AEwAGoVChMI_qGZ48DpxgIVUjCICh2MXQIs#v=snippet&q=each%20year%27s%20
            top-performing&f=false

1070 bri.li/1070 or www.marketwatch.com/story/the-first-shall-be-last-2013-01-04

1071 bri.li/1071 or ssrn.com/abstract=8036

1072 bri.li/1072 or ssrn.com/abstract=980430

1073 bri.li/1073 or cache.financialinvestigator.nl/upload/fi_43a1c02c/files/downloads/article3.pdf

1074 bri.li/1074 or www.hec.unil.ch/agoyal/docs/HireFire_JoF.pdf

1075 bri.li/1075 or ssrn.com/abstract=3034686

1076 bri.li/1076 or finance.martinsewell.com/fund-performance/BerkGreen2004.pdf

1077   bri.li/1077 or us.spindices.com/documents/spiva/spiva-us-mid-year-2017.pdf
1078   bri.li/1078 or www.marketwatch.com/story/the-dow-is-arguably-the-best-active-fund-ever-engineered-2016-12-22/print
1079   bri.li/1079 or www.ino.com/blog/2015/03/did-you-know-the-dow-jones-has-crushed-the-sp-500-over-the-past-30-year/
1080   bri.li/1080 or www.aaii.com/journal/article/a-closer-look-at-funds-that-focus-on-the-dow
1081   bri.li/1081 or johncbogle.com/wordpress/wp-content/uploads/2011/09/NMS-9-12-12.pdf
1082   bri.li/1082 or books.google.com/books?id=GkrQBGUJb-OC&pg=PT35&lpg=PT35&dq=el-erian+Diversification+alone+is+no+longer+suffi
            cient+to+temper+risk&source=bl&ots=XPhyH4GuoZ&sig=oo1koaDMZ4oHewVaxSlDv-_nmwE&hl=en&sa=X&ei=vwdhVYPSFpf
            goASa2oPIBw&ved=0CD8Q6AEwBQ#v=onepage&q=el-erian%20Diversification%20alone%20is%20no%20longer%20sufficient%20
            to%20temper%20risk&f=false
1083   bri.li/1083 or Marketwatch.com/Search?m=Column&mp=Paul%20B.%20Farrell
1084   bri.li/1084 or seekingalpha.com/article/4003556-beating-couch-potato-20-portfolios-outperform-scott-burnss-simple-asset-allocation
1085   bri.li/1085 or Marketwatch.com/lazyportfolio
1086   bri.li/1086 or www.marketwatch.com/lazyportfolio/portfolio/second-grader-starter
1087   bri.li/1087 or www.myplaniq.com/LTISystem/jsp/portfolio/ComparePortfolio.action?withCompare=true&portfolioString=P_1361%2CP_17645
1088   bri.li/1088 or www.myplaniq.com/LTISystem/jsp/portfolio/ComparePortfolio.action?withCompare=true&portfolioString=P_407%2CP_17465
1089   bri.li/1089 or www.marketwatch.com/lazyportfolio/portfolio/bernsteins-no-brainer
1090   bri.li/1090 or www.myplaniq.com/LTISystem/jsp/portfolio/ComparePortfolio.action?withCompare=true&portfolioString=P_36809%2CP_33676
1091   bri.li/1091 or www.marketwatch.com/lazyportfolio/portfolio/margaritaville
1092   bri.li/1092 or www.myplaniq.com/LTISystem/jsp/portfolio/ComparePortfolio.action?withCompare=true&portfolioString=P_33690%2CP_33692
1093   bri.li/1093 or www.myplaniq.com/LTISystem/jsp/portfolio/ComparePortfolio.action?withCompare=true&portfolioString=P_18357%2CP_18333
1094   bri.li/1094 or www.wsj.com/articles/how-much-stock-is-too-much-1402075902
1095   bri.li/1095 or www.wsj.com/articles/how-much-stock-is-too-much-1402075902
1096   bri.li/1096 or en.wikipedia.org/wiki/Great_Recession_in_the_United_States
1097   bri.li/1097 or en.wikipedia.org/wiki/Sailing_faster_than_the_wind
1098   bri.li/1098 or cxoadvisory.com/momentum-strategy
1099   bri.li/1099 or theideafarm.com/about/
1100   bri.li/1100 or paulmerriman.com/the-ultimate-buy-hold-strategy-2014/
1101   bri.li/1101 or www.myplaniq.com/articles/20131107-tactical-and-strategic-portfolios-vs-fundadvice-ultimate-buy-and-hold/
1102   bri.li/1102 or www.newyorker.com/magazine/2009/01/05/doing-it
1103   bri.li/1103 or www.thoughtco.com/grace-hopper-quotes-3530092
1104   bri.li/1104 or en.wikiquote.org/wiki/Damon_Runyon
1105   bri.li/1105 or www.cxoadvisory.com/gurus/
1106   bri.li/1106 or CXOAdvisory.com/4811/individual-gurus/cramer-offers-you-his-protection/
1107   bri.li/1107 or CXOAdvisory.com/4815/individual-gurus/jim-cramer-comments-on-our-evaluations-of-his-advice/
1108   bri.li/1108 or CXOAdvisory.com/18886/momentum-investing/simple-asset-class-etf-momentum-strategy-performance/
1109   bri.li/1109 or CXOAdvisory.com/momentum-strategy/
1110   bri.li/1110 or cxoadvisory.com/momentum-strategy/
1111   bri.li/1111 or CXOAdvisory.com/28418/momentum-investing/sacems-portfolio-asset-addition-testing/
1112   bri.li/1112 or CXOAdvisory.com/28423/momentum-investing/sacems-portfolio-asset-exclusion-testing/
1113   bri.li/1113 or CXOAdvisory.com/26124/momentum-investing/simple-asset-class-momentum-strategy-applied-to-mutual-funds/
1114   bri.li/1114 or cxoadvisory.com/25549/calendar-effects/optimal-monthly-cycle-for-simple-asset-class-etf-momentum-strategy/
1115   bri.li/1115 or CXOAdvisory.com/25767/calendar-effects/effects-of-execution-delay-on-simple-asset-class-etf-momentum-strategy/
1116   bri.li/1116 or money.usnews.com/investing/articles/2016-08-23/5-reasons-why-youre-bad-at-investing
1117   bri.li/1117 or ssrn.com/abstract=962461
1118   bri.li/1118 or www.advisorperspectives.com/dshort/updates/Monthly-Moving-Averages.php
1119   bri.li/1119 or ssrn.com/abstract=962461
1120   bri.li/1120 or hq.ssrn.com/rankings/Ranking_display.cfm?RequestTimeout=5000&TRN_gID=7&TMY_gID=5&order=DESC&runid=46024
1121   bri.li/1121 or www.advisorperspectives.com/dshort/updates/Monthly-Moving-Averages.php
1122   bri.li/1122 or ssrn.com/abstract=962461
1123   bri.li/1123 or cxoadvisory.com/25549/calendar-effects/optimal-monthly-cycle-for-simple-asset-class-etf-momentum-strategy/
1124   bri.li/1124 or quoteinvestigator.com/2011/05/13/einstein-simple/
1125   bri.li/1125 or vanguard.com/bogle_site/lib/sp19970401.html

1126 bri.li/1126 or johncbogle.com/wordpress/wp-content/uploads/2011/09/NMS-9-12-12.pdf

1127 bri.li/1127 or etf.com/etf-education-center/21017-why-are-etfs-transparent-and-tax-efficient.html

1128 bri.li/1128 or personal.vanguard.com/us/funds/snapshot?FundId=0585&FundIntExt=INT

1129 bri.li/1129 or therichest.com/celebnetworth/celebrity-business/investors/john-bogle-net-worth/

1130 bri.li/1130 or forbes.com/profile/edward-johnson/

1131 bri.li/1131 or www.morningstar.com/cover/videocenter.aspx?id=718639

1132 bri.li/1132 or wjpm.iijournals.com/content/42/1/119

1133 bri.li/1133 or books.google.com/books?id=gRdOBrus_9wC&printsec=frontcover&dq=jason+zweig&hl=en&sa=X&ei=jLSlVKqMDo61oQSFwIGA
         BQ&ved=0CCUQ6AEwAQ#v=snippet&q=%22if%20it%20went%20way%20down%22&f=false

1134 bri.li/1134 or QuoteInvestigator.com/2011/10/31/compound-interest

1135 bri.li/1135 or Snopes.com/quotes/einstein/interest.asp

1136 bri.li/1136 or earlyretirementextreme.com/ere-book

1137 bri.li/1137 or www.newretirement.com/retirement/retired-at-30-a-true-story-of-successfully-saving-for-retirement/

1138 bri.li/1138 or www.epi.org/publication/retirement-in-america/

1139 bri.li/1139 or webapps.dol.gov/elaws/faq/esa/flsa/028.htm

1140 bri.li/1140 or www.dol.gov/whd/state/certification.htm

1141 bri.li/1141 or rothira.com/roth-iras-for-kids

1142 bri.li/1142 or ObliviousInvestor.com/roth-ira-withdrawal-rules

1143 bri.li/1143 or irs.gov/publications/p929#en_US_2016_publink1000273225

1144 bri.li/1144 or archive.li/nwByn

1145 bri.li/1145 or irs.gov/retirement-plans/plan-participant-employee/retirement-topics-ira-contribution-limits

1146 bri.li/1146 or irs.gov/retirement-plans/amount-of-roth-ira-contributions-that-you-can-make-for-2017

1147 bri.li/1147 or www.kitces.com/blog/benefits-of-attending-college-signaling-theory-bryan-caplan-case-against-education/

1148 bri.li/1148 or www.kiplinger.com/article/college/T042-C001-S001-how-roth-iras-affect-financial-aid-eligibility.html

1149 bri.li/1149 or www.irs.gov/publications/p590b/ch02.html#en_US_2014_publink1000231057

1150 bri.li/1150 or MarottaOnMoney.com/fund-a-teenagers-million-dollar-retirement

1151 bri.li/1151 or awealthofcommonsense.com/2016/07/misconceptions-about-diversification/

1152 bri.li/1152 or books.google.com/books?id=UEIUAQAAMAAJ&dq=editions%3Avy9EGXfdb3sC&source=gbs_book_other_versions

1153 bri.li/1153 or en.wikipedia.org/wiki/Claude_Shannon

1154 bri.li/1154 or books.google.com/books?id=xz4y3u-qMO4C&pg=PA307&dq=%22William+Poundstone%22+%22Fortune%E2%80%99s+Formu
         la%22+%22Claude+Shannon%22+%22return+on+his+stock+portfolio%22&hl=en&sa=X&ved=0ahUKEwjm3cLzn6DWAhXH5IQKH
         bOKB3QQ6AEIJzAA#v=onepage&q=%22William%20Poundstone%22%20%22Fortune%E2%80%99s%20Formula%22%20%22Claude%20
         Shannon%22%20%22return%20on%20his%20stock%20portfolio%22&f=false

1155 bri.li/1155 or ssrn.com/abstract=983112

1156 bri.li/1156 or gestaltu.blogspot.com/2012/02/volatility-harvesting-and-importance-of.html

1157 bri.li/1157 or www.kitces.com/blog/wealth-limits-diversification-too-soon-concentration-redwood-bush-pear-tree/

1158 bri.li/1158 or www.theverge.com/2017/8/15/16148370/bill-gates-microsoft-shares-sale-2017

1159 bri.li/1159 or www.dualmomentum.net/2013/10/momentumthe-only-practical-anomaly.html

1160 bri.li/1160 or SSRN.com/abstract=911960

1161 bri.li/1161 or www.dualmomentum.net/2013/10/momentumthe-only-practical-anomaly.html

1162 bri.li/1162 or SSRN.com/abstract=2292544

1163 bri.li/1163 or systematicrelativestrength.com/2013/04/18/the-wonders-momentum/

1164 bri.li/1164 or books.google.com/books?id=nnG-CgAAQBAJ&pg=PA130&dq=10-asset-universe+54-percent+adam+butler&hl=en&sa=X&ved=0a
         hUKEwia2MPr5brWAhVLzFQKHX4DBEQQ6AEIJzAA#v=onepage&q=10-asset-universe%2054-percent%20adam%20butler&f=false

1165 bri.li/1165 or books.google.com/books?id=nnG-CgAAQBAJ&pg=PA130&dq=10-asset-universe+54-percent+adam+butler&hl=en&sa=X&ved=0a
         hUKEwia2MPr5brWAhVLzFQKHX4DBEQQ6AEIJzAA#v=onepage&q=10-asset-universe%2054-percent%20adam%20butler&f=false

1166 bri.li/1166 or www.researchaffiliates.com/en_us/publications/articles/541_timing_smart_beta_strategies_of_course_buy_low_sell_high.html

1167 bri.li/1167 or www.researchaffiliates.com/content/dam/ra/documents/Timing_Smart_Beta_Of_Course_Buy_Low_Sell_High_Final.pdf

1168 bri.li/1168 or ssrn.com/abstract=2503174

1169 bri.li/1169 or seekingalpha.com/article/2765385-individual-stock-momentum-that-dog-wont-hunt?page=2

1170 bri.li/1170 or docs.lhpedersen.com/DemystifyingManagedFutures.pdf

1171 bri.li/1171 or works.bepress.com/brooke_harrington/5/

1172 bri.li/1172 or www.snopes.com/quotes/jefferson/banks.asp

1173 bri.li/1173 or en.wikipedia.org/wiki/Financial_crisis_of_2007％E2％80％9308

1174 bri.li/1174 or www.newsweek.com/floridas-foreclosure-nightmare-269526

1175 bri.li/1175 or www.cbsnews.com/news/robo-signing-of-mortgages-still-a-problem

1176 bri.li/1176 or www.gpo.gov/fdsys/pkg/GPO-FCIC/pdf/GPO-FCIC.pdf

1177 bri.li/1177 or www.huffingtonpost.com/2013/11/07/william-dudley-big-banks_n_4235834.html

1178 bri.li/1178 or www.bloomberg.com/news/articles/2014-07-30/bofa-on-brink-of-burying-countrywide-woes-as-accord-near

1179 bri.li/1179 or www.bloomberg.com/news/articles/2012-02-09/u-s-mortgage-servicers-in-26b-settlement

1180 bri.li/1180 or www.bloomberg.com/news/articles/2015-05-22/ubs-s-godfather-of-leniency-made-one-offer-fraud-cops-refused

1181 bri.li/1181 or www.fhfa.gov/Media/PublicAffairs/Pages/FHFAs-Update-on-Private-Label-Securities-Actions-71217.aspx

1182 bri.li/1182 or www.housingwire.com/articles/36939-judge-approves-goldman-sachs-272-million-toxic-mortgage-settlement

1183 bri.li/1183 or www.justice.gov/opa/pr/bank-america-pay-1665-billion-historic-justice-department-settlement-financial-fraud-leading

1184 bri.li/1184or www.justice.gov/opa/pr/justice-department-federal-and-state-partners-secure-record-7-billion-global-settlement

1185 bri.li/1185 or www.justice.gov/opa/pr/credit-suisse-sentenced-conspiracy-help-us-taxpayers-hide-offshore-accounts-internal-revenue

1186 bri.li/1186 or www.justice.gov/opa/pr/justice-department-announces-deutsche-bank-suisse-sa-reaches-resolution-under-swiss-bank

1187 bri.li/1187 or www.justice.gov/opa/pr/goldman-sachs-agrees-pay-more-5-billion-connection-its-sale-residential-mortgage-backed

1188 bri.li/1188 or www.justice.gov/opa/pr/justice-department-federal-and-state-partners-secure-record-13-billion-global-settlement

1189 bri.li/1189 or www.justice.gov/opa/pr/morgan-stanley-agrees-pay-26-billion-penalty-connection-its-sale-residential-mortgage-backed

1190 bri.li/1190 or www.justice.gov/opa/pr/ubs-securities-japan-co-ltd-plead-guilty-felony-wire-fraud-long-running-manipulation-libor

1191 bri.li/1191 or www.justice.gov/opa/pr/wells-fargo-bank-agrees-pay-12-billion-improper-mortgage-lending-practices

1192 bri.li/1192 or www.justice.gov/opa/pr/us-trustee-program-reaches-816-million-settlement-wells-fargo-bank-na-protect-homeowners

1193 bri.li/1193 or www.nytimes.com/interactive/2015/04/23/business/dealbook/db-libor-timeline.html

1194 bri.li/1194 or www.sec.gov/spotlight/enf-actions-fc.shtml

1195 bri.li/1195 or economix.blogs.nytimes.com/2012/01/17/measuring-the-top-1-by-wealth-not-income/

1196 bri.li/1196 or www.barrons.com/articles/americas-top-40-wealth-management-firms-1506132481

1197 bri.li/1197 or www.barrons.com/articles/americas-top-40-wealth-management-firms-1506132481

1198 bri.li/1198 or online.wsj.com/public/resources/documents/Top40WealthManagementFirms2017.pdf

1199 bri.li/1199 or online.wsj.com/public/resources/documents/PentaTop40WealthManagersTable.pdf

1200 bri.li/1200 or www.amazon.com/The-Four-Pillars-Investing-Portfolio/dp/0071747052/ref=sr_1_1?ie=UTF8&qid=1405693100

1201 bri.li/1201 or www.amazon.com/The-Four-Pillars-Investing-Portfolio/dp/0071747052/ref=sr_1_1?ie=UTF8&qid=1405693100

1202 bri.li/1202 or www.efficientfrontier.com/t4poi/intro.htm

1203 bri.li/1203 or m.kiplinger.com/article/investing/T047-C000-S002-8-things-you-must-know-about-the-new-broker-rule.html

1204 bri.li/1204 or www.rollingstone.com/politics/news/the-great-american-bubble-machine-20100405

1205 bri.li/1205 or www.rollingstone.com/politics/news/the-great-american-bubble-machine-20100405

1206 bri.li/1206 or www.spiegel.de/international/europe/greek-debt-crisis-how-goldman-sachs-helped-greece-to-mask-its-true-debt-a-676634.html

1207 bri.li/1207 or www.businessinsider.com/goldman-sachs-shorted-greek-debt-after-it-arranged-those-shady-swaps-2010-2

1208 bri.li/1208 or www.businessinsider.com/the-incredible-story-of-the-jefferson-county-bankruptcy-one-of-the-greatest-financial-ripoffs-of-all-time-2011-10

1209 bri.li/1209 or www.rollingstone.com/politics/news/looting-main-street-20100331

1210 bri.li/1210 or www.rollingstone.com/politics/news/looting-main-street-20100331

1211 bri.li/1211 or www.sec.gov/news/press/2009/2009-232.htm

1212 bri.li/1212 or www.nytimes.com/2015/04/13/business/dealbook/wall-street-banks-mutual-funds-can-lag-on-returns.html

1213 bri.li/1213 or dealbook.nytimes.com/2014/09/08/brokers-battle-deutsche-bank-over-selling-in-house-products/

1214 bri.li/1214 or www.nytimes.com/2015/04/13/business/dealbook/wall-street-banks-mutual-funds-can-lag-on-returns.html

1215 bri.li/1215 or www.nytimes.com/2015/04/13/business/dealbook/wall-street-banks-mutual-funds-can-lag-on-returns.html

1216 bri.li/1216 or isbn.nu/9780061241895

1217 bri.li/1217 or www.linkedin.com/pulse/5-disruptive-ideas-advisors-adam-butler

1218 bri.li/1218 or www.barrons.com/articles/SB51367578116875004693704580480471482826474

1219 bri.li/1219 or www.nytimes.com/2014/11/20/science/bankers-honesty-study-nature.html

1220 bri.li/1220 or www.econ.uzh.ch/dam/jcr:ffffffff-9758-127f-0000-0000327a03c6/SummaryStudyE.pdf

1221 bri.li/1221 or www.wsj.com/articles/why-i-fired-my-financial-adviser-1409323717

1222 bri.li/1222 or www.nytimes.com/interactive/2016/05/29/business/how-much-ceos-made-last-year.html

1223 bri.li/1223 or www.forbes.com/sites/zackomalleygreenburg/2016/07/13/full-list-the-worlds-highest-paid-celebrities-of-2016/

1224 bri.li/1224 or www.ibtimes.com/what-carried-interest-tax-loophole-2100059

1225 bri.li/1225 or www.marketwatch.com/story/how-hedge-fund-geniuses-got-beaten-by-monkeys-again-2015-06-25/print

1226 bri.li/1226 or www.mebfaber.com/wp-content/uploads/2009/02/wir-winter-2009-february.pdf

1227 bri.li/1227 or ssrn.com/abstract=1354070

1228 bri.li/1228 or www.institutionalinvestorsalpha.com/Article/3552805/The-2016-Rich-List-of-the-Worlds-Top-Earning-Hedge-Fund-Managers.html

1229 bri.li/1229 or visualizingeconomics.com

1230 bri.li/1230 or www.nytimes.com/2016/06/04/business/dealbook/finra-arbitration-case-offers-a-peek-into-a-murky-world.html

1231 bri.li/1231 or wealthmanagement.com/commentary/streamlined-finra-arbitration-system-are-you-kidding-me

1232 bri.li/1232 or www.arbitrationnation.com/when-can-a-party-recover-attorneys-fees-incurred-confirming-an-arbitration-award/

1233 bri.li/1233 or www.financial-planning.com/broker/fp-50-broker-dealer-data

1234 bri.li/1234 or www.justice.gov/usao-wdnc/pr/stockbroker-pleads-guilty-securities-fraud-operating-14-million-ponzi-scheme

1235 bri.li/1236 or www.bizjournals.com/triad/news/2016/07/08/local-criminal-defense-attorney-has-license.html

1236 bri.li/1235 or www.finra.org/arbitration-and-mediation/arbitration-awards-online?keyword=15-01288

1237 bri.li/1237 or www.finra.org/arbitration-and-mediation/arbitration-awards-online?keyword=04-07012

1238 bri.li/1238 or www.finra.org/arbitration-and-mediation/arbitration-awards-online?search=09-00992&field_document_type_tax_tid=All&field_
       forum_tax_tid=All&field_core_official_dt_value%5Bmin%5D%5Bdate%5D=&field_core_official_dt_value%5Bmax%5D%5Bdate%5D=&
       field_case_id_txt_value=

1239 bri.li/1239 or www.finra.org/arbitration-and-mediation/arbitration-awards-online?keyword=11-01425

1240 bri.li/1240 or www.investmentnews.com/article/20160122/FREE/160129972/attorney-schlichter-preps-new-round-of-401-k-suits

1241 bri.li/1241 or www.barnesandnoble.com/w/a-fool-and-his-money-john-rothchild/1003033750

1242 bri.li/1242 or archive.fortune.com/magazines/fortune/fortune_archive/2007/07/23/100134937/index.htm

1243 bri.li/1243 or www.nber.org/cycles.html

1244 bri.li/1244 or us.spindices.com/documents/spiva/persistence-scorecard-june-2014.pdf?force_download=true

1245 bri.li/1245 or www.nytimes.com/2014/07/20/your-money/who-routinely-trounces-the-stock-market-try-2-out-of-2862-funds.html

1246 bri.li/1246 or finance.yahoo.com/news/why-this-mutual-fund-manager-is-trouncing-the-competition-152643576.html

1247 bri.li/1247 or us.spindices.com/documents/spiva/persistence-scorecard-june-2014.pdf?force_download=true

1248 bri.li/1248 or www.nytimes.com/2015/03/15/your-money/how-many-mutual-funds-routinely-rout-the-market-zero.html

1249 bri.li/1249 or bloomberg.com/news/articles/2017-11-24/longest-s-p-500-rally-ever-it-s-wall-street-s-official-forecast

1250 bri.li/1250 or fool.com/investing/general/2015/02/25/the-blind-forecaster.aspx

1251 bri.li/1251 or insightalliance.com/articles/1352-the-realistic-response-to-expert-optimists

1252 bri.li/1252 or online.wsj.com/articles/for-s-p-strategists-forecasts-fall-short-1406486263

1253 bri.li/1253 or gestaltu.blogspot.com/2009/09/statistics-of-prediction.html

1254 bri.li/1254 or blogs.wsj.com/economics/2008/12/01/nber-makes-it-official-recession-started-in-december-2007/

1255 bri.li/1255 or en.wikipedia.org/wiki/Bear_Stearns#Start_of_the_crisis_%E2%80%93_two_subprime_mortgage_funds_fail

1256 bri.li/1256 or www.awordinyoureye.com/jokes6thset.html

1257 bri.li/1257 or www.investorhome.com/quotes/qow234.htm

1258 bri.li/1258 or www.scribd.com/doc/162606509/Kitces-Report-May-2008

1259 bri.li/1259 or corporate.morningstar.com/us/documents/targetmaturity/LowBondYieldsWithdrawalRates.pdf

1260 bri.li/1260 or portfolioconstructionforum.edu.au/obj/articles/Investing%20in%20the%201990s%200ccams%20Razor%20Revisited.pdf

1261 bri.li/1261 or jpm.iijournals.com/content/42/1/119

1262 bri.li/1262 or cnbc.com/2017/03/22/jack-bogle-believes-the-stock-market-will-return-only-4-annually-over-the-next-decade.html

1263 bri.li/1263 or jpm.iijournals.com/content/42/1/119

1264 bri.li/1264 or ssrn.com/abstract=2222008

1265 bri.li/1265 or www.hussmanfunds.com/comment/mc180201/

1266 bri.li/1266 or philosophicaleconomics.com/2013/12/shiller

1267 bri.li/1267 or en.wikipedia.org/wiki/Tobin%27s_q

1268 bri.li/1268 or cowles.yale.edu/cfdp-427

1269 bri.li/1269 or www.advisorperspectives.com/dshort/updates/Market-Cap-to-GDP.php

1270 bri.li/1270 or ssrn.com/abstract=2222008

1271 bri.li/1271 or books.google.com/books?id=VSTIAAAAQBAJ&pg=PA99&lpg=PA99&dq=being+without+an+opinion+is+so+painful+to+human+
nature+that+most+people+will+leap+to+a+hasty+opinion+rather+than+undergo+it&source=bl&ots=YMp-8i7dFA&sig=kNYRz
11jU1oozdETGrKeCOT4kWs&hl=en&sa=X&ved=0CC8Q6AEwA2oVChMIlvnAhqHhxgIVCVyIChOAYgfx#v=snippet&q=%22being%20with
out%20an%20opinion%20is%20so%20painful%20to%20human%20nature%20that%20most%20people%20will%20leap%20to%20a%20
hasty%20opinion%20rather%20than%20undergo%20it%22&f=false

1272 bri.li/1272 or www.wellcome.ac.uk/News/Media-office/Press-releases/2010/WTX058430.htm

1273 bri.li/1273 or ssrn.com/abstract=2444503

1274 bri.li/1274 or www-03.ibm.com/ibm/history/ibm100/us/en/icons/deepblue/

1275 bri.li/1275 or www.techrepublic.com/article/ibm-watson-the-inside-story-of-how-the-jeopardy-winning-supercomputer-was-born-and-what-it-
wants-to-do-next/

1276 bri.li/1276 or www.cxoadvisory.com/2122/individual-investing/actual-index-options-trading-results/

1277 bri.li/1277 or advisorperspectives.com/commentaries/2013/12/16/absolute-return-letter-squeaky-bum-time

1278 bri.li/1278 or books.google.com/books?id=9juFAwAAQBAJ&pg=PA39&dq=%22on+flinching%22+%22thick+glass-plate%22&hl=en&sa=X&ei=y
3siVOSOMoO7ogSmkICIBw&ved=0CDIQ6AEwAA#v=onepage&q=%22on%20flinching%22%20%22thick%20glass-plate%22&f=false

1279 bri.li/1279 or blogs.psychcentral.com/mentoring-recovery/2013/08/yes-your-survival-instinct-is-stronger-than-you-are/

1280 bri.li/1280 or en.wikipedia.org/wiki/Stanford_marshmallow_experiment

1281 bri.li/1281 or csinvesting.org/2012/01/28/greenblatt-discusses-magic-formula-and-the-psychology-of-investing/

1282 bri.li/1282 or GothamAssetManagement.com/Documents/Brochure.pdf

1283 bri.li/1283 or csinvesting.org/wp-content/uploads/2012/09/greenbackd-case-for-quantitative-value-eyquem-global-strategy.pdf

1284 bri.li/1284 or pdfs.semanticscholar.org/f022/58c85fa3a1d612543e350568c50e749ebbca.pdf

1285 bri.li/1285 or jasonkelly.com/books/3sig/

1286 bri.li/1286 or en.wikipedia.org/wiki/Tragedy_of_the_commons

1287 bri.li/1287 or ssrn.com/abstract=2484322

1288 bri.li/1288 or thebamalliance.com/blog/bollinger-band-blues-another-anomaly-disappears-post-publication/

1289 bri.li/1289 or ssrn.com/abstract=281665

1290 bri.li/1290 or ssrn.com/abstract=283156

1291 bri.li/1291 or ncbi.nlm.nih.gov/pmc/articles/PMC1444800/

1292 bri.li/1292 or ritholtz.com/2015/04/margin-debt-hits-an-all-time-high-so-what/

1293 bri.li/1293 or czep.net/weblog/52cards.html

1294 bri.li/1294 or www.cxoadvisory.com/3873/calendar-effects/sell-in-may-over-the-long-run/

1295 bri.li/1295 or books.google.com/books?id=jbD47VkOHAEC&printsec=frontcover&dq=%22evidence-based+technical+analysis%22&hl=en&sa=X&ved
=0ahUKEwiL8Y6KyIPNAhVR9WMKHQzoBykQ6AEIHTAA#v=onepage&q=%22evidence-based%20technical%20analysis%22&f=false

1296 bri.li/1296 or books.google.com/books?id=jbD47VkOHAEC&pg=PT339&dq=%22an+enhanced+version+of+white%27s+reality+check%22+%22mon
te+carlo+permutation+method%22&hl=en&sa=X&ved=0ahUKEwi7hvyux4PNAhUS22MKHSpKCiUQ6AEIHTAA#v=onepage&q=%22an%20
enhanced%20version%20of%20white%27s%20reality%20check%22%20%22monte%20carlo%20permutation%20method%22&f=false

1297 bri.li/1297 or books.google.com/books?id=jbD47VkOHAEC&pg=PT383&dq=%22the+best+rule+out+of+the+6,402+examined%22&hl=en&sa=X
&ved=0ahUKEwjXpPKWxIPNAhUP7GMKHdqTCsMQ6AEIHTAA#v=onepage&q=%22the%20best%20rule%20out%20of%20the%20
6%2C402%20examined%22&f=false

1298 bri.li/1298 or jfec.oxfordjournals.org/content/3/4/606.short

1299 bri.li/1299 or books.google.com/books?id=jbD47VkOHAEC&pg=PT390&dq=%22none+of+the+rules+produced+statistically+significant+gains%22
&hl=en&sa=X&ved=0ahUKEwjDxfakzYPNAhVRyWMKHYpXALUQ6AEIHTAA#v=onepage&q=%22none%20of%20the%20rules%20pro
duced%20statistically%20significant%20gains%22&f=false

1300 bri.li/1300 or books.google.com/books?id=jbD47VkOHAEC&pg=PT18&dq=%22trends+in+industry+groups+and+sectors%22&hl=en&sa=X
&ved=0ahUKEwjA-a7xzoPNAhVCMGMKHe_hAEYQ6AEIJjAA#v=onepage&q=%22trends%20in%20industry%20groups%20and%20
sectors%22&f=false

1301 bri.li/1301 or thereformedbroker.com/2016/08/30/everyone-is-a-closet-technician-2/

1302 bri.li/1302 or webcache.googleusercontent.com/search?q=cache:gXb2-qulr1UJ:https://www.quirky.com/
forumstopic/35557%3Fpage%3D3D3&hl=en&gl=us&strip=1&vwsrc=0

1303 bri.li/1303 or www-03.ibm.com/ibm/history/ibm100/us/en/icons/deepblue

1304 bri.li/1304 or techrepublic.com/article/ibm-watson-the-inside-story-of-how-the-jeopardy-winning-supercomputer-was-born-and-what-it-wants-
to-do-next/

1305 bri.li/1305 or cxoadvisory.com/2122/individual-investing/actual-index-options-trading-results/

1306 bri.li/1306 or online.wsj.com/articles/look-whos-beating-the-market-1403888067

1307 bri.li/1307 or pressroom.vanguard.com/nonindexed/7.5.2013_The_bumpy_road_to_outperformance.pdf

1308 bri.li/1308 or jasonzweig.com/fee-only-financial-advisers-who-dont-charge-fees-alone/

1309 bri.li/1309 or jasonzweig.com/some-fee-only-advisers-charge-commissions-too/

1310 bri.li/1310 or www.cfp.net/news-events/latest-news/2017/10/12/cfp-board-imposes-public-discipline

1311 bri.li/1311 or books.google.com/books?id=aeCEAAAAQBAJ&pg=PA190&dq=get+wise+to+your+advisor&hl=en&sa=X&ei=Y_JBVNKyK8etogSUhIHYCQ&ved=0CCgQ6AEwAA#v=onepage&q=mind-numbing%20legalese&f=false

1312 bri.li/1312 or books.google.com/books?id=WVe3b1DFLoMC&pg=PA129&lpg=PA129&f=false#v=onepage&q&f=false

1313 bri.li/1313 or www.fool.com/investing/mutual-funds/2010/10/18/its-time-to-take-back-your-10-billion.aspx

1314 bri.li/1314 or barrons.com/articles/schwabs-robo-service-grabbed-5-3-billion-in-first-year-1452118508

1315 bri.li/1315 or investorjunkie.com/39634/schwab-intelligent-portfolios-review/

1316 bri.li/1316 or www.etf.com/sections/features-and-news/td-ameritrade-drops-major-no-fee-etfs?nopaging=1

1317 bri.li/1317 or barrons.com/articles/why-direct-sold-mutual-funds-often-beat-those-peddled-by-advisors-1428719781

1318 bri.li/1318 or invest.ameritrade.com/grid/p/site#r=jPage/https://research.ameritrade.com/grid/wwws/etfs/commissionfree/commissionfree.asp?YYY600_4TasO+9+jFjDGVndajH8hGRpR1jqHraXrOU2hFcCywh47RBav/zTk2P1QeqaQjff8AGld92gnlj5GLLp790fPjWrQN86V9Eq&c_name=invest_VENDOR

1319 bri.li/1319 or invesco.com/portal/site/us/financial-professional/etfs/product-detail?productId=PDBC

1320 bri.li/1320 or www.barrons.com/articles/interactive-brokers-takes-top-spot-in-online-broker-ranking-1521854071

1321 bri.li/1321 or cnbc.com/id/47358931

1322 bri.li/1322 or www.chegg.com/homework-help/interactive-session-organizationsthe-flash-crash-machines-go-chapter-11.4iso-problem-2csq-solution-9780132142854-exc

1323 bri.li/1323 or www.google.com/url?sa=t&rct=j&q=&esrc=s&source=web&cd=7&ved=0ahUKEwixocKE_rPYAhVH3WMKHSgcAa4QFghMMAY&url=http%3A%2F%2Fwww.barrons.com%2Farticles%2Fthe-great-etf-debacle-explained-1441434195&usg=AOvVaw2EnAmc2ozeUC6LTR4T2jQE

1324 bri.li/1324 or eepurl.com/cjSYNb

1325 bri.li/1325 or awealthofcommonsense.com/market-earthquakes/

1326 bri.li/1326 or www.vanguard.com/pdf/icrpr.pdf

1327 bri.li/1327 or resource.fpanet.org/resource/09BBF2F9-D5B3-9B76-B02E27EB8731C337/daryanani.pdf

1328 bri.li/1328 or www.cxoadvisory.com/momentum-strategy (paid registration required)

1329 bri.li/1329 or twitter.com/biiimurray/status/447851038696275968

1330 bri.li/1330 or en.wikipedia.org/wiki/Death_%26_Taxes

1331 bri.li/1331 or issuu.com/einfohq/docs/money_usa__december_2017_einfohq (Page 27)

1332 bri.li/1332 or finance.zacks.com/roth-ira-law-created-6969.html

1333 bri.li/1333 or www.kitces.com/blog/understanding-the-two-5-year-rules-for-roth-ira-contributions-and-conversions

1334 bri.li/1334 or www.kitces.com/to-roth-or-not-to-roth-may-2009-issue-of-the-kitces-report

1335 bri.li/1335 or www.forbes.com/sites/deborahljacobs/2012/03/20/how-facebook-billionaires-dodge-mega-millions-in-taxes/

1336 bri.li/1336 or www.washingtonpost.com/blogs/worldviews/wp/2015/02/11/chart-u-s-defense-spending-still-dwarfs-the-rest-of-the-world

1337 bri.li/1337 or prosperitynow.org/sites/default/files/resources/Upside_Down_to_Right-Side_Up_2014.pdf

1338 bri.li/1338 or www.taxpolicycenter.org/UploadedPDF/1001542-Spending-In-Disguise-Marron.pdf

1339 bri.li/1339 or prosperitynow.org/sites/default/files/resources/Upside_Down_to_Right-Side_Up_2014.pdf

1340 bri.li/1340 or prosperitynow.org/sites/default/files/resources/Upside_Down_to_Right-Side_Up_2014.pdf

1341 bri.li/1341 or www.nytimes.com/2015/03/18/business/economy/taxes-take-away-but-also-give-back-mostly-to-the-very-rich.html

1342 bri.li/1342 or taxfoundation.org/2018-tax-brackets/

1343 bri.li/1343 or www.irs.gov/Individuals/Net-Investment-Income-Tax

1344 bri.li/1344 or jobsearch.about.com/od/increase/fl/minimum-wage-rates-2015.htm

1345 bri.li/1345 or www.savingtoinvest.com/2015-tax-brackets-projected-changes/

1346 bri.li/1346 or www.taxcreditsforworkingfamilies.org/child-tax-credit/

1347 bri.li/1347 or www.linkedin.com/in/denise-olivier-6028812

1348 bri.li/1348 or 20somethingfinance.com/savers-tax-credit/

1349 bri.li/1349 or www.irs.gov/retirement-plans/plan-participant-employee/retirement-savings-contributions-savers-credit

1350 bri.li/1350 or www.irs.gov/Retirement-Plans/Plan-Participant,-Employee/Retirement-Topics-IRA-Contribution-Limits

1351 bri.li/1351 or www.irs.gov/Retirement-Plans/Plan-Participant,-Employee/Retirement-Topics-What-Happens-When-an-Employee-has-Elective-Deferrals-in-Excess-of-the-Limits%3F

1352 bri.li/1352 or sepira.com/calculator.html

1353 bri.li/1353 or www.ebri.org/publications/benfaq/index.cfm?fa=retfaq14
1354 bri.li/1354 or www.dol.gov/agencies/ebsa/employers-and-advisers/plan-administration-and-compliance/reporting-and-filing/e-file/tophat-plan-
          filing-instructions
1355 bri.li/1355 or www.irs.gov/pub/irs-tege/eotopicm97.pdf
1356 bri.li/1356 or www.savingforcollege.com/compare_529_plans/
1357 bri.li/1357 or www.collegesavings.org/planComparison.aspx
1358 bri.li/1358 or www.fidelity.com/saving-for-college/compare-plans
1359 bri.li/1359 or www.ablenrc.org
1360 bri.li/1360 or www.irs.gov/retirement-plans/rmd-comparison-chart-iras-vs-defined-contribution-plans
1361 bri.li/1361 or www.aaii.com/journal/article/converting-to-a-roth-ira-can-minimize-rmds
1362 bri.li/1362 or www.aaii.com/journal/article/converting-to-a-roth-ira-can-minimize-rmds
1363 bri.li/1363 or https://www.betterment.com/resources/retirement/401ks-and-iras/roth-ira-rules-smart-ways-to-avoid-taxes-on-a-conversion
1364 bri.li/1364 or www.forbes.com/sites/kellyphillipserb/2014/10/30/irs-announces-2015-tax-brackets-standard-deduction-amounts-and-more/
1365 bri.li/1365 or https://www.betterment.com/resources/retirement/401ks-and-iras/roth-ira-rules-smart-ways-to-avoid-taxes-on-a-conversion
1366 bri.li/1366 or www.demos.org/publication/retirement-savings-drain-hidden-excessive-costs-401ks
1367 bri.li/1367 or www.aon.com/human-capital-consulting/thought-leadership/retirement/2013_Trends_Experience_DC_Survey.jsp
1368 bri.li/1368 or www.demos.org/publication/retirement-savings-drain-hidden-excessive-costs-401ks
1369 bri.li/1369 or money.usnews.com/money/retirement/articles/2011/07/11/7-signs-of-a-good-401k-plan?page=2
1370 bri.li/1370 or www.brightscope.com/401k-rating/43642/United-Parcel-Service-Inc/473079/Upsipa-Defined-Contribution-Money-Purchase-Pension-Plan/
1371 bri.li/1371 or www.nytimes.com/2014/03/30/business/a-lone-ranger-of-the-401-k-s.html
1372 bri.li/1372 or blogs.wsj.com/totalreturn/2015/03/26/another-suit-on-401k-fees-is-settled/
1373 bri.li/1373 or consumerreports.org/cro/magazine/2013/09/how-to-grow-your-savings/index.htm
1374 bri.li/1374 or en.wikipedia.org/wiki/Federal_government_of_the_United_States
1375 bri.li/1375 or www.myplaniq.com/LTISystem/f401k_view.action?ID=708
1376 bri.li/1376 or myplaniq.com/LTISystem/jsp/portfolio/ViewPortfolio.action?ID=23749&follow=true
1377 bri.li/1377 or myplaniq.com/LTISystem/paypal__pricing.action
1378 bri.li/1378 or www.vanguard.com/pdf/ISGIRA9.pdf
1379 bri.li/1379 or www.physicianonfire.com/backdoor/
1380 bri.li/1380 or www.madfientist.com/after-tax-contributions/
1381 bri.li/1381 or thefinancebuff.com/rollover-after-tax-to-roth.html
1382 bri.li/1382 or thefinancebuff.com/after-tax-contributions-in-solo-401k.html
1383 bri.li/1383 or fairmark.com/retirement/roth-accounts/roth-conversions/isolating-basis-for-roth-conversion/
1384 bri.li/1384 or frankadvising.com/wp-content/uploads/2014/10/How-to-Implement-Investment-Location-to-Generate-Alpha-SPDR.pdf
1385 bri.li/1385 or www.onefpa.org/journal/Pages/AUG17-A-3-Step-Procedure-for-Computing-Sustainable-Retirement-Savings-Withdrawals.aspx
1386 bri.li/1386 or i-orp.com/dividend/index.html
1387 bri.li/1387 or www.forbes.com/sites/ashleaebeling/2017/12/21/final-tax-bill-includes-huge-estate-tax-win-for-the-rich-the-22-4-million-exemption/
1388 bri.li/1388 or www.kiplinger.com/article/taxes/T055-C001-S003-how-to-minimize-taxes-when-you-inherit-an-ira.html
1389 bri.li/1389 or www.kitces.com/blog/evaluating-the-tax-deferral-and-tax-bracket-arbitrage-benefits-of-tax-loss-harvesting
1390 bri.li/1390 or www.kitces.com/blog/wealthfront-tax-loss-harvesting-white-paper-how-not-to-calculate-tax-alpha
1391 bri.li/1391 or www.kitces.com/blog/the-taxation-of-social-security-benefits-as-a-marginal-tax-rate-increase
1392 bri.li/1392 or www.kitces.com/blog/how-ira-withdrawals-in-the-crossover-zone-can-trigger-the-3-8-medicare-surtax-on-net-investment-income
1393 bri.li/1393 or www.kitces.com/blog/how-the-premium-assistance-tax-credit-for-health-insurance-impacts-the-marginal-tax-rate
1394 bri.li/1394 or www.kitces.com/blog/evaluating-exposure-to-the-alternative-minimum-tax-and-strategies-to-reduce-the-amt-bite
1395 bri.li/1395 or www.kiplinger.com/article/retirement/T039-C001-S003-what-you-ll-pay-for-medicare-in-2015.html
1396 bri.li/1396 or www.houselogic.com/home-advice/taxes-incentives/property-tax-exemptions
1397 bri.li/1397 or www.forbes.com/sites/deborahljacobs/2012/03/26/why-and-how-congress-should-curb-roth-iras/
1398 bri.li/1398 or www.wsj.com/articles/SB10001424052970204468004577168972507188592
1399 bri.li/1399 or www.businesswire.com/news/home/20120120005824/en/PENSCO-Presidential-Candidate-Mitt-Romney-Tax-Deferred-Account
1400 bri.li/1400 or selfdirectedira.nuwireinvestor.com/list-of-self-directed-ira-custodians/
1401 bri.li/1401 or www.forbes.com/sites/deborahljacobs/2012/03/20/how-facebook-billionaires-dodge-mega-millions-in-taxes/
1402 bri.li/1402 or www.foxbusiness.com/features/interested-in-a-self-directed-ira-you-better-know-your-stuff

1403 bri.li/1403 or www.marketwatch.com/story/self-directed-iras-risky-smart-or-both-2013-05-27

1404 bri.li/1404 or www.fool.com/investing/ira/2009/01/08/why-you-need-a-self-directed-ira.aspx

1405 bri.li/1405 or books.google.com/books?id=V6JYAAAMAAJ&pg=PA2&lpg=PA2&dq=bagehot+%22stupid+money%22+%22stupid+people%22&source=bl&ots=frZRe78tRd&sig=OGBZf1OC65JrJcmlXU4KKg6i4GM&hl=en&ei=52ykTs6TAoq6tgfyw6iWBQ&sa=X&oi=book_result&ct=result&resnum=2&ved=0CCEQ6AEwAQ#v=onepage&q&f=false

1406 bri.li/1406 or www.kitces.com/blog/advisor-fintech-product-distribution-channel-robo-advisor-model-marketplace/

1407 bri.li/1407 or www.investmentnews.com/article/20160509/FREE/160509928/startup-robo-advisers-grapple-with-client-acquisition-costs

1408 bri.li/1408 or fsc.org.nz/site/fsc/files/FAAR%202015/Morningstar%20-%20Hungry%20Robo-Advisors%20Are%20Eyeing%20Wealth%20Management%20Assets%20We....pdf

1409 bri.li/1409 or www.cnbc.com/2016/06/14/is-the-twilight-of-the-robo-advisor-already-at-hand.html

1410 bri.li/1410 or research.wealthfront.com/whitepapers/advanced-indexing/#7-back-tested-results

1411 bri.li/1411 or www.roboadvisorpros.com/november-2017-robo-advisor-news-vanguard-biggest-robo/

1412 bri.li/1412 or www.marketwatch.com/story/heres-the-advice-you-get-from-vanguards-new-robot-human-hybrid-2015-05-18

1413 bri.li/1413 or books.google.com/books?id=UcIkAwAAQBAJ&printsec=frontcover&dq=flash+boys&hl=en&sa=X&ei=Xz8QVLPYGKiEjALMt4DoAw&ved=0CDgQ6AEwAA#v=snippet&q=flash%20boys%20%24225%20billion&f=false

1414 bri.li/1414 or books.google.com/books?id=UcIkAwAAQBAJ&printsec=frontcover&dq=flash+boys&hl=en&sa=X&ei=Xz8QVLPYGKiEjALMt4DoAw&ved=0CDgQ6AEwAA#v=snippet&q=flash%20boys%2030%20percent&f=false

1415 bri.li/1415 or www.businessinsider.com/the-fastest-traders-on-wall-street-are-in-trouble-2017-8

1416 bri.li/1416 or www.middletonco.com/cutting-through-the-noise/

1417 bri.li/1417 or www.wsj.com/articles/retiring-in-2065-are-far-off-target-date-funds-worthwhile-1502539200

1418 bri.li/1418 or www.wsj.com/articles/retiring-in-2065-are-far-off-target-date-funds-worthwhile-1502539200

1419 bri.li/1419 or www.towerswatson.com/en/Insights/IC-Types/Ad-hoc-Point-of-View/2013/08/Understanding-smart-beta

1420 bri.li/1420 or www.etf.com/sections/features/19816-ferri-vs-arnott-is-smart-beta-real.html?nopaging=1

1421 bri.li/1421 or www.thenatureofmarkets.com/why-forex-traders-lose-money-market-research-2017/

1422 bri.li/1422 or https://financefeeds.com/ibfx-banned-us-market-detailed-look-nfas-reasons/

1423 bri.li/1423 or www.forbes.com/sites/greatspeculations/2017/03/01/learn-why-the-nfa-barred-fxcm-and-what-it-means-for-forex-traders/

1424 bri.li/1424 or www.followingthetrend.com/2014/01/etfs-are-not-what-you-think-they-are/

1425 bri.li/1425 or jamesetf.com

1426 bri.li/1426 or insightshares.com/prid/

1427 bri.li/1427 or www.forbes.com/sites/jeffkauflin/2017/12/06/portfolio-placebos/#6b837e44c045

1428 bri.li/1428 or etfdb.com/type/investment-style/socially-responsible/?search[inverse]=false&search[leveraged]=false#etfs__expenses&sort_name=expense_ratio&sort_order=desc&page=1

1429 bri.li/1429 or en.wikipedia.org/wiki/Interfaith_Center_on_Corporate_Responsibility

1430 bri.li/1430 or en.wikipedia.org/wiki/As_You_Sow

1431 bri.li/1431 or en.wikipedia.org/wiki/Ceres_(organization)

1432 bri.li/1432 or personal.vanguard.com/pdf/ISGDCA.pdf

1433 bri.li/1433 or personal.vanguard.com/pdf/ISGDCA.pdf

1434 bri.li/1434 or www.dallasnews.com/business/columnists/scott-burns/20150502-tax-takes-toll-on-middle-income-social-security-recipients.ece

1435 bri.li/1435 or www.dallasnews.com/business/columnists/scott-burns/20150502-tax-takes-toll-on-middle-income-social-security-recipients.ece

1436 bri.li/1436 or medicare.gov/your-medicare-costs/part-b-costs/part-b-costs.html

1437 bri.li/1437 or kitces.com/blog/required-minimum-distribution-rmd-calculation-tax-rules-ira-401k-403b/

1438 bri.li/1438 or kitces.com/blog/minimize-delay-required-minimum-distribution-rmd-mandatory-withdrawal-obligations

1439 bri.li/1439 or www.irs.gov/uac/About-Publication-915

1440 bri.li/1440 or www.irs.gov/pub/irs-pdf/p590b.pdf

1441 bri.li/1441 or individual.troweprice.com/public/Retail/Retirement/Required-Minimum-Distributions/Calculate-My-RMD

1442 bri.li/1442 or www.ssa.gov/oact/cola/examplemax.html

1443 bri.li/1443 or seekingalpha.com/article/4142059-december-2017-median-household-income

1444 bri.li/1444 or www.ssa.gov/policy/docs/quickfacts/stat_snapshot/

1445 bri.li/1445 or www.irs.gov/uac/About-Publication-915

1446 bri.li/1446 or www.irs.gov/pub/irs-pdf/p590b.pdf

1447 bri.li/1447 or www.calcxml.com/calculators/how-much-of-my-social-security-benefit-may-be-taxed

1448 bri.li/1448 or www.kiplinger.com/article/retirement/T051-C000-S001-which-states-tax-social-security.html

1449 bri.li/1449 or books.google.com/books?id=KPsdDAAAQBAJ&printsec=frontcover&dq=The+Art+of+Trading&hl=en&sa=X&ved=0ahUKEwid3NDnx
czNAhVL1GMKHbbsDIoQ6AEIODAE#v=onepage&q=The%20elements%20of%20good%20trading%20are%20cutting%20losses&f=false

1450 bri.li/1450 or kitces.com/blog/how-has-the-4-rule-held-up-since-the-tech-bubble-and-the-2008-financial-crisis/

1451 bri.li/1451 or www.kitces.com/march-2012-issue-of-the-kitces-report-expanding-the-framework-of-safe-withdrawal-rates/

1452 bri.li/1452 or www.kitces.com/march-2012-issue-of-the-kitces-report-expanding-the-framework-of-safe-withdrawal-rates/

1453 bri.li/1453 or www.kitces.com/march-2012-issue-of-the-kitces-report-expanding-the-framework-of-safe-withdrawal-rates/

1454 bri.li/1454 or www.kitces.com/march-2012-issue-of-the-kitces-report-expanding-the-framework-of-safe-withdrawal-rates/

1455 bri.li/1455 or www.kitces.com/march-2012-issue-of-the-kitces-report-expanding-the-framework-of-safe-withdrawal-rates/

1456 bri.li/1456 or projectmagma.net/~melekor/uploads/AAA/Adaptive%20Asset%20Allocation%20A%20Primer.pdf

1457 bri.li/1457 or www.kitces.com/march-2012-issue-of-the-kitces-report-expanding-the-framework-of-safe-withdrawal-rates/

1458 bri.li/1458 or www.retailinvestor.org/pdf/Bengen1.pdf

1459 bri.li/1459 or www.bls.gov/opub/reports/consumer-expenditures/2015/home.htm

1460 bri.li/1460 or www.brainyquote.com/quotes/quotes/p/peterdevri106585.html

1461 bri.li/1461 or www.thornburg.com/pdf/TH1858_LadderVsBarbell.pdf

1462 bri.li/1462 or www.marketwatch.com/story/heres-the-income-portfolio-you-want-to-own-when-interest-rates-rise-2015-02-20/print

1463 bri.li/1463 or am.jpmorgan.com/us/en/asset-management/gim/adv/insights/guide-to-the-markets/viewer

1464 bri.li/1464 or www.nytimes.com/2015/04/12/business/mutfund/questioning-the-seaworthiness-of-bond-funds.html?_r=0

1465 bri.li/1465 or www.invesco.com/portal/site/us/investors/etfs/strategies/bulletshares/#tab_tab3-products

1466 bri.li/1466 or www.ishares.com/us/products/etf-product-list#!type=ishares&tab=yields&view=list&fst=50587

1467 bri.li/1467 or www.invesco.com/portal/site/us/investors/etfs/strategies/bulletshares/#tab_tab3-products

1468 bri.li/1468 or www.ishares.com/us/products/etf-product-list#!type=ishares&tab=yields&view=list&fst=50587

1469 bri.li/1469 or www.standardandpoors.com/en_US/web/guest/article/-/view/sourceId/504352#ID545

1470 bri.li/1470 or siepr.stanford.edu/sites/default/files/publications/17-048.pdf

1471 bri.li/1471 or www.nact.org/resources/2014_SP_Global_Corporate_Default_Study.pdf

1472 bri.li/1472 or www.nact.org/resources/2014_SP_Global_Corporate_Default_Study.pdf

1473 bri.li/1473 or www.jstor.org/discover/10.2307/745492?uid=2129&uid=2&uid=70&uid=4&sid=21104218662901

1474 bri.li/1474 or books.google.com/books?id=JS9HpSYncTMC&pg=PA14&lpg=PA14&dq=soros+%22market+prices+are+always+wrong%22&sou
rce=bl&ots=DSBb84TQCp&sig=3x5Xq-atKR9gAeyv5aNLo8NPQyE&hl=en&sa=X&ei=krBcVffAEIXKsAXw5YLoCA&ved=0CDMQ6A
EwAw#v=onepage&q=soros%20%22market%20prices%20are%20always%20wrong%22

1475 bri.li/1475 or www.ncbi.nlm.nih.gov/pmc/articles/PMC2917363/

1476 bri.li/1476 or www.economist.com/blogs/babbage/2012/11/qa-samuel-arbesman

1477 bri.li/1477 or books.google.com/books?id=nXho71uvKBsC&printsec=frontcover&dq=%22half-life+of+facts%22&hl=en&sa=X&ved=0CCsQ6AEwA
GoVChMI44DLlvOGyQIVSNRjCh0avQP8#v=onepage&q=It%20takes%2050%20years%20to%20get%20a%20wrong%20idea%20out%20
of%20medicine&f=false

1478 bri.li/1478 or skepdic.com/zombieidea.html

1479 bri.li/1479 or www.economist.com/blogs/babbage/2012/11/qa-samuel-arbesman

1480 bri.li/1480 or zombiecon.wikidot.com/

1481 bri.li/1481 or www.researchgate.net/publication/247884597_Consulting_to_the_Ultra_Affluent

1482 bri.li/1482 or www.math.ust.hk/~maykwok/courses/ma362/07F/markowitz_JF.pdf

1483 bri.li/1483 or en.wikibooks.org/wiki/Principles_of_Finance/Section_1/Chapter_7/Modern_Portfolio_Theory#History

1484 bri.li/1484 or nobelprize.org/nobel_prizes/economics/laureates/1990/markowitz-lecture.pdf

1485 bri.li/1485 or www.math.ust.hk/~maykwok/courses/ma362/07F/markowitz_JF.pdf

1486 bri.li/1486 or en.wikipedia.org/wiki/Modern_portfolio_theory#Risk-free_asset_and_the_capital_allocation_line

1487 bri.li/1487 or en.wikipedia.org/wiki/Modern_portfolio_theory#Criticisms

1488 bri.li/1488 or ssrn.com/abstract=908569

1489 bri.li/1489 or books.google.com/books?id=gRdOBrus_9wC&printsec=frontcover&dq=jason+zweig&hl=en&sa=X&ei=jLSIVKqMDo61oQSFwIGA
BQ&ved=0CCUQ6AEwAQ#v=snippet&q=%22if%20it%20went%20way%20down%22&f=false

1490 bri.li/1490 or www.wsj.com/articles/SB123093692433550093

1491 bri.li/1491 or books.google.com/books?ei=mdGlVPDRD8P1oASuj4D4Aw&id=XOOWMES6YvUC&dq=%22intelligent+asset+allocator%22&focus=
searchwithinvolume&q=%22would+have+tanked%22

1492 bri.li/1492 or thepfengineer.com/2016/02/14/basic-portfolio-construction/

1493 bri.li/1493 or www.jstor.org/stable/2977928

1494 bri.li/1494 or books.google.com/books?id=H3CxAAAAIAAJ&q=%22the+asset+pricing+model+is+not+consistent+with+the+data%22&dq=%22the+asset+pricing+model+is+not+consistent+with+the+data%22&hl=en&sa=X&ved=0ahUKEwjAjtX3rprYAhVDxGMKHQqLCJgQ6AEIKDAA

1495 bri.li/1495 or ssrn.com/abstract=908569

1496 bri.li/1496 or www.nber.org/chapters/c11393

1497 bri.li/1497 or www.ivey.uwo.ca/cmsmedia/3775518/the_cross-section_of_expected_stock_returns.pdf

1498 bri.li/1498 or www.nytimes.com/1992/02/18/business/market-place-a-study-shakes-confidence-in-the-volatile-stock-theory.html

1499 bri.li/1499 or www.lapasserelle.com/escem/finance1/13_portfolios_(2)/Modern%20Portfolio%20Theory%20criticisms.htm

1500 bri.li/1500 or www.sunrisecapital.com/wp-content/uploads/2013/02/Futures_Mag_Sortino_0213.pdf

1501 bri.li/1501 or books.google.com/books?id=ZNTjEbOcPpQC&printsec=frontcover&dq=The+Sortino+Framework+for+Constructing+Portfolios&hl=en&sa=X&ved=0CDAQ6AEwAGoVChMIy7Ww39mYyQIVxOmICh1zdAlg#v=onepage&q=more%20than+2040%25%20of%20the%20time&f=false

1502 bri.li/1502 or pmpt.me/2012/01/25/pmpt-marries-prospect-theory

1503 bri.li/1503 or www.tangotools.com/ui/fkbook.pdf

1504 bri.li/1504 or mutualfundobserver.com/discuss/discussion/6694/the-ulcer-index-and-martin-ratio

1505 bri.li/1505 or tangotools.com/ui/ui.htm

1506 bri.li/1509 or www.aaii.com/journal/article/2013-Stock-Screens-The-Year-of-the-Bulls#10

1507 bri.li/1507 or boards.fool.com/MessagePrint.aspx?mid=24866511

1508 bri.li/1508 or www.tangotools.com/ui/ui.htm

1509 bri.li/1509 or tangotools.com/ui/ui.htm

1510 bri.li/1510 or simple.wikipedia.org/wiki/Standard_deviation#More_examples

1511 bri.li/1511 or www.the300club.org/wp-content/uploads/2015/12/300_Club-Bob_Maynard_Managing_risk_in_a_complex_world.pdf

1512 bri.li/1512 or mebfaber.com/2013/03/21/you-are-not-a-good-investor/

1513 bri.li/1513 or gallery.mailchimp.com/6750faf5c6091bc898da154ff/files/The_Capitalism_Distribution_12.12.12_1_.pdf

1514 bri.li/1514 or onlinelibrary.wiley.com/doi/10.1111/j.1540-6261.1970.tb00518.x/full

1515 bri.li/1515 or e-m-h.org/Basu1977.pdf

1516 bri.li/1516 or www.journals.uchicago.edu/doi/abs/10.1086/260832

1517 bri.li/1517 or www.jstor.org/stable/1802789

1518 bri.li/1518 or books.google.com/books?id=Rv-DULmRx2YC&pg=PA8&lpg=PA8&dq=%22efficient+markets+hypothesis+represents+one+of+the+most+remarkable+errors%22&source=bl&ots=NkUCAVE1dZ&sig=tswSFnqe_h3iDXQ3NU6xVypYMOk&hl=en&sa=X&ved=2ahUKEwiIwvuuxsjcAhUxCjQIHTSWDQcQ6AEwAHoECAAQAQ#v=onepage&q=%22efficient%20markets%20hypothesis%20represents%20 one%20of%20the%20most%20remarkable%20errors%22&f=false

1519 bri.li/1519 or www.barrypopik.com/index.php/new_york_city/entry/id_be_a_bum_on_the_street_with_a_tin_cup_if_the_markets_were_always_efficie

1520 bri.li/1520 or www.talkativeman.com/never-be-a-price-taker/

1521 bri.li/1521 or www.top1000funds.com/wp-content/uploads/2014/05/The-Arbitrage-Theory-of-Capital-Asset-Pricing.pdf

1522 bri.li/1522 or www.jstor.org/stable/2327087?seq=1#page_scan_tab_contents

1523 bri.li/1523 or onlinelibrary.wiley.com/doi/10.1111/j.1540-6288.1994.tb00817.x/abstract

1524 bri.li/1524 or onlinelibrary.wiley.com/doi/10.1111/j.1540-6288.1994.tb00817.x/abstract

1525 bri.li/1525 or ssrn.com/abstract=2459086

1526 bri.li/1526 or en.wikipedia.org/wiki/Merton_Miller

1527 bri.li/1527 or www.gsb.stanford.edu/stanford-gsb-experience/news-history/professor-william-sharpe-shares-nobel-prize-economics

1528 bri.li/1528 or books.google.com/books?id=GSBcQVd3MqYC&pg=PA277&dq=%22black+swan%22+%22Nobel+Committee+could+have+tested+the+Sharpe+and+Markowitz+models%22&hl=en&sa=X&ei=IE-tVOGmJ9jSoAT314L4BQ&ved=0CB8Q6AEwAA#v=onepage&q=%22black%20swan%22%20%22The%20Nobel%20Committee%20could%20have%20tested%20the%20Sharpe%20and%20Markowitz%20models%22&f=false

1529 bri.li/1529 or www.bloomberg.com/news/2010-10-08/taleb-says-crisis-makes-nobel-panel-liable-for-legitimizing-economists.html

1530 bri.li/1530 or en.wikipedia.org/wiki/Nobel_Memorial_Prize_in_Economic_Sciences#Alternative_names

1531 bri.li/1531 or en.wikipedia.org/wiki/Nobel_Memorial_Prize_in_Economic_Sciences#Controversies_and_criticisms

1532 bri.li/1532 or www.bauer.uh.edu/rsusmel/phd/jegadeesh-titman93.pdf

1533 bri.li/1533 or onlinelibrary.wiley.com/doi/10.1111/j.1540-6261.1997.tb03808.x/full?viewType=Print&viewClass=Print

1534 bri.li/1534 or www8.gsb.columbia.edu/rtfiles/Heilbrunn/Schloss Archives for Value Investing/vi/02basu_83_earnings_yield.pdf

1535 bri.li/1535 or ssrn.com/abstract=1970693

1536 bri.li/1536 or www.aaii.com/journal/article/is-outperforming-the-market-alpha-or-beta#4

1537 bri.li/1537 or ssrn.com/abstract=2503174

1538 bri.li/1538 or www.business.unr.edu/faculty/liuc/files/BADM742/Banz_sizeeffect_1980.pdf

1539 bri.li/1539 or www.sciencedirect.com/science/article/pii/0304405X81900192

1540 bri.li/1540 or www.researchaffiliates.com/Our%20Ideas/Insights/Fundamentals/Pages/223_Finding_Smart_Beta_in_the_Factor_Zoo.aspx

1541 bri.li/1541 or onlinelibrary.wiley.com/doi/10.1111/0022-1082.00192/abstract

1542 bri.li/1542 or books.google.com/books?id=e5yzAwAAQBAJ&pg=PA29&dq=%22wealth+management%22+andrew+ang&hl=en&sa=X&ved=0C DAQ6AEwAGoVChMI8pqZt-ibyQIVjJSICh1VRAuA#v=onepage&q=%22since%20the%20mid-1980s%22&f=false

1543 bri.li/1543 or www.sciencedirect.com/science/article/pii/S0927539800000086

1544 bri.li/1544 or books.google.com/books?id=NMwswtk5UZAC&dq=%22what+works+on+wall+street%22+fourth+edition&focus=searchwithinvol ume&q=%22impossible+to+buy%22

1545 bri.li/1545 or www.ifa.com/12steps/step9/monthly_rolling_periods/

1546 bri.li/1546 or books.google.com/books?id=rWW8AwAAQBAJ&printsec=frontcover&dq=asset+management+andrew+ang&hl=en&sa=X&ved=0a hUKEwjLroLZop7JAhVQXIgKHaXvBp4Q6AEINjAB#v=snippet&q=%22risk%20of%20the%20value%20strategy%22&f=false

1547 bri.li/1547 or books.google.com/books?id=oY8fAQAAQBAJ&pg=PT114&dq=mandelbrot+spanish+authorities&hl=en&sa=X&ved=0CCQQ6A EwAWoVChMI3Kex14OfyAIVkjqIChOuTgpg#v=onepage&q=mandelbrot%20spanish%20authorities&f=false

1548 bri.li/1548 or www.businessinsider.com/cost-of-missing-10-best-days-in-sp-500-2015-3

1549 bri.li/1549 or www.onefpa.org/journal/Pages/Missing%20the%20Ten%20Best.aspx

1550 bri.li/1550 or books.google.com/books?id=zg91TAIs6bgC&pg=PA96&lpg=PA96&dq=fama+%22drama+only+once+every+seven+thousand+ years%22&source=bl&ots=YmpXxSfJEK&sig=N6BZT9ZSeFBI7CUaW-Qsc_-Ac9A&hl=en&sa=X&ved=0ahUKEwjXlYGbobXaAhX mjlQKH VU5DOY Q6AEIKDAA#v=onepage&q=fama%20%20drama%20only%20once%20every%20seven%20thousand%20years%22&f= false

1551 bri.li/1551 or books.google.com/books?id=zg91TAIs6bgC&pg=PA249&lpg=PA249&dq=mandelbrot+%22you+can+side step+its+worst+punch es%22&source=bl&ots=YmpXxSfMDP&sig=wvS4HrpQDZ2wkBamMEg7KMdfgbM&hl=en&sa=X&ved=0ahUKEwiT7 2norXaAhXI6J8KH cOTAIgQ6AEIKDAA#v=onepage&q=mandelbrot%20%22you%20can%20sidestep%20its%20worst%20punches%22&f=false

1552 bri.li/1552 or en.wikipedia.org/wiki/Normal_distribution#History

1553 bri.li/1553 or en.wikipedia.org/wiki/Paul_L%C3%A9vy_%28mathematician%29

1554 bri.li/1554 or www.nobelprize.org/nobel_prizes/economic-sciences/laureates/2003/advanced-economicsciences2003.pdf

1555 bri.li/1555 or www.investresolve.com/blog/dynamic-asset-allocation-for-practitioners-part-1-universe-selection/

1556 bri.li/1556 or ssrn.com/abstract=1914673

1557 bri.li/1557 or etf.com/sections/index-investor-corner/swedroe-downside-momentum?nopaging=1

1558 bri.li/1558 or books.google.com/books?id=hC_qBQAAQBAJ&dq=editions:2uSnx79bcVsC&hl=en&sa=X&ved=0CB0Q6AEwAGoVChMI6azYuriWyAI VDimICh2SwAXx

1559 bri.li/1559 or www.wsj.com/articles/the-trick-to-making-better-forecasts-1443235983

1560 bri.li/1560 or www.economist.com/news/21589145-how-sort-best-rest-whos-good-forecasts

1561 bri.li/1561 or www.etfscreen.com/blog/contact-us/

1562 bri.li/1562 or stockcharts.com/docs/doku.php

1563 bri.li/1563 or www.myplaniq.com/LTISystem/f401k_view.action?ID=5837

1564 bri.li/1564 or www.bogleheads.org/blog/william-bernsteins-cowards-portfolio/

1565 bri.li/1565 or www.myplaniq.com/LTISystem/jsp/portfolio/ViewPortfolio.action?ID=407

1566 bri.li/1566 or socialize.morningstar.com/NewSocialize/forums/t/183963.aspx

1567 bri.li/1567 or bri.li/morning

1568 bri.li/1568 or www.myplaniq.com/LTISystem/jsp/portfolio/ComparePortfolio.action?withCompare=true&portfolioString=P_36809%2CP_33676

1569 bri.li/1569 or www.myplaniq.com/LTISystem/jsp/portfolio/ComparePortfolio.action?withCompare=true&portfolioString=P_33690%2CP_33692

1570 bri.li/1570 or www.myplaniq.com/LTISystem/jsp/portfolio/ComparePortfolio.action?withCompare=true&portfolioString=P_1361%2CP_17645

1571 bri.li/1571 or www.myplaniq.com/LTISystem/jsp/portfolio/ComparePortfolio.action?withCompare=true&portfolioString=P_20970%2CP_20965

1572 bri.li/1572 or www.myplaniq.com/LTISystem/jsp/portfolio/ComparePortfolio.action?withCompare=true&portfolioString=P_37035%2CP_33624

1573 bri.li/1573 or www.myplaniq.com/LTISystem/jsp/portfolio/ComparePortfolio.action?withCompare=true&portfolioString=P_20508%2CP_21403

1574 bri.li/1574 or www.myplaniq.com/LTISystem/jsp/portfolio/ComparePortfolio.action?withCompare=true&portfolioString=P_20933%2CP_28414

1575 bri.li/1575 or www.myplaniq.com/LTISystem/jsp/portfolio/ComparePortfolio.action?withCompare=true&portfolioString=P_18357%2CP_18333

1576 bri.li/1576 or www.myplaniq.com/LTISystem/jsp/portfolio/ComparePortfolio.action?withCompare=true&portfolioString=P_407%2CP_17465

Glossary
Cash is a four-letter word

active investing Frequently changing one's portfolio based on opinions. Compare *mechanical investing.* CH. 16

after-tax account A savings plan in which contributions are not tax-deductible but permissible withdrawals are tax-free. Examples: Roths and HSAs. Compare *before-tax account.* CH. 19

amygdala An emotional part of the brain, often called the lower mind or reptilian brain. Compare *prefrontal cortex.* CH. 14

annualized rate of return The growth rate of a straight line from a portfolio's start value to its end value. Abbreviated ann'd. Identical to *compound annual growth rate* (CAGR). Compare *average annual return.* CH. 1

arbitration A private process to resolve financial disputes; usually required by brokerages, among other firms. CH. 11

armchair investor A person who pays little attention to the market until hearing that it has sunk into a bear market. Compare *informed investor.* CH. 1

asset class A category of securities—such as stocks, bonds, real estate, commodities, and precious metals—that sometimes goes up and down in price differently than other categories. Various systems typically divide the world's investable securities into 9 to 13 asset classes. CH. 1

asset rotation A portfolio strategy that remains 100% invested at all times in at least three different asset classes and gradually tilts toward those with the strongest momentum. Compare *market timing.* CH. 3

attic Those asset classes in the top half of performance rankings over the past 3 to 12 months. Such assets tend to perform better than other assets in the coming month or more. Compare *basement.* CH. 10

average annual return A deceptive way to compute an equity portfolio's return, which always exaggerates the growth. Compare *annualized rate of return.* CH. 1

Baby Bear Portfolio A starter portfolio that holds only two ETFs, 50% US stocks and 50% US bonds, to keep trading costs low for people with under $10,000 of investable assets. CH. 7

backdoor Roth An investor's contribution to a Roth account through an employer's Qualified Plan, enabling larger transactions than could be made directly into the Roth. CH. 19

backtester A computer program that uses actual historical prices of securities to estimate the return of various portfolio strategies. Compare *simulator.* CH. 1

bargain brokerage An online brokerage that offers trades commission-free or as low as $4. Examples: Robinhood.com and FolioInvesting.com. CH. 17

basement Those asset classes in the lower half of the performance rankings over the past 3 to 12 months. Such assets tend to perform poorly or crash in the coming month or more. Compare *attic.* CH. 10

bear market A decline of 20% or more after a bull market. CH. 1

before-tax account A savings plan in which contributions are tax-deductible but withdrawals are taxed. Examples: 401(k)s and traditional IRAs. Compare *after-tax account.* CH. 19

behavioral economics A Nobel Prize–winning body of science showing that humans make decisions about money irrationally rather than completely logically. CH. 1

behavioral pain point A level of financial loss—thought to average around 25%—that compels investors to throw in the towel and liquidate a portfolio. CH. 16

bid-ask spread The difference at any given moment between the price someone would pay if buying a security and the price someone would receive if selling that security. Example: The ask price for XYZ is $50.05, but the bid price is only $49.95. The spread gives professional market makers a profit motive to keep an exchange's trading almost instantaneous. CH. 17

bond ETF See *defined-maturity bond ETF.* CH. 23

bond ladder A portfolio of individual bonds or defined-maturity bond ETFs that mature in different years, providing stability of principal and yield no matter how interest rates may change. CH. 23

bond-like volatility Financial strategies that never have losses greater than Treasury bonds (approximately –40% at worst). Compare *market-like returns.* CH. 1

bounce The first 10 months of a new bull market, on average, when equities typically rise faster than at any other time in a bear-bull market cycle. CH. 16

Buffett Buffer Keeping a portfolio's losses small during bear markets, as Warren Buffett does, providing a cushion. This buffer allows the portfolio to outperform the S&P 500 over complete bear-bull market cycles, even though the portfolio lags the index during bull markets. CH. 2

bull market A gain of 20% or more after a bear market. CH. 1

business cycle One round of an economy's expansion/boom and contraction/recession, in either order. Each phase is often said to occur approximately six months later than an equity market's bull and bear phases. Compare *market cycle.* CH. 2

buy-and-hope Purchasing risk assets, such as the S&P 500, and holding them until they deliver an intolerable loss and the investor liquidates, harming performance. CH. 3

C is for customer service

correlation The percentage of days or months that one asset rises in price when a different asset also rises. Asset classes with a low correlation to each other can give a portfolio a greater return with lower volatility than either asset class by itself. CH. 9

crash A decline of 30% or more. A severe crash is a decline of 40% or more. CH. 1

data-mining bias Testing hundreds or thousands of investing strategies reveals by random chance one that performed best but won't work in the future. CH. 15

day trader A speculator who seeks to profit from small changes in security prices intraday. CH. 1

defined-maturity (DM) bond ETF An exchange-traded fund that offers hundreds of bonds in a single security and provides the certainty of a specific maturity date. CH. 23

deviation The extent to which a portfolio's growth varies from a straight line. BONUS CH.

disinvest To remove your capital from an undesirable financial entity. CH. 11

diversification Allocating a portfolio so it contains at least three different asset classes at all times for stability and growth. CH. 9

downer portfolio A financial strategy that loses 30% or more every few years, such as the S&P 500 and Lazy Portfolios. The crashes compel investors to liquidate their portfolios and lock in their losses. CH. 3

drawdown Any decline in a security's price since its all-time high. A portfolio's drawdowns will always be larger if measured between daily closes rather than monthly closes. Compare *maximum drawdown*. CH. 1

dynamic asset allocation (DAA) Holding percentages of asset classes that gradually increase and decrease according to a mechanical formula as market conditions change. Also called tactical asset allocation and Muscular Portfolios. Compare *static asset allocation*. CH. 3

cash In Wall Street terms, money held in a money-market fund, short-term Treasury bills, a demand-deposit checking account, etc. These instruments offer a low return but a high degree of safety, plus immediate access to principal with no waiting period. "Cash" is distinct from currency hidden under a mattress, which has no return. CH. 9

commodities Investable assets, such as oil and gas, agricultural products, precious and base metals, and other physical goods. Also called hard assets or alternative investments (along with real estate) to distinguish them from stocks and bonds. CH. 1

compound annual growth rate (CAGR) The growth rate of a straight line from a portfolio's start value to its end value. Identical to *annualized rate of return*. CH. 1

compounding The mathematical fact that a portfolio growing at a constant rate—with the gains retained in the portfolio—will generate a larger number of dollars every year. CH. 8

core principles of Muscular Portfolios Compounding, diversification, and momentum are the three essential components of investing. CH. 16

correction A decline of 10% to 19.9% during a bull market. CH. 1

Dynamic Portfolio Model (DPM) A principle that requires investors to remain 100% invested at all times in the three asset classes with the strongest momentum. BONUS CH.

effective tax rate The percentage of a filer's gross income that is paid to the IRS after all deductions, exemptions, and credits. Always lower than the *marginal tax rate.* CH. 19

equities Tradable stocks. CH. 1

ETF See *exchange-traded fund.* CH. 1

evidence-based investing Any financial strategy based on the latest academic research, especially the Fama-French-Carhart papers on momentum, company size, and value. CH. 1

exchange-traded fund (ETF) A security that tracks a market index and trades during the day like a stock. Compare *mutual fund.* CH. 1

expected return The theoretical payoff from any series of gains after a large number of repetitions. Example: From 1900 to 2016, the average expected return of equities across 20 markets was 3.2 percentage points higher than intermediate-term bonds (Dimson 2017). CH. 9

factors Market metrics that have some tendency to predict an asset's price change in the next month or more. The primary factor is momentum. CH. 10

fee-only adviser A professional who works for investors for a fee and agrees in writing not to accept commissions or kickbacks from securities firms to promote their products. Not to be confused with a "fee-based adviser," who accepts kickbacks in addition to investor fees. CH. 16

financial freedom Your ability to quit unwanted jobs and do anything you wish when your portfolio has grown large enough. CH. 8

gain The difference between a security's start price and its end price. Compare *return.* CH. 2

gentle shadowing A portfolio gaining approximately two-thirds as much as the S&P 500 during a bull market. Informed investors accept this lag in exchange for outperformance during the subsequent bear market and thus over the complete bear-bull market cycle. CH. 16

golden zero Long-term capital gains that incur an income tax rate of 0%. This is possible for households who generate large enough deductions and after-tax balances to keep the "taxable income" on their IRS Form 1040 down to middle-class levels. CH. 19

Goldilocks investing A research project to find and publish Muscular Portfolios. CH. 1

growth stock A company whose share price divided by various measures of its earning power puts it in the upper half of all companies. Also called "glamour stock." Compare *value stock.* CH. 6

hard assets Real estate, commodities, precious metals, and other physical invest-able assets, as opposed to stocks and bonds. Also called alternative investments. CH. 1

headline price A security's price series that ignores dividends and inflation. CH. 1

headline return A security's rate of return that ignores dividends and inflation. CH. 1

health savings account (HSA) A tax-deferred plan that requires an investor to have a high-deductible health insurance policy. It acts as a "super Roth" to shelter income, because contributions are tax-deductible and permissible withdrawals incur no tax. CH. 19

hedge fund A financial firm that implies it will deliver superior returns but charges high fees, typically 1% to 2% of assets plus 5% to 20% of any gains. CH. 1

I is for investment committee

index fund A security that tracks an asset class, such as an index of stocks, bonds, or gold. The fund may be organized as an ETF, a mutual fund, a limited partnership, etc. CH. 1

Index Investing Revolution The disruptive effect of three 21st-century megatrends: bargain brokerages, ultra-low-cost ETFs, and a new scientific consensus on momentum. CH. 1

indicator Two or more market metrics computed as a ratio, which doesn't always work out as you'd hoped. Compare *price*. CH. 15

individually managed plan A savings plan run by an individual, such as a traditional IRA, Roth, or HSA. Not to be confused with *Qualified Plans* run by employers, such as 401(k)s, or *self-directed IRAs* run by special financial custodians. CH. 19

informed investor A person who studies the latest scientific research on investing. Compare *armchair investor*. CH. 1

investing universe See *menu*. CH. 5

investor's remorse The tendency of investors to regret starting to follow a financial strategy with serious money, when it underperforms their expectations for the first two years or so. CH. 9

IRA (Individual Retirement Arrangement) A savings plan that offers a tax deduction for contributions but requires withdrawals after age 70½ that incur ordinary tax rates. Also called a traditional IRA. Compare *HSA* and *Roth*. CH. 19

IRA-to-Roth conversion A movement of an investor's funds from various before-tax accounts (IRA, SEP IRA, etc.) into an after-tax account, such as a Roth, incurring ordinary income tax. CH. 19

Ivy 5 A global tactical asset allocation (GTAA) portfolio with a menu of five asset classes and a hedging rule. Presented in a 2006 academic paper and a 2009 book, *The Ivy Portfolio*. CH. 6

large-cap stock A company with total shares outstanding (market capitalization) between approximately $10 and $200 billion. Large-caps are smaller than mega-caps but larger than mid-caps, small-caps, micro-caps, and nano-caps. Compare *small-cap stock*. CH. 6

Lazy Portfolio An investing strategy that typically holds five or more index funds in a specified proportion that never changes. Exception: Lazy Portfolio authors often advise investors to increase the allocation to bonds every year to keep the percentage equal to their age or some similar formula. Authors usually recommend an annual rebalance to the original proportions. CH. 3

linear scale A market-graph axis that increases by addition. Example: $100, $200, $300, $400. Compare *ratio scale*. CH. 3

liquidate To convert the risk assets in one's portfolio to cash, typically when an investor can no longer stand the pain of a bear market. CH. 1

liquidity The ability to find a buyer or seller of a security quickly, even during market panics. Most index ETFs have high liquidity, because their underlying assets are highly liquid. CH. 1

Long Night of the Portfolio Virtually every investing strategy that outperforms the S&P 500 in the long run significantly underperforms the index for five years in a row. CH. 16

long-termism An investor's dedication to evaluate portfolio performance only over time periods of one full bear-bull market cycle or longer. Compare *short-termism.* CH. 2

lunatics Participants in stock exchanges, who tend to drive market prices up during predictable periods in the lunar cycle. CH. 15

Mama Bear Portfolio A Muscular Portfolio with a menu of nine asset classes and a Momentum Rule that picks the three strongest ETFs to hold each month. CH. 5

marginal tax rate The percentage that a filer pays the IRS on the highest dollar of taxable income. Almost no one pays the marginal rate on gross income, after subtracting deductions, exemptions, and credits. Compare *effective tax rate.* CH. 19

market cycle One bear market and one bull market in equities, in either order. Also called primary cycle. Compare *business cycle.* CH. 2

market-cycle graph A chart of financial results that shows a security's return during bear markets and bull markets separately. Lines restart at 0% or $100 at the beginning of each half-cycle. CH. 2

market-like returns Financial strategies with returns within 1 percentage point of the S&P 500's total return or better over complete bear-bull market cycles. Compare *bond-like volatility.* CH. 1

market-like returns with bond-like volatility Financial strategies that deliver within 1% of the S&P 500's total return over complete bear-bull market cycles with losses no greater than Treasury bonds (about –40% at worst). The basis for Muscular Portfolios and the Baby Bear Portfolio. CH. 1

market timing Switching a portfolio from 100% invested in stocks to 100% invested in cash and back based on an indicator. Compare *asset rotation.* CH. 1

Martin ratio A ranking system that gives higher scores to portfolios that achieve better returns with smaller losses. A replacement for the rebutted Sharpe ratio. BONUS CH.

maximum drawdown The single largest decline in a security's price during a given period of years. The maximum drawdown will always be larger if measured between daily closes rather than monthly closes. Compare *drawdown.* CH. 1

mean In statistics, an arithmetic average. See also *reversion to average.* CH. 9

mechanical investing Following a computerized financial formula without allowing a human mind to second-guess it. Distinct from *active investing, passive investing,* and other portfolio management styles. CH. 16

megatrend A historical development that disrupts and changes many aspects of society or an industry. CH. 1

menu A list of asset classes that a portfolio may choose from. Also called investing universe. CH. 5

Modern Portfolio Theory (MPT) A rebutted 1952 paper which stated that a "tangency portfolio" would be the best strategy for investors. More correctly called Markowitz Portfolio Theory. BONUS CH.

momentum The tendency of an asset class that has risen in price during the past 3 to 12 months to continue to rise for an additional month or more. CH. 10

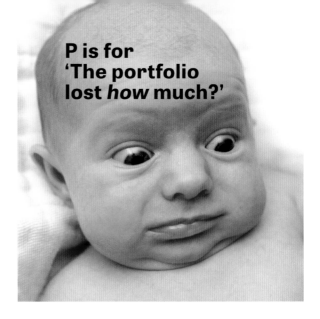

momentum factor The most effective of several academic market metrics, such as company size and value, that predict to some extent a security's future price trend. CH. 1

Momentum Rule The specific formula used by a Muscular Portfolio to determine which asset classes have the best odds of rising over the next one month. CH. 1

money-market fund A security that pays a low return—like that of short-term Treasury bills—but offers a high degree of safety and immediate access to principal with no waiting period. See also _cash._ CH. 9

Muscular Portfolio A mechanical investing formula designed by a financial expert, using a Momentum Rule on nine or more ETFs, that is fully disclosed free of charge and without mandatory registration. CH. 1

MuscularPortfolios.com A free website that displays the ETF momentum rankings for strategies like the Mama Bear Portfolio and the Papa Bear Portfolio. CH. 4

mutual fund A security that holds stocks or other financial vehicles but can only be bought or sold at the close of the market. Compare _exchange-traded fund._ CH. 1

nominal Not inflation-adjusted. Memory aid: <u>no</u>t <u>m</u>odified for <u>in</u>flation at <u>all</u>. Compare _real._ CH. 1

one-half down, two-thirds up A mathematical truth that a portfolio losing only half as much as the S&P 500 during down months and gaining only two-thirds as much in up months tends to beat the index over complete bear-bull market cycles. CH. 2

overgrazing The tendency for a market indicator that once had some predictive value to stop working when the technique becomes more widely used. CH. 15

pain point See _behavioral pain point._ CH. 16

Papa Bear Portfolio A Muscular Portfolio with a menu of 13 asset classes and a Momentum Rule that picks the three strongest ETFs to hold each month. CH. 6

passive investing Allocating one's portfolio among different asset classes in percentages that never change. Compare _mechanical investing._ CH. 16

patience An investor's skill in allowing a diversified portfolio to underperform the S&P 500 during bull markets, in the expectation that the portfolio will outperform during bear markets and over complete bear-bull market cycles. CH. 2

pension fund A financial institution that invests workers' contributions in hopes of providing the employees with retirement income. CH. 1

persistance A financial strategy's tendency to have good performance in the future after good performance in the past. Persistence requires a track record of 15 years or more. Exception: Bad performance has a strong tendency to repeat, even after only one year. CH. 2

prefrontal cortex A logical part of the brain, often called the higher mind. Compare _amygdala._ CH. 14

price The sum of all the greed and fear in the world about a security at a particular time. Price is a more reliable factor than any indicator, which can stop working at any time. Compare *indicator.* CH. 15

price return A security's rate of return, incorrectly ignoring dividends. Compare *total return.* CH. 1

primary cycle See *market cycle.* CH. 2

Qualified Plan A savings plan recognized by the IRS and administered by an employer. Examples: A 401(k) plan for private companies, 457(b) for government agencies, and 403(b) for tax-exempt nonprofits. Compare *individually managed plan.* CH. 19

randomness Unpredictability, which exists in at least three forms: predictably random, predictably chaotic, and wildly chaotic. CH. 13

rate of return See *return.* CH. 2

ratio scale A market-graph axis that increases geometrically, so constant rates of return are shown as straight lines. Example: $100, $200, $400, $800. Useful when portfolio values quadruple or more over the time period of a graph. Also called a semi-logarithmic or semilog scale. Compare *linear scale.* CH. 3

real Adjusted for inflation. Compare *nominal.* CH. 1

real total return A security's annualized rate of return, correctly adjusted for inflation and the reinvestment of dividends. CH. 1

reallocation date A day of the month that an investor chooses for portfolio tune-ups, with changes in rankings determined by a Momentum Rule. CH. 5

rebalance To restore the original allocation percentages of the assets in a portfolio. CH. 18

recovery time The period it takes a portfolio to return back to even after a loss. Recovery time increases geometrically. A 25% loss requires a 33.3% gain, while a 50% loss requires a 100% gain. CH. 2

reinvestment of dividends The use of periodic distributions from stocks or bonds to immediately purchase more of the same stock or bond. CH. 1

required minimum distributions (RMDs) Mandatory withdrawals you must make from IRAs and Qualified Plans after age 70½. Not required from Roths or HSAs. CH. 21

return A security's annualized rate of return. Identical to *compound annual growth rate* (CAGR). Compare *gain.* CH. 2

reversion to average The tendency of an investing strategy that has had a hot streak to experience a cold streak. Also called reversion to the mean. CH. 9

risk The likelihood of an intolerable loss—the kind that compels investors to liquidate their portfolios near the bottom of a bear market. CH. 16

risk assets Securities—such as stock, bond, and commodity ETFs—that fluctuate in price more than a risk-free asset, such as a money-market fund. CH. 1

risk-free rate The return offered by short-term government bonds, such as 4-week Treasury bills, that are considered to have no default risk or interest-rate risk. BONUS CH.

risk profile A number, typically 1 to 9, which a broker determines from an investor questionnaire. It has little value in predicting when an investor will throw in the towel and liquidate. CH. 13

robo-adviser A computerized firm that charges an annual fee, typically to hold investors' money in an unchanging allocation like a Lazy Portfolio. CH. 20

Rogues' Gallery Nine giant Wall Street banks that paid $150 billion in settlements for consumer fraud during the 2007–2009 global financial crisis. CH. 11

rollover A transfer of an investor's funds from a Qualified Plan, such as a 401(k), into an individually managed account, such as a traditional IRA. CH. 19

Roth IRA A savings plan that offers no tax deduction for contributions but incurs no tax on permissible withdrawals. Compare *HSA* and *IRA*. CH. 19

S&P 500 An index of approximately 500 mostly large-cap US companies. The index is tracked by ETFs such as SPY and VOO and mutual funds such as VFINX. CH. 2

S&P 500 envy An irrational lust to make a diversified portfolio outperform the S&P 500 at all times, even during periods when the index is one of the world's strongest asset classes. CH. 1

safe withdrawal rate (SWR) The percentage you can safely withdraw from your savings each year after you quit your job without exhausting the account during your lifetime. The first-year amount is typically increased for inflation each year thereafter. CH. 22

seasoned The owner of a Roth is "seasoned" (can withdraw gains without tax or penalty) after age 59½ and after holding any Roth in five tax years. CH. 19

securities Any financial instruments—such as stocks, bonds, and ETFs—that trade on an exchange. Distinct from physical currencies, coins, etc. CH. 1

self-directed IRA An account managed by a special financial custodian that allows investors to hold real estate, precious metals, and other assets in an IRA that most brokerages do not. Not to be confused with *individually managed plans,* such as Traditional IRAs and Roths, or *Qualified Plans* run by employers. CH. 19

semilog scale See *ratio scale.* CH. 3

Sharpe ratio See *Martin ratio.* BONUS CH.

short-termism The human tendency to evaluate portfolio performance over statistically insignificant time periods such as 1, 3, or 5 years, or anything shorter than one full bear-bull market cycle. Compare *long-termism.* CH. 2

shorting Borrowing stock shares and selling them in hopes of buying them back at a lower price and reaping a profit. Prohibited in Muscular Portfolios. BONUS CH.

simulator A computer program that uses theoretical historical prices of asset classes to estimate the return of various portfolio strategies. Compare *backtester.* CH. 1

small-cap stock A company with total shares outstanding (market capitalization) between approximately $300 million and $2 billion. Smaller than mid-caps, large-caps, and mega-caps but larger than micro-caps and nano-caps. Compare *large-cap stock.* CH. 6

smart beta A type of ETF that seeks to tilt its portfolio toward a particular market factor, such as equal-weight, company size, or value, with little or no adaptation to changing market conditions. CH. 20

spread See *bid-ask spread.* CH. 17

starter portfolio A financial strategy that holds only two to four ETFs in fixed proportions to keep trading costs low for people with under $10,000 of investable assets. Example: The Baby Bear Portfolio. CH. 7

static asset allocation (SAA) Holding fixed percentages of asset classes. Also called strategic asset allocation or Lazy Portfolios. Compare *dynamic asset allocation.* CH. 3

Strategy Sanity Twelve features that informed investors require portfolio strategies to have. Examples: No losses over 25%, no math required, fully disclosed free of charge without mandatory registration. CH. 3

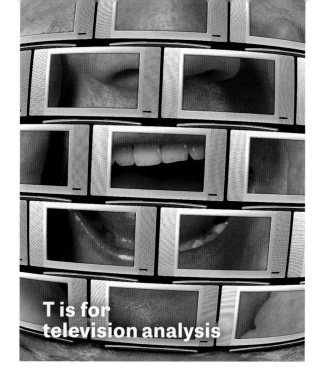

T is for
television analysis

tactical asset allocation (TAA) See *dynamic asset allocation*. CH. 3

target-date fund A mutual fund or ETF that allocates more and more of an investor's principal to bonds on a rigid schedule as the investor grows older. CH. 20

tax harvesting Two tax-reduction methods: tax-loss harvesting (using losses to offset gains) and tax-gain harvesting (selling securities in increments to reduce tax). CH. 19

Tax Torpedo An ordinary income tax that applies to 85% of your Social Security benefit if your income exceeds a certain level. CH. 21

tilt A shift in a Muscular Portfolio toward assets with good odds of prices rising and away from assets with poor odds. Similar to a captain who tacks a sailboat as the wind changes. CH. 3

total return A security's rate of return including the reinvestment of dividends. Compare *price return*. CH. 1

Ulcer Index A formula that scores portfolios on the depth and duration of their losses, not their mere up and down variability. Used in calculating the *Martin ratio*. A replacement for standard deviation. BONUS CH.

value stock A company whose share price divided by various measures of its earning power puts it in the lower half of all companies. Compare *growth stock*. CH. 6

VBINX The Vanguard Balanced Index mutual fund, which holds at all times 60% US stocks and 40% US bonds, similar to the Baby Bear Portfolio (which is 50/50). CH. 2

VFINX The Vanguard Five Hundred Index mutual fund, which tracks the S&P 500. CH. 2

volatility The deviation of a security's growth from a straight line. CH. 16

wealth-preservation portfolio An ultra-conservative financial strategy that holds at all times 80% in bond ETFs for predictable income and 20% in a Muscular Portfolio for growth. Intended for households with a few million dollars of investable assets. Example: The End Game Portfolio. CH. 23

yeti portfolio A mythical financial strategy that promises to always return more than the S&P 500 during up months and lose less than the index during down months. Cannot exist, because any such model would quickly be overused and stop working. CH. 1

zombie ideas Economic myths—such as, "to get more gain, you must take more risk"—that eat into our brains long after the original theories have been disproven. BONUS CH.

Index

Note: **Boldface** numerals indicate a significant discussion or definition.

KEY CONCEPTS

LIVINGSTON'S LAW

MUST-READS

N

O

P

Dedication

This book is dedicated to my wife, the visual artist and Fulbright Scholar **Margie Livingston (margie.net)**, without whose support this six-year labor of love would never have been completed.

Acknowledgments—it takes a village to publish a book

PUBLICA PRESS & FRIENDS
Brian Livingston
  president
Jennifer Munro
  developmental editor
Roberta Scholz
  copyeditor
Brent Scheffler
  Web development

BENBELLA BOOKS
Glenn Yeffeth
  CEO
Adrienne Lang
  deputy publisher
Leah Wilson
  editor in chief
Alexa Stevenson
  senior editor
Sarah Avinger
  art director
Aaron Edmiston
  graphic design
Monica Lowry
  production director
Jessika Rieck
  senior production editor
Rachel Phares
  publishing associate
Jennifer Canzoneri
  marketing director
Lindsay Marshall
  publishing associate
Heather Butterfield
  senior marketing mgr.
Erica Harmon
  marketing assistant
Alicia Kania
  senior publishing associate

EXPERT CONTRIBUTIONS
Brad Barber & Terrance Odean
Jack Bogle
Mebane Faber
John W. Gelm/
  bid-ask spread data
Jane Hodges/
  WSJ researcher-reporter
Stephen Jones
Steve LeCompte
Jill Mislinski/
  Advisor Perspectives
Timothy Pew/
  MrLasers.com
Dan Sotiroff/
  ThePFEngineer.com

ACRYLIC PAINTINGS & COLLAGE
Jed Dunkerley

COMIC ILLUSTRATING
Randy Wood

DATA PROVIDER
Hugh Todd/
  ETFScreen.com

DESIGN CONSULTING
John D. Berry
Karen Mason Creative

EXCEL CONSULTING
Jon Peltier

INFOGRAPHICS
Pieter Tandjung

OF COUNSEL
Malcolm Harris
Gloria Wakayama
Fred Wilf

PHOTOGRAPHIC CONSULTING
Robert Wade

PUBLIC RELATIONS CONSULTING
Johanna Ramos-Boyer
David Ratner
Tess Woods

BETA READERS
AAII Puget Sound Chapter
  Board of Directors
Maurice Fuller
Dave Gaba
Dennis Gibb/
  SweetwaterInv.com
John Hedtke/
  Hedtke.com
Thom Heileson
Kristi Heim
Bryce James/
  SmartPortfolios.com
Barbara Johnston
Woody & Add Leonhard
Ben Livingston
Archana Murthy
Kristan Olivas
Mark Roth
Rich Nichols
Ray Rondeau
John Shelton
Mai-Liis Todd

Disclosures

The author has no business relationship at this writing with any of the parties mentioned in the text, with the following caveats:

He is a paying subscriber to the newsletters and/or websites of CXO Advisory, The Idea Farm, My Plan IQ, and ETFScreen.com, and may from time to time purchase other subscriptions that pose no conflict of interest.

He keeps the majority of his personal wealth in the Mama Bear, Papa Bear, and Baby Bear Portfolios, and therefore will have at any given time a position in exchange-traded funds (ETFs) that are on those strategies' menus.

He wrote the spreadsheet formulas that were used to calculate the after-tax returns of the Muscular Portfolios in Chapter 19. He donated the formulas free of charge to be integrated into the Quant simulator, so other researchers might use them.

The MuscularPortfolios.com website links to fee-only, fiduciary-only registered investment advisers (RIAs) who have pledged to manage Muscular Portfolios for clients at a reasonable cost. The site currently charges a token fee of $1 per two years to defray the cost of Web hosting. Neither the author nor the site receives anything else from RIAs or their clients who take advantage of such services.

ETFScreen.com delivers market data to MuscularPortfolios.com, which provides promotional consideration.

The author periodically gives presentations to groups about the Dynamic Portfolio Model and is compensated for these appearances by a speaker's bureau.

Future caveats that apply to the first edition of this book will be listed at MuscularPortfolios.com/1e.

About the author

FIGURE ATA-1
While traveling in Switzerland in 2012, the author evaluates strategies competing to become the Mama Bear Portfolio

Brian Livingston is an investigative journalist now focusing directly on the investment industry.

Based in New York City from 1984 to 1991, he was the assistant IT manager of UBS Securities, a computer consultant for Morgan Guaranty Trust Co. (now JPMorgan Chase), and technology adviser to the investment bank Lazard Frères (now Lazard Ltd.).

As a consumer advocate exposing the dark side of high tech, he wrote more than 1,000 articles from 1991 to 2010 as a contributing editor of *PC World*, CNET, *InfoWorld*, and *eWeek*, and edited the *Windows Secrets Newsletter*, which grew to more than 400,000 subscribers. He also authored or coauthored 11 books in the *Windows Secrets* series (John Wiley & Sons), selling more than 2.5 million copies.

The 6th Annual Internet Content Summit in New York City named him Entrepreneur of the Year in 2006 for his creation of a profitable "pay what you wish" subscription model for delivering information to consumers. He is a recipient of the Award for Technical Excellence from the National Microcomputer Managers Association.

Livingston is president of the Seattle regional chapter of the American Association of Individual Investors (AAII). He is a member of Investigative Reporters & Editors and the National Writers Union.

Photo credits

Photos are copyright or copyleft by their respective owners.

FW-1 Steven Miller/SMB Magazine

1-1 Juniors Bildarchive/Alamy
1-2 Colourbox
1-3 Franck Boston/Shutterstock
1-6 Eva Kröcher/Creative Commons
1-8 Wavebreak Media/123RF
1-12 Aleksander Kovaltchuk/Dreamstime
1-13 Gualtiero Boffi/Dreamstime
1-15 Sean Gallup/Burda Media/Getty Images
1-16 Barbara Tversky
1-19 (1st) Gennadiy Poznyakov/123RF
1-19 (2nd) Nerthuz/Shutterstock
1-19 (3rd) Fat Camera/iStock
1-23 123ucas/123RF

2-1 Alphaspirit/123RF
2-4 Kent Sievers/Shutterstock
2-10 HulbertRatings.com/Creative Commons

3-1 Comaniciu Dan/123RF
3-8 Ivan Reka/123RF

4-2 Can Yesil/Shutterstock

5-3 Mary LeCompte/CXO Advisory

6-3 Ringo Chiu/Zuma Press/Alamy

7-3 Ken Cedeno/Bloomberg/Getty Images

8-1 Newco500/123RF
8-2 Dragon Images/Shutterstock

9-1 Katsiaryna Hurava/123RF

10-1 Wikichops/Creative Commons
10-3 Ralf Roletschek/Creative Commons

11-1 Kial/iStock
11-5 Felix Lipov/123RF
11-6 Xiaohuan/123RF
11-9 Adam Gregor/Shutterstock

14-5 Rosa Jay/Shutterstock
14-6 Brian A. Smith/Shutterstock

15-1 Beaniebeagle/Dreamstime
15-2 Oz Photo/Shutterstock
15-3 William Potter/Shutterstock
15-4 EGD/Shutterstock
15-5 Dolgachov/123RF

15-6 Paul Fleet/Shutterstock
15-7 Stocksnapper/123RF
15-8 Beeboys/Shutterstock

16-1 Arina Zaiachin/123RF
16-3 Sergey Soldatov/123RF
16-5 Mikhail Kusayev/123RF

17-1 (1st) Ken Wolter/Shutterstock
17-1 (2nd) Jonathan Weiss/Shutterstock
17-1 (3rd) Roman Tiraspolsky/Shutterstock
17-1 (4th) Peter L. Gould/Shutterstock

18-1 Tsung-lin Wu/Dreamstime

19-1 Dave Bredesen/Dreamstime
19-5 Eric Baker/Shutterstock
19-6 Steve Jennings/Creative Commons
19-11 Flair Images/Dreamstime
19-12 Gunnar Pippel/Shutterstock
19-22 Paulus Rusyanto/Dreamstime
19-24 Maksym Yamelyanov/123RF

20-1 Katrin Photo/Shutterstock
20-2 Tatiana Shepeleva/123RF
20-3 Kjetil Kolbjornsrud/Shutterstock
20-4 DNY59/iStock
20-7 Kaspri/Dreamstime
20-12 Ababaka/Dreamstime

22-1 Mars Evis/Shutterstock

BC-1 Duplass/Shutterstock
BC-5 Blaine Ohigashi/DailyBruin.com
BC-8 Alphaspirit/Dreamstime
BC-9 Jim Rice/Getty Images
BC-10 Peter Foley/Bloomberg/Getty Images
BC-13 Steve Jurvetson/Creative Commons
BC-16 Hans Mehlin/Nobel Foundation

AW-1 Odua Images/Shutterstock

G-1 Kues/Shutterstock
G-2 Maleo/Shutterstock
G-3 Nuwat Phansuwan/Shutterstock
G-4 TBC Photography/Dreamstime
G-5 Ken Tannenbaum/Shutterstock

ATA-1 Margie Livingston